MW00830410

{THE JOHN WALVOORD PROPHECY COMMENTARIES}

Revelation

John F. Walvoord
Edited by Philip E. Rawley & Mark Hitchcock

MOODY PUBLISHERS
CHICAGO

Original edition published in 1966, under the title of *The Revelation of Jesus Christ*.

Edited by Christopher Reese
Interior design: Ragont Design
Cover design: Tan Nguyen
Cover image: iStock photo

Library of Congress Cataloging-in-Publication Data

Walvoord, John F.
    The John Walvoord prophecy commentaries : Revelation / John F. Walvoord,
  Philip E. Rawley, Mark Hitchcock.
        p. cm.
    Includes bibliographical references and index.
    ISBN 978-0-8024-7312-7
    1. Bible. N.T. Revelation—Commentaries. I. Rawley, Philip E. II. Hitchcock, Mark.
  III. Title. IV. Title: Revelation.
  BS2825.53.W35 2011
  228'.07—dc22

                                                                2010047804

We hope you enjoy this book from Moody Publishers. Our goal is to provide high-quality, thought-provoking books and products that connect truth to your real needs and challenges. For more information on other books and products written and produced from a biblical perspective, go to www.moodypublishers.com or write to:

Moody Publishers
820 N. LaSalle Boulevard
Chicago, IL 60610

9 10 8

Printed in the United States of America

To my wife, Sarah,
my lifelong and only love

To my daughter, Bethany,
the child for whom we prayed

To my son, Philip,
the best a dad ever had

To my daughter-in-law, Denise Hill Rawley,
God's gift to our family

To my grandson, Micah Ryan Rawley,
the light of all our lives

—Philip E. Rawley

Philip E. Rawley is a former Moody Publishers textbook editor, one of the founding editors and writers for *Today in the Word*, and a freelance writer living in Rockwall, Texas. He is a graduate of the University of South Florida (BA) and Dallas Theological Seminary (ThM). Phil and his wife, Sarah, have two children and a grandson.

Mark Hitchcock graduated from law school in 1984 and worked for a judge at the Oklahoma Court of Criminal Appeals. After a clear call to full-time ministry, Mark attended Dallas Theological Seminary, graduating in 1991. Since that time he has served as senior pastor of Faith Bible Church in Edmond, Oklahoma. He completed his PhD at Dallas Theological Seminary in 2005 and serves as an adjunct faculty member at DTS in the Bible Exposition Department. He has authored over twenty books related to end-times Bible prophecy.

Contents

	Foreword	7
	Preface	9
	Introduction	13
1.	The Things That You Have Seen	37
2.	The Letters to Ephesus, Smyrna, Pergamum, and Thyatira	51
3.	The Letters to Sardis, Philadelphia, and Laodicea	77
4.	The Church in Heaven	97
5.	The Lamb and the Seven-Sealed Book	109
6.	The Beginning of the Great Day of God's Wrath	119
7.	The Saints of the Great Tribulation	137
8.	The Seventh Seal and the Beginning of the Trumpets	149
9.	The Fifth and Sixth Trumpets: The First and Second Woes	157
10.	The Mighty Angel with the Little Scroll	169
11.	The Two Witnesses and the Seventh Trumpet	177
12.	The Conflict in Heaven and on Earth	191
13.	The Two Beasts	203
14.	The Victory of the Lamb and His Followers	219
15.	The Vision of the Seven Last Plagues	231
16.	The Bowls of God's Wrath	239
17.	The Destruction of Ecclesiastical Babylon	253
18.	The Fall of Babylon	269
19.	The Second Coming of Christ	281
20.	The Reign of Christ	297
21.	The New Heaven and the New Earth	325
22.	Concluding Revelations and Exhortations	341
	Bibliography	353
	Subject Index	355
	Scripture Index	379

Foreword

In the last few weeks before my father died we had time to celebrate his life, tell stories about past family events, and dream a little about the future. His mind and memory were sharp and he was as upbeat and confident as ever. He was 92 years of age, had lived a full life, and had served well the Lord he loved.

The doctors had given him six weeks to live, and in that time we relived many a family story. He was visited by a parade of his close friends, many influential leaders he had taught and mentored. From his hospital room were days filled with warm memories and laughter, and an occasional hymn echoed down the hall.

My father had a list of things he entrusted to me as his oldest son. But in the last week of his life, the conversation turned to the seventy years he had dedicated to the study of the Bible. And in all that time, he explained, four key books of the Bible had been the subject of his most intense study; *Revelation, Daniel, Matthew,* and *1st and 2nd Thessalonians.* He shared stories about how they were first written, taught, and eventually published.

I remember many of those times. Every summer our family piled into our car and drove across the U.S. and sometimes into Canada. We went from one Bible conference to another, but a lot of that time was spent on the road. And always somewhere in the car was a cardboard box filled with books.

Many nights Dad put us to bed and quietly went into a motel bathroom to read and take notes. Then when he was ready he would dictate an entire chapter, footnotes and all. So whether on the road or at home, this scholarly work was often done late at night and early in the morning. And it continued all his life.

His dream in those final conversations was that his work and biblical insights would live on after him. He remembered how the commentaries and works of some of the great teachers of the Bible lived on for generation after generation. Would his commentaries survive to teach others after his death?

My father explained he had chosen Moody Publishers (then known as Moody Press) to publish his first commentary on *Revelation* for one very important reason. He knew he could trust them to keep the commentary in print as long as it was needed.

So in those last weeks of my father's life, our discussions produced one more assignment. Could I find a way to fulfill his dream to keep these works alive for the generations of students he would not be able to teach in the classroom?

From the seed of that dream has grown the new Walvoord Commentary series. The team that took up that dream is made up of men my father knew and trusted. And as he would have guessed, it was championed by Greg Thornton, vice president of Moody Publishers.

Phillip Rawley agreed to take the lead as the editor of the series. And he took on the assignment with much more than the word "editor" implies. Phil was both a student of my father's and a friend. As far back as twenty five years ago he collaborated with me to help my father with a project that became *All The Prophecies of the Bible*. Since then we have worked together on many writing projects.

But I believe this may have been one of Phil Rawley's most important tasks. He was much more than an editor. In many instances he took up the mantle of the writer who could best capture the way my father would have explained his biblical insights to a new generation of students.

Dr. Mark Hitchcock also agreed to join the team. Because of Mark's interest in prophecy, he and my father often had lunch to discuss key issues in biblical prophecy. Mark is a great admirer of my father's work and a prolific author in his own right who had written more than fifteen books on prophecy and end-time events before we met. Mark was a natural choice to work with me to research and write *Armageddon, Oil, and Terror* shortly after my father's death. In that process we became close friends in the quest to turn my father's ideas and notes into an entirely new work. It was an amazing journey.

Dr. Hitchcock has collaborated on *Revelation* and has taken on the lion's share of expanding my father's work and class notes, previously published as *The Thessalonian Epistles*, into a full commentary for this series. He is a thorough scholar who fully understands my father's teaching from the Epistles.

Dr. Charles Dyer also became an important part of the team. He is an author and teacher who has been greatly influenced by my father as one of his students and later a colleague in the administration of Dallas Theological Seminary. As an Old Testament scholar, Dr. Dyer has taken up the task of revising my father's commentary on *Daniel*, and has also agreed to work on *Matthew's Gospel* for two reasons. First, most of Jesus' teaching on prophecy is best understood in its Old Testament context. Second, Dr. Dyer is as familiar with the Holy Land and the setting of *Matthew* as anyone I know. He will, I am sure, make both Daniel and the events of *Matthew's Gospel* come alive for every reader of the Walvoord Commentary series.

So now, almost a decade after my father's death, his legacy will live on in this new series of biblical commentaries. I am sure he would have been proud of the men who have taken up his torch and are passing it to a new generation of Bible students. As a great man of "The Book," my father is greater still because those who follow in his footsteps remain true to his vision and faithful to the exposition of God's Word.

John Edward Walvoord
January 2011

Preface

When I entered Dallas Theological Seminary in the fall of 1976 to begin work on my master of theology degree, I had little concept of the four wonderful years that lay ahead of me.

Many of my professors were the men who wrote the books from which we studied. One man in particular seemed larger than life to me, and not only because he was a very tall, impressive person. Dr. John F. Walvoord was the seminary's president and resident expert on Bible prophecy. I and about eighty other students would sit under his teaching in large lecture classrooms—the only way Dr. Walvoord could commit time to teaching along with his enormous administrative duties.

I can still remember Dr. Walvoord's lectures as he poured forth information with an encyclopedic knowledge of God's prophetic Word concerning how each part related to the others. We students often had a hard time keeping up, partly because most of us were beginners when it came to any substantive, scholarly knowledge of Bible prophecy. I am sure my fellow students despaired as much as I did of ever having a fraction of the insight Dr. Walvoord had on the prophetic Scriptures.

My seminary experiences were over thirty years ago, and the fraction of Bible prophecy knowledge I acquired has grown. But still, after years as a writer and editor on biblical themes, I was both honored and a bit intimidated when asked to serve as general editor on the revised version of Dr. Walvoord's commentaries on key prophetic books.

And when I was given the opportunity to be the reviser of his commentary on Revelation, my intimidation almost outweighed the honor of helping to preserve Dr. Walvoord's careful work for new generations of Bible students. I didn't feel any less intimidated knowing that his original work on Revelation was 340 densely packed pages with small type and extensive footnotes.

But I plunged in, and now the work is done. I had a lot of great help and encouragement along the way. I am tremendously indebted to Dr. Walvoord's son and my fellow Dallas Theological Seminary alum, Dr. John E. Walvoord, and to Mr. Greg Thornton, vice president of publications at Moody Bible Institute, for their leadership on this entire project, future volumes of which are still to come. John E., as we call him, is deeply committed to preserving his father's legacy and work. He is also a former mentor of mine. Greg is a friend of friends who started working at Moody Press in 1981, the same year that I came to be textbook editor.

Dr. Mark Hitchcock, another fellow Dallas Theological Seminary graduate and pastor who is a prolific prophetic author in his own right, read every word of the *Revelation* manuscript and made a number of helpful suggestions and additions, along with contributing many of the charts throughout the book.

Finally, my assistant and daughter, Bethany Rawley, spent countless hours combing through the original manuscript. Her task was to find every verse, partial verse, and even single words of quotation from the King James Version, and replace them with the text of the English Standard Version. With help like this, any remaining mistakes are mine.

In the preface to his original work, Dr. Walvoord wrote,

No other book of the New Testament evokes the same fascination as the book of Revelation. Attempts at its exposition are almost without number, yet there continues the widest divergence of interpretation. Because the book reveals truth relative to every important fundamental of Christian theology, it is inevitable that its interpretation be influenced by the contemporary confusion in biblical scholarship especially in the realm of eschatology. In some sense, the book is the conclusion to all previous biblical revelation and logically reflects the interpretation of the rest of the Bible. The expositor is faced with innumerable hermeneutical decisions before beginning the task of understanding the peculiar contribution of the book of Revelation, an undertaking made more difficult by the fact that his decisions not only color the exposition of the book itself but also in a sense constitute an interpretation of all that precedes it in the Scriptures.

It is implicit in any orthodox Protestant approach to the Scriptures to hold that the Bible was intended to be understood. What is true of other Scriptures is also true of the book of Revelation. However, it is too much to assume that the book, like the Old Testament apocalyptic books and prophecy generally, was intended to be comprehended fully by believers in the early church. As history unfolds and as prophecy is fulfilled in the future, much will be understood that could be only dimly comprehended by the first readers of the book. But even to early Christians, the main facts were clear.

The expositor of the Revelation is inevitably forced to choose one of the systems of interpretation which have emerged in the history of the church as a proper approach to this last book of the Bible. The author has assumed that this book should be interpreted according to the normal rules of hermeneutics rather than as a special case. The prophetic utterance of the book has therefore been taken in its ordinary meaning unless the immediate context or the total revelation of the book indicates that terms are being used in a symbolic sense, as they frequently are in apocalyptic writings. Instead of assuming that the interpretation should be nonliteral unless there is proof to the contrary, the opposite approach has been taken, namely, that terms should be understood in their ordinary meaning unless contrary evidence is adduced. Hence stars are stars, earthquakes are earthquakes, et cetera, unless it is clear that something else is intended. The result has been a more literal interpretation of prophecy and revelation in general and a clearer picture of end-time events than is frequently held by expositors.

In offering this new exposition of the book of Revelation, an attempt has been made to provide a norm for premillennial interpreters of the Bible. In many cases alternative views are offered even though they differ from the interpretation of the author. It is too much to hope that the interpretation will persuade all readers. But if added light is cast upon the Word of God, and the Christian hope is enriched thereby, the author's expectation will have been realized. Most of all may the Lord Jesus Christ, the subject of the revelation of the book, be glorified in this attempt to understand what John saw and heard on the Isle of Patmos.

To this I can only add, amen.

Philip E. Rawley
Rockwall, Texas
July 31, 2010

Introduction

AUTHORSHIP AND OCCASION

The opening verses of Revelation plainly claim the book was written by John, identified almost universally in the early church as the apostle John. The apostolic authorship of the book has, nevertheless, been questioned ever since the time of Dionysius of Alexandria in the third century.

Dionysius challenged the traditional view that John the apostle was the author on several grounds, including the fact that John did not identify himself as the apostle of Jesus, but rather as a "servant," and that Revelation did not match the other authentic writings of John.[1]

Beginning with Dionysius, those who object to Johannine authorship or to inclusion of the Revelation in the canon have tended to magnify the problems of grammar, as well as what Dionysius considered many instances of incorrect Greek usage. Impartial scholarship has admitted that there are expressions in Revelation which do not correspond to accepted Greek usage, but this problem is not entirely confined to this book of the Bible. Conservative scholarship has insisted that infallibility in divine revelation does not necessarily exclude expressions which are not normal in other Greek literature and that such instances do not mar the perfection of the truth that is transmitted. It is important to note, however, that some of the supposedly bad grammar in Revelation was used in contemporary *Koine* literature, as is revealed by discoveries in the Papyri.

The arguments for rejecting the apostolic authorship of Revelation stem largely from the theological climate of the third century. At that time, the Alexandrian school of theology, including Dionysius, opposed the doctrine of the millennial kingdom which is plainly taught in chapter 20 with its reference to the thousand years. An attack by them on the authorship of John tended to weaken the force of this prophecy. Many scholars, motivated by other reasons, have advanced the theory that the John of Revelation was John the Presbyter or John the Elder, mentioned by Papias in a statement preserved in the writing of Eusebius. Another author considered but rejected by Dionysius was John Mark.

The substantiating evidence for any other author than John the apostle, however, is almost entirely lacking. While notable scholars can be cited in support of divergent views, the proof dissipates upon examination. It seems clear that the early church attributed the book to John the apostle.[2] The first commentary on Revelation to be preserved, written by Victorinus, regards John the apostle as the author. Though the book of Revelation was not commonly received by the church as canonical until the middle of the second century, it is most significant that the Johannine authorship was not questioned until the strong antichiliastic influence arose in the Alexandrian school of theology at the end of the second century.

The evidence for the Johannine authorship is based first on the fact that four times the writer calls himself by the name John (1:1, 4, 9; 22:8). Describing himself as a "servant" (1:1) and "your brother and partner in the tribulation and the kingdom, and the patient endurance that are in Jesus" (1:9), John never states that he is an apostle. Taking into consideration, however, that in the fourth gospel there is a similar anonymity, this does not seem to be strange. Most conservative expositors regard the name John as genuine rather than a pseudonym as is common in nonscriptural apocalyptic books. There is really no solid evidence against accepting John the apostle as the author, and there is much that confirms it. In fact, it may be argued that the reference to John without further identification would presume a familiarity on the part of the readers that would make naming him unnecessary.

The evidence for John the apostle hangs largely on the question whether he was actually sent into exile on the island of Patmos, as the author of this book claims (1:9). There is good historical evidence in support of this contention. Clement of Alexandria refers to the apostle John as returning from the Isle of Patmos.[3] Eusebius not only affirms John's return from the isle but dates it immediately following the death of Domitian, which occurred in A.D. 96.[4]

Irenaeus adds his confirming word when he states that John lived in Ephesus after returning from Patmos until the reign of Trajan.[5] Though the Scriptures do not dogmatically confirm that John the apostle is the author, the existing evidence is heavily in favor of this conclusion.

DATE OF COMPOSITION

Related to the total problem is the question of the date of the book. Two main dates for the composition of Revelation have been proposed by the majority of scholars: the early or Neronic date (A.D. 65), during the reign of the emperor Nero and the late or Domitianic date (A.D. 95), during the reign of Domitian. The evidence for determining which of these views is correct can be divided into two categories: external and internal evidence. Both lines of evidence point strongly in the direction of the late or Domitianic date (A.D. 95) as the correct view.

The external evidence can best be understood by the chart on the next page placing the witnesses for each date side by side.

The first clear, unambiguous witness to the Neronic date is a one-line attribution in the Syriac translation of the New Testament c. A.D. 500. There are only two other external witnesses to the early date: Arethas (c. 900) and Theophylact (d. 1107).

The late date, on the other hand, has an unbroken line of support from many of the greatest, most reliable luminaries in church history beginning in A.D. 150. Moreover, Clement of Alexandria, Tertullian, and Origen all support the late date; however, they are not included in the chart since they don't *specifically* say that John was banished by Domitian. Thus, the external evidence from church history points emphatically to the A.D. 95 date for the composition of Revelation. It has been the dominant view of the church for 1,900 years.

In addition, there are two key lines of internal evidence from within Revelation that also favor the Domitianic date for its writing.

SUMMARY OF THE EXTERNAL EVIDENCE

Witnesses for the A.D. 95 Date	Witnesses for the A.D. 65 Date
Hegesippus (A.D. 150)	
Irenaeus (180)	
Victorinus (c. 300)	
Eusebius (c. 300)	
Jerome (c. 400)	
Sulpicius Severus (c. 400)	
The Acts of John (c. 650)	
Primasius (c. 540)	Syriac Version of NT (c. A.D. 500)
Orosius (c. 600)	
Andreas (c. 600)	
Venerable Bede (700)	
	Arethas (c. 900)
	Theophylact (d. 1107)

THE CONDITION OF THE SEVEN CHURCHES

One of the key internal arguments for the late date of Revelation is the condition of the seven churches of Asia Minor in Revelation 2–3, which show all the symptoms of the second generation of those churches. The period of Paul's great mission seems to lie in the past. Consider these clues on the date of Revelation from three of the churches addressed in chapters 2–3.

The Church of Ephesus

If John wrote Revelation in A.D. 64–67, then the letter to the church of Ephesus in Revelation 2:1–7 overlaps with Paul's two letters to Timothy who was the pastor of the church when Paul wrote to him. In fact, if Revelation was written in 64–66, then it is very likely that Paul wrote 2 Timothy after

John wrote to the church. Yet Paul makes no mention of the loss of first love or the presence of the Nicolaitans at Ephesus in his correspondence with Timothy. Neither does he mention these problems in his Ephesian epistle which was probably written in A.D. 62.

Jesus' statement to the church of Ephesus in Revelation 2:2 that it had guarded itself well against error does not fit what we know of this church in Nero's day (Acts 20:29–30; 1 Tim. 1:3–7; 2 Tim. 2:17–18). Those who support the early date often respond by noting that error can erupt very quickly in a church. As an example they sometimes cite the churches of Galatia, who "are so quickly deserting him who called you" (Gal. 1:6). But there is a great difference between the condition and maturity of the Galatian churches after Paul's brief visit there on his first missionary journey, and the church of Ephesus where Paul headquartered for three years, where Apollos taught, where Priscilla and Aquila ministered, and where Timothy pastored for several years.

Moreover, Revelation 2:1–7 makes no mention of the great missionary work of Paul in Asia Minor. On his third journey Paul headquartered in Ephesus for three years and had a profound ministry there. If John wrote in A.D. 64–67 then the omission of any mention of Paul in the letters to the churches of Asia Minor is inexplicable. However, if John wrote thirty years later to the second generation in the churches, then the omission is easily understood.

The Church of Smyrna

Apparently, the church of Smyrna did not even exist during the ministry of Paul. Polycarp was the bishop of Smyrna. In his letter to the Philippians, written about A.D. 110, Polycarp says that the Smyrnaeans did not know the Lord during the time Paul was ministering.

> But I have not observed or heard of any such thing among you, in whose midst the blessed Paul labored, and who were his letters of recommendation in the beginning. For he boasts about you in all the churches— those alone, that is, which at that time had come to know the Lord, for we had not yet come to know him. (11.3)

Polycarp is saying that Paul praised the Philippian believers in all the churches, but that during Paul's ministry in the A.D. 50s and 60s the church of Smyrna did not even exist.

The Church of Laodicea

The church of Laodicea is the only one of the seven churches (and possibly Sardis) that does not have one thing to commend. In his letter to the Colossians, probably written in A.D. 60–62, Paul indicates that the church was an active group (Col. 4:13). He mentions the church there three times in this letter (2:1; 4:13, 16). It would certainly take more than two to seven years for the church to depart so completely from its earlier acceptable status that absolutely nothing good could be said about it. Laodicea is also described in Revelation as flourishing economically. Jesus quotes the church as saying, "I am rich, I have prospered, and I need nothing." Yet the city suffered devastation in an earthquake that occurred in A.D. 60. After the earthquake the Laodiceans refused all aid and assistance from Rome, preferring to rebuild their devastated city from their own resources.

Tacitus, the Roman historian, in his *Annals* (14.27), describes this independent spirit. "In the same year, Laodicea, one of the famous Asiatic cities, was laid in ruins by an earthquake, but recovered by its own resources, without assistance from ourselves." The extent of the damage to Laodicea and the length of time it took to reconstruct the city are powerful evidence of the late date for Revelation.

Most of the main ruins that survive today in Laodicea are from buildings erected during the time of earthquake reconstruction. The great public buildings destroyed in the earthquake were rebuilt at the expense of individual citizens and were not finished until about the year A.D. 90. The completion date of the stadium can be precisely dated to the latter part of A.D. 79 and the inscriptions on several other buildings indicate that they too can be dated to this same period. New gates and fortifications seem to have culminated the rebuilding of Laodicea. It is likely that the great triple gate (Syrian gate) and towers were not finished until A.D. 88–90.

Since the rebuilding of Laodicea after the earthquake occupied a complete generation, it is highly problematic to claim that Laodicea was rich, wealthy, and in need of nothing in A.D. 64–67. During those years the city was in the early stages of a rebuilding program that would last another twenty-five years. However, if Revelation was written in A.D. 95 the description of Laodicea in Revelation 3:14–22 would fit the situation exactly. By this time the city was completely rebuilt with its own resources, enjoying prosperity and prestige, and basking in the pride of its great accomplishment.

THE BANISHMENT OF JOHN TO PATMOS

Revelation 1:9 states that when John received the Revelation he was exiled on the island of Patmos. Church history consistently testifies that both Peter and Paul were executed in Rome near the end of Nero's reign. Those who hold to the early date for the writing of Revelation maintain that during this same time the apostle John was banished to Patmos by Nero. But why would Nero execute Peter and Paul and banish John? This seems inconsistent. The different sentences for Peter and Paul as compared with John argue for the fact that they were persecuted under different rulers. Moreover, there is no evidence of Nero's use of banishment for Christians.

Since Domitian was the second Roman emperor after Nero to persecute Christians, and since banishment was one of his favorite modes of punishment, John's exile to Patmos is much more likely under Domitian than Nero.

Taking into account all the relevant evidence, both external and internal, the strongest view is that the apostle John wrote the book of Revelation in the year A.D. 95 while exiled by the Roman emperor Domitian to the island of Patmos. In any case, there is little tendency among scholars who accept the inspiration of the Revelation to place the date later, as some liberal scholars have attempted to do. In many cases the theological bias against the chiliastic teaching of the book of Revelation seems to be the actual motive in rejecting the apostolic authorship. The date must be before the death of Domitian, who was assassinated in A.D. 96, as the apostle was apparently released from his exile shortly after this.

In contrast to other apocalyptic books, the revelation recorded by John is presented as having a solid historical basis in his exile on Patmos. It was there these visions were given to him, and in obedience to the command to write them and send them to the seven churches, John recorded these prophecies. It would seem entirely reasonable that in the midst of persecution the church should be given a book of such assurance as that embodied in the content of Revelation, which holds before them both an explanation as to why persecution is permitted but also a promise of ultimate triumph and reward.

INSPIRATION AND CANONICITY

Because Revelation was addressed to seven different churches, it would be only natural that each of these churches would want its own copy, and thus the circulation of the entire book would be given a good start. The circulation and wide use of the book as Scripture are evident by the beginning of the third century.

It is true, nevertheless, that Revelation was slow in gaining universal recognition as Scripture. Important among the reasons for this is opposition to the chiliasm that is expressly taught in Revelation 20. Other theological objections arose from various sects that for the most part were heretical. The more orthodox churches seem to have had less difficulty in accepting it as Scripture. The reasons for a slower reception arose principally from the unusual character of this book, the only apocalyptic book in the New Testament. Critics also were quick to point to grammatical difficulties and to cite apparent discrepancies. But the fact is that the early Western church, in spite of certain objections, generally accepted Revelation by the end of the second century, and the Eastern church soon followed suit.

INTERPRETATION

Most of the difficulty in the interpretation of this last book in the Scriptures has come from treating it as an ordinary piece of literature produced by a variety of human authors. With such presuppositions, the book becomes a literary monstrosity devoid of any real revelation from God.

When approached as divinely inspired and to be interpreted by the phraseology and symbolism of other portions of the Bible, the depth and breadth of Revelation become immediately apparent. The book offers knowledge far beyond human ability and claims revelation not only in relation to spiritual and moral truths, as in the letters to the seven churches, but revelation extending to visions of heaven and earth and prophetic revelation of the future, including the eternal state. If a human invention, the book is of little value; if divinely inspired, it is an open door into precious eternal truth.

If the inspiration of the book and its apostolic authorship are accepted, there still remain, however, serious exegetical problems illustrated in the variety of approaches found in conservative scholarship. These have often been divided into four categories.

1. *The nonliteral or allegorical approach.* This point of view, originating in the Alexandrian school of theology represented in Clement of Alexandria and Origen, regarded Revelation as one great allegory going far beyond the natural symbolism that is found in the book. They understood in a nonliteral sense much of what other expositors interpreted literally. They were motivated by their antichiliastic premises, which led them to take in a nonliteral sense anything that would teach a millennial reign of Christ on earth. They claimed that their view was the true "spiritual" interpretation as opposed to the literalism of their opponents.

The Alexandrian school in the early church is generally regarded as heretical. Its leaders undoubtedly influenced such men as Jerome and Augustine and was responsible for turning the early church from its chiliastic position. The interpretative method of the Alexandrians has found little favor with modern interpreters, but there is a persistent tendency to return to some use of this method to avoid the premillennial implications of the book of Revelation, if understood more literally.

The more moderate form of allegorical interpretation, following Augustine, has achieved respectability and regards the book of Revelation as presenting in a symbolic way the total conflict between Christianity and evil, or, as Augustine put it, the City of God versus the City of Satan.

2. *The preterist approach.* Adherents to this approach maintain that Revelation is a record of the conflicts of the early church with Judaism and paganism. The events of Revelation 4–20 are viewed primarily as a description of the Jewish war, its culmination in the destruction of Jerusalem in A.D. 70, and the persecution of the early church. Though some in the early church may have had similar views, credit is usually given to the Jesuit Luis de Alcazar (1554–1613) for its origin. There are two main camps under the preterist banner: full preterism (also known as consistent, orthodox, or hyperpreterism) and partial preterism.

Full preterism holds that Jesus returned in A.D. 70 in the clouds of judgment against unbelieving Israel and that all Bible prophecy, including Revelation, was fulfilled by A.D. 70. According to this view, believers are living now in the new heaven and new earth. Full preterists maintain that there is no future second coming of Christ, no final resurrection, and no final judgment. For these reasons, this brand of preterism is outside the pale of orthodoxy.

Partial preterism, while agreeing with full preterists that Jesus returned in the clouds of judgment against apostate Israel in A.D. 70, does hold that there will be a future second coming, resurrection, and final judgment. R. C. Sproul, a popular advocate of the partial preterist position, defines it as "an eschatological viewpoint that places many or all eschatological events in the past, especially during the destruction of Jerusalem in A.D. 70."[6] Partial preterists view the seals, trumpets, and bowls as descriptions of the judgment against the Jewish people in the land, the Beast of Revelation as Nero, Babylon in Revelation 17–18 as the city of Jerusalem, and the coming of Christ in Revelation 19 as his "cloud coming" in A.D. 70 to destroy Jerusalem through the Roman army. In general, the preterist view tends to destroy any prophetic significance of the book, which becomes a literary curiosity with little prophetic meaning. To arrive at these conclusions, contemporary preterists follow a mixture of literal and symbolical/allegorical methods of interpretation, rejecting a consistent, literal method of interpretation.

Since preterists view Revelation as a prophecy about the events of A.D. 67–70, for their view to be viable, Revelation must have been written in

A.D. 65–66. This date is highly problematic, as previously discussed in this introduction.

Hendriksen dismisses both the historical and the futurist interpretations of the book of Revelation on the assumption that the book was intended for the use of first-century Christians to whom a detailed prophecy of the entire church age would have been meaningless. Hendriksen instead seems to follow the view that the book is a symbolic word of encouragement to early Christians suffering persecution, and a general assurance of ultimate triumph in Christ;[7] hence, he is only partially a preterist.

Contemporary liberal works usually follow a combination of the preterist and nonliteral methods of interpretation, disregarding the strictly historical interpretation as well as the futurist. Even universalists have attempted commentaries on Revelation in which they explain away all judgment upon sin and make all future judgment contemporary.

3. *The historical approach.* Adherents to this theory consider Revelation a symbolic presentation of the total of church history, culminating in the second advent. Though it had earlier disciples, Joachim de Fiora, a Roman Catholic scholar of the twelfth century, is largely responsible for this approach as he was also the originator of the first forms of postmillennialism. This method of interpreting Revelation achieved considerable stature in the Reformation because of its identification of the pope and the papacy with the beasts of Revelation 13. But as Ryrie says, "Dogmatism and contradiction abound among those who attempt to interpret the book in this way."[8]

Indeed, as many as fifty different interpretations of the book of Revelation have appeared, varying with the time and circumstances of the expositor. The very multiplicity of such interpretations and identifications of the personnel of Revelation with a variety of historical characters is its own refutation.

4. *The futuristic approach.* Limited to conservative expositors who are often premillennial, this point of view regards Revelation as futuristic beginning with chapter 4 and therefore subject to future fulfillment. Some have attempted to make even chapters 1, 2, and 3 futuristic and the seven churches as future assemblies, but the great majority of futurists begin with chapter 4.

Under this system of interpretation, the events of chapters 4 through 18 relate to the period just preceding the second coming of Christ. This is generally regarded as a period of seven years with emphasis on the last three-and-one-half years, labeled the "great tribulation." Chapter 19, therefore, refers to the second coming of Christ to the earth, chapter 20 to the future millennial kingdom that will follow, and chapters 21 and 22 to events either contemporary with or subsequent to the millennium.

In contrast to the other approaches to Revelation, the futuristic position allows a more literal interpretation of the book's specific prophecies. Though recognizing the frequent symbolism in various prophecies, the events foreshadowed by these symbols and their interpretation are regarded as being fulfilled in a literal way. Hence, the various judgments of God are actually poured out on the earth as contained in the seals, trumpets, and bowls. Chapter 13 is considered a prophecy of the future world empire with its political and religious heads represented by the two beasts of this chapter. The prostitute of chapter 17 is the final form of the church in apostasy. In a similar way, all other events of Revelation relate to the climax of history contained in the second coming of Christ.

Critics of this position often argue that if the main body of Revelation deals with the period immediately preceding the second coming of Christ, it robs the reader of immediate blessing. But much of the Bible's prophecy deals with the distant future, including the Old Testament promises of the coming Messiah, the prophecies of Daniel concerning the future world empires, predictions relating to the coming kingdom on earth, as well as countless other prophecies. If the events of chapters 4 through 19 are future, even from our viewpoint today, they teach the blessed truth of the ultimate supremacy of God and the triumph of righteousness. The immediate application of distant events is familiar in Scripture, as for instance 2 Peter 3:10–12, which speaks of the ultimate dissolution of the earth. Nevertheless the succeeding passage makes an immediate application: "Therefore, beloved, since you are waiting for these, be diligent to be found by him without spot or blemish, and at peace" (v. 14).

Though the premillennial conclusions of the futuristic view seem to have been held by the New Testament church, the early fathers did not in any clear or consistent way interpret Revelation as a whole in a futuristic sense. In fact, it can be demonstrated that the principal error of the Fathers was that they attempted to interpret the book as being fulfilled contemporaneously in the trials and difficulties of the church. Subsequent history has shown that the events which would have naturally followed did not come to pass, and the assumption of contemporaneous fulfillment was thereby discredited. The futuristic school has gained a hold upon a large segment of interpreters of prophecy in conservative evangelicalism largely because the other methods have led to such confusion of interpretation and have tended to make Revelation a hopeless exegetical problem.

The futurist approach is rejected by most amillenarian and postmillenarian scholars, but is normally held by contemporary premillenarians who tend to follow the futuristic form of interpretation. Though many difficulties and obscurities remain, the futuristic school has the advantage of offering a relatively clear understanding of the principal events of future fulfillment, and tends to treat Revelation as a more normative piece of literature than the other interpretative frameworks.

One of the common assumptions of those who reject the futurist position is that the Revelation is essentially the creation of John's own thinking and was understandable to those of his generation, though it is obscure to the modern reader. The difficulty with this view is twofold: (1) Prophecy, as given in the Scripture, was not necessarily understandable by the writer or his generation, as illustrated in the case of Daniel (Dan. 12:4, 9). It is questionable whether the great prophets of the Old Testament always understood what they were writing (cf. 1 Pet. 1:10–12). (2) It is of the nature of prophecy that it often cannot be understood until the time of the generation that achieves fulfillment. The assumption, therefore, that Revelation was only understandable in the first generation is without basis.

The second and third chapters of the book, however, are primarily a message to the seven historic churches of Asia. Inasmuch as these exhortations are set in the prophetic context of the chapters that follow, the book of Revelation is best seen to be designed for the church at large. If it were not for Revelation, the New Testament canon would have ended with an obviously unfinished character.

Revelation is in many respects the capstone of futuristic prophecy of the entire Bible and gathers in its prophetic scheme the major themes of prophecy which thread their way through all of Scripture. The scope and plan of the book indicate that its primary intent was to prepare the way for the second coming of Christ. The book, therefore, has a special relevance for the generation that will be living on earth at that time. Because that event is undated, it constitutes a challenge to each succeeding generation of believers.

APOCALYPTIC CHARACTER

Revelation, beginning as it does with the Greek word *apokalypsis* ("uncovering," "revelation"), by its very title is apocalyptic in character—that is, a book that claims to unfold the future, the unveiling of that which would otherwise be concealed. The nature of such a revelation requires a supernatural understanding of future events. Although Revelation is the only apocalyptic book of the New Testament, many other apocalyptic works preceded its appearance, and there were others that followed.

A sharp distinction should be observed between apocalyptic works outside the Bible and apocalyptic works that are Scripture, whose writing was guided by the inspiration of the Holy Spirit. Apocalyptic literature outside the Bible can be classified as *pseudepigrapha*. These were works pretending to emanate from characters of the Bible who are cast in the role of predicting the future. The actual authors, however, often lived long after the character to whom the work is ascribed. Among the most important pseudepigrapha are Ascension of Isaiah, Assumption of Moses, Book of Enoch, Book of Jubilees, the Greek Revelation of Baruch, Letters of Aristeas, III and IV Maccabees, Psalms of Solomon, Secrets of Enoch, Sibylline Oracles, the Syriac Revelation of Baruch, and Testament of the Twelve Patriarchs. These works are usually dated as beginning about 250 B.C. and as continuing into the period following the apostolic church. A great many other apocalyptic works are sometimes cited as of lesser importance, including the Revelations of Adam, Elijah, and Zephaniah, and Testament of Abram, Isaac, and Jacob.

It is characteristic of apocalyptic literature outside the Bible to have a pessimistic view of the contemporary situation and to paint the future in glowing terms of blessing for the saints and doom for the wicked. The real author's name is never divulged in apocalyptic works outside the Bible.

Apocalyptic portions of the Scriptures stand in sharp contrast. The more prominent apocalyptic works of the Old Testament are Isaiah, Ezekiel, Daniel, Joel, and Zechariah. Liberal scholars have sometimes drawn unfair comparisons between the apocalyptic writers outside the Bible and those within the canon. For instance, a common assumption is that the book of Daniel was not actually written by Daniel, as the book purports to be, in the sixth century B.C., but rather in the period of the second century when much of the book of would have been history. This, however, has been refuted by conservative scholarship, and the apocalyptic character of Scriptural books is not a just ground for denying the historical content or the authorship indicated. It is an unwarranted assumption to conclude from the pseudoauthorship of apocalyptic writings outside the Bible that the same principle also applies to Scripture.

The Revelation of John stands in sharp contrast not only to apocalyptic writings outside the Bible which preceded it but also to the Christian apocalypses that followed, such as Anabaticon and Pauli, the Revelations of St. Steven and Thomas, the Decree of Gelasius, the Revelation of Peter (which for a brief time in the early church seems to have been considered genuine), the Revelation of Paul, a Spurious Revelation of John, the Revelation of Sedrach, and the Revelation of the Virgin. The reverent student, however, has little difficulty distinguishing the superlative and inspired character of the genuine Revelation of John from these later apocalyptic writings.

SYMBOLISM

Symbolism occurs throughout Scripture as a vehicle for divine revelation, but it is undoubtedly true that the final book of the New Testament, because of its apocalyptic character, contains more symbols than any other book in the New Testament. In this it is similar to Daniel to which, in many respects, it is a counterpart, and also to Ezekiel and Zechariah. Many apocalyptic books appeared prior to, as well as contemporary with, the book of Revelation. The fact that Revelation was included in the canon and all other contemporary apocalyptic books were excluded is itself a testimony to the special character of Revelation.

The symbolism of Revelation has been explained in various ways. One of the most probable and popular, however, is that it was necessary to state opposition to the Roman Empire during the persecutions of Domitian in symbolic terms that would not be easily understood by the Roman authorities. This was also important because the emperor Domitian gradually applied to himself all the attributes of God and established a form of religion that was anti-Christian. Domitian's claim to divine attributes appears on the coins that were issued during his reign and used as an important propaganda vehicle to communicate to the people Domitian's assumption of divinity.

Almost every aspect of nature is used as a vehicle of the symbolism of Revelation, as well as grotesque unnatural forms. Hence, from the animal world, frequent symbols appear, such as the horses of Revelation 6, the living creatures seen in heaven, Christ as the Lamb, and the calf, the locust, the scorpion, the lion, the leopard, the bear, the frog, the eagle, the vulture, birds, fish, as well as unnatural beasts, such as those in Revelation 13. There is also allusion to the botanical world, and trees and grass are mentioned in a context of reference to earth, sky, and sea. The sun, moon, and stars in the heavens; the thunder, lightning, and hail of the atmospheric heavens; as well as rivers and seas on earth often form a vehicle of divine revelation. Various forms of humanity are also mentioned, such as the mother and child of Revelation 12, the prostitute of Revelation 17, and the wife of Revelation 19. Weapons of war such as swords are named as well as reapers with their sickles. Trumpeters with their trumpets are introduced along with the flute and harp. In many cases John had to use unusual expressions to describe scenes in heaven and on earth that transcend normal human experience.

Some items allude either to ancient Near Eastern background or to the geography of the Bible, but much of the imagery found in the book of Revelation is also familiar to students of Daniel, Ezekiel, and Zechariah. The golden lampstand of the churches of Asia has some correspondence to the lampstand of the tabernacle and temple. Allusions to the heavenly tabernacle and temple, to the altar, ark, and censer, all have Old Testament background. Many geographic descriptions also refer to Old Testament names and places such as the River Euphrates, Sodom, Armageddon (the hill of Megiddo), Jerusalem, Babylon, Egypt, and to Old Testament characters such as Balaam and Jezebel. In many cases there are indirect allusions to Old Testament ideas and situations. In the center is Christ as the Lamb and Lion of the tribe of Judah and the Root of David. The twelve tribes of Israel are also mentioned.

It is nevertheless true that much of Revelation's imagery is new, created as a vehicle for the divine revelation that John was to record. To attempt, as many writers have done, to consider this symbolism as allusion to extrabiblical apocalyptic literature is to press the matter beyond its proper bounds. It is also true that some items, while partially symbolic, may also be intended to be understood literally, as in numerous instances where reference is made to stars, the moon, the sun, rivers, and seas. While there will never be complete agreement on the line between imagery and the literal, the patient exegete must resolve each occurrence in some form of consistent interpretation.

Numbers are very prominent in the book: 2, 3, 3½, 4, 5, 6, 7, 10, 12, 24, 42, 144, 666, 1,000, 1,260, 1,600, 7,000, 12,000, 144,000, 100,000,000, and 200,000,000. These numbers may be understood literally, but even when understood in this way, they often carry with them a symbolic meaning. Hence the number seven, used fifty-four times, more than any other number in the book, refers to seven historical churches in the opening chapter. Yet by the very use of this number (which speaks of completion or perfection) the concept is conveyed that these were representative churches which in some sense were complete in their description of the normal needs of the church. There were not only seven churches but seven lampstands, seven stars, seven spirits of God, seven seals on the scroll, seven angels with seven trumpets, seven bowls containing the seven last plagues, seven thunders, seven thousand killed in the earthquake of chapter 12, a dragon with seven heads and seven crowns, the beast of chapter 13 with seven heads, seven mountains of chapter 17, and the seven kings.

Next in importance to the number seven and in the order of their frequency are the numbers twelve, ten, and four. Some of this stems from the fact that there are twelve tribes of Israel. Twelve thousand were sealed from each of the twelve tribes. The elders of chapter 4 are twice twelve or twenty-four. The New Jerusalem is declared to be 12,000 furlongs wide and long, and its wall twelve times twelve, or 144 cubits in height. Clearly, the use of these numbers is not accidental. Though the symbolism is not always obvious, the general rule should be followed to interpret numbers literally unless there is clear evidence to the contrary. The numbers nevertheless convey more than their bare numerical significance.

Of special importance is the reference to forty-two months or 1,260 days, describing the precise length of the great tribulation. This is in keeping with the anticipation of Daniel 9:27 that the last half of the seven-year period would be a time of unprecedented trouble. Endless speculation has also risen over the number 666, describing the beast out of the sea in Revelation 13:18. The most natural and simple explanation of this number, however, is that the beast is characterized by the number six, just falling short of the number seven and signifying that he is only a man after all. Possibly the threefold occurrence of the number six is in vague imitation of the Trinity, formed by his association with the devil and the false prophet.

The wide use of symbols is attended, however, by frequent interpretations in Revelation itself either by direct reference or by implication. Symbols can often be explained also by usage elsewhere in Scripture. The list on the next page may be helpful.

In addition, the lake of fire is described as the second death (20:14). Jesus Christ is the root and offspring of David (22:16), and also the Lamb, who is Lord of lords and King of kings (17:14).

In many instances, where symbols are explained, they establish a pattern of interpretation that casts a great deal of light upon the meaning of the book as a whole. This introduces a presumption that, where expressions are not explained, they can normally be interpreted according to their natural

SYMBOL	MEANING
The seven stars (1:16)	seven angels (1:20)
The seven lampstands (1:13)	seven churches (1:20)
The hidden manna (2:17)	Christ in glory (cf. Ex. 16:33–34; Heb. 9:4)
The morning star (2:28)	Christ returning before the dawn, suggesting the church's rapture before the establishment of the kingdom (cf. Rev. 22:16; 2 Pet. 1:19)
The key of David (3:7)	the power to open and close doors (Isa. 22:22)
The seven lamps of fire	the sevenfold Spirit of God (4:5)
The living creatures (4:7)	the attributes of God
The seven eyes	the sevenfold Spirit of God (5:6)
The odors of the golden bowls	the prayers of the saints (5:8)
The four horses and their riders (6:1ff.)	successive events in the developing tribulation
The fallen star (9:1)	the angel of the abyss, probably Satan (9:11)
The great city (11:8), Sodom, and Egypt (11:8),	Jerusalem (in contrast to the new Jerusalem, the heavenly city)
The stars of the sky (12:4)	fallen angels (12:9)
The woman and the child (12:1–2)	Israel and Christ (12:5–6)
Satan	the great dragon, the old serpent, and the devil (12:9; 20:2)
The time, times, and half a time (12:14)	1,260 days (12:6)
The beast out of the sea (13:1–10)	the future world ruler and his empire
The beast out of the earth (13:11–17)	the false prophet (19:20)
The prostitute (17:1)	the great city (17:18), as Babylon the great (17:5), as the one who sits on seven hills (17:9), is usually interpreted as apostate Christendom
The waters (17:1) on which the woman sits	the peoples of the world (17:15)
The ten horns (17:12)	ten kings associated with the beast (13:1; 17:3, 7–8, 11–13, 16–17)
Fine linen	the righteous deeds of the saints (19:8)
The rider of the white horse (19:11–16, 19)	Christ, the King of kings

meaning unless the context clearly indicates otherwise. The attempt to interpret all of the book of Revelation symbolically ends in nullifying practically all the details of the book and leaving them unexplained.

The difficulties of interpreting Revelation have often been made far greater than they really are. They frequently yield to patient study and comparison with other portions of Scripture. The study of Revelation is an endless task but offers rich rewards to the patient student.

THEOLOGY

Few books of the Bible provide a more complete theology than Revelation. Because of its apocalyptic character, the emphasis of the book is eschatological in the strict sense of dealing with last things (note "the words of this prophecy," Rev. 1:3). More specifically, however, it is Christological, as the material of the book relates to the "revelation of Jesus Christ." The objective is to reveal Jesus Christ as the glorified One in contrast to the Christ of the Gospels, who was seen in humiliation and suffering. The climax of the book is the second coming of Jesus Christ. Events preceding the second coming constitute an introduction, and all events that follow constitute an epilogue. The wide range of Revelation, however, deals with many subjects not specifically eschatological or Christological. Indeed, there are major contributions in all important fields of theology.

Bibliology. The doctrine of Scripture in Revelation is deduced mostly by implication in that there are frequent allusions to other books of the Bible. A special blessing is pronounced upon the reader and hearer in a context that refers to the book as "the word of God and . . . the testimony of Jesus Christ" (Rev. 1:2). John claims divine authority and inspiration both for the book itself and for the revelation it contains. Revelation, however, is not only Scripture itself but is saturated with Old Testament references. Wiersbe says that of the 404 verses of Revelation, 278 contain references to the Old Testament.[9] The fact that the Revelation is saturated with Old Testament references tends to tie the book to the rest of Scripture and makes it a fitting climactic volume, a terminal for major lines of Scriptural revelation.

32

Theology proper. Apart from its eschatology, the Revelation contributes more to the doctrine of God than to any other field. The study of its contribution to the doctrine of the Father, the Son, and the Holy Spirit would itself merit a full volume. God is presented in all the majesty of the Yahweh of the Old Testament, who is holy, true, omnipotent, omniscient, and eternal. There is emphasis on God's righteousness and His judgment upon sin, with comparatively little mention made of His love and mercy. The character of God is in keeping with His main role in Revelation as the Judge of all.

Though there is reference to both the Father and the Spirit, the central revelation concerns Christ, in keeping with the title of the book. Many allusions are made to His human origin as coming from the tribe of Judah and the house of David and to His humiliation while on earth as represented in the symbol of a slain lamb. Always, however, Christ is depicted as triumphant over death, the eternal One of infinite power and majesty who is worthy of all honor and adoration. Before His glorified humanity the apostle falls as one dead.

The supreme revelation is continued in chapter 19 where He is described as descending from heaven as King of kings and Lord of lords to slay the evil, deliver the righteous, and accomplish His glorious purpose in the earth. Though Revelation contains no defense of the deity of Christ, no book of the Bible is plainer in its implications, for here indeed is the eternal God who became man. This is confirmed by His relationship to God the Father described in 4:2–3 and 5:1, 7. Complementing the revelation of Christ is that of the Spirit through whom John received the revelation (1:10) and who appears frequently in various symbols, as in the seven horns and seven eyes of 5:6, the seven spirits of 1:4 and 4:5, and who is seen in special relationship to Christ in 3:1 and 5:6. It is fitting that the book of Revelation should close with another reference to the Spirit in 22:17, climaxing other indirect references to the Spirit throughout the book.

Anthropology and hamartiology. The emphasis on the doctrines of man and of sin in Revelation is apparent. Humanity is revealed in its utter need of the grace of God as righteously deserving the judgment of God for sin. Few books of the Bible describe the human race in greater depravity and as the object of more severe divine judgment. The acme of human blasphemy and evil is portrayed in the beast and the false prophet who are the supreme demonstration of Satan's handiwork in the human race.

Angelology. No other book in the New Testament speaks more often of angels than Revelation. They are the principal vehicle of communication to John of the truth that he is recording. The holy angels are seen in power and majesty in sharp contrast to the wicked or fallen angels also described in the book. Angels are prominent in the scenes of heaven in chapters 4 and 5, and they reappear to sound the seven trumpets in chapters 8 through 11. The truth of chapter 11 concerning the two witnesses is transmitted to John through an angel, and the warfare against the evil angels is described dramatically in chapter 12. The seven bowls of God's wrath are also administered by the angels in chapters 15 and 16, and the judgment upon Babylon is related to angelic ministry. Angels apparently accompany the Lord in His second coming in chapter 19. The final message of the book recorded in chapter 22 comes to John through the ministry of angels.

Soteriology. God's redemptive purpose is constantly in view in Revelation, beginning with the reference in 1:5 to Christ as the One who "loves us and has freed us from our sins by his blood." His crucifixion is mentioned in 1:7, and constant allusions follow as Christ is presented as the slain Lamb, as the One who redeemed mankind by His blood out of every kindred, tongue, and nation in 5:9, and the One whose blood can make white the robes of the martyrs in 7:14. It is because of His finished work in sacrifice that the Spirit and bride of 22:17 can invite anyone who chooses to take of the water of life without cost. Salvation is ascribed to God three times (7:10; 12:10; 19:1). Emphasis is on the doctrine of redemption, and the saints are declared to be a redeemed people.

Ecclesiology. A major contribution to the doctrine of the church is found in the opening chapters of Revelation with the incisive letters to the seven churches. Here the emphasis is on practical truth and holy living, in keeping with their relationship to Christ, the Head of the church. Reference to the New Testament church is not found in chapters 4 through 18, but the church as the wife of the Lamb reappears in 19:7–8 and is included in the mention of the apostles in the description of the new Jerusalem, which the church shares with believers of other ages.

The word *ekklēsia*, when used in a religious sense referring to believers in the body of Christ, is nowhere found in Revelation from 3:14 to 22:16; rather, the general word *hagios* ("saint") is used to include the saved of all ages. This tends to support the concept that the church is raptured before events pictured beginning in chapter 4. The true church is in contrast to the prostitute of chapter 17, and it is to be distinguished from the saints described as Jews or Gentiles. The church's unique hope—the rapture—in contrast to other believers, is alluded to only obliquely and is not the main substance of chapters 4–19.

Eschatology. Undoubtedly, the principal contribution of Revelation is in the realm of eschatology. Here is presented not only the eschatology of the church in a few scattered references to the doctrine of the rapture (2:25; 3:10–11), but the majestic completion of the prophetic program of the Gentiles and Daniel's program for Israel, both culminating in the second coming of Christ. Nowhere else in Scripture is there more detailed description of the period just before the second coming with special reference to the great tribulation. The events immediately preceding and following the second coming are also spelled out in detail.

Here alone the millennial kingdom is declared to be one thousand years in length, and a clear distinction is made between the millennium and the eternal state. Emphasis in the book is on the triumphant second coming of Christ. Prominent also are the doctrine of divine judgment of sin, the doctrine of resurrection, and the doctrine of reward. No book of Scripture more specifically sets out the believer's eternal hope in Christ in the new heaven and earth and gives greater assurance of God's triumph over evil, rebellion, and unbelief.

Revelation is the eschatological center of the New Testament. Every major theme of prophecy is treated to some extent in this book, with special attention to completion or fulfillment of God's prophetic program. For this reason Revelation cannot be understood apart from the sixty-five books that precede it, although it is in itself a Bible in miniature.

NOTES

1. Robert L. Thomas, *Revelation 1–7: An Exegetical Commentary* (Chicago: Moody, 1992), 2–4.

2. Thomas, *Revelation 1–7*, 10.

3. Clement, "Who Is the Rich Man?", XLII, *Ante-Nicene Fathers*, II, 603.

4. Eusebius, "Ecclesiastical History," III, xx, *The Fathers of the Church*, I, 168.

5. Irenaeus, "Against Heresies," III, iii, 4, *Ante-Nicene Fathers*, I, 416.

6. R. C. Sproul, *The Last Days According to Jesus* (Grand Rapids: Baker, 1998), 228.

7. William Hendriksen, *More Than Conquerors* (Grand Rapids: Baker, 1967), 11–15.

8. Charles C. Ryrie, *Revelation*, rev. ed. (Chicago: Moody, 1996), 9.

9. Warren Wiersbe, *Wiersbe's Expository Outlines on the New Testament* (Wheaton, IL: Victor, 1992), 791.

1 The Things That You Have Seen

PROLOGUE (1:1–3)

1:1 The revelation of Jesus Christ, which God gave him to show to his servants the things that must soon take place. He made it known by sending his angel to his servant John,

The opening words of the book of Revelation immediately reveal Jesus Christ as its futuristic and central theme, presenting Him in His present and future glory. The book's prophetic character is indicated in the words "the revelation of Jesus Christ" that concerns "things that must soon take place." The word *revelation* is the translation of the Greek word *apokalypsis* (the basis of the English word *apocalypse*) without the article, meaning a "revelation, disclosure, or unveiling." It is a revelation of truth *about* Christ, a disclosure of future events surrounding His second coming when Christ will be revealed. It is also a revelation which comes *from* Christ.

The title, "The Revelation to John," merely identifies the human author, whom we believe to be the apostle John (see Introduction; John's name appears three other times in this book, 1:4, 9; 22:8). The subject actually is a revelation *of* Jesus Christ, described as given by God the Father to Christ the Son and then revealed "to his servant." The revelation of the Father to the Son is a common theme in John's Gospel (John 3:34–35; 5:20–24; 7:16; 8:28; 12:49; 14:10, 24; 16:15; 17). The substance of the revelation, "things that must soon take place," is similar to expressions in Daniel 2:28–29, 45 and Revelation 4:1; 22:6.

That which Daniel said would occur "in the latter days" (2:28) is here described as "soon" (Gr., *en tachei*), "quickly or suddenly coming to pass," indicating the rapid progression of events once they begin to occur. The idea is not that the event may occur soon, but that when it does, it will be sudden (cf. Luke 18:8; Acts 12:7; 22:18; 25:4; Rom. 16:20). A similar word, *tachys*, is translated "soon" seven times in Revelation (2:16; 3:11; 11:14; 22:6–7, 12, 20).

Revelation 1:1 also says this revelation came from Christ "by sending his angel to his servant John." The progression of the revelation was from God the Father to Christ the Son to the angel, who communicated the message to John. The name of the angel is not given, though Gabriel has been suggested (cf. Dan. 8:16; 9:2, 21–22; Luke 1:26–31). The reference to John as a "servant" (v. 1) rather than as an apostle is not unusual considering the way other New Testament apostles referred to themselves (cf. Rom. 1:1; Phil. 1:1; Titus 1:1; James 1:1; 2 Pet. 1:1; Jude 1).

1:2 who bore witness to the word of God and to the testimony of Jesus Christ, even to all that he saw.

The expression "bore witness" in verse 2 means "to testify." The book of Revelation is not only the Word of God in that it originates in God, but John testifies to his reception of it. It has the added weight of being "the testimony of Jesus Christ," and John was faithful to record everything he saw. He was an eyewitness.

1:3 Blessed is the one who reads aloud the words of this prophecy, and blessed are those who hear, and who keep what is written in it, for the time is near.

An unusual feature of the opening verses is the special blessing in verse 3, which is addressed to the reader [singular], and to those [plural] who hear and keep the words of the prophecy. This structure reflects the situation of the early church. Copies of the various New Testament books were not readily available, so the letters were read aloud in the assembly (cf. Col. 4:16; 1 Thess. 5:27; 1 Tim. 4:13).[1] The blessing on both the reader and the hearers is fulfilled as they "keep" or observe what is written (which is emphasized again in 22:7). Revelation is the only book of Scripture containing such a direct promise of blessing. This blessing is the first of seven in the book (1:3; 14:13; 16:15; 19:9; 20:6; 22:7, 14).

Revelation is described by the phrase "the words of this prophecy," implying that the book as a whole is prophetic. The importance of the prophecy is emphasized by the phrase "for the time is near." The Greek word for "time" here is *kairos*, which means a season of time in contrast to the terms *hōra*, "hour," and *chronos*, which means time as on a calendar or clock. The next great event on God's prophetic calendar, the imminent return of Jesus Christ to rapture His church, is near from the standpoint of prophetic revelation and could occur at any moment. Our task is to be obedient and expectant!

FOUR AGES IN REVELATION

Chapters	Age	Years
Chapter 1–3	Church Age	? Years
Chapter 4–19	Tribulation Age	7 Years
Chapter 20	Kingdom Age	1,000 Years
Chapter 21–22	Eternal Age	Endless

SALUTATION (1:4–8)

1:4 John to the seven churches that are in Asia: Grace to you and peace from him who is and who was and who is to come, and from the seven spirits who are before his throne,

The recipients of Revelation were the seven churches in Asia, that is, the Roman province of Asia Minor, which is part of modern-day Turkey. We will discuss these in more detail when we consider Revelation chapters 2–3.

John's greeting of "grace . . . peace" is also common to Paul's letters. These two words capture the richness of the Christian faith. Grace is God's attitude toward believers, coupled with His loving gifts—which will never change. Peace refers to our relationship with God—which includes both the peace made with God at salvation and our ongoing relationship with Him, which we can enjoy, or fail to enjoy, as we walk or fail to walk in obedience to God.

The eternal God, the source of all grace and peace, is introduced as the One "who is and who was and who is to come." Because of subsequent references to Christ and the Holy Spirit, this is best understood as referring to God the Father. The concept of past, present, and future corresponds to the three-fold chronological division of the book itself (1:19) and is used to help us grasp the timelessness of the Godhead (this phrase also occurs with variations in 1:8; 4:8; 11:17; 16:5).

Joining the Father in salutation are "the seven spirits who are before his throne." Some consider the term an allusion to the Holy Spirit (cf. Isa. 11:2–3). Others believe these were seven angels in places of high privilege before the throne of God (cf. Rev. 3:1; 4:5; 5:6). The word *spirit* is commonly used of evil spirits, that is, demons or fallen angels; of the human spirit (cf. Mark 8:12); and occasionally of holy angels (cf. Heb. 1:7, 14). Those who favor the seven spirits as referring to the Holy Spirit find justification in Isaiah 11. The message originates in God the Father and the Spirit.

1:5–6 and from Jesus Christ the faithful witness, the firstborn of the dead, and the ruler of kings on earth. To him who loves us and has freed us from our sins by his blood and made us a kingdom, priests to his God and Father, to him be glory and dominion forever and ever. Amen.

This greeting also comes from Jesus Christ in His character as the faithful witness (cf. 3:14), the firstborn of the dead—referring to His resurrection—and as the ruler of the kings of the earth. As the faithful Witness, Jesus fulfilled the role of a prophet (John 18:37). In contrast to those who had been restored to life only to die again, Christ is the first to receive a resurrection body, which is immortal (cf. Acts 26:23).

Just as Christ is "the firstborn of all creation" (Col. 1:15), indicating that He was before all creation in time, so Christ is first also in resurrection. As Christ is first (cf. "firstfruits," 1 Cor. 15:20) so others are to follow Christ in His resurrection. Later in Revelation we read that Christ and all the righteous dead are included in "the first resurrection" (Rev. 20:5–6). The wicked dead are raised last, after the millennium (20:12–13).

Jesus' witness and His resurrection are now past. His role as the Ruler of all the earth's kings and kingdoms is still future, to be achieved after His victory over the beast and the false prophet (Rev. 19), fulfilling Isaiah 9:6–7 and many other verses (cf. Ps. 72:11 and Zech. 14:9). But the special emphasis here is what Jesus has already accomplished for believers, because He "loves us" or "keeps on loving us," and "has freed us from our sins" (the aorist tense in Greek, once for all) by His own blood.

Just as Christ has the right to rule, though He has not yet taken His throne as King, so believers have been made both a kingdom and a priesthood (cf. Rev. 5:10). As a kingdom, we are under Christ's sovereign rule (Col. 1:13), and as a priesthood we have the privilege of direct access to God (1 Pet. 2:9). The only proper response to such a glorious reality is to offer a doxology of praise to God, as John does at the end of verse 6, sealing it with "Amen" ("So be it").

1:7 Behold, he is coming with the clouds, and every eye will see him, even those who pierced him, and all tribes of the earth will wail on account of him. Even so. Amen.

John's doxology is followed by an equally glorious announcement: the second coming of Jesus Christ. The use of the present tense depicts a future act that is so certain to be fulfilled it can be spoken of as already happening. Christ was received by a cloud in His ascension (Acts 1:9), and so He will come again in the clouds of heaven (Matt. 24:30; 26:64; Mark 13:26; 14:62; Luke 21:27).

There is no indication that the world as a whole will see Christ at the time of the rapture of the church (cf. 1 Thess. 4:16–18, where believers will be caught up "in the clouds to meet the Lord in the air," v. 17). But when Jesus comes back to establish His kingdom, all will see Him, including both those who "pierced him" and all the peoples of earth. Of course, Jesus' crucifiers who were responsible for His death on Calvary are dead, but this term doesn't have to be limited to them. According to Zechariah 12:10, the nation of Israel will look on Jesus when He returns and mourn its rejection of Him as Messiah, although many Jews will be saved during the tribulation. The wailing of the Gentile nations will in large part be not a cry of repentance, but one of terror at judgment.

To this John adds, "Even so, Amen." This is a powerful statement of the certainty of Christ's coming and the events surrounding it. The NET Bible seeks to capture this force with the rendering, "This will certainly come to pass! Amen."[2] Jesus is called "the Amen" in Revelation 3:14.

1:8 "I am the Alpha and the Omega," says the Lord God, "who is and who was and who is to come, the Almighty."

God now speaks, declaring Himself to be the Alpha and the Omega, the first and last letters of the Greek alphabet. The description of the Father

---

JESUS CHRIST IS THE CENTRAL FIGURE OF REVELATION 1:1–8. HE IS:

1. The Source of revelation (v. 1).

2. The Channel of the Word and the testimony of God (v. 2).

3. The faithful Witness, the Firstborn of the dead, and the Ruler of earth's kings (v. 5).

4. The God of grace who loves us, has cleansed our sins, and has made us a kingdom and a priesthood (vv. 5, 6).

5. The coming King whose return will be powerful and glorious (v. 7).

6. The Almighty God of eternity past and future (v. 8).

given in verse 4 is then repeated here, concluding with the title "the Almighty," a word that occurs nine times in Revelation. It is probable that verse 8 applies to Christ, even as verse 4 does to God the Father, since Christ is the eternal Second Person of the Godhead (cf. Rev. 22:12–13).

THE VISION OF CHRIST GLORIFIED (1:9–18)

1:9 I, John, your brother and partner in the tribulation and the kingdom and the patient endurance that are in Jesus, was on the island called Patmos on account of the word of God and the testimony of Jesus.

It's clear that John was not writing to the believers in the seven churches of Asia Minor as their superior or simply an uninvolved witness to the events that would impact them. Far from it; he was their fellow believer in Jesus and their fellow sufferer for the Lord's sake. As the longest-surviving apostle, John was well known to these churches, and he felt a very close bond with them in their time of tribulation. And like them, he was also called to patiently endure hardship for Christ. John himself, of course, was also enduring a trial as a lonely exile on the island of Patmos.

This small island, rocky and forbidding in its terrain, about ten miles long and six miles wide, is located in the Aegean Sea southwest of Ephesus just beyond the island of Samos. Early church fathers such as Irenaeus, Clement of Alexandria, and Eusebius state that John was sent to this island as an exile under the ruler Domitian. (See Introduction.) According to Victorinus, John, though aged, was forced to labor in the mines located at Patmos. Early sources also indicate that about A.D. 96, at Domitian's death, John was allowed to return to Ephesus when the emperor Nerva was in power.

It was in these bleak circumstances, shut off from friends and human fellowship, that John was given the most extensive revelation of future things shown to any writer of the New Testament. Although John's persecutors could confine his body, they could not imprison the Holy Spirit or silence the testimony of Jesus!

1:10–11 I was in the Spirit on the Lord's day, and I heard behind me a loud voice like a trumpet saying, "Write what you see in a book and send it to the seven churches, to Ephesus and to Smyrna and to Pergamum and to Thyatira and to Sardis and to Philadelphia and to Laodicea."

John was carried beyond normal sense into a state where God could reveal supernaturally the contents of this book. Ezekiel (Ezek. 2:2; 3:12, 14; etc.), Peter (Acts 10:10–11; 11:5), and Paul (Acts 22:17–18) had similar experiences.

Some Bible commentators say the expression "on the Lord's day" refers to the first day of the week,[3] the day of Christ's resurrection and Christians' day of worship, while others believe it is a reference to "the day of the Lord" as used in the Old Testament—an extended period of time in which God deals in judgment and rules over the earth. Although it is common today to refer to Sunday as "the Lord's day," it is not used this way in the Bible. The New Testament consistently refers to Christ's resurrection as occurring on "the first day of the week," never as "the Lord's day" (Matt. 28:1; Mark 16:2, 9; Luke 24:1; John 20:1, 19; Acts 20:7; 1 Cor. 16:2). Ryrie notes, "[The word] 'Lord's' is an adjective . . . used only here and in 1 Corinthians 11:20 in the New Testament. Unless this is a reference to Sunday, there is no place in the New Testament where this expression is used for that day, since the usual designation is 'the first day of the week.'"[4] So John was projected forward to the future day of the Lord as he received the revelation of the unfolding of the end times.

The voice John heard was undoubtedly the voice of Christ, who had identified Himself in verse 8. John is given the command to write what he sees, a command given twelve times throughout the book (in 10:4 John is told not to write). The message of the entire book is to be sent to each of the seven churches of Asia Minor along with the particular message to the individual church. The seven churches are mentioned in the order of the letters of chapters 2 and 3, following the circular route that a messenger would take in visiting each church to deliver the messages.

1:12 Then I turned to see the voice that was speaking to me, and on turning I saw seven golden lampstands,

In the tabernacle and later in the temple at Jerusalem, one of the items of furniture was a seven-branched lampstand, a single stand with three lamps on each side and one lamp in the center forming the central shaft. It would seem from the description here that instead of one lampstand with seven lamps there are seven separate lampstands, each made of gold and arranged in a circle.

The symbolism of the lampstands is explained in verse 20. They represent the seven churches and are significant symbols of the churches in their principal function of giving light. The golden metal, as in the tabernacle and Solomon's temple, represents the deity and glory of Christ, and the implied olive oil is symbolic of the Holy Spirit.

1:13–16 and in the midst of the lampstands one like a son of man, clothed with a long robe and with a golden sash around his chest. The hairs of his head were white, like white wool, like snow. His eyes were like a flame of fire, his feet were like burnished bronze, refined in a furnace, and his voice was like the roar of many waters. In his right hand he held seven stars, from his mouth came a sharp two-edged sword, and his face was like the sun shining in full strength.

Christ is portrayed as in the midst of the lampstands, that is, in the midst of the churches. His title, "son of man," frequently appears in the Gospels, but only twice in Revelation (here and in 14:14). The title emphasizes Jesus' humanity and Messianic character, and He used it more than any other term to refer to Himself.

This description of Christ has special significance in light of the events that are portrayed in Revelation. His long robe and sash are the clothing of a priest and judge. His snow-white hair corresponds to the vision of God in

Daniel 7:9, which also describes the throne of God as "fiery flames" and "burning fire." This is a picture of the deity of Christ, who possesses all the attributes of God. His eyes as a flame of fire speak of the searching righteousness and divine judgment upon all that is impure. The bronze of His feet symbolizes divine judgment as embodied in the Old Testament type of the bronze altar and other items of bronze used in connection with sacrifice for sin (cf. Ex. 38:30). The picture of Christ standing ready to judge and purify is completed by the description of His voice as the thundering voice of the Son of God revealing the majesty and power before which human authority must bow.

Three additional aspects of this initial revelation are mentioned in verse 16. The seven stars Christ holds in His hand are identified in verse 20 as "the angels of the seven churches." Since the word *angel* means "messenger, one who is sent," it is best to understand these angels not as divine beings, but as the leaders in these churches who are responsible for their spiritual welfare. These messengers representing the churches are in Christ's right hand, indicating possession, protection, and sovereign control.

Christ is also described as having a sharp two-edged sword coming out of His mouth, representing divine judgment (cf. 19:15). As the ancient Roman historian Vegetius stated, the Romans were accustomed to using the sword as a principal weapon of offense. They were instructed to use it in such a way as not to expose themselves to a thrust from their enemy. They were to employ the sword in a stabbing action, since a stroking movement with its edge would seldom kill an enemy. So as used here in Revelation, the term implies killing the wicked.[5] The particular word used for *sword* (Gr., *rhomphaia*) here refers to a long and heavy sword, mentioned five other times in Revelation (2:12, 16; 6:8; 19:15, 21). This is a weapon of devastating judgment.

The final reference to Christ in verse 16 is to the brilliant glory of His face. The bright light which seems to accompany the glory of God blinded Paul on the road to Damascus, and is both a terror to unbelievers and a blessing to believers. In 1 John 3:2, this same apostle assured us: "We know that when he [Christ] appears we shall be like him, because we shall see him as he is."

1:17–18 When I saw him, I fell at his feet as though dead. But he laid his right hand on me, saying, "Fear not, I am the first and the last, and the living one. I died, and behold I am alive forevermore, and I have the keys of Death and Hades."

The majesty and the glory of the vision he saw so overwhelmed John that he fell on his face before Jesus. John was the apostle who had enjoyed such intimate fellowship with Jesus on earth, even leaning on Him at the Last Supper. But now John is in the presence of the risen and glorified Son of God, whose power and majesty are no longer veiled and whose righteousness is revealed to be a consuming fire.

The revelation of God and His glory on other occasions in the Bible had a similar stunning effect, as illustrated in the cases of Abraham (Gen. 17:3), Manoah (Judg. 13:20), Ezekiel (Ezek. 3:23; 43:3; 44:4), Daniel (Dan. 8:17; 10:8–9, 15–17), and the disciples at Jesus' transfiguration (Matt. 17:6). Those who do not fall down before God at the revelation of His glory and majesty are brought to immediate self-judgment and reverent fear as illustrated in the cases of Gideon (Judg. 6:22–23), Job (Job 42:5–6), Isaiah (Isa. 6:5), Zacharias (Luke 1:12), and Peter (Luke 5:8). In compassion toward the disciple whom He loved, Christ laid His hand on John and told him not to be afraid.

The eternal nature of Christ as the Son of God and Second Person of the Godhead is described in the expression "the first and the last." As the eternal God, Jesus is the One who lives (present tense, i.e., "lives continually"), who died at one time, and who is now resurrected and is "alive forevermore." And as the One who conquered death, Jesus also has "the keys of Death and Hades."

This is a statement of Christ's sovereign authority over both physical death and life after death. The Greek word *hades* is commonly translated "hell" in older versions of the Bible. But it is rightly translated here because Hades refers to the intermediate state and is distinguished in Scripture from the lake of fire, or *gehenna*, which refers to the eternal state.

In His death and resurrection, Christ stripped Satan of any authority he may have had over death (cf. Heb. 2:14–15). Because Christ alone holds the key or authority over death, no one can die without divine permission even though afflicted by Satan and in trial and trouble—a word of comfort to all suffering believers. And because Christ is in authority over Hades, He is also sovereign over the life to come.

JOHN COMMISSIONED TO WRITE (1:19–20)

1:19–20 "Write therefore the things that you have seen, those that are and those that are to take place after this. As for the mystery of the seven stars that you saw in my right hand, and the seven golden lampstands, the seven stars are the angels of the seven churches, and the seven lampstands are the seven churches."

Here in verse 19 is a three-part outline of Revelation. Though many outlines have been suggested for the book, none seems to be more practical or illuminating than the one given here.[6] The things referred to as having already been seen are those we have just studied in chapter 1. The second division, "those [things] that are," includes chapters 2 and 3 with the seven messages of Christ to the churches. This contemporary situation gives the historical context for the revelation that follows. The third division, "those [things] that are to take place after this," would include the bulk of the book, comprising chapters 4 through 22.

The advantage of this outline is that it deals in a natural way with the material. In fact, we can say that this outline is the only one that allows Revelation to speak for itself without artificial manipulation and that leads to a futurist interpretation. It is worth noting that practically all other approaches to Revelation produce widely differing interpretations with little uniformity. The futurist school at least agrees on some of its main lines of interpretation.

The concluding verse in chapter 1 gives the key to the symbolism of the preceding revelation. As noted earlier, the mystery of the seven stars is revealed to represent the messengers to the churches, and the seven golden lampstands are the churches themselves.

Perhaps the most important thing we can say at this point is that the revelation embodied in this book, though often presented in symbols, is designed to *reveal* truth, not to hide it. Symbols in Revelation refer to something literal. There is a reality behind the symbols. Though all the symbols are not explained, in the great majority of cases the symbols are interpreted in one way or another in the Word of God. So even though many people say that Revelation is too hard to understand, or too filled with symbolism to be meaningful in today's world, that is simply not the case. God gave us His revelation for our understanding, our obedience, our warning, and our encouragement.

Chapter 1, emphasizing as it does the glory of Christ, is in essence the theme of the entire book moving progressively to the climax—the second coming of Christ in power and glory to the earth in chapter 19. The spiritual significance of Christ and His coming to judge the world is applied in chapters 2 and 3 to the spiritual problems of the contemporary church, and forms the second major division of the entire book.

NOTES

1. Thomas interestingly notes that books like Revelation that an apostle designated for public reading also helped the church in later years to distinguish writings that were intended to be part of the canon of Scripture from the many other writings in circulation at the time that claimed have to apostolic authority. See Robert L. Thomas, *Revelation 1–7: An Exegetical Commentary* (Chicago: Moody Publishers, 1992), 62–63.
2. Michael H. Burer, W. Hall Harris III, Daniel B. Wallace, eds., *New English Translation: Novum Testamentum Graece* (Dallas: NET Bible Press, 2003), 633.
3. For the argument that "the Lord's day" refers to Sunday, the first day of the week and the day of Christian worship, see Thomas, *Revelation 1–7*, 89–91.
4. Charles C. Ryrie, *Revelation*, rev. ed. (Chicago: Moody, 1996), 19.
5. Flavius Vegetius Renatus, *The Military Institutions of the Romans*, trans. Lt. John Clark (Westport, CT: Greenwood Press, 1985), 19–21.
6. See Lewis S. Chafer, *Systematic Theology* (Dallas: Dallas Seminary Press, 1947), vol. 4, 297.

2 The Letters to Ephesus, Smyrna, Pergamum, and Thyatira

The second major division of Revelation begins with this chapter. As we noted, chapter 1 seems to fulfill the command of 1:19, "Write therefore the things that you have seen." Beginning in chapter 4, the material deals with "those that are to take place after this" (1:19). In chapters 2 and 3 the messages to the seven churches refer to "those [things] that are" (cf. 1:19). These messages contain divine revelation and exhortation pertaining to the present age, which is the church age, and so they are some of the most incisive and penetrating passages in the entire New Testament relating to church doctrine and Christian living.

THE SEVEN CHURCHES

1. Ephesus – the Orthodox, but Lost-love Church
2. Smyrna – the Suffering Church
3. Pergamum – the Compromising Church
4. Thyatira – the Tolerant, Permissive Church
5. Sardis – the Dead Church
6. Philadelphia – the Faithful Church
7. Laodicea – the Lukewarm, Useless Church

Since the seven letters of Revelation 2 and 3 are written to all churches at all times and in all places, it is regrettable that these messages of encouragement, rebuke, and warning are not more carefully studied by modern-day

Christians. Their incisive character and denunciation of departure from biblical morality and theology have tended to keep them out of the mainstream of contemporary teaching, to the church's loss. Many of the problems and evils that exist in the church today are a direct outgrowth of the neglect of Christ's instruction to these seven churches.

There has been some debate concerning the theological significance of these seven churches. Clearly, there were many other churches Christ could have selected, including more prominent ones such as Rome, Antioch, Colossae, or even Jerusalem. One reason these seven churches were chosen may have to do with their geographical location in Asia Minor. There is a geographical progression in the order they are presented, beginning at Ephesus, moving north to Smyrna, then farther north to Pergamum, then east to Thyatira, south to Sardis, east to Philadelphia, and southeast to Laodicea. It is also no doubt significant that the number was limited to seven, since this is the number of completeness in Scripture.

It is also obvious that each church the risen Lord addressed needed a particular message to address its particular condition or spiritual need. At the same time, these churches' issues also illustrated conditions that were common in local churches at that time as well as throughout later history. This is why the messages here are applicable to churches in many different settings and historical ages. There are also personal messages of exhortation included, making the messages equally applicable to individual Christians. In fact, each message ends with a personal exhortation beginning with the phrase, "He who has an ear, let him hear."

Many Bible teachers also believe that the conditions in these seven churches represent the chronological development of church history viewed spiritually. They note that Ephesus seems to be characteristic of the apostolic period in general and that the progression of evil climaxing in Laodicea seems to indicate the final state of apostasy of the church in the last days. There is certainly some merit to this view, although it is a deduction from the text rather than being stated explicitly.

The idea that the churches of Revelation 2 and 3 give us the historical sweep of church history from the first century to today does not mean that the characteristics of each church are found only in succeeding generations of the church. In other words, while the modern-day church exhibits many of the problems of Laodicea (the last age of the church in this view), there are also traits from the other churches present.[1] With those cautions in mind, there does seem to be a remarkable progression in the messages, suggesting that the order of the messages appears to be divinely selected to give prophetically the main movement of church history. This view is in keeping with the futurist interpretation of Revelation that this commentary has adopted.

From a study of other passages we do understand that this age will end not with progressive improvement and a trend toward righteousness and peace, but with a movement toward failure and apostasy in the professing church (2 Tim. 3:1–5), as symbolized in the church of Laodicea. This slide will culminate in the apostate Christendom of the great tribulation that will be destroyed. At the same time, God is also fulfilling His divine plan in calling out a true church designed to be a holy bride for His Son. To this true body of believers is given the promise of the rapture before the final tragic scenes of the tribulation begin to unfold.

**STRUCTURE OF LETTERS
TO THE SEVEN CHURCHES**

THE COMMISSION

THE CHARACTER

THE COMMENDATION
(letters to Sardis and Laodicea lack this)

THE CONDEMNATION
(letters to Smyrna and Philadelphia lack this)

THE CORRECTION

THE CALL

THE CHALLENGE

While the message to each church is distinctive, there are similarities among the seven. Each begins with the expression, "I know your works." Each offers a promise "to the one who conquers." Although there is variation in the order, each has the same concluding sentence: "He who has an ear, let him hear what the Spirit says to the churches." The Lord Jesus is also described in each message, but His description differs in keeping with the message addressed to the church.

THE LETTER TO EPHESUS:
THE CHURCH THAT LOST ITS LOVE (2:1–7)

2:1 "To the angel of the church in Ephesus write: 'The words of him who holds the seven stars in his right hand, who walks among the seven golden lampstands.'"

Christ the Sovereign Judge. The first letter is addressed to the angel or messenger of the church of Ephesus. The Greek word *angelos*, which has been transliterated in the English word *angel*, is frequently used in the Bible of angels. However, in several instances this word referred to human messengers (Matt. 11:10; Mark 1:2; Luke 7:24, 27; 9:52). It is best understood here as referring to human messengers to these seven churches, who were probably the pastors or prophets through whom the message was to be delivered to the congregation.

The messenger of the church at Ephesus, which at that time was a large metropolitan city, was undoubtedly an important person and Christian leader of the time. Ephesus was the most prominent city in the Roman province of Asia Minor at this time and already had a long history of Christian witness. In fact, Ephesus is the only one of the seven churches that is mentioned in the book of Acts (chapter 19) and was also a recipient of one of Paul's epistles.[2] The account of the riot in Ephesus resulting from Paul's preaching of the gospel (Acts 19:28–41) is an amazing testimony to the power and effectiveness of early Christian witness in this important city.

After Paul's ministry at Ephesus came to a close, evidence indicates that

Timothy for many years led the work as superintendent of the churches in the area. There is reason to believe that the apostle John himself, now exiled on Patmos, had succeeded Timothy as the pastor at large in Ephesus. It was to this church and to Christians living in Ephesus at the close of the first century, some thirty years after Paul, that the first of the seven messages is addressed.

Christ is introduced in the message to Ephesus as the One who "holds the seven stars in his right hand, who walks among the seven golden lampstands." This portrayal of Christ corresponding to that given early in the first chapter of Revelation is a symbolic presentation of the fact that Christ holds the messengers of these churches in His right hand, a place of sovereign protection as well as divine authority over them. The word for "hold" (Gr., *kratōn*) means to "to hold authoritatively." The messengers, therefore, are held in divine protection and under divine control, echoing what John had written earlier about the security of the believer (John 10:28–29).

2:2–3 "'I know your works, your toil and your patient endurance, and how you cannot bear with those who are evil, but have tested those who call themselves apostles and are not, and found them to be false. I know you are enduring patiently and bearing up for my name's sake, and you have not grown weary.'"

Commendation of doctrine and diligence. As He who walks among the churches' lampstands, Christ is the ever-present One who observes the testimony of the churches of Asia. His message is based on His knowledge of their notable and commendable works. He mentions the hard work and patience of the church in Ephesus, their abhorrence of those who were evil, and their detection of false teachers. These characteristics are sorely needed in the church today where too often we see a failure to serve the Lord patiently, along with the tendency to compromise both with moral and theological evil. The Ephesian church is commended by Christ for turning from both moral corruption and theological error.

The patient way these believers were bearing their burdens is a strong contrast to their refusal to bear with evil. They were patiently enduring for the right reason, "for my [Christ's] name's sake," which provided them with the endurance in doing right for which Christ commended them. (Recall the apostle Paul's exhortation in Gal. 6:9, "Let us not grow weary of doing good.") This church in Ephesus had served Christ well.

2:4–5 "'But I have this against you, that you have abandoned the love you had at first. Remember therefore from where you have fallen; repent, and do the works you did at first. If not, I will come to you and remove your lampstand from its place, unless you repent.'"

Indictment for lack of devotion. In spite of these desirable traits, Christ declared that the church at Ephesus had failed in holding to its first love. The translation "the love you had at first" shows the emphasis of the Greek text. The word for "love" (Gr., *agapēn*) is the deepest and most meaningful word for love in the Greek language. Though the Ephesians had not departed completely from their love for God, it no longer had the intensity or meaning it once had—which is a very serious condition.[3]

The church's problem evidently was not a lack of faith, which would be a defect in either intellect or in theology. Neither is there any indication that the problem was in the area of the will, as if the believers had had never yielded themselves completely to God and thus had not been filled with the Spirit. Instead of the mind or the will, their failure was a matter of the heart. The passion they once had for Christ had grown cold.

This was not always the case. In his letter to the Ephesians about thirty years earlier, Paul wrote: "Because I have heard of your faith in the Lord Jesus and your love toward all the saints, I do not cease to give thanks for you, remembering you in my prayers" (Eph. 1:15–16).

But now the church at Ephesus was in its second generation of Christians, those who had come into the church in the years since Paul had ministered among them. Though they continued to work faithfully as those before them, their love for Christ was missing. The importance of the fervency and purity of this love is revealed in the final words of Paul's letter to the Ephesians:

"Grace be with all who love our Lord Jesus Christ with love incorruptible" (6:24).

The Ephesians' cooling of heart that had overtaken them was a dangerous forerunner of spiritual apathy that later was to erase all Christian testimony in this important center of the early church, as we will see below. The pattern is sadly familiar in church history: a cooling of the church's love for Christ, then its replacement by a love for the things of the world, resulting in compromise and spiritual corruption, followed by a departure from the faith and loss of effective spiritual testimony.

Other portions of Scripture warn of the danger of fading love for God. Paul wrote, "The love of money is a root of all kinds of evils. It is through this craving that some have wandered away from the faith" (1 Tim. 6:10). John warned, "Do not love the world or the things in the world. If anyone loves the world, the love of the Father is not in him" (1 John 2:15), and again, "Little children, keep yourselves from idols" (1 John 5:21). Even loved ones can stand between us and our love for God. Christ Himself said, "Whoever loves father or mother more than me is not worthy of me, and whoever loves son or daughter more than me is not worthy of me" (Matt. 10:37).

To correct this problem, the Lord commanded the church at Ephesus to take three urgent steps. The first was, "Remember therefore from where you have fallen." Going back to the place of departure from God is the first step. For the Ephesian Christians, this meant remembering the love for Christ which once burned in their hearts. So often spiritual defection comes from forgetting what was once known.

The second command is to repent. This is the Greek word *metanoēson*, meaning "to change the mind." The Ephesians were to have a different attitude toward Christ and reclaim their former love for Him. The third command is the outgrowth of the first two: "Do the works you did at first." A true love for God is always manifested in the works it produces. The Ephesian believers were faithful workers, but they were not merely bondslaves of Jesus Christ; they had given their hearts to the Savior in a love relationship.

The seriousness of these commands is evident in the last part of verse 5. If the Ephesians did not obey Christ in these things, they could expect sudden judgment and removal of their lampstand. The meaning seems to be that He would remove the church as a testimony for Christ—which, as we have seen, ultimately happened. The church at Ephesus retained its vigor for several centuries and was not only the seat of Eastern bishops but also the meeting place of the church's third General Council which took place in A.D. 431. Ephesus declined as a city, however, after the fifth century, and the Turks deported its remaining inhabitants in the fourteenth century. The city, now uninhabited, is one of the most important ruins in that area, located seven miles from the sea due to accumulation of silt which has stopped up the harbor of this once important seaport.

2:6 "'Yet this you have: you hate the works of the Nicolaitans, which I also hate.'"

Commendation for hating the enemies of truth. Coupled with the exhortation to repent is the final word of approbation in verse 6 in which the Ephesian church is commended for hating the deeds of the Nicolaitans. There is much speculation concerning the precise identity of this group and the nature of their error.[4] The Nicolaitans apparently were a sect, and some have interpreted their name as meaning "conquering of the people" (from Gr. *nikaō*, meaning "to conquer," and *laos*, meaning "the people"). This view considers the Nicolaitans as the forerunners of the clerical hierarchy superimposed upon the laity and robbing them of spiritual freedom. Others have considered them as a licentious sect advocating complete freedom in Christian conduct including participation in heathen feasts and free love. A third view connects this group with Nicolaus, the proselyte of Antioch (Acts 6:5), one of the seven original deacons.

Whatever the identity and practices of the Nicolaitans, the fact that Christ said He also hated their works speaks very strongly about the terrible nature of what they believed and/or did. Christ's hatred is that of a holy God against whatever counterfeits and distorts the purity of biblical truth. It is not wrong for Christians to hate the enemies of God (cf. Ps. 139:21–22).

2:7 "'He who has an ear, let him hear what the Spirit says to the churches. To the one who conquers I will grant to eat of the tree of life, which is in the paradise of God.'"

The invitation and promise. Christ's letter to the Ephesians closes with an invitation and a promise to those who conquer: "He who has an ear, let him hear what the Spirit says to the churches. To the one who conquers I will grant to eat of the tree of life, which is in the paradise of God."

It is important to note that this promise, and those that follow to the other six churches, are not only for a special group of Christians called "conquerors." Instead, this is a description of what should be the normal Christian life for every true follower of Christ. In his first epistle John asks, "Who is it that overcomes the world except the one who believes that Jesus is the Son of God?" (1 John 5:5). In other words, those in the Ephesian church who had overcome the unbelief and sin of the world are promised the right to the tree of life that is in the paradise of God.

This tree, first mentioned in the Garden of Eden in Genesis 3:22, is later found in the midst of the street of the new Jerusalem, where it bears its fruit for the abundant health and life of the nations (Rev. 22:2). It is especially appropriate that those who hate the world's evil deeds and idolatrous worship are given the reward of abiding in the abundant life that is in Christ in the eternity to come. The gracious nature of the promise is designed to restore and rekindle that love of Christ known in the early days of the church.

The letter to the church at Ephesus reminds us how easily the church's early days of passionate love for Christ can grow cold as the years go by. But Christ never meant for our duty to Him, even faithful duty, to replace our love for Him. The church's "first love" for Jesus Christ has to be continually nurtured, and serve as the genuine motivation for service to our Lord.

THE LETTER TO SMYRNA:
THE CHURCH IN SUFFERING (2:8–11)

The city of Smyrna was about thirty-five miles north of Ephesus. It was a wealthy city, second only to Ephesus in the entire area and, like Ephesus, a seaport. But unlike Ephesus, Smyrna is still a large city (modern-day Izmir, Turkey's third-largest city).

It was once one of the finest cities of Asia. Unger notes, "The city was called 'the glory of Asia' because of its planned development, its beautiful temples and ideal harbor."[5] In this large and flourishing commercial center was the little church to which this message was sent. Smyrna is mentioned only here in Scripture, but from other literature it is evident that this city was noted for its wickedness and opposition to the gospel in the first century.

2:8 "And to the angel of the church in Smyrna write: 'The words of the first and the last, who died and came to life.'"

Christ the Eternal One. In describing Himself as "the first and the last," Christ is relating Himself to time and eternity. He is the eternal God who has always existed in the past and who will always exist in the future. In keeping with this attribute He is also portrayed as the One who was dead, literally, the One "who became dead," referring to His death on the cross. He is also the One who is alive, literally, "who lives," referring to His resurrection.

Thus Christ is the eternal One, a description that is prominent in Revelation 1. This church is reminded that even the eternal Son of God willingly became subject to the rejection and persecution of evil people—just as the church was suffering. But like Christ, whom even death could not hold, the church should also anticipate ultimate victory.

These truths about the Person and work of Christ were chosen to encourage the church at Smyrna in its suffering. The word *Smyrna* itself means "myrrh," a sweet perfume used in embalming dead bodies, and included in the holy anointing oil used in the tabernacle worship in the Old Testament (Ex. 30:23). It was also a common perfume and is mentioned as used by the bridegroom in the Song of Solomon 3:6. And in Psalm 45:8, the heavenly bridegroom is described this way: "Your robes are all fragrant with myrrh and aloes and cassia." The fragrance of Christ as the bridegroom is thus represented typically by the myrrh.

2:9 "'I know your tribulation and your poverty (but you are rich) and the slander of those who say that they are Jews and are not, but are a synagogue of Satan.'"

Commendation of faithfulness in trial. Christ assures the believers at Smyrna that He knows of their oppression by their enemies and its resulting affliction. The word used for "poverty" is the word for abject poverty, not just being poor. It may be that they were drawn from a poor group of people, but it is more probable that their extreme poverty was because they had been robbed of their possessions as part of their persecution and affliction. Christ quickly reminds them, however, "But you are rich," bringing to mind those who are "the poor of this world [yet] rich in faith" (James 2:5, using the same Greek words for poverty and riches).

The persecutors of the believers at Smyrna probably included pagans, who naturally would be offended by the peculiarities of the Christian faith. Two other foes specifically named were hostile Jews and Satan himself. Paul distinguished between those who were Jews "outwardly," or physically, and those who were Jews "inwardly," or spiritually (Rom. 2:28–29). The Jews' hostility against Paul himself was well known.

Ryrie confirms the Jews' hostility toward Christians in Smyrna: "When Polycarp [the bishop of Smyrna] was martyred in A.D. 155, these Jews eagerly assisted by gathering *on the Sabbath* wood and fagots for the fire in which he was burned" (author's emphasis).[6] It has always been this way in the church; false religion has been most zealous in opposing that which is true. The Smyrna Christians found few friends in the hostile world around them.

2:10–11 "'Do not fear what you are about to suffer. Behold, the devil is about to throw some of you into prison, that you may be tested, and for ten days you will have tribulation. Be faithful unto death, and I will give you the crown of life. He who has an ear, let him hear what the Spirit says to the churches. The one who conquers will not be hurt by the second death.'"

The exhortation and promise. Their present persecution, however, was only a taste of the suffering to come. Christ predicted that the devil would do everything in his power to stamp out this church's testimony in his domain. Christ indicated that these believers would be thrown into prison, would be tried, and would have tribulation "for ten days." Christ's exhortation is "Do not fear what you are about to suffer." The promise is "the crown of life."

Biblical interpreters differ on the significance of the "ten days." Some believe it refers to the church period that Smyrna represents, which would be the persecution the church suffered in the second and third centuries under pagan Rome. Others believe it is symbolic of a limited period of time. There are Bible passages where ten is a short period of time (cf. Gen. 24:55; Acts 25:6). It is clear in any case that the church at Smyrna could expect further persecution, including imprisonment for some of their number. The length of their trial, whether interpreted literally or not, is short in comparison with the eternal blessings that would be theirs when their days of trial were over.

The problem of human suffering is as old as humanity. It is not difficult to understand why the ungodly suffer, but what about Christ's own, as in the case of the Smyrna church? The answer to this question is largely bound up in the doctrine of the sovereignty of God. The Bible does help us with these explanations:

1. In some cases, suffering for a child of God may be disciplinary as indicated in God's dealings with the church at Corinth (1 Cor. 11:30–32; cf. Heb. 12:3–13).
2. Suffering may also be preventive, such as Paul's thorn in the flesh (2 Cor. 12:7). Through this affliction Paul was kept from pride in the revelation.
3. A third reason for suffering is that we may learn obedience. Suffering teaches us what we could not learn otherwise (cf. Rom. 5:3–5). Even Christ "learned obedience through what he suffered" (Heb. 5:8).
4. Suffering also allows us to bear a better testimony for Christ. This was true of Paul: "For I will show him how much he must suffer for the sake of my name" (Acts 9:16).

The experience of the church at Smyrna, therefore, though certainly not to be desired, was designed by an infinitely wise and loving God for their good as well as for the better testimony of the gospel.

To this suffering church Christ addresses two exhortations that are His watchword to all believers in similar circumstances. First, "Do not fear what you are about to suffer," which literally translated is, "Stop being afraid." They had nothing really to fear in this persecution because it could not rob them of their priceless eternal blessings in Christ. They were in the hands of God, and no one could snatch them from Him (cf. John 10:28–29). Whatever was permitted was by His wise design.

Second, Christ exhorts them, "Be faithful unto death," which translated literally is, "Become faithful even unto death." Up to this time, apparently no believer had died. But even though their lives might be sacrificed, their real riches could not be touched because they were heavenly. Faithfulness to death would result in the crown of life. This is not to be understood as a crown or a reward accompanying eternal life, but eternal life itself—"the crown which is life." This promise had to be encouraging to John also in his own bleak circumstances on Patmos.

We mentioned above the martyrdom of Polycarp of Smyrna. According to the anonymous *Martyrdom of Polycarp* written in the era of the church fathers, his famous statement upon being told to renounce Christ was, "Eighty and six years have I served the Lord, and He never wronged me: How then can I blaspheme my King and Savior?" The faithfulness of Polycarp to the end seems to have characterized this church in Smyrna in its entire testimony.

The concluding promise to the church at Smyrna is, "The one who conquers will not be hurt by the second death," the judgment at the great white throne (Rev. 20:11–15). The world in its rejection of Christ can inflict physical death on believers, which continues to happen in the twenty-first century as in the first. But those who die in Christ are not subject to the second death, eternal suffering in hell—the sad end of those who die without faith in Jesus Christ as Savior and Lord. Paul understood this promise and looked forward to being with Christ after death (cf. Phil. 1:21–23; 2 Tim. 4:6–8).

Just as the church at Ephesus in large measure is representative of the spiritual state of the church at the close of the first century, so the trials of the church in Smyrna symbolize the persecution the early church endured until the emperor Constantine granted Christians freedom of worship in the Roman Empire at the beginning of the fourth century.

It is noteworthy that Christ's message to the church of Smyrna contains no rebuke. The very trials that afflicted them assured them of deliverance from any lack of fervency for the Lord, which plagued the church at Ephesus, and kept them from any impurity or compromise with evil. It is true in every age that the purifying fires of affliction cause the church's testimony to burn all the more brilliantly.

THE LETTER TO PERGAMUM: THE COMPROMISING CHURCH (2:12–17)

2:12 "And to the angel of the church in Pergamum write: 'The words of him who has the sharp two-edged sword.'"

Christ the Judge of compromise. Pergamum was a prominent city, located in the western part of Asia Minor north of Smyrna and about twenty miles from the Mediterranean Sea. It was a wealthy city with many temples devoted to idol worship and full of statues, altars, and sacred groves, which made Pergamum an important religious center where the pagan cults of Athena, Asklepios, Dionysus, and Zeus were prominent. Among its treasures was a large library of two hundred thousand volumes, later sent to Egypt as a gift from Anthony to Cleopatra.

One of the products for which Pergamum was famous was paper, or parchment, which seems to have originated here, the paper itself being called *pergamena.* One of the prominent buildings was the magnificent temple of Asklepios, a pagan god whose idol was in the form of a serpent. Although the glory of the ancient city has long since vanished, a city named Bergama is located atop the ruins of the old city. A nominal Christian testimony has continued in the town to modern times.

In this atmosphere completely adverse to Christian testimony was situated the little church to which Christ addressed this letter. Here Christ is introduced as the One who "has the sharp two-edged sword," a description given to Him earlier, in 1:16. Here there is added emphasis by the repeated use of the article, literally "the sword, the two-edged one, the sharp one." This is a long spear-like sword, apparently referring to the double-edged character of the Word of God. Reference is made to this spear-like sword seven times in the Bible (Luke 2:35; Rev. 1:16; 2:12, 16; 6:8; 19:15, 21).

The last two references in Revelation 19, where it speaks of the sword proceeding from the mouth of Christ in keeping with the introductory description in 1:16, seem to make plain that the sword here refers to God's Word. Its representation as a double-edged sword indicates on the one hand the way God's Word, by its promises and message of salvation, cuts loose the chains of sin and condemnation that bind the helpless sinner. On the other hand, the same Word is the means of condemnation and rejection for those who refuse the message of grace. The Word of God is both the instrument of salvation and the instrument of death—a pertinent message to the church at Pergamum, which needed to be reminded of the difference between those who were true Christians and those who rejected the gospel.

2:13 "'I know where you dwell, where Satan's throne is. Yet you hold fast my name, and you did not deny my faith even in the days of Antipas my faithful witness, who was killed among you, where Satan dwells.'"

Commendation for holding fast. Christ begins His message with a word of commendation to this church, which existed "where Satan's throne is" and again "where Satan dwells." These are references to satanic power in the evil religious character of the city of Pergamum, made plain in the persecution of Antipas, one of the church's number. We know nothing about this Antipas; his name means "against all," which may indicate that he stood alone against the forces of evil and paid for his faithfulness with his life.

In spite of their evil environment the Pergamum Christians have held fast to Christ's name and have not denied the faith. The reference to "my name" seems to embody a personal loyalty and faith in the Lord Jesus Christ; in addition to this they have not denied the body of Christian truth that accompanies faith in Christ, called by Christ "my faith." Christ's commendation of the faithfulness of the church at Pergamum is a challenge to Christians today to stand true when engulfed by the evil of this present world, the apostasy within the ranks of religion, and the temptation to compromise their stand for the truth.

> **2:14–15** "'But I have a few things against you: you have some there who hold the teaching of Balaam, who taught Balak to put a stumbling block before the sons of Israel, so that they might eat food sacrificed to idols and practice sexual immorality. So also you have some who hold the teaching of the Nicolaitans.'"

Rebuke for compromise. But the Lord also indicated that all was not well in Pergamum. Two blots on their record labeled them as the compromising church: the doctrines of Balaam and the Nicolaitans.

The story of the false prophet Balaam is found in Numbers 22–25. Balaam was hired by the kings of the Midianites and the Moabites to curse the children of Israel. Balaam was never successful in cursing Israel, and he was later killed by the Israelites (Num. 31:8). In that same chapter we learn for the first time that Balaam had advised King Balak to corrupt Israel by tempting them to sin through intermarriage with pagan women and the resulting inducement to worship idols (31:15–16). The doctrine of Balaam therefore was the teaching that the people of God should intermarry with the heathen and compromise in the matter of idolatrous worship. This is in contrast to "the way of Balaam" and "the error of Balaam," that is, selling his prophetic gift for money (2 Pet. 2:15; Jude 11).

Undoubtedly intermarriage with pagans and spiritual compromise were real issues in Pergamum where civic and religious life were so entwined. It would have been very difficult for Christians in this city to have any kind of social contact with the outside world without becoming involved with the worship of idols or intermarriage with non-Christians. No doubt some social contacts or intermarriages would lead to Christians participating in pagan feasts with their immorality that was so much a part of idolatrous worship. Apparently there were some in the Pergamum church who felt that Christians had liberty in this matter. But Christ's absolute condemnation of the doctrine of Balaam is a clear testimony to the fact that Christians must at all costs remain pure and separate from defilement with the world, its religion, and its moral standards. In a similar way they were rebuked for embracing the doctrine of the Nicolaitans, the same group that Christ commended the Ephesian church for hating (see discussion at 2:6).

What God hates the Christian ought to hate as well. The modern tendency to compromise on issues of morality and theology and to downplay their importance had its counterpart in the early church of Pergamum. The word of Christ to this church is a stern warning to modern Christians to examine their morality and faith, and to follow the Word of God where this conflicts with the standards of men.

The temptation and failure foreshadowed at Pergamum is all too evident in church history. With the so-called conversion of the Roman emperor Constantine, the persecution that the church had previously endured was replaced by a period in which the church was favored by the government. The edicts of persecution that had characterized the previous administration were repealed and Christians were allowed to worship according to the dictates of their conscience.

Under these circumstances it soon became popular to be a Christian, and the conscience of the church was quickly blunted. It became increasingly difficult to maintain a clear distinction between the church and the world and to preserve the purity of biblical doctrine. Though some benefit was gained by the successful defense of biblical truth by the Council of Nicea in A.D. 325, the history of the three centuries that followed is a record of increasing corruption of the church, departure from biblical doctrine, and an attempt to combine Christian theology with pagan philosophy.

As a result the church soon lost its hope of the early return of Christ, and biblical simplicity was replaced by a complicated church organization that substituted human creeds and worship of Mary, the mother of our Lord, for true biblical doctrine. The church committed the same sin of which Israel was guilty in the Old Testament: the worship of idols and union with the unbelieving world.

> **2:16** "'Therefore repent. If not, I will come to you soon and war against them with the sword of my mouth.'"

Warning to repent. In this abrupt command, Christ issued a sharp word to the church at Pergamum—and their modern counterparts. Even though many in the church at Pergamum had been faithful and one of their number had died as a martyr, it was still true that the church was being invaded by an evil so serious that Christ warned He would fight against it. There is no alternative to continued impurity and compromise with the truth but divine judgment. The apostasy that is seen in its early stage in the church at Pergamum has its culmination in the still-future apostate church in Revelation 17, which is ultimately brought into divine judgment by Christ, the Head of the church.

> **2:17** "'He who has an ear, let him hear what the Spirit says to the churches. To the one who conquers I will give some of the hidden manna, and I will give him a white stone, with a new name written on the stone that no one knows except the one who receives it.'"

Invitation and promise. As in His messages to the other churches, Christ gives a promise and an invitation to the conqueror. The promise has three elements. First, the believer is assured that he will eat from the hidden manna. Just as Israel received manna from heaven as its food in the wilderness, replacing the onions and garlic of Egypt, so for the true believer in the Lord Jesus there is the hidden manna, that bread from heaven that the world does not know or see—the present spiritual food of believers as well as a part of their future heritage. This seems to refer to the benefits of fellowship with Christ and the spiritual strength that comes from this fellowship.

The second element of the promise is a white stone, possibly a brilliant diamond. There has been a lot of speculation about the identity and purpose of this stone, possibly as an inscribed invitation to a banquet.[7] Whatever the exact nature of the stone, it certainly indicates being accepted or favored by Christ, a wonderful assurance especially for those who have been rejected by the evil world and are the objects of its persecution.

The third promise is the new name, which is unknown until the time it is given. This is an individual name given to the believer, symbolizing the personal heritage of the glories of heaven and the assurance of eternal salvation. We are reminded by this passage that God's purpose is to separate believers from all evil and compromise and to have them as His inheritance throughout eternity. The new name that Christ gives speaks to this relationship.

THE LETTER TO THYATIRA:
THE CHURCH TOLERATING APOSTASY (2:18–29)

2:18 "And to the angel of the church in Thyatira write: 'The words of the Son of God, who has eyes like a flame of fire, and whose feet are like burnished bronze.'"

Christ the Holy One. The fourth message of Christ was addressed to the church in Thyatira, a small, thriving town located about forty miles southeast of Pergamum. The city had been established as a Macedonian colony by Alexander the Great after the destruction of the Persian empire. Located in a rich agricultural area, Thyatira was famous for the manufacture of purple dye, and numerous references are found in secular literature of the period to the trade guilds that manufactured cloth.[8] This is reflected in the only other biblical mention of Thyatira, the conversion of a woman named Lydia, "a seller of purple goods" (Acts 16:14–15) who was converted under the preaching of Paul.

Since there is no record in Scripture of any evangelistic effort in Thyatira, it may be that the gospel was first brought to the city through the testimony of Lydia. Her role indicates that she was a representative of the thriving trade in purple cloth originating in Thyatira. Though Lydia was probably deceased by this time, Christ directed the longest of the seven letters to this small Christian church that may have been the fruit of her witness. But all was not well in Thyatira; this is one of Christ's most severe letters.

Christ is introduced in verse 18 as the righteous Judge who, knowing all things, can uncover every evil (cf. 1:13–15 for a similar description). The difference here is in the Lord's title, the Son of God, rather than Son of Man as in chapter 1. Since each description of Christ is significant to His message to each church, this restatement of His deity is important. The church at Thyatira was tolerating a departure from the true worship of Christ that was so serious that He responded with burning indignation and purifying judgment. His feet are described as being like fine brass, a word used only here in the Bible. Its exact character is not known, but its brilliant appearance enhanced the revelation of Christ as a glorious judge.

2:19 "'I know your works, your love and faith and service and patient endurance, and that your latter works exceed the first.'"

Commendation of works, faith, and love. In the commendations of the churches at Smyrna and at Pergamum, Christ did not mention their works. Smyrna's commendation centered on their faithful suffering, while in Pergamum the commendation related to the difficult place in which the church was giving its testimony. In Thyatira, however, works are mentioned because their works were prominent, and of these the omniscient Christ was fully aware.

It is remarkable that this church was commended for its love and for the increase in the quality of its works, or service. None of the three preceding churches was praised for its love. But in spite of these most commendable features, the church at Thyatira was guilty of terrible sin that Christ deals with decisively.

2:20–23 "'But I have this against you, that you tolerate that woman Jezebel, who calls herself a prophetess and is teaching and seducing my servants to practice sexual immorality and to eat food sacrificed to idols. I gave her time to repent, but she refuses to repent of her sexual immorality. Behold, I will throw her onto a sickbed, and those who commit adultery with her I will throw into great tribulation, unless they repent of her works, and I will strike her children dead. And all the churches will know that I am he who searches mind and heart, and I will give to each of you according to your works.'"

Indictment for spiritual wickedness. Here is a sweeping indictment of the church's toleration of a woman in its midst whose teaching and influence led the church to commit sexual immorality and eat things sacrificed to idols. It is possible that there was a woman leader in the church at Thyatira and that her dominant position may have been derived from the fact that Lydia, another woman, had brought them the message in the first place. But this woman, called Jezebel, led the Christians at Thyatira to participate in idolatry by eating things sacrificed to idols and by taking part in the immorality that was a central feature of idol worship.

Was this woman's name actually Jezebel? Probably not, but in her sinful practices she was fulfilling the role of the historic Jezebel in the Old Testament, who corrupted her husband, Ahab, and all of Israel by attempting to combine the worship of God with the worship of the idol Baal. She did what she could to stamp out all true worship of the Lord and influenced her weak husband to the extent that the Bible says, "Ahab did more to provoke the Lord, the God of Israel, to anger than all the kings of Israel who were before him" (1 Kings 16:33). Jezebel's name became synonymous with subtle corruption, immorality, and idolatry.

The Jezebel in Thyatira had a similar influence upon the church and broke down all boundaries of moral separation from the evil world. She also had refused to repent even though she was given time, another clue to her evil nature. The judgment Christ pronounces against her is fearsome, made even more stark by the present-tense verb "I will throw" (Gr., *ballō*), used here for an emphatic future as if Christ were already in the process of executing His judgment on her and those who committed adultery with her.

Though sexual immorality in general is frequently mentioned in the book of Revelation, this is the only place where adultery is indicated, a reference to the violation of the marriage vow. Those in Thyatira who had sinned in this way had not only violated the moral law of God, but had sinned against their covenant relationship with God that bound them to inward as well as outward purity.

Christ also predicts that Jezebel's children will be killed—a judgment of such unmistakable character that no church would have any doubt about Christ's ability to search people's innermost beings and deliver the appropriate judgment for sin. These solemn words are applicable to anyone who dares to corrupt the purity of the truth of God and spoil the worship of the Lord with idolatrous and pagan practices.

The message to the church in Thyatira seems to foreshadow that period of church history known as the Middle Ages, preceding the Protestant Reformation. In that period the church became corrupt as it sought to combine Christianity with pagan philosophy and religious rites so that many of the church rituals of that period are directly traceable to comparable ceremonies in pagan religion. During this period also there began the exaltation of Mary, the mother of our Lord, which has tended to exalt her to the plane of a female deity and a co-redemptrix with Christ. The church was taught that intercession to God should be made through Mary, apart from whose favor there could be no salvation.

The prominence of a woman prophetess in the church at Thyatira anticipates the prominence of this unscriptural exaltation of Mary. Along with this, the church experienced spiritual depravity, and idols in the form of religious statues were introduced. Gross physical and spiritual immorality resulted, similar to the church at Thyatira. But also like Thyatira, many noble qualities can be found in the church in the Middle Ages. Individual believers were often characterized by a true love for God and selfless service and faith.

The idolatry being tolerated in Thyatira also foreshadows the departure from the scriptural doctrine of the finished sacrifice of Christ. In the Middle Ages the false teaching of the continual sacrifice of Christ was advocated, transforming the observance of the elements of the Lord's Supper into another sacrifice of Christ. This fundamental error of the church in the Middle Ages has been corrected in modern Protestantism by the recognition of the bread and the cup as symbols, but not the sacrifice itself, which Christ performed once and for all on the cross of Calvary. In contrast to the false doctrine exalting the Virgin Mary, Christ introduces Himself to the church of Thyatira as the Son of God, the One to whom alone we owe our redemption and in whose hands alone our final judgment rests.

2:24–25 "'But to the rest of you in Thyatira, who do not hold this teaching, who have not learned what some call the deep things of Satan, to you I say, I do not lay on you any other burden. Only hold fast what you have until I come.'"

Exhortation to the godly remnant. Here for the first time in the messages to the seven churches a group is singled out within a local church as being the continuing true testimony of the Lord. The godly remnant consists of those who did not follow the doctrine of Jezebel or know the "deep things" of Satan. This is a reference to the satanic system of belief and practice often seen in false cults that competes with the true Christian faith. Just as there are the deep things of God (1 Cor. 2:10) that are taught by the Holy Spirit, so there are the deep things of Satan that result from his work.

Christ gives a limited responsibility to the godly remnant. Jezebel and her followers are so evil that they are destined for judgment, but the true Christians are urged to hold fast to what they already have and await the coming of the Lord. Here is the first reference in the messages to the seven churches of the coming of Christ for His church as the hope of those who are engulfed by an apostate system.

2:26–29 "'The one who conquers and who keeps my works until the end, to him I will give authority over the nations, and he will rule them with a rod of iron, as when earthen pots are broken in pieces, even as I myself have received authority from my Father. And I will give him the morning star. He who has an ear, let him hear what the Spirit says to the churches.'"

The invitation and promise. Christ closes His message to the church at Thyatira with a promise to the conquerors that those who keep His works unto the end will be given a responsible position of judgment over the nations. Closely following the prediction of a second coming is this second reference in Revelation to the millennial reign of Christ (cf. 1:6–7). The overcoming Christians are promised places of authority, sharing Christ's rule over the nations of the world.

The word for "rule" (Gr., *poimanei*) means literally "to shepherd." The rule of Christ's faithful ones in the millennium will not be simply that of executing judgment, but also that of administering mercy and direction to those who are the sheep as contrasted to the goats (Matt. 25:31–46). The power to rule in this way was given to Christ by His heavenly Father (John 5:22).

To the conquerors also is given the promise of "the morning star." While various explanations of this expression have been given, it seems to refer to Christ Himself (cf. Rev. 22:16) in His role as the returning One who will rapture the church before the dark hours preceding the dawn of the millennial kingdom.

This letter closes with the familiar invitation to individuals who have ears to hear. Beginning with this letter, this exhortation comes last in contrast to its position before the promise to conquerors in preceding letters. The word of Christ to the church of Thyatira is therefore addressed to any who will hear, who find themselves in similar need of this searching exhortation.

NOTES

1. John MacArthur, *The MacArthur New Testament Commentary: Revelation 1–11* (Chicago: Moody, 1999), 55.

2. Wilbur M. Smith, *The Wycliffe Bible Commentary*, Charles F. Pfeiffer and Everett F. Harrison, eds. (Chicago: Moody, 1990), 1503.

3. The New English Translation notes that the word translated "abandoned" can be used of divorce, "so the imagery here is very strong." See Michael H. Burer, W. Hall Harris III, Daniel B. Wallace, eds., *New English Translation: Novum Testamentum Graece* (Dallas: NET Bible Press, 2003), 634.

4. See Robert L. Thomas, *Revelation 1–7: An Exegetical Commentary* (Chicago: Moody, 1992), 148–50; MacArthur, *Revelation 1–11*, 61.

5. Merrill F. Unger, *The New Unger's Bible Handbook*, rev. Gary N. Larson (Chicago: Moody, 1984), 652.

6. Charles C. Ryrie, *Revelation*, rev. ed. (Chicago: Moody, 1996), 28.

7. Alan F. Johnson, *Revelation*, The Expositor's Bible Commentary, Frank E. Gaebelein, ed., vol. 12 (Grand Rapids: Zondervan, 1981), 442.

8. Thomas, *Revelation 1–7*, 207.

The Letters to Sardis, Philadelphia, and Laodicea

The third chapter of Revelation contains Christ's final three messages to the churches of Asia. The first is to the church in Sardis, a city located in West Asia Minor, about fifty miles east of Smyrna and thirty miles southeast of Thyatira. It was an important and wealthy city located on the commercial trade route running east and west through the kingdom of Lydia, of which Sardis was the capital. It was also the place where gold and silver coins were first struck.[1]

Much of Sardis's wealth came from its textile manufacturing and dye industry and its jewelry trade. Most of the city practiced pagan worship, and there were many mystery cults or secret religious societies. The magnificent Temple of Artemis dating from the fourth century B.C. was one of its points of interest and still exists as an important ruin. The remains of a Christian church building, which have been discovered immediately adjacent to the temple, testify of post-apostolic Christian witness to this evil, pagan city noted for its loose living. The church to which the letter was addressed continued its existence until the fourteenth century, but it was never prominent. Today the village of Sart exists amid the ancient ruins.

THE LETTER TO SARDIS:
THE CHURCH THAT WAS DEAD (3:1–6)

3:1 "And to the angel of the church in Sardis write: 'The words of him who has the seven spirits of God and the seven stars. I know your works. You have the reputation of being alive, but you are dead.'"

Christ the Possessor of the Spirit. The message addressed to the messenger of the church of Sardis is notable for several reasons. Like the letter to Laodicea (3:14–22) it is a message of rebuke and censor, and it is almost devoid of any commendation such as those Christ spoke to the other churches. The reason for the sad condition in Sardis was that the people were surrounded by the grossest form of pagan idolatry. Apparently, instead of standing out against its ungodly surroundings, the church at Sardis had made peace with the idolatry and had lost its witness. This peace, however, was "the peace of the dead" as Ryrie points out.[2]

It is worth noting that Christ is described here as having, or possessing, "the seven spirits of God," whereas in 1:4 they are said to be before the Father's throne. This is an apparent allusion to the sevenfold character of the Holy Spirit as given in Isaiah 11:2–5. A similar description is found later in Revelation 5:6.

Thus Christ is introduced to the church at Sardis as the Possessor of the sevenfold Spirit of God, insuring His righteous judgment of the wicked. Christ also has the star, or the messenger of this church in His possession, making the message being delivered all the more authoritative. The same description of Christ as holding the seven stars in His right hand was given in the letter to the church at Ephesus (2:1) to make clear that the leaders of the church are responsible to no human representative of Christ, but must give account directly to the Lord Himself.

Christ can judge His church righteously because nothing is hidden from His omniscient gaze. While we human beings are limited in what we can see, Christ sees the heart and so can say to this church, "You have the reputation of being alive, but you are dead." Sardis evidently was considered to be a spiritual church and one that had an effective ministry and testimony for God. From the divine standpoint, however, it was actually dead as far as spiritual life and power were concerned. This searching judgment of Christ also speaks to the modern church, which often is full of activity even though there is little that speaks of Christ and spiritual life and power. Barclay observes that a church "is in danger of death when it begins to worship its own past . . . when it is more concerned with forms than with life . . . when it loves systems more than it loves Jesus Christ . . . when it is more concerned with material than spiritual things."[3]

3:2–3 "'Wake up, and strengthen what remains and is about to die, for I have not found your works complete in the sight of my God. Remember, then, what you received and heard. Keep it, and repent. If you will not wake up, I will come like a thief, and you will not know at what hour I will come against you.'"

Indictment and warning. Though the church at Sardis was dead in the sight of God, it is obvious from verse 2 that there were some in the church who still had true life and spirituality. But it was tenuous, because it needed to be strengthened before it died. Christ's indictment could be literally translated as, "not any of your works have I found complete before God." Those who still had true spiritual life are warned to be watchful against a further invasion of spiritual deadness.

The previous history of Sardis should have warned them concerning the possibility of sudden and unexpected judgment. Although the situation of the city was ideal for defense, as it stood high above the valley of Hermus and was surrounded by deep cliffs almost impossible to scale, Sardis had twice before fallen because of overconfidence and failure to watch. In 549 B.C. the army of the Persian king Cyrus scaled the cliffs under the cover of darkness. In 214 B.C. the armies of Antiochus the Great captured the city by the same method as the defenders carelessly guarded only the one known approach to the city.[4] At the time it received this letter, Sardis was in a period of decline compared to its former glory, having been reduced by these invasions.

The spiritual history of the Sardis church corresponded to the political history of the city. Christ's warning to be watchful surely called to mind the occasions when Sardis failed to watch for the enemy. If they refuse to heed His exhortation, Christ promises that He will come upon them as a thief, meaning that He will come unexpectedly with devastating suddenness and bring judgment upon them. The same symbolism is used to describe the Lord's second coming (cf. 1 Thess. 5:2–4), but this figure of a thief coming is not related to that event. The judgment upon the church at Sardis, however, is going to be just as unexpected, sudden, and irrevocable as that related to the second coming.

3:4–6 "'Yet you have still a few names in Sardis, people who have not soiled their garments, and they will walk with me in white, for they are worthy. The one who conquers will be clothed thus in white garments, and I will never blot his name out of the book of life. I will confess his name before my Father and before his angels. He who has an ear, let him hear what the Spirit says to the churches.'"

Invitation and promise to the godly remnant. To those individuals in the Sardis church who conquer by remaining true to Christ, the promise is given that they will be clothed in white garments, which were worn in the ancient world at weddings and other festive occasions. White also represents the purity of God's people as they are clothed in the righteousness of Christ. Those who share the marriage supper of the Lamb, the victorious Christ, are seen in white robes (Rev. 19:7–9).

The saints' white garments are thus a token of their acceptance by God. This is accompanied by the promise that their name will never be blotted out of the book of life. To some, this verse seems to indicate that a believer's name *could* be blotted out, which is contrary to the Bible's clear teaching of the believer's eternal security. To make the continuance of our salvation depend upon works is gross failure to comprehend that salvation is by grace alone. If it depended upon the believer's perseverance, the name would not have been written there in the first place.

Does this verse teach the possibility of the loss of salvation? If so, it hardly sounds like a promise. MacArthur states, "Incredibly, although the text says just the opposite, some people assume that this verse teaches that a person's name can be erased from the book of life. They thus foolishly turn a promise into a threat."[5] The implication of the passage is that those who put their trust in Christ and thus conquer by faith have the privilege of being recognized as the saints of God throughout eternity—even saints from the church at Sardis where so much was offensive to their holy Lord.

In keeping with the view that the seven churches of Revelation foreshadow the church in later ages, some consider Sardis picturing the church in the time of the Protestant Reformation. A great mass of Christendom was dead even though it had a name that it lived. During those years only a small believing remnant took their stand for true biblical revelation and trusted in Christ as Savior. The characteristics of the church in Sardis remarkably parallel those of the Roman church that sparked the Reformation. This fact seems to confirm that the message delivered to this first-century church was prophetic of the future of the church at large during this period.

The message is therefore a series of exhortations not only to the church of the first century but to those who need the same exhortations in every century. Those who take Christ's warnings seriously and accept His invitation to faithfulness are sometimes a godly remnant within the established church as a whole. It was true at Sardis, true at the time of the Protestant Reformation, and is becoming increasingly true in the twenty-first century.

THE LETTER TO PHILADELPHIA:
THE CHURCH FAITHFUL TO CHRIST (3:7–13)

The city of Philadelphia, known in modern times as Alasehir, is located in Lydia some twenty-eight miles southeast of Sardis and was named after a king of Pergamum, Attalus Philadelphus, who built the city. The word *Philadelphia*, meaning "brotherly love," is found six other times in the New Testament (Rom. 12:10; 1 Thess. 4:9; Heb. 13:1; 1 Pet. 1:22; 2 Pet. 1:7 [bis]). Here the word occurs for the seventh and final time, but only here is it used of the city bearing this name.

Philadelphia had a long history and several times was almost completely destroyed by earthquakes. The most recent rebuilding was in A.D. 17. Grapes were one of the principal crops, and, in keeping with this, Dionysus was one of the chief objects of pagan worship. Through the centuries a nominal Christian testimony continued in this city of Philadelphia and prospered even under Turkish rule.

The message addressed to the church at Philadelphia has the unusual characteristic of being almost entirely one of praise, similar to that received by the church at Smyrna, but in sharp contrast to the messages to Sardis and Laodicea.

> **3:7** "And to the angel of the church in Philadelphia write: 'The words of the holy one, the true one, who has the key of David, who opens and no one will shut, who shuts and no one opens.'"

Christ the holy and sovereign God. Christ as the preeminently Holy One is qualified to call the Christians of Philadelphia to a life of faith in Him and a corresponding life of holiness. Peter wrote, "But as he who called you is holy, you also be holy in all your conduct" (1 Pet. 1:15). As the One who is true, Christ is also the Author of truth in contrast to all error or false doctrine. This verse brings out the great truth that right doctrine and right living go together. There can be no holiness without truth.

Christ is also presented as the One who has the key of David and with it absolute authority to open and shut. Christ had been declared in 1:18 to "have the keys of Death and Hades." Here the allusion seems to be to Isaiah 22:22 where, speaking of Eliakim the son of Hilkiah, it is recorded that "I will place on his shoulder the key of the house of David. He shall open, and none shall shut; and he shall shut, and none shall open." Eliakim had the key to all the treasures of the king, so when he opened the door it was opened, and when he closed the door it was closed. Christ has the key to truth and holiness as well as to opportunity, service, and testimony. The Philadelphia church, surrounded by paganism and wickedness, needed the assurance Christ gives that He has the power to bring about His sovereign will.

> **3:8–9** "'I know your works. Behold, I have set before you an open door, which no one is able to shut. I know that you have but little power, and yet you have kept my word and have not denied

my name. Behold, I will make those of the synagogue of Satan who say that they are Jews and are not, but lie—behold, I will make them come and bow down before your feet, and they will learn that I have loved you.'"

Commendation and promised victory. Once again, Christ assures His church that He knows their works; that is, that the entire picture of the church's spiritual condition and service is open before Him. This church's faithfulness is rewarded with the promise of an open door that no one can shut.

This image of an open door is used by Paul to describe opportunities for gospel witness and missionary activity (1 Cor. 16:9; 2 Cor. 2:12; Col. 4:3). Mounce suggests that the open door refers to the open door faithful believers in Philadelphia have into Christ's messianic kingdom, even though they had been shut out of the local synagogue by Jews who opposed the gospel.[6] But the first interpretation seems to better fit in the context of Christ's commendation of this church's faithful testimony. The church's witness was divinely ordained by God and assured by His power and sovereignty.

Some have interpreted the expression "little power" as a word of rebuke rather than commendation. But while it is obviously short of a full commendation, the thrust of the passage is that Christ recognizes in the Philadelphian church a degree of spiritual power that comes from God and that assured them that their testimony would continue. The church is also commended for guarding the truth of God as it was committed to them.

Another commendable quality of the church at Philadelphia was their loyalty to the name of Christ in their public confession of faith in Him. As a result of their faithfulness in witness, Christ promises that their adversaries, described as "the synagogue of Satan," will be forced to acknowledge that the Philadelphians were true servants of God. This reference to the synagogue of Satan is to unbelieving Jews who were opposing the witness of the gospel in Philadelphia and making it difficult for the Christians to bear a good testimony before the pagan world.

The church will always encounter Satanic opposition when it attempts to faithfully declare the gospel and stand for Christ. Those believers today who are experiencing such affliction and persecution may be assured that however violent the opposition and however direct the efforts to thwart the work of God, in the end there will be victory for the cause of Christ.

3:10–11 "'Because you have kept my word about patient endurance, I will keep you from the hour of trial that is coming on the whole world, to try those who dwell on the earth. I am coming soon. Hold fast what you have, so that no one may seize your crown.'"

Promise of deliverance from the hour of trial. Because of their faithfulness, the Christians in Philadelphia are promised that they will be kept from the hour of trial that will come upon the earth as a divine judgment. It should be noted that this deliverance is not only from trial but from a period of time in which the trial exists, "the hour of trial." If the expression had been simply "deliverance from trial," conceivably it could have meant only partial deliverance.

The expression seems as strong as possible that the Philadelphian church would be delivered from this period, which is the great tribulation, Daniel's seventieth week (cf. Dan. 9:25–27). As Bailey notes, "One purpose [of the tribulation] is to bring retribution on the world to punish sin."[7] This pouring out of God's wrath is not the future the Bible promises to the church, for Paul says believers are not "destined" for wrath (1 Thess. 5:9).

Many have observed also that the preposition "from" (Gr., *ek*) is best understood as "out of" rather than simply "from." As the horrors of this tribulation period are unfolded in the following chapters of Revelation, it is evident that the promise here to the church at Philadelphia is one of deliverance from this time of trouble.

The event in view here that will deliver the true church from the tribulation is the rapture, which must occur prior to the tribulation for this promise to have its full force. What is said emphasizes deliverance *from* rather than deliverance *through.* Thus the pretribulational view of the rapture of the church seems to fit best with the biblical context in Revelation 3:10.

As far as the Philadelphian church was concerned, the rapture of the church was presented to them as an imminent hope. If the rapture had occurred in the first century preceding the tribulation that the book of Revelation describes, they were assured of deliverance. By contrast, those sealed out of the twelve tribes of Israel in 7:4 clearly go through the time of trouble. This implies the rapture of the church before the time of trouble referred to as the great tribulation. Such a promise of deliverance would seemingly have been impossible if the rapture were delayed until the end of the tribulation prior to the second coming of Christ and the establishment of His millennial kingdom.

This passage therefore provides support for the hope that Christ will come for His church before the time of trial and trouble described in Revelation 6–19. This time of tribulation will overtake the entire world, as God inflicts His wrath upon unbelieving Gentiles as well as upon Christ-rejecting Jews.

The Lord's coming is compared to an imminent event, one that will come suddenly without announcement. In view of this expectation the church at Philadelphia is urged to hold fast to their testimony for Christ in order to receive their reward at His coming. The expression "soon" is to be understood as something that is sudden and unexpected, not necessarily immediate.

The coming of Christ to establish a kingdom on earth is a later event following the predicted time of tribulation that is unfolded in Revelation. By contrast, the coming of Christ for His church in the rapture (1 Thess. 4:13–17) is portrayed here, as elsewhere in the book, as an event that is not separated from us by any series of events, but is one of constant expectation in the daily walk of the believer. If the church at Philadelphia foreshadows a future period of church history just as other churches seem to do[8], the promises given to this church can be taken as given to all churches bearing a true witness for Christ even down to the present day.

3:12–13 "'The one who conquers, I will make him a pillar in the temple of my God. Never shall he go out of it, and I will write on him the name of my God, and the name of the city of my God, the new Jerusalem, which comes down from my God out of heaven, and my own new name. He who has an ear, let him hear what the Spirit says to the churches.'"

Invitation and promised reward. As with the faithful in the other churches to whom Christ spoke, the Christians of Philadelphia are also promised blessing and reward to come. The entire heavenly city is considered a temple, so these believers will be permanent like a pillar in the temple, and, speaking figuratively, they will stand when all else has fallen. This promise may have had extra meaning to the people of Philadelphia, since their city had been destroyed by an earthquake in A.D. 17. The city had frequent experience with earthquakes, in fact, so the people could appreciate a promise of Christ's ability to make them stand firm.

The promise "Never shall he go out of it" seems to mean that they will no longer be exposed to the temptations and trials of this life and will have their permanent residence in the very presence of God. Those who remain true to Christ are also promised three new names. The expression "new Jerusalem" is a reference to the future eternal city described in Revelation 21 and 22. As these believers have been faithful to their Lord in the present age, so they will be rewarded with full tokens of their salvation in eternity.

Finally, the church of Philadelphia is given the invitation to hear "what the Spirit says to the churches." The challenge to all who hear today is to receive Jesus Christ as Savior and, having received Him, to bear a faithful witness for Him. This will confirm their salvation and their possession of eternal life with God. True believers can not only look forward to present but also future deliverance from this world and the enjoyment of all the privileges of eternity because of the Lord's provision.

THE LETTER TO LAODICEA:
THE CHURCH WITH UNCONSCIOUS NEED (3:14–22)

The seventh and concluding message to the churches of Asia is addressed to the church in Laodicea, a city founded by Antiochus II in the middle of the third century B.C. and named after his wife Laodice. It was situated about forty miles southeast of Philadelphia on the road to Colossae. Under Roman rule Laodicea had become wealthy and had a profitable business in the production of wool cloth. When destroyed by an earthquake about A.D. 60, it was able to rebuild without any outside help. Its economic sufficiency tended to lull the church to sleep spiritually, and though there is mention of the church as late as the fourteenth century, the city as well as the church is now in ruins.

There is no evidence that Paul ever visited the church in Laodicea, but it is evident that he knew some of the Christians there from his reference in Colossians 2:1 where he speaks of his "great struggle" for the Christians both at Colossae and at Laodicea (cf. also the greeting to the Laodicean church, Col. 4:15). Some believe that the epistle to the Ephesians was also sent to the Laodiceans. In any event the church had had a long history, and at the time this letter was addressed to it by Christ it was a well-established church.

3:14 "And to the angel of the church in Laodicea write: 'The words of the Amen, the faithful and true witness, the beginning of God's creation.'"

Christ the eternal and faithful Witness. Christ describes Himself here in an unusual way as "the Amen." The frequent use of "Amen," meaning "so be it," was a feature of Christ's teachings during His ministry on earth. As a title for Christ it indicates His sovereignty and the certainty of the fulfillment of His promises. As Paul wrote the Corinthians, "For all the promises of God find their Yes in him. That is why it is through him that we utter our Amen to God for his glory" (2 Cor. 1:20). When Christ speaks, it is the final word, and His will is always done.

Christ is called the faithful and true Witness in contrast to the church in Laodicea, which was neither faithful nor true. Christ had been earlier introduced as "the faithful witness" in 1:5 and as "the true one" in 3:7. The fact that Christ is both a faithful and a true witness gives special solemnity to the words that follow. Christ is also described as "the beginning of the creation of God." As "the beginning" (Gr., *archē*), He is not the first of creation but He is before all creation.

No doubt the Laodiceans were familiar with the letter to Colossae that must have been in their possession for at least a generation. There Christ is described as "the image of the invisible God, the firstborn of all creation" (Col. 1:15), and as "the beginning, the firstborn from the dead" (1:18). In a similar way Christ declares in Rev. 21:6, "I am Alpha and Omega, the beginning and the end." As the Laodiceans had reveled in material riches, Christ reminds them that all of these things come from Him who is the Creator.

> **3:15–16** "'I know your works: you are neither cold nor hot. Would that you were either cold or hot! So, because you are lukewarm, and neither hot nor cold, I will spit you out of my mouth.'"

The indictment of being lukewarm. This message contains no commendation, and begins with the most scathing rebuke to be found in any of the seven letters. The fact that the letter, like all the others, is addressed to the minister of the church is noteworthy here since some commentators have suggested that Paul's ministry companion Archippus may have been the minister of the church in Laodicea. Paul had strictly charged Archippus, "See that you fulfill the ministry that you have received in the Lord" (Col. 4:17). In verse 15, Paul had sent greetings to the church in Laodicea and stated in the following verse that the Colossians should also read a letter they would receive from the Laodiceans. Though it cannot be determined whether this is a letter now lost or a reference to the epistle to the Ephesians, there seems to be concern on the part of Paul even at that time, a generation earlier, for the spiritual state of the Laodicean church. It is improbable that Archippus was still pastor, however, as thirty years or more had elapsed since Colossians was written.

The church's sad state is described by the word translated "lukewarm," used only here in the New Testament. It is one of three spiritual states that Christ refers to here. The others are cold, which describes the unbelieving world's reaction to the gospel of Jesus Christ, or hot, as those who show genuine spiritual fervor and leave no question as to their faith in Christ.

The normal transition is from a state of coldness to a state of spiritual warmth, which is the experience of many believers. The apostle Paul himself at one time was cold toward Christ and bitter in his persecution of Christians; but once he met Christ on the Damascus road, the opposition and lack of interest were immediately dissolved and replaced by the fervent heat of a flaming testimony for the Lord.

But as the church at Laodicea makes clear, this progression is not guaranteed. Some people may display a mild interest in the things of God at one time. They may be professing Christians who attend church but whose attitude and actions raise questions concerning the reality of their spiritual life. They have been touched by the gospel, but it is not clear whether they really belong to Christ. Such was the case of the church at Laodicea. This was the reason for Christ's sharp word of rebuke. This church could not be classified with the worldly who were cold, or totally unconcerned about the things of Christ. And it certainly could be not be classified with those who were "on fire" in their testimony for the Lord. This intermediate state of being lukewarm is the reason that Christ cannot bear their taste in His mouth. There is something about lukewarmness that is utterly obnoxious to God.

The person who is untouched by the gospel and makes no pretense of putting his trust in Christ is actually a more hopeful case for true repentance than the one who makes some profession but by his life illustrates that he does not really know Christ. There is no one further from the truth in Christ than the one who makes an idle profession without real faith. The church at Laodicea is a sad picture of much of the professing church in the world throughout history, and serves as an illustration of those who participate in outward religious worship without the inner reality. How many have outwardly conformed to requirements of the church without a true state of being born again into the family of God? How many church members are far from God yet by their membership in the professing church have satisfied their own hearts and have been lulled into a sense of false security?

The indifference embodied in the term "lukewarm" in this passage seems to extend to the convictions the Laodicean church had about the central doctrines of the Christian faith. If a church's shepherds never make clear the necessity of the new birth, and do not proclaim accurately the depravity and sin of the human heart and the divine remedy provided alone in the salvation offered by Christ, one can hardly expect the church itself to be better than those who lead it. The result is "churchianity," membership in an organization without biblical Christianity and without membership in the Body of Christ accompanied by the new birth.

Having said this, it is worth noting that none of the sins mentioned in the preceding churches' letters are mentioned as being present in Laodicea. But there are also no commendations for good works here, either. Apparently, being half-heartedly indifferent to the things of Christ is sin enough to make a church intolerable to God.

3:17–18 "'For you say, I am rich, I have prospered, and I need nothing, not realizing that you are wretched, pitiable, poor, blind, and naked. I counsel you to buy from me gold refined by fire, so that you may be rich, and white garments so that you may clothe yourself and the shame of your nakedness may not be seen, and salve to anoint your eyes, so that you may see.'"

Their poverty amid wealth. A lukewarm attitude toward the things of God is often accompanied by the exaltation of material wealth in contrast to spiritual riches. The Laodiceans were guilty on this point. They even boasted, "I have need of nothing." Their lack of economic need seems to have blinded their eyes to their deep spiritual needs, as described graphically by Christ. They are "wretched," a term Paul uses in reference to himself in Romans 7:24. They are "to be pitied," the same phrase Paul uses in 1 Corinthians 15:19 of one who has no hope of resurrection. In describing the Laodiceans as "poor" Christ indicates that they are extremely poor, that is, reduced to begging. In addition, they are "blind" (unable to perceive spiritual things) and "naked" (stripped of clothes, or without proper clothes), here referring to spiritual clothing—the righteousness that comes from God. Their spiritual poverty was the exact opposite of their material wealth.

This sense of self-sufficiency lulled the church at Laodicea into a false sense of contentment. The Laodiceans are typical of the modern world, which revels in that which the natural eye can see but is untouched by the gospel and does not see beyond the material world to the unseen and real eternal spiritual riches. To these who were in such unconscious need, Christ addresses a word of admonition. He could have commanded the church to repent, but with a touch of irony, He advises the church to buy from Him gold, garments, and salve.

These were things the Laodiceans could not buy in the marketplace, however, for Christ was referring to the spiritual counterparts of these physical items the church could easily have afforded. The gold they needed to obtain from Christ was the true riches—more specifically, that which corresponds to the glory of God. They were to have white garments, speaking of the righteousness that God provides. The merchants of Laodicea were famous for their manufacture of a certain black garment that was widely sold. They grew their own glossy black wool used in making this garment. There may be a reference to the contrast between that which the merchants could provide, a black garment, and a white garment that God alone could supply. In any case the white garment alone would be a satisfactory covering of their spiritual nakedness before God.

Christ also advised them to anoint their eyes with salve because they lacked spiritual insight. Laodicea had a famous school of medicine, and either produced or distributed an eye ointment known as "Phrygian powder."[9] Laodicea was famous for this ointment, but it was powerless to cure spiritual blindness. This church seems to have been blind to the things of God. There are few passages in Scripture more searching, more condemning, more pointed than the message to church at Laodicea, and few messages are more needed by the church today, which in many respects sadly parallels the spiritual state of this ancient church.

3:19 "'Those whom I love, I reprove and discipline, so be zealous and repent.'"

Warning to repent. To anyone in the Laodicean church who will listen, Christ warns of the need for repentance. Obviously this verse is not addressed to those who are still cold, those who are still out of Christ, those who make no pretense of putting their trust in Him. It is directed rather to those who profess to follow Christ and who in some sense may be classified as belonging to Him. God is not seeking to discipline those who make no pretense of following Him, but rather deals with those who claim to be His children. These are the objects of God's divine chastening just as children are corrected by a faithful father.

The exhortation is addressed to "those whom I love." The word used for "love" is not *agapaō*, the self-sacrificing love of God, but *phileō*, or "brotherly love," a term for affection with less depth. Although in some cases the choice between *phileō* and *agapaō* may be insignificant, it seems here that John deliberately chose the former word, rather than *agapaō*, which he had used in the same context (v. 9), to express a personal affection that was more in line with the discipline that is also part of God's love. The word translated "reprove" could also be translated "expose, convict, or punish." It is not simply a verbal rebuke, but is effective in dealing adequately with the person who is reproved. These are also disciplined, a term that means to train or educate a child. It is evident that Christ has in mind here those few in the Laodicean church who are actually born again but whose lives have taken on the same lukewarm characteristics as those around them. The fact that they are reproved and disciplined is evidence that they are true children of God (cf. Heb. 12:3–11).

Though lukewarmness should never exist in those who have believed in Christ, Christians are sometimes indistinguishable from those who are merely making an idle profession. A lot of attention has been given to polls revealing that today, even those who identify themselves as born-again Christians are little better off than the world in terms of their rate of divorce and other ills. But "the Lord knows those who are his" (2 Tim. 2:19). The Scripture makes clear that if a Christian will discipline himself and put away sin (cf. 1 Cor. 11:31–32), God will not be required to bring chastening judgment upon him. If he will not judge himself, however, God will deal with him.

3:20–22 "'Behold, I stand at the door and knock. If anyone hears my voice and opens the door, I will come in to him and eat with him, and he with me. The one who conquers, I will grant him to sit with me on my throne, as I also conquered and sat down with my Father on his throne. He who has an ear, let him hear what the Spirit says to the churches.'"

Invitation and promise. We have seen that the seven churches of Revelation offer a prophetic panorama of the condition of the church throughout its history. This foreshadowing has special relevance for us in the case of the Laodicean church, which is representative of the church in the last days that are upon us.

This means we need to take Christ's warning and gracious invitation seriously. He is seen as standing outside the door of the church, awaiting an invitation to come in. This is true of any local church, for Christ must be invited to come in and become the center of worship, adoration, and love. But it is also true of the human heart. No one is saved against his will. No one is compelled to obedience who wants to be rebellious. The gracious invitation is extended, however, that if one opens the door—the door of faith, the door of worship, the door of love—Christ will enter and close fellowship will result.

Some have found in this imagery a parallel to the scene in the Song of Solomon chapter 5 where the bridegroom stands outside the door and knocks in the middle of the night, attempting to awaken the bride so she will open the door to him. A similar idea is found in Luke 12:35–36 relative to the second coming of Christ: "Stay dressed for action and keep your lamps burning, and be like men who are waiting for their master to come home from the wedding feast, so that they may open the door to him at once when he comes and knocks." Thomas believes the return of the Lord is in view here, seeing this as the "eschatological door through which Christ will enter at His second advent."[10] The point in all these illustrations is that Christ does not force Himself upon anyone, but awaits our invitation to be admitted.

The Scriptures do not elaborate on the nature of the fellowship Christ seeks with us, except that the word for "eat" indicates the main meal of the day, the one to which an honored guest would be invited. The significant thing is that the one who invites Christ in will sit down at the same table with Him and enjoy the same spiritual food. Christ is to become the center of our fellowship and that upon which we feed. This is a rich feast, a foreshadowing of that fellowship with Christ we will enjoy throughout eternity.

The promise that the one who conquers will sit with Christ on His throne is made to all genuine Christians who overcome by faith and are victorious over the world (1 John 5:4). What amazing condescension by Christ! Not only does He graciously await an invitation, but He graciously promises that those who display true devotion to Him will share His glory.

What a wonderful invitation. The day will come, however, when the invitation will be closed and Christ will come not for fellowship, but in power and glory, leading the armies of heaven, no longer awaiting any human decision. He will take control, judging those who did not invite Him to come in and rewarding those who opened the door and received Him.

Notice also here that Christ's present position is contrasted with His future millennial reign. Now Christ is sharing the Father's throne and glory. The day will come, however, when He will establish His own throne on the earth (Matt. 25:31) that will be the fulfillment of the predicted throne of David in the Old Testament. Then He will rule with power and glory not only over the nation Israel, but over all nations. In that future time when His sovereignty will be manifested to the entire world, those who put their trust in Him will reign with him as His bride, as the ones who have identified themselves with Christ in this present age of grace.

In the church at Laodicea there was so much that was obnoxious to God and so little that was commendable. Yet Christ extended His personal invitation to them even as He extends to all who will receive it today. This invitation involves recognizing Him as Savior and Lord and entering fully into the blessings of the Christian life.

CONCLUSION TO THE SEVEN CHURCHES

The church at Ephesus represents *the danger of losing our first love* (2:4), that fresh devotion to Christ that characterized the early church. The church at Smyrna represents *the danger of fear of suffering* and was exhorted, "Do not fear what you are about to suffer" (2:10). With persecution against believers worldwide so strong today, the church can take heart that Christ is aware of her suffering. The church at Pergamum illustrates *the constant danger of doctrinal compromise* (2:14–15), often the first step toward complete defection. The modern church that has forsaken so many fundamentals of biblical faith needs to heed this warning!

The church at Thyatira is a monument to *the danger of moral compromise* (2:20). The church today may well take heed to the departure from moral standards that has invaded the church itself. The church at Sardis is a warning against *the danger of spiritual deadness* (3:1–2), of orthodoxy without life, of mere outward appearance. The church at Philadelphia commended by our Lord is nevertheless warned against *the danger of not holding fast* (3:11), and exhorted to keep "my word about patient endurance," to maintain the "little power" that they did have and to wait for their coming Lord. The final message to the church at Laodicea is a telling indictment, a warning against *the danger of lukewarmness* (3:15–16), of self-sufficiency, of being unconscious of desperate spiritual need. Each of these messages is amazingly relevant and pointed in its analysis of what our Lord sees as He stands in the midst of His church.

The present age is an age of grace, an age in which God is testifying concerning Christ and His work, an age in which those who wish to hear may receive Christ and be saved. The invitation given long ago to the seven churches of Asia to hear what the Spirit says is extended to humanity today. A loving God wants people to hear and believe, turn from their idols of sin and self, and look in faith to the Son of God, who loved them and gave Himself for them.

NOTES

1. Robert H. Mounce, *The Book of Revelation*, rev. ed., New International Commentary on the New Testament (Grand Rapids: Eerdmans, 1997), 92.

2. Charles C. Ryrie, *Revelation*, rev. ed. (Chicago: Moody, 1996), 32.

3. William Barclay, *Letters to the Seven Churches* (London: S.C.M. Press Limited, 1957), 87–88.

4. Robert L. Thomas, *Revelation 1–7: An Exegetical Commentary* (Chicago: Moody, 1992), 240–41.

5. John MacArthur, *The MacArthur New Testament Commentary: Revelation 1–11* (Chicago: Moody, 1999), 115.

6. Mounce, *The Book of Revelation*, 101.

7. Mark L. Bailey in *The Road to Armageddon*, Charles R. Swindoll, John F. Walvoord, J. Dwight Pentecost, eds. (Nashville: Word, 1999), 69.

8. Tony Evans, *The Best Is Yet to Come* (Chicago: Moody, 2000), 137.

9. Alan F. Johnson, *Revelation*, The Expositor's Bible Commentary, vol. 12, Frank E. Gaebelein, ed. (Grand Rapids: Zondervan, 1981), 456.

10. Thomas, *Revelation 1–7*, 321.

4 ⟩ The Church in Heaven

THE INVITATION FROM HEAVEN (4:1)

4:1 After this I looked, and behold, a door standing open in heaven! And the first voice, which I had heard speaking to me like a trumpet, said, "Come up here, and I will show you what must take place after this."

Chapter 4 introduces the third major section of the book of Revelation, following the divinely inspired outline of 1:19: "the things that you have seen [chapter 1], the things that are [chapters 2–3] and those that are to take place after this [chapters 4–22]." Beginning here, the revelation has to do with the consummation of this age.

The view that the book of Revelation beginning with 4:1 is future, from the standpoint of the twenty-first century, is a broad conclusion growing out of the lack of correspondence of these prophecies to anything that has been fulfilled. A natural interpretation of this section that understands these prophecies as literal events would require that they be viewed as future. The futuristic concept is supported by the close similarity in the Greek of the expression in 1:19, "[the things] that are to take place after this" and the clause in 4:1, "what must take place after this."

Chapters 4 and 5 are the introduction and background of the tremendous sweep of prophetic events predicted in the rest of the book. If chapter 4 and succeeding chapters relate to the future, they provide an important clue concerning the interpretation of the vision and the prophetic events that unfold in those chapters. One of the principal reasons for confusion in the study of Revelation has been the failure to grasp this point. If Revelation has no chronological structure and is merely a symbolic presentation of moral truth, its prophetic significance is reduced to a minimum. Or if, as preterists teach, the predictions of this section of Revelation are already fulfilled in the early persecution of the church, it also robs the book of any prophecy of the future. (For discussion of the various systems of interpretation of the book of Revelation, see the introduction.)

But a literal interpretation of the prophecies beginning in chapter 4 precludes the possibility that they are fulfilled in any historic event. If the events anticipated in Christ's promise to show us what is to take place are indeed valid prophecy, they should be regarded as a prediction of events that will occur at the end of the age. This demands the futurist view of Revelation.

The expression "after this" in 4:1 identifies the revelation as subsequent to that of chapters 2 and 3. John now is being introduced to a new field of prophecy. As he watched, he saw a door opened into the very presence of God in heaven. The reference to heaven is not to our atmosphere, or to the vastness of space, but to that which is beyond the natural eye that the best of telescopes cannot reveal. This is the third heaven (cf. 2 Cor. 12:2–4), the immediate presence of God.

John also hears a voice that he described as the same voice he had heard earlier in Revelation 1:10 and following. It is described as the voice of a trumpet, inviting John to enter heaven. The command does not anticipate any self-effort on the part of John to enter heaven, but is rather an announcement of the purpose of God to show what would take place in the future. The implication is that the prophecies now to be unfolded will occur after the events of the present age.

The invitation to John to "come up here" is so similar to that which the church anticipates at the rapture that many have connected the two expressions. It is clear from the context that this is not an explicit reference to the rapture of the church, as John was not actually translated; in fact, he was still in his natural body on the island of Patmos. He was translated into scenes of heaven only temporarily. Though there is no authority for connecting the rapture with this expression, this sequence does seem to typify the order of events: that is, the church age first, then the rapture, then the church in heaven.

Though the rapture is mentioned in letters to two of the churches (cf. 2:25; 3:11), the rapture as a doctrine is not a part of the prophetic foreview of the book of Revelation. This is in keeping with the fact that the book as a whole is not occupied primarily with God's program for the church. Instead, the primary objective is to portray the events leading up to and climaxing in the second coming of Christ and the prophetic kingdom and the eternal state that ultimately will follow.

From a practical standpoint, however, the rapture may be viewed as having already occurred before the events of chapter 4 and following chapters of Revelation unfold. The word *church*, so prominent in chapters 2 and 3, does not occur again until 22:16, though the church is undoubtedly in view as the wife of the Lamb in Revelation 19:7. She is not a participant in the scenes of the tribulation that form the major content of Revelation.

It seems that the church as the body of Christ is out of the picture, and saints who come to know the Lord in this period are described as saved Israelites or saved Gentiles, never by terms that are characteristic of the church. Saints mentioned from this point on do not lose their racial background as is commonly done in referring to the church where Jew and Gentile are one in Christ. At the beginning of chapter 4, then, the church may be considered as in heaven and not related to events that will take place on the earth in preparation for Christ's return in power and glory.

THE VIEWING OF GOD'S THRONE (4:2–3)

4:2–3 At once I was in the Spirit, and behold, a throne stood in heaven, with one seated on the throne. And he who sat there had the appearance of jasper and carnelian, and around the throne was a rainbow that had the appearance of an emerald.

From the beginning of verse 2, John finds himself in heaven "in the Spirit" in much the same way as he indicated in 1:10, only this time his location is changed. Though actually on Patmos, he is experiencing being in the presence of God and seeing these glorious visions. The first object that appears to his startled eyes is a throne in heaven with One sitting upon it. The primary impression John has is that of color, and he describes the presence of the One in terms of the colors of precious stones.

Without reference to other portions of Scripture, this verse would be obscure except as a general expression of the glory of God. The details furnished, however, though not explained by John, undoubtedly have a deep significance. It is first of all important to note that this is a throne in heaven, a reminder of the sovereignty of God who is far removed from the petty struggles of earthly government. Here is the true picture of the universe as being subject to the dominion of an omnipotent God.

The precious stones mentioned also seem to have meaning. The jasper stone is described in chapter 21 as being clear like crystal, which would seem to indicate that it may be what we would today call a diamond. The carnelian, or the sardius, is a beautiful red like a ruby.[1]

The significance, however, goes far beyond the color. Though the clear jasper might refer to the purity of God and the carnelian to His redemptive purpose, according to the Old Testament these stones had a relationship to the tribes of Israel. Each tribe of Israel had a designated stone, and the high priest had these twelve stones on the breastplate of his garments when he stood before the altar. This symbolized the fact that he as the high priest was representing all twelve tribes before the throne of God.

Significantly, the jasper and the carnelian are the first and last of these twelve stones (cf. Ex. 28:17–21). The jasper represented Reuben, the first-born of Jacob. The carnelian represented Benjamin, the youngest of Jacob's twelve sons. In other words, these two stones represented the first and the last, and therefore may be regarded as including all the other stones in between; that is, the whole of the covenanted people.

Furthermore, the names Reuben and Benjamin have significance. The word *Reuben* means "behold, a son." The word *Benjamin* means "son of my right hand." In both cases these terms seem to have a double meaning: first, the fact that though Christ is the representative of Israel, He is also the Son of God. Like Reuben, Christ is the first begotten son. And like Benjamin, Christ is also the "son of my right hand" in relation to God the Father. The person whom John sees on the throne looking like a jasper and carnelian is, therefore, God in relation to the nation Israel. MacArthur sees the significance of this as symbolic of the fact that, although the tribulation will be a time of terrible wrath and judgment, God's covenant relationship with Israel will remain intact.[2]

In the description of the foundation of the New Jerusalem in Revelation 21:19–20, we find the jasper, the carnelian, and the emerald—to which John compared the rainbow around the throne. It is evident that these stones have a special significance of glory and majesty that are characteristic of God on His throne. That this is God the Father seems certain because Jesus is represented in this heavenly scene as the Lamb in chapter 5.

THE TWENTY-FOUR ELDERS (4:4)

4:4 Around the throne were twenty-four thrones, and seated on the thrones were twenty-four elders, clothed in white garments, with golden crowns on their heads.

John's attention is next directed to twenty-four thrones upon which the twenty-four elders are seated. There have been a number of suggestions made as to the identity of these heavenly beings. Some regard them as a representative body of all the saints of all ages. Others regard them as representative only of the church, the Body of Christ. Still a third view is that they represent an order of angels.

The fact that they are a representative group, however, seems to be clear from the parallel of the Old Testament where the priesthood was represented by twenty-four orders of priests. There were actually thousands of priests in Israel's day of ascendancy under David and Solomon, but they all could not minister at the same time. Accordingly, they were divided into twenty-four orders, each of which was represented by a priest. The priest Zechariah, father of John the Baptist, was a part of this priestly rotation system when he was chosen to offer incense in the temple and was visited by the angel Gabriel (cf. Luke 1:8–20).

When these priests met together, even though there were only twenty-four, they represented the whole priesthood and at the same time the whole of the nation of Israel. In a similar way the twenty-four elders mentioned in the book of Revelation may be regarded as a representative body. John saw them wearing white garments with golden crowns on their heads. There are two kinds of crowns in Revelation, involving two different Greek words. One is the crown of a ruler or a sovereign (Gr., *diadem*), which is a crown of governmental authority. The other is the crown of a victor (Gr., *stephanos*), such as was awarded in the Greek games when a person won a race or some contest. This crown "refers to a wreath consisting either of foliage or of precious metals formed to resemble foliage and worn as a symbol of honor, victory, or as a badge of high office."[3]

The elders wore the *stephanos*, the crown of a victor, rather than that of a sovereign. It was made of gold, indicating that the elders had been rewarded for victory accomplished. It is significant that the elders already have their victors' crowns. If this passage is regarded as chronologically before the time of the tribulation that succeeding chapters unfold, it would seem to eliminate the angels, since their judgment and reward seems to come later. For the same reason the elders do not seem to be a proper representation of Israel, for Israel's judgment also seems to come at the end of the tribulation, not before. Only the church, which is raptured before chapter 4, is properly complete in heaven and eligible for reward at the judgment seat of Christ. The crowns of gold on the heads of the twenty-four elders would be fitting at this point and would seem to confirm the idea that these may be representative of the church in glory. (See chapter 5 for further discussion of the elders' identity.)

THE SEVEN SPIRITS OF GOD (4:5)

4:5 From the throne came flashes of lightning, and rumblings and peals of thunder, and before the throne were burning seven torches of fire, which are the seven spirits of God,

The awe-inspiring scene described by John is in keeping with the majesty of the throne and the dignity of the twenty-four elders. The sights and sounds he recorded are prophetic of the righteous judgment of God upon a sinful world, and call to mind a similar display of God's majesty at the giving of the Mosaic law (cf. Ex. 19:16). Here these manifestations are a fitting preliminary to the awful judgments that are to follow in the great tribulation as God deals with the earth in righteousness.

John's attention is also directed to seven torches of fire that are burning before the throne. These are identified as "the seven Spirits of God" mentioned earlier in 1:4 and 3:1. These are best understood as a visible representation of the Holy Spirit, symbolizing the perfection and completeness of His activities.[4]

Ordinarily, the Holy Spirit is not humanly visible unless embodied in some way. When the Spirit descended on Christ on the occasion of His baptism, the people saw "the Spirit of God descending like a dove" and resting on Jesus (Matt. 3:16). On the day of Pentecost, the coming of the Spirit was made visible by the tongues of fire that appeared (cf. Acts 2:3). The seven torches of fire, therefore, are the means by which John is informed of the presence of the Holy Spirit. Indeed, we can conclude that all three Persons of the Trinity are present in this heavenly scene, each in His particular form of revelation.

THE FOUR LIVING CREATURES (4:6–8)

4:6–8 and before the throne there was as it were a sea of glass, like crystal. And around the throne, on each side of the throne, are four living creatures, full of eyes in front and behind: the first living creature like a lion, the second living creature like an ox, the third living creature with the face of a man, and the fourth living creature like an eagle in flight. And the four living creatures, each of them with six wings, are full of eyes all around and within, and day and night they never cease to say, "Holy, holy, holy, is the Lord God Almighty, who was and is and is to come!"

The sea of glass and the four living creatures add to the majesty of this revelation of the throne of God. Other than describing the sea as like crystal, John gives us no explanation of its meaning. But as he seems to do elsewhere in Revelation, John expects the reader to draw conclusions from similar scenes elsewhere in the Bible. There may be an analogy or comparison here to the sea of brass in the Old Testament tabernacle or to the sea in the temple. Both were washstands, designed for the cleansing of the priests, and contained water used for various ceremonial rites. This may represent typically the sanctifying power of the Word of God.

Exodus 24:10 describes a scene in which Moses, Aaron, and the elders of Israel have a vision of God, with a pavement under His feet that is described as perfectly clear. But we cannot be certain about the interpretation of the sea of glass.

John is occupied at this point with the incredible four living creatures he saw. They are full of eyes, and each of them has six wings. The translation "creature" is quite inaccurate. The Greek word is *zōon*, which means "living ones." An entirely different word, *therion*, meaning "a creature," such as a wild animal, is used in Revelation 13 to speak of the beast coming out of the sea. The emphasis here is on the quality of life and the attributes that relate to it.

There has been much speculation about the identity of these living ones and the significance of their presence and ministry in this heavenly scene. Some interpret the four living creatures as representative of the attributes or qualities of God. This is probably the best interpretation. Just as the Holy Spirit is represented by seven torches, the attributes of God are represented by the four living ones. The fact that the creatures are full of eyes can signify the omniscience and omnipresence of God who knows all and sees all.

In a similar way the four creatures' depictions are respectively a lion, a calf, a man, and an eagle, which are considered different aspects of divine majesty. All of these are supreme in their respective categories. The lion is the king of beasts and represents majesty and omnipotence. The calf or ox, representing the most important of domestic animals, signifies patience and continuous labor. Man is the greatest of all God's creatures, especially in intelligence and rational power. The eagle is greatest among birds and is symbolic of sovereignty and supremacy.

Comparison has also been made of the four living creatures to the four Gospels, which present Christ in four major aspects of His person. As the lion, He is the Lion of the tribe of Judah, represented as the King of Matthew. As the calf or ox, He is the Servant of Jehovah, the faithful One of Mark. As man, He is the human Jesus, presented in the Gospel of Luke. As the eagle, He is the divine Son of God presented in the Gospel of John.

Taken in general, on this view, the four living creatures are representative of God; as with the seven torches, they are a physical embodiment of that which would be otherwise invisible to the natural eye. To John the scene was unmistakably one of majestic revelation.

An alternative explanation is that the four living creatures are angels whose function is to bring honor and glory to God. Angels who appear in Scripture vary widely in their appearance, and this explanation is a plausible one. Angels are frequently seen in the Bible, especially in apocalyptic books such as Ezekiel and Revelation. The fact that the living creatures have six wings as do the seraphim of Isaiah 6:2–3 adds weight to the interpretation that they are angels.

In addition, the living creatures in Revelation 4 and the seraphim of Isaiah 6 have a similar function in that both ascribe holiness to the Lord Almighty, or Lord of hosts (cf. Isa. 6:3). In any case, the ministry of the living creatures emphasizes the holiness and eternality of God. Their presence in this heavenly scene does much to add to the overall impression of the majesty, holiness, sovereignty, and eternity of God.

THE WORSHIP OF THE LIVING
CREATURES AND THE ELDERS (4:9–11)

4:9–11 And whenever the living creatures give glory and honor and thanks to him who is seated on the throne, who lives forever and ever, the twenty-four elders fall down before him who is seated on the throne and worship him who lives forever and ever. They cast their crowns before the throne, saying, "Worthy are you, our Lord and God, to receive glory and honor and power, for you created all things, and by your will they existed and were created."

Though it is stated earlier that the living creatures do not rest in their praise of God's holiness, according to verse 9 they periodically give special glory and honor and thanks to the Lord. On such occasions, the twenty-four elders join with them in worship and fall down before God on His throne. In their worship, they cast their victors' crowns before the throne, declaring that God is worthy of glory and honor and power because all things have been created by Him according to His perfect will.

The closing scene of chapter 4 brings out several important truths. It is evident that the living ones are designed to give glory to God sitting upon His throne. The emphasis of their praise is on the divine attributes and worthiness of God.

The worship of the twenty-four elders has a more particular focus. They not only worship and recognize these attributes of God, but support their worship by recognition of the fact that God is the sovereign Creator of the universe and, as such, is sovereign over it. In other words, they recognize not only the attributes, but the works of God that reveal His attributes. By casting their crowns before the throne they testify that if it had not been for God's grace, salvation, and goodness, they could not have had victory over sin and death. Here the creature honors, and is subject to, his Creator.

The world today does not give such honor to the Lord God. Though all people benefit from God's goodness and live in the universe He created, they tend to neglect the worship of God. One of the important aims of Revelation is to trace the divine movement of history toward the goal of universal recognition of God. This purpose of God, especially as related to the Son of God, is also spelled out in Philippians 2:9–11:

Therefore God has highly exalted him and bestowed on him the name that is above every name, so that at the name of Jesus every knee should bow, in heaven and on earth and under the earth, and every tongue confess that Jesus Christ is Lord, to the glory of God the Father.

Someday all people will recognize the exalted name of Jesus, whether they are the redeemed in heaven or the lost in hell. Revelation 4 seems to anticipate this future day by revealing an intimate glimpse of heaven where all created beings join in a symphony of praise and honor and worship to the Almighty God. The worthiness of God to receive such praise is related to His sovereign right to rule as the One who sits upon the throne.

The twenty-four elders bear witness to His majesty and glory, His holiness and power, and the eternity of the One "who was and is and is to come." All creatures owe their very existence to Him as their Creator. Chapter 4 is a fitting introduction to what follows in the next chapter, where the glory of Christ as our Redeemer and the Lamb that is slain is an added reason for praise. The person who finds in the Scriptures the revelation of our great God, and who bows before Him now in this day of grace, is wise!

NOTES

1. Ryrie notes interestingly that the sardius was found in the city of Sardis and named for it. Charles C. Ryrie, *Revelation*, rev. ed. (Chicago: Moody, 1996), 42.

2. John MacArthur, *The MacArthur New Testament Commentary: Revelation 1–11* (Chicago: Moody, 1999), 148.

3. Michael H. Burer, W. Hall Harris III, Daniel B. Wallace, eds., *New English Translation: Novum Testamentum Graece* (Dallas: NET Bible Press, 2003), 638.

4. Wilbur M. Smith, *The Wycliffe Bible Commentary*, Charles F. Pfeiffer and Everett F. Harrison, eds. (Chicago: Moody, 1990), 1505.

The Lamb and the Seven-Sealed Book

THE SEVEN-SEALED BOOK
IN THE RIGHT HAND OF GOD (5:1–4)

5:1–4 Then I saw in the right hand of him who was seated on the throne a scroll written within and on the back, sealed with seven seals. And I saw a strong angel proclaiming with a loud voice, "Who is worthy to open the scroll and break its seals?" And no one in heaven or on earth or under the earth was able to open the scroll or to look into it, and I began to weep loudly because no one was found worthy to open the scroll or to look into it.

As he continues to receive a vision of the throne in heaven, John is now introduced to an item of central importance: a book that contains the prophecy of impending events to be unfolded in Revelation. The book is actually a scroll that is given prominence by the fact that it is in the right hand of God. The importance and comprehensive character of the revelation contained is indicated by the fact that the book is written on both sides of the parchment. Further, the document is made impressive by seven seals, apparently fixed on the edges of the scroll in such a way that the seals must be successively broken if the scroll is to be unrolled and read. Wills in the Roman world were sometimes sealed seven times[1], although the number may also simply represent the importance and completely inviolable nature of the scroll. If this is a will, it is a reference to the inheritance that Christ will receive from His Father, which is the kingdom (cf. Ps. 2).

John's attention is directed to this book by the pronouncement of a strong angel. The adjective "strong" indicates that an important angel is selected for this pronouncement (cf. 10:1 and 18:21, where the same word is translated "mighty"). The two angels named in Scripture are Michael and Gabriel, but this angel is not identified by name.

The proclamation is given with a loud voice as the angel asks, "Who is worthy to open the scroll and break its seals?" John then records that no one in all of creation was found worthy. This is another indication that the contents of this scroll are impressive and require the power of God for their revelation as well as for the execution of their program. John says he wept because it seemed the scroll's contents would remain a mystery. This dramatic presentation of the seven-sealed scroll was designed to impress upon John the importance of its contents and of the revelation contained within it.

THE LAMB WHO IS
WORTHY TO RECEIVE THE BOOK (5:5–7)

5:5–7 And one of the elders said to me, "Weep no more; behold, the Lion of the tribe of Judah, the Root of David, has conquered, so that he can open the scroll and its seven seals." And between the throne and the four living creatures and among the elders I saw a Lamb standing, as though it had been slain, with seven horns and with seven eyes, which are the seven spirits of God sent out into all the earth. And he went and took the scroll from the right hand of him who was seated on the throne.

John's distress is short-lived, because one of the twenty-four elders in this heavenly vision tells him that there is indeed One who is worthy to break the seals and open the scroll. What follows is a magnificent description of Christ, "the Lion of the tribe of Judah, the Root of David." The allusion to the lion is a reference to Genesis 49:9–10, where it is predicted that the future ruler of the earth would come from the tribe of Judah, the lion tribe, which is the tribe into which Jesus was born.

Reference to Christ as the Root of David stems from the prophecy of Isaiah 11:1: "There shall come forth a shoot from the stump of Jesse, and a branch from his roots shall bear fruit" (cf. Isa. 11:10). It is declared that He "has conquered," a reference to Christ's victory on the cross (cf. Rev. 3:21).[2] Christ's victory is the focus of this announcement, since the verb comes first in the Greek sentence for emphasis. Thus, translated literally, it is, "Behold, He has conquered, the Lion of the tribe of Judah, the Root of David."

Christ's victory over sin, death, and the grave has earned Him the right to take the scroll and break its seven seals. The Scriptures seem to distinguish between opening the scroll (which would involve beginning the process of unrolling it) and the complete authority to break all the seven seals successively. It implies that Christ is completely worthy and has full authority and sovereignty over the contents of the scroll.

With this introduction, John fixes his gaze upon One portrayed as a Lamb standing in the midst of the throne and of the four living creatures. The Lamb is described as having been slain—a clear reference to Christ's ministry as the "Lamb of God, who takes away the sin of the world!" (John 1:29). The word for "Lamb" is a diminutive that has reference to the Passover lamb sacrificed by Israelites.[3] While a lion speaks of strength, a lamb speaks of meekness, a perfect description of Christ in His first coming as the Lamb who submitted to death, and in His second coming as a conquering Lion. This is the only place in Revelation where Christ is referred to as a lion.

The horns seem to speak of the prerogative of a king (cf. Dan. 7:24; Rev. 13:1). The seven eyes are "the seven Spirits of God," no doubt another reference to the sevenfold Spirit of God. The Holy Spirit was sent by Christ into the world (cf. John 16:7).

Christ takes the scroll out of the right hand of the One sitting upon the throne, who is clearly God the Father. In the act of receiving the scroll, it is made evident that judgment and power over the earth are committed to Christ the Son of God. Daniel 7:13–14 is a parallel passage that reveals the ultimate triumph of Christ when the kingdoms of the world are given to Him:

I saw in the night visions, and behold, with the clouds of heaven there came one like a son of man, and he came to the Ancient of Days and was presented before him. And to him was given dominion and glory and a kingdom, that all peoples, nations, and languages should serve him; his dominion is an everlasting dominion, which shall not pass away, and his kingdom one that shall not be destroyed.

In that future day complete authority over the world will be realized by Christ, an authority that He will exercise both in the judgments that precede His second coming and in His reign for one thousand years that will follow His second advent. Once again in the scroll of Revelation the focus is upon Christ, the central character of the scroll and the One whose glory is supremely revealed in the unfolding pages of its prophecies.

THE LAMB WHO IS
WORTHY OF WORSHIP (5:8–10)

5:8–10 And when he had taken the scroll, the four living crea-tures and the twenty-four elders fell down before the Lamb, each holding a harp, and golden bowls full of incense, which are the prayers of the saints. And they sang a new song, saying, "Worthy are you to take the scroll and to open its seals, for you were slain, and by your blood you ransomed people for God from every tribe and language and people and nation, and you have made them a kingdom and priests to our God, and they shall reign on the earth."

The four living creatures and the twenty-four elders recognized the importance of this scene by falling down and worshiping the Lamb. This should make it clear that this Being is not merely a prophet or an exalted angel, but the Lord Jesus Christ in all the majesty of His deity, even as He is portrayed here in His sacrificial role as the Lamb who died on the cross.

The living creatures and the elders hold harps, which are symbols and instruments of divine worship, and also golden bowls of incense said to be "the prayers of the saints." The same Lamb of God who suffered the abuse of the soldiers and the scoffing of the crowd as well as the agony on the cross is here being given His rightful worship. Apart from the trumpet, the harp (or lyre) is the only instrument mentioned in heavenly worship and was employed commonly in the worship of the Old Testament.

The reference of the saints' prayers suggests the importance of prayer in the earthly scene. Later in the scroll, testimony is made to the continued witness on earth of those who trust in Christ during the time of dreadful tribulation. Their prayers are said to be like sweet incense before the throne of God. The symbolism of bowls of incense representing the prayers of the saints is reflected in Psalm 141:2, where David cried to the Lord, "Let my prayer be counted as incense before you, and the lifting up of my hands as the evening sacrifice!"

The living creatures and elders also sing a new song praising Christ for His work of redemption and for making His people a kingdom of priests ("a royal priesthood," 1 Pet. 2:9). This couplet of reigning and being priests occurs two other times in Revelation (1:6; 20:6) and may have been part of an early hymn. We should note that there is a textual problem in the Greek of verse 10 concerning whether the pronoun is "them" or "us," and whether the verb is the future tense "shall reign" or the present tense "are reigning." The use of "them" is almost certainly the original reading, and "shall reign" is to be preferred. As MacArthur says, "The use of 'them' instead of 'us' indicates the vastness and comprehensiveness of redemption. The twenty-four move beyond themselves to sweep up all the saints of all the ages into praise and adoration."[4]

In the comment on Revelation 4:4 we observed that there are different views of the identity of the twenty-four elders. The translation presented here in the *English Standard Version* (ESV), which is also found in other popular translations such as the *New International Version* (NIV) and the *New American Standard Bible* (NASB), leaves open the question of whether the elders are angels or representatives of redeemed humanity, since they are not identified specifically as being among the redeemed. The song of verses 9–10 is worthy of angels as well as redeemed people.

But in view of the fact that the elders are pictured as having crowns of gold and clothed in white raiment, as if they are already a complete people judged and rewarded, the weight of evidence is still in favor of considering them as representatives of the church, the Body of Christ. The alternative suggestion that they are angels, however, is possible. Adherents of this view point out that the "crowns" could be representative of government of the universe in which angels participate (cf. Col. 1:16).

One further observation can be made about this issue. The song of redemption would be entirely normal for saints, but would be rather unusual if the angels were involved. Nowhere else in the Bible are angels pictured as singing since sin entered the world. In the early joy of creation, before it was spoiled by sin, Job refers to the time "when the morning stars sang together and all the sons of God shouted for joy" (Job 38:7). The morning stars are commonly identified with the angels. Since Adam's sin, however, there is no further record of angels singing. The angels praised God at the birth of Christ (Luke 2:13–14), but this seems to have been a recital of words, not a song.

The phrase "on the earth" at the end of verse 10 is significant, referring to the earthly millennial reign of Christ in which the church will participate. In this glorious earthly scene to follow the dark hour of the tribulation, the church will share the glory of Christ as joint heirs with Christ and partakers of His sovereign rule.

The controversy over verse 10 should not obscure the marvelous symphony of praise that is ascribed to the Lamb. The new song is one that could not have been sung prior to His redemptive act on the cross. He is declared to have the right to rule, not simply in virtue of His deity, but in His victory over sin and death. The right to the scroll has been secured by conquering death and providing a complete sacrifice for sin. Christ's redemption is also worldwide. No language, people group, or nation is excluded.

THE WORSHIP OF THE ANGELS (5:11–12)

5:11–12 Then I looked, and I heard around the throne and the living creatures and the elders the voice of many angels, numbering myriads of myriads and thousands of thousands, saying with a loud voice, "Worthy is the Lamb who was slain, to receive power and wealth and wisdom and might and honor and glory and blessing!"

John introduces the exaltation of the Lamb in verse 11 with the familiar words "Then I looked, and I heard." Forty-four times in Revelation he declares that he saw something, and twenty-seven times he says, "I heard." The scene is described as concentric circles, with the Lamb in the center. He is surrounded by the living creatures and the elders, with an innumerable host of angels around them on every side, all joined in one mighty symphony of praise.

The seven attributes ascribed to the Lamb sum up the worship and adoration of these heavenly beings. This great chorus of praise is a prelude to the mighty scenes that will unfold when in succeeding chapters the seven-sealed scroll is unrolled.

THE WORSHIP OF ALL CREATION (5:13–14)

5:13–14 And I heard every creature in heaven and on earth and under the earth and in the sea, and all that is in them, saying, "To him who sits on the throne and to the Lamb be blessing and honor and glory and might forever and ever!" And the four living creatures said, "Amen!" and the elders fell down and worshiped.

All the rest of creation now joins in this chorus of blessing and praise to the One on the throne and to the Lamb. Climaxing the scene of worship, the four living creatures pronounce their amen, and the twenty-four elders once again fall down and worship. With this awe-inspiring introduction, the groundwork is laid for the unfolding revelation beginning in chapter 6, when the scene shifts once again from heaven to the earth.

The beauty and wonder of this scene are a startling contrast to the dark clouds of divine judgment portrayed as falling upon the earth in the tribulation as revealed in the chapters that follow. The scenes of earth are always dark in comparison to the glory of heaven. The Christian engulfed by temptation, persecution, and trial can take heart in the fact that our Lord also suffered and was tried, and that He in triumph ascended on high, having completed His earthly work. Those who follow in His steps while in the world may endure many afflictions, but they are assured that they will share with the Lord in His glory and His grace throughout all eternity.

The scene of chapter 5 can be considered prophetic of future events in which the church of Jesus Christ will be with Him in heaven. Those who have received Jesus Christ as Savior and who have entered into the blessings of His redemptive work will be numbered among the tens of thousands pictured as giving their worship and praise to the Savior. That which John saw in prophetic vision will be the future experience of raptured believers as they wait with Christ in heaven for the consummation events of the age and the establishment of His kingdom.

For many Christians heaven is an unreal place. Even God's people tend to be occupied too much with the things of this world, which can be seen and touched and felt. Too often goals in life have little to do with eternity's values. Though we have not been given the privilege of glimpsing heaven as did the apostle John, what he saw is plainly written in the Word of God, and we can see through his eyes the glorious picture of the majesty that surrounds the Lord in heaven. By comparison, earth is revealed to be temporary and transitory, and its glory and glitter are tarnished.

Revelation puts earth and heaven in proper perspective, the scenes of earth ending in the tragic denouement of the great tribulation, and the scenes of heaven fulfilled both in the millennial glory and in the eternal state. The true occupation of the child of God should be one of praise and worship of the God of glory while awaiting the fulfillment of His prophetic Word.

Thus, with the heavenly side of the picture revealed in chapters 4 and 5, the narrative in John's vision now turns to the earth in chapter 6. The same Lord and Redeemer who is the object of worship and praise in heaven is also the righteous Judge of the wicked earth and the One by whose authority the terrible events of the tribulation unfold. In the light of these future events, how important is the decision that faces every human soul. Today is the day of grace as the Scriptures make plain. Those who hear and respond to the divine invitation have the promise of blessing throughout eternity and deliverance from the time of judgment that will fall upon those who neglect to enter into the safety of salvation in their day of opportunity.

NOTES

1. Walter C. Kaiser and Duane Garrett, eds., *The Archaeological Study Bible* (Grand Rapids: Zondervan, 2005), 205.

2. Robert L. Thomas, *Revelation 1–7: An Exegetical Commentary* (Chicago: Moody, 1992), 387.

3. John MacArthur, *The MacArthur New Testament Commentary: Revelation 1–11* (Chicago: Moody, 1999), 167.

4. John MacArthur, *Because the Time Is Near* (Chicago: Moody, 2007), 123. For an excellent discussion of the textual problem of Rev. 5:10, see Michael H. Burer, W. Hall Harris III, Daniel B. Wallace, eds., *New English Translation: Novum Testamentum Graece* (Dallas: NET Bible Press, 2003), 884.

6 | The Beginning of the Great Day of God's Wrath

INTRODUCTION

Chapter 6 of Revelation marks an important milestone in the progressive revelation of the end of the age. In chapter 5 John is introduced to the seven-sealed book or scroll in God the Father's hand. In chapter 6 the first six seals are opened with resultant tremendous events occurring on the earth. The interpretation of these events depends upon the understanding of other portions of the prophetic Word. If the events portrayed are taken in any literal sense, it should be clear that they describe events yet future—in the words of Christ, "the things that are to take place after this" (1:19).

This commentary holds the pretribulational view that the church has already been raptured, translated to heaven, before the outpouring of God's wrath. Though the book of Revelation itself does not determine this important question with finality, it is significant that the church that was so prominent in chapters 2 and 3 is not mentioned again until 22:16, except as the wife of the Lamb at the close of the tribulation. Nowhere in scenes of earth that describe the end time (chaps. 6–19) is the church pictured as involved in the earthly struggle.

Further, the hope of the rapture mentioned to the church of Thyatira and the church at Philadelphia does not appear in the detailed prophetic program that unfolds in the book of Revelation. This lends credence to the conclusion that the rapture of the church has occurred before the events pictured beginning with chapter 4. Benware points to the promises of 1 Thessalonians 1:10 and 5:9–10 that believers will be delivered from God's wrath and says these passages "point to the protection and removal of the church during these days of the wrath of God."[1]

Expositors usually agree that there is some relation between the events at the end of the age and Daniel's seventieth week, to be understood as the last seven years of Israel's program prophesied in Daniel 9:27. Many have believed that the events of earth in Revelation 6–19 coincide with the seven years of Israel's program culminating in the second coming of Christ. They assume that Revelation gives a panoramic view of the entire seven years, even though there is no explicit proof of this in the book itself. There is evidence, however, that the events pictured in the seals, trumpets, and bowls are instead a concentrated prophecy of the latter half of this week: a period of three-and-a-half years, designated as a time of wrath and the great tribulation, and introducing the second coming of Christ. Evidence for this is presented as the exposition unfolds.

There is a remarkable parallel between the progress of chapter 6 as a whole and the description given by our Lord of the end of the age in Matthew 24:4–31 (see accompanying chart). In both passages the order is (1) war (Matt. 24:6–7; Rev. 6:3–4); (2) famine (Matt. 24:7; Rev. 6:5–6); (3) death (Matt. 24:7–9; Rev. 6:7–8); (4) martyrdom (Matt. 24:9–10, 16–22; Rev. 6:9–11); (5) the sun darkened, the moon darkened, and the stars falling (Matt. 24:29; Rev. 6:12–14); and (6) a time of divine judgment (Matt. 24:32–25:26; Rev. 6:15–17).

PARALLELS BETWEEN MATTHEW 24 AND REVELATION 6–7

Matthew 24	Revelation 6–7
False Christs (24:4–5)	The rider on the white horse (6:1–2)
Wars and rumors of wars (24:6–7a)	The rider on the red horse (6:3–4)
Famine (24:7b)	The rider on the black horse (6:5–6)
Famines and plagues (24:7b; cf. Luke 21:11)	The rider on the pale horse (6:7–8)
Persecution and martyrdom (24:9–10)	Martyrs (6:9–11)
Terrors and great cosmic signs (24:29; cf. Luke 21:11)	Terror (6:12–17)
Worldwide preaching of the gospel (24:14)	Ministry of the 144,000 (7:1–8)

Thus, any exposition of Revelation must have presuppositions based upon a study of the entire Word of God and consider the question of whether prophecy should be interpreted with the same degree of literalness as other portions of Scripture. Though Revelation abounds in signs and symbols, it was intended to be interpreted with far greater literalness than has been commonly applied. Such an approach yields a remarkable picture of the end of the age that coincides with other prophetic revelation.

The picture before us, then, is God's revelation of the dramatic and terrible judgment that will climax the present age. This constitutes a warning to those who are living carelessly in unbelief to beware lest this present age engulf them. The prophecy of the end of the age is a spur to Christians to snatch souls from the fire and thus prepare them for the coming of the Lord.

THE SHIFTING SCENES OF REVELATION

Beginning in Revelation 6:1, the scene shifts from heaven back to earth. This alternating between heaven and earth occurs throughout Revelation. Here are the major scene shifts.

Earth	Rev. 1–3
Heaven	**Rev. 4–5**
Earth	Rev. 6:1–8
Heaven	**Rev. 6:9–11**
Earth	Rev. 6:12–16
Heaven	**Rev. 7:1–8:6**
Earth	Rev. 8:7–11:14
Heaven	**Rev. 11:15–12:4**
Earth	Rev. 12:5–14:20
Heaven	**Rev. 15:1–8**
Earth	Rev. 16–18
Heaven	**Rev. 19:1–10**
Earth	Rev. 19:11–20:10
Heaven	**Rev. 20:11–22:21**

This alternating pattern reveals to us that the God who sits on the throne in heaven is in complete control of what transpires on earth. The events happening on earth—no matter how frightening and devastating—are neither haphazard nor random. They are ordered by the One seated on His throne. Heaven rules on earth. God's people are to view what is happening on earth from God's viewpoint rather than from man's. Every generation of believers can draw comfort and strength by looking at things from this perspective.

THE FIRST SEAL: ANTICHRIST (6:1–2)

6:1–2 Now I watched when the Lamb opened one of the seven seals, and I heard one of the four living creatures say with a voice like thunder, "Come!" And I looked, and behold, a white horse! And its rider had a bow, and a crown was given to him, and he came out conquering, and to conquer.

As the first seal is opened, John in his vision hears the noise of thunder, a symbolic token of a coming storm. On a warm summer day one can hear thunder in the distance even though the sun is still shining, a sign that a storm is approaching.

The seals seem to unfold successively in a chronological pattern. Out of the seventh seal will come another series of seven trumpets, and out of the seventh trumpet will come another series of seven bowls of the wrath of God. Actually, however, the seven seals contain the whole revelation, since all the trumpets and bowls are comprehended in the seventh seal. The seven-sealed book therefore is the comprehensive program of God culminating in the second coming of Christ.

It is important to note that this revelation indicates a succession of events, though not all expositors have agreed on this conclusion. Some believe that the seals, trumpets, and bowls are a symbolic presentation of the whole of human history. The decision to reject the historical school of interpretation in favor of the futuristic approach is most important in understanding the subsequent chapters of Revelation. While many arguments can be cited pro and con, the final choice must be based upon the judgment as to which provides the most sensible and self-consistent interpretation of Revelation. The historical school does not meet the test of providing such a self-consistent interpretation. At least fifty different systems of interpretation have arisen from the historical view.

THE SEVEN SEAL JUDGMENTS

First Seal (6:1–2)	White Horse: Antichrist
Second Seal (6:3–4)	Red Horse: War
Third Seal (6:5–6)	Black Horse: Famine
Fourth Seal (6:7–8)	Pale Horse: Death and Hell
Fifth Seal (6:9–11)	Martyrs in Heaven
Sixth Seal (6:12–17)	Universal Upheaval and Devastation
Seventh Seal (8:1–2)	The Seven Trumpets

While even in the futurist school minor variations will be found in various expositors, the general conclusion that these chapters picture definite future events is the important coherent factor. The subsequent exposition of Revelation must be its own proof that the futuristic school provides a sensible explanation of the major events prophesied in the book. Many of the historical interpretations have already been proven false by historical developments. The ultimate proof of the futuristic interpretation will be in future events.

The noise of thunder captures John's attention, and he witnesses the scene unfolding before him. John says he looked, and then he adds the word "behold" to indicate the startling character of the vision: a white horse on which a man is sitting. He is carrying a bow, has been given a crown, and his purpose is to conquer.

No explanation is given of this vision. In many cases the reader of Revelation is not left to his own ingenuity but is given the meaning of what is beheld. Here, however, the appeal is to a general knowledge of Scripture. Because no specific interpretation of the vision is given, more diverse explanations have been given of verse 2 than probably any other portion of the entire book.

Of the many possibilities, two stand out as worthy of mention. Some believe the rider of the white horse is none other than Christ Himself. This is characteristic of the historical school of interpretation that regards the Revelation as history rather than prophecy. However, some of this school regard this scene as future and as picturing Christ as the ultimate Victor of the ages.

There are three main reasons it is difficult to envision Christ as the rider on the white horse in Revelation 6:2. First, this is out of order chronologically, for Christ comes on a white horse not at the beginning but at the end of the tribulation. Second, the four horses and their riders have an essential likeness to each other. The other three horsemen are all evil powers of tragedy and destruction. Christ cannot be put on the same level as the other three horsemen. Third, Christ is the Lamb who is opening the seals in Revelation 6:1. He is the only one worthy to do so (5:2–8) and remains in control of their contents. It would be strange for Him to open the seal judgments and also constitute the contents of one of the seals.

A more plausible explanation is that the rider of the white horse is none other than the "prince who is to come" of Daniel 9:26, who is to head up the revived Roman Empire and ultimately become the world ruler. He is Satan's masterpiece and the counterfeit of all that Christ is or claims to be. He is therefore cast in the role of a conqueror, which seems to be the significance of the white horse. In biblical times, it was customary for a conqueror to ride in triumph on a white horse.

While the dispute as to the identity of the rider cannot be finally settled, especially in the brief compass of this discussion, his identification as the world ruler of the tribulation, the same individual described as the beast out of the sea in Revelation 13, is preferred.[2]

The fact that the rider has a bow, symbolic of distant victory, but no arrows has been taken to mean a bloodless victory, but this interpretation cannot be dogmatically held. He is, however, given the crown of a victor, not the crown of a sovereign. The emphasis is not so much on his authority as on his victory, as confirmed by the latter part of verse 2. Though he is in fact destined to be a world ruler, the emphasis is on the temporary victory that is his.

THE SECOND SEAL: WAR (6:3–4)

6:3–4 When he opened the second seal, I heard the second living creature say, "Come!" And out came another horse, bright red. Its rider was permitted to take peace from the earth, so that men should slay one another, and he was given a great sword.

As the Lamb opens the second seal, John observes another horse and rider with the power to disrupt peace and cause people to kill one another, as indicated by the "great sword" given to the rider. Ryrie notes that the giving of the sword to the rider is an indication that the event is under God's control—an encouraging reminder.[3] Some have identified this second rider as the false prophet who works in conjunction with the world ruler, the Antichrist, who rides the first horse. The difficulty with this interpretation is that it does not properly account for the riders on the third and fourth horses.

If the first seal is a period of peace (though this seems to be contradicted by the fact that the rider of the first horse conquers), when the second seal is broken, military warfare breaks out and peace is taken from the world. The constant tension among nations and the ambitions of rulers have their climax in this period before Christ comes. Though "wars and rumors of wars" (Matt. 24:6) are characteristic of the age, it is evident that warfare occupies a large place in the consummation of the age with a resultant great loss of life. There apparently is a series of wars, the greatest of which is underway at the time of the second coming. The hope of permanent peace by means of the United Nations and other human efforts is doomed to failure.

THE THIRD SEAL: FAMINE (6:5–6)

6:5–6 When he opened the third seal, I heard the third living creature say, "Come!" And I looked, and behold, a black horse! And its rider had a pair of scales in his hand. And I heard what seemed to be a voice in the midst of the four living creatures, saying, "A quart of wheat for a denarius, and three quarts of barley for a denarius, and do not harm the oil and wine!"

In the aftermath of war a great famine is revealed. John records that he sees a black horse and one sitting on the horse with a pair of balances in his hand used to weigh different commodities. The Roman denarius was worth about fifteen cents. In the wage scale of that time, it was common for a person to receive one denarius for an entire day's work. For such a coin, one measure of wheat or three measures of barley could be purchased in the vision here.

The explanation seems to be this: A measure of wheat is approximately what a laboring man would eat in one meal. If he used his denarius to buy barley, a cheaper grain, he would have enough from his day's wages to buy three good meals of barley. If he bought wheat, a more precious grain, he would be able to buy enough for only one meal. There would be no money left to buy other things, such as oil or wine, which were considered essential in biblical times.

To put this scenario in ordinary language, the situation would be such that a person would have to spend a day's wages for a loaf of bread with no money left to buy anything else. The symbolism therefore indicates a time of famine when life will be reduced to the barest necessities, for famine is almost always the aftermath of war. The somber picture is emphasized by the color of the horse, black being the symbol of suffering (cf. Lam. 5:10 KJV).

THE FOURTH SEAL: DEATH (6:7–8)

6:7–8 When he opened the fourth seal, I heard the voice of the fourth living creature say, "Come!" And I looked, and behold, a pale horse! And its rider's name was Death, and Hades followed him. And they were given authority over a fourth of the earth, to kill with sword and with famine and with pestilence and by wild beasts of the earth.

With the opening of the fourth seal a dramatic picture of divine judgment upon the world is unfolded. John introduces the vision with the same dramatic expression he uses in verse 2, indicating that what he sees again startles him. This horse is literally a pale green, like young vegetation, the same word being used to describe the color of the grass in Mark 6:39 and Revelation 8:7; 9:4. In the context, it is a ghastly color.

The Greek word for the horse's color is *chlōros*—from which we derive our English word *chlorine*. *Chlōros* usually denotes a pale green color and is used elsewhere in Revelation to describe the color of grass and vegetation (8:7; 9:4) In Revelation 6:8, it pictures a decomposing corpse. Robert Thomas describes the grotesque color of the fourth horse as "the yellowish green of decay, the pallor of death. It is the pale ashen color that images a face bleached because of terror. It recalls a corpse in the advanced state of corruption."[4]

The rider is pictured as Death and that which follows as Hades, the abode of the dead. These riders have startling power over one-fourth part of the earth, to kill with the sword, hunger, and wild animals.

There are three main views on the identity of the "wild beasts of the earth" in Revelation 6:8. First, it's possible that this refers to actual wild animals that will become especially ferocious during the tribulation as their normal food supplies are disrupted. They will look for prey and take advantage of the defenseless as God uses them to terrorize and destroy. Another view is that this term is a reference to brutal military and political leaders of the end times. This view is based on the fact that the same phrase "wild beasts," which in the Greek is *thērion*, is used thirty-eight times in Revelation, and every other time refers to the coming Antichrist or his henchman, the false prophet. A third view is that this is a reference to pandemic plagues such as swine flu, bird flu, AIDS, Ebola, etc. that come from animals. Whatever the final fulfillment, this will add to the misery of earth's darkest hour.

The area covered by this judgment, described as the earth, though sometimes used only of the promised land given to Israel, is a general word referring to the inhabited world and in this context apparently extends to the entire earth.

By any standard of comparison this is an awesome judgment. If one-fourth of the world's population is destroyed in the fourth seal, it would be the greatest destruction of human life ever recorded. The population of the human race in Noah's day undoubtedly was far less than the figure here cited as dying. If such a judgment would fall upon a world population of approximately six billion people, it would mean the deaths of 1,500,000,000 people. It should be clear from this description that the divine judgments being meted out to the earth are not trivial in character but describe a period of world history awful beyond any words, a period without precedent in its character and extent.

The fact that this devastating judgment comes at this stage casts light on the important problem of determining when in the sequence of Revelation the great tribulation predicted by our Lord (Matt. 24:15–25) begins in relationship to the seal judgments.

If the revelation of the final stage of Israel's predicted program is considered future, as recorded in Daniel 9:27, the last seven years or the seventieth week of Daniel's prophecy will immediately precede the second coming of Christ. According to Daniel 9:27 the seven-year period is divided into two halves: the first three-and-a-half years in which Israel is apparently protected under a covenant with the Gentile world ruler, the prince mentioned in Daniel 9:26, and the last three-and-a-half years in which there is unprecedented trouble. In this period, Israel becomes the object of persecution instead of being protected from her enemies.

The prophet Daniel speaks of this period again when he predicts in Daniel 12:1:

"At that time shall arise Michael, the great prince who has charge of your people. And there shall be a time of trouble, such as never has been since there was a nation till that time. But at that time your people shall be delivered, everyone whose name shall be found written in the book."

Jeremiah the prophet refers to the same event in Jeremiah 30:7 when he declares, "Alas! That day is so great there is none like it; it is a time of distress for Jacob; yet he shall be saved out of it."

Other Old Testament passages bear witness to the awful character of this future time of trouble (cf. Joel 2:1–3). Since the judgment described in the fourth seal is unparalleled, it seems to correspond with greater accuracy to the latter half of Daniel's seventieth week than to the earlier half and for that reason must be the time of great tribulation that Christ declared would exceed by far anything the world had previously known.

So great will be the trial of that period that Christ exhorted those living in Israel at that time to flee to the mountains to escape their persecutors:

> "For then there will be great tribulation, such as has not been from the beginning of the world until now, no, and never will be. And if those days had not been cut short, no human being would be saved. But for the sake of the elect those days will be cut short." (Matt. 24:21–22)

If the supreme mark of this great tribulation is unprecedented trouble, the fourth seal certainly qualifies as describing this period. Though some expositors believe the great tribulation does not begin until chapter 11, on the basis of the preceding evidence many have concluded that the great tribulation must begin much earlier, possibly as early as the first seal of Revelation 6. Though the book of Revelation itself does not state specifically what event begins the great tribulation, the characteristics unfolded in the fourth seal would indicate the great tribulation is underway at the time. The wars and famines predicted in the second and third seals are not unfamiliar events in the history of the world, but never before since the time of Noah has a judgment so devastating been enacted as to destroy one-fourth of the earth's population at one stroke.

Though it is impossible to settle this question conclusively, some believe that the rider on the white horse in the first seal is a picture of the prince (Dan. 9:26) at that stage in his career when he assumes control over the entire world (Dan. 7:23; Rev. 13:7), which seems to coincide with the beginning of the great tribulation. Though he comes as a false prince of peace who will bring order to a troubled world, the peace is short-lived and is followed by war, famine, and death, as well as the devastating judgments of God recorded later in Revelation. The fifth and sixth seals advance the narrative and describe the period specifically as "the great day of their wrath" (6:17), which almost certainly is a reference to the great tribulation.

From this introduction to the judgments portrayed in Revelation, it should be evident that the world is facing a time of trouble never known before. The dream of the optimist for a world becoming increasingly better scientifically, intellectually, morally, and religiously does not fit the pattern of God's prophetic Word. The ultimate triumph of God is assured, and as Revelation makes plain, Christ will reign over the earth and bring in a kingdom of peace and righteousness after the time of trouble has run its course. First, however, there must be the awful time of the great tribulation.

There is much in the modern world that seems to point toward just such a period. Today's "weapons of mass destruction" have the ability to destroy life on a frightening scale. Distance is no longer a barrier to waging war, and the world never seems to be short of madmen bent on mass murder and conquest. The darkness of the human hour is in sharp contrast to the bright hope of the imminent return of Christ for His church as an event preceding the time of trouble.

THE FIFTH SEAL:
THE MARTYRED SOULS IN HEAVEN (6:9–11)

6:9–11 When he opened the fifth seal, I saw under the altar the souls of those who had been slain for the word of God and for the witness they had borne. They cried out with a loud voice, "O Sovereign Lord, holy and true, how long before you will judge and avenge our blood on those who dwell on the earth?" Then they were each given a white robe and told to rest a little longer, until the number of their fellow servants and their brothers should be complete, who were to be killed as they themselves had been.

Here the scene shifts from earth to heaven and John sees a vision of those who will be martyred for their faith in Christ. They are described as being under the altar, in keeping with the fact that the blood of the sacrifices of the Old Testament was poured out under the altar (Ex. 29:12; Lev. 4:7). John hears them crying with a loud voice asking why God has not judged their persecutors.

The introduction of these martyred dead in heaven at this point immediately after the fourth seal seems to imply that these martyrs have come from the tribulation scene on the earth. There have been many martyrs in every generation, and it was said that more people died for their testimony for Christ in the twentieth century than in any previous century of the church. There are several reasons, however, for believing that a greater period of martyrdom is yet ahead. If the church has already been raptured, the dead in Christ have been raised from the dead before the time pictured here, and those pictured do not include the martyrs of the present dispensation.

The plea of these martyrs for righteous judgment indicates that their persecutors are still living. In answer to their question as to how long it will be, the reply is given in verse 11 that there is still a little time required for the fulfillment of God's program, that still additional martyrs must be added to their number. In a word, they are to wait until the time of Christ's return in power and glory when God will deal in summary judgment with the earth.

The revelation of the fifth seal makes clear that in the future time of tribulation it will be most difficult to declare one's faith in the Lord Jesus. It may very well be that the majority of those who trust Christ as Savior in that day will be put to death. This is confirmed in chapter 7 where another picture of the martyred dead of the tribulation is given, and in chapter 13 where death is inflicted on all who will not worship the beast. Those who trust in Christ in that day will be forced to stand the acid test of being faithful even unto death.

The white robe given to each of the martyrs is symbolic of righteousness. This introduces another question often debated by theologians: what kind of a body will saints have in heaven before their own bodies are raised from the dead? If the martyred dead pictured here are those who have come from the tribulation, it is clear that they will not receive their resurrection bodies until the end of the tribulation, according to Revelation 20:4.

Verse 11 suggests an answer to this question. These martyrs have not been raised from the dead and have not received their resurrection bodies. Yet the fact that they are given robes would almost demand that they have bodies of some kind. It is not the kind of body that Christians now have, nor is it the resurrection body of flesh and bones of which Christ spoke after His own resurrection. It is a temporary body suited for their presence in heaven but replaced in turn by their everlasting resurrection body given at the time of Christ's return.

The introduction of these martyred saints in heaven also has bearing upon the chronology of chapter 6. In support of the common interpretation that the seals cover the entire seven years of Daniel's seventieth week (Dan. 9:27), it is sometimes pointed out that two classes of martyrs are here mentioned: those already slain, and those who are yet to be slain. It has been inferred, accordingly, that those previously slain were killed in the first half of Daniel's seventieth week, whereas those who are yet to be slain will perish in the great tribulation or the last half of the week.

There is no reason, however, why the last three-and-a-half years could not have the same distinction—that is, certain martyrs at the beginning as contrasted with martyrs at the end. The ultimate decision depends on whether there is unprecedented tribulation prior to the fifth seal as seems to be clearly indicated in this context, and the fact that Revelation never speaks of a seven-year period, only of a period of three-and-a-half years, forty-two months, or a similar designation. The ultimate decision depends upon what evidence is considered decisive.

THE SIXTH SEAL:
THE DAY OF DIVINE WRATH (6:12–17)

6:12–17 When he opened the sixth seal, I looked, and behold, there was a great earthquake, and the sun became black as sackcloth, the full moon became like blood, and the stars of the sky fell to the earth as the fig tree sheds its winter fruit when shaken by a gale. The sky vanished like a scroll that is being rolled up, and every mountain and island was removed from its place. Then the kings of the earth and the great ones and the generals and the rich and the powerful, and everyone, slave and free, hid themselves in the caves and among the rocks of the mountains, calling to the mountains and rocks, "Fall on us and hide us from the face of him who is seated on the throne, and from the wrath of the Lamb, for the great day of their wrath has come, and who can stand?"

It would be difficult to paint any scene more moving or more terrible than that described at the opening of the sixth seal. All the elements of a great catastrophic judgment of God are present. This is an awe-inspiring scene, but what does it mean prophetically? Students of Revelation have had difficulty interpreting this passage, and the tendency has been to regard these judgments as symbolic rather than real. This is because of a reluctance to accept a literal interpretation of these judgments falling on the earth at this time. Thus the disturbances of the heavens are taken to refer to changes in human government, and disturbances in the earth as referring to the upsetting of tradition and commonly fixed ideas.

But there are a number of reasons for preferring to take this passage in its literal meaning. While this is not the final breakup of the world as described later in Revelation, when a further period of terrible judgments will be poured on the world, it does seem to indicate that beginning with the sixth seal God is undertaking a direct intervention into human affairs. The judgments of war, famine, and death, and the martyrdom of the saints have largely originated in human decision and evil. The judgment described here, however, originates in God as a divine punishment inflicted upon a blasphemous world.

In view of the catastrophic and climactic character of the period, there is no good reason that there should not be precisely the disturbances in the heavens and earthquakes mentioned here. This is borne out by the response of the world's people, both the great and mighty and the ordinary. In terror they hide themselves in dens and in the mountains to escape the wrath of God. Note that these people realize the nature and the source of their judgment, that it is God who is wreaking this destruction on the earth.

It is questionable whether changes in human government or affairs would have brought such a striking transformation in the hearts of these wicked people. As is often the case with desperate people, instead of availing themselves of the grace of God, they attempt to hide from His wrath by seeking escape in death. But their hope is futile, for death is not an escape but merely a change from one state to another. Those who escape through death from the immediate judgment of God are destined for eternal judgment at the great white throne.

The elements of divine judgment pictured here are common in the prophecies pertaining to the end of the age. Christ Himself predicted earthquakes (Matt. 24:7). Both earthquakes and the sun becoming black are intimated by Joel (Joel 2:2, 10, 30–31). The heavens departing as a scroll are mentioned in Isaiah 34:4 (cf. also Isa. 13:6–13). The resulting impression upon the unbelieving world is that the time of the judgment of God has come.

It is apparent that the unbelieving world had some foreboding that their blasphemous unbelief and worship of the beast are in defiance of the true God. They therefore seek refuge from the One sitting on the throne and apparently realize that the day of divine wrath has come. The world today that is so indifferent to the claims of God, so bent upon pleasure, luxury, and fame, will face in that day its terrible need. Success in the world is of no help here; no one escapes.

The day of God's wrath is not a twenty-four-hour day, but a period of unspecified length. The day of wrath in one sense is the whole period of the great tribulation, when God will deal in direct judgment with the world, climaxing with the return of Christ in power and glory and divine judgment upon all who oppose His coming. The day of wrath is at the beginning of the day of the Lord, that extended period when God is going to deal directly in governing the entire world. It is significant that early in Revelation the day of wrath is declared as having already come. It is another evidence that the great tribulation is already underway.

The day of wrath is in contrast to our present day of grace. Though God in every dispensation deals with believers and saves them by grace, the present age is supremely designed to manifest grace not only as the way of salvation but as the way of life. Today God is not attempting to bring divine judgment to bear upon sin. Though there may be some forms of immediate retribution, for the most part God is not settling accounts now. The righteous are not rewarded nor are the wicked judged in a final sense today. This day of grace will be followed by the day of the Lord that features early in its progress the day of wrath.

In contrast to the judgments that are inflicted upon a Christ-rejecting world, believers in this present age are promised escape from the judgment that the world richly deserves (cf. John 3:18, 36). The person who trusts in Christ is not only forgiven in this world but he has eternal life and is a member of God's family. By contrast the unbeliever shall never see life, but abides under the wrath of God that in due time will be inflicted.

The book of Revelation discredits those who teach that God is so loving and kind that He will never judge people who have not received His Son. Though the modern mind is reluctant to accept the fact that God will judge the wicked, the Bible clearly teaches that He will. The Scriptures reveal a God of love as clearly as they reveal a God of wrath who will deal with those who spurn the grace of Christ. The passage before us is a solemn word that there is inevitable judgment ahead for those who will not receive Christ by faith.

The close of Revelation 6 advances the narrative to a new high in the progress of the book. In some sense this chapter is the outline of the important facts of the period of great tribulation, and the rest of the events of the Revelation are comprehended in the seventh seal introduced in chapter 8.

Chapter 6 closes with a pointed question: "Who can stand?" The answer is obvious: only those who avail themselves of the grace of God, even though they suffer a martyr's death in this future tragic period. Those who can stand are described in the next chapter, including the 144,000. The revelation given here emphasizes the importance of receiving God's grace today with the bright prospect of the Lord coming for His own.

NOTES

1. Paul Benware, *Understanding End Times Prophecy* (Chicago: Moody, 2006), 224.

2. For the view that the rider is not the Antichrist, but the personification of a growing force or movement that will be at work in the tribulation, see Robert L. Thomas, *Revelation 1–7: An Exegetical Commentary* (Chicago: Moody, 1992), 422; and John MacArthur, *The MacArthur New Testament Commentary: Revelation 1–11* (Chicago: Moody, 1999), 178.

3. Charles C. Ryrie, *Revelation*, rev. ed. (Chicago: Moody, 1996), 55.

4. Thomas, *Revelation 1–7* (Chicago: Moody, 1992), 436.

7 The Saints of the Great Tribulation

In contrast to chapter 6, which seems to give the chronological sequence of major events of the great tribulation, chapter 7 does not advance the narrative but directs attention to two major groups of saints in the tribulation. The opening portion of the chapter pictures the 144,000 representative of the godly remnant of Israel on earth in the great tribulation. The latter part of the chapter describes a great multitude of martyred dead in heaven, those who died as a testimony to their faith from every nation and language on earth.

The question has often been asked: Will anyone be saved after the rapture? The Scriptures clearly indicate that a great number of both Jews and Gentiles will trust in the Lord after the church is caught up to glory. Though the children of God living on earth will be translated when Christ comes for His church, immediately a testimony will be raised up to the name of Christ through new converts among Jews and Gentiles. Though these are never described by the term "church," they are constantly called saints—those set apart as holy to God and saved through the sacrifice of Christ. God will never leave Himself without a witness as long as it is possible for people to be saved.

The presence of saved people in the world after the rapture has puzzled some because according to 2 Thessalonians 2:7 "he who now restrains" sin, often identified as the Holy Spirit, is said to be removed from the world. The question then is, How can people be saved in the tribulation if the Holy Spirit is taken out of the world? The answer, of course, is that the Holy Spirit is removed from the world in the same sense in which He came on the day of Pentecost.

People were saved before the day of Pentecost, when the Spirit of God came to indwell the church, and it should be clear from other Scriptures that the Holy Spirit is omnipresent. He has always been in the world and always will be, in keeping with His divine attribute of omnipresence as the Third Person of the Trinity. Though His special ministries that are characteristic of the present dispensation may cease, the Holy Spirit will continue to minister as He did before Pentecost.

There is a parallel in the fact of the incarnation of Jesus Christ. Throughout the Old Testament, Christ was present in the world, but it was not His particular field of operation—though He ministered as the Angel of Yahweh (cf. Josh. 5:13–15). In due time, according to the plan of God, Christ was born in Bethlehem and ministered as God's unique revelation of Himself to mankind. Then He ascended into heaven, yet at the same time told His disciples, "I am with you always" (Matt. 28:20). While Jesus' special earthly work was completed with His sacrifice on the cross and His resurrection, He nevertheless continued to work in the world in His omnipresence as God.

Likewise the Holy Spirit is resident in the world now just as Christ was resident in the world between His birth and ascension. When the present age ends and the Holy Spirit is caught up with the church, the situation will return to that which was true before the day of Pentecost. The Holy Spirit will continue to be working in the world, but in some particulars in a different way. There is good reason to believe, however, that the Holy Spirit will lead people to Christ, and many will be saved during the tribulation. Revelation 7 is so plain on this that no one should question whether people will be saved after the rapture.

THE VISION OF THE FOUR ANGELS (7:1–3)

7:1–3 After this I saw four angels standing at the four corners of the earth, holding back the four winds of the earth, that no wind might blow on earth or sea or against any tree. Then I saw another angel ascending from the rising of the sun, with the seal of the living God, and he called with a loud voice to the four angels who had been given power to harm earth and sea, saying, "Do not harm the earth or the sea or the trees, until we have sealed the servants of our God on their foreheads."

This scene gives a strong implication that the judgment of God is impending. The winds of heaven speak of His judgment,[1] but prior to its infliction on the earth God wants to set apart and protect His servants. In the verses that follow, 12,000 from each of the twelve tribes of Israel are protected by the angelic seal. It is implied that these who are thus sealed have been saved in the time of trouble pictured in Revelation, and by this means are being set apart as a special divine remnant to be a testimony to God's grace and mercy during this time of judgment.

There are many precedents in Scripture for such a protection of God's own. When God sent the flood upon the earth, He separated Noah and his family from the rest of the human race and the flood did not hurt them (cf. Gen. 7:1). When God destroyed Jericho, He protected Rahab and her household (cf. Josh. 6:22–23). In a similar way, in the time of great tribulation, protection will be given to this group of 144,000 Israelites. The matter is so significant to God that the names of the tribes and the number to be saved from each are given in detail.

THE SEALING OF THE TWELVE TRIBES (7:4–8)

7:4–8 And I heard the number of the sealed, 144,000, sealed from every tribe of the sons of Israel: 12,000 from the tribe of Judah were sealed, 12,000 from the tribe of Reuben, 12,000 from the tribe of Gad, 12,000 from the tribe of Asher, 12,000 from the tribe of Naphtali, 12,000 from the tribe of Manasseh, 12,000 from the tribe of Simeon, 12,000 from the tribe of Levi, 12,000 from the tribe of Issachar, 12,000 from the tribe of Zebulun, 12,000 from the tribe of Joseph, 12,000 from the tribe of Benjamin were sealed.

Some commentators have tried to make this list a symbolic reference to the church rather than to Israel.[2] But such spiritualization ignores the plain statement of the text that the twelve tribes of Israel are in view. Israel's tribes are still in existence, and God certainly knows who they are. The genealogical records of the nation were lost in the destruction of the second temple by the Romans in A.D. 70, but today there are a number of groups from India to South Africa to South America claiming to be remnants of the "lost tribes" of Israel, and with modern DNA identification techniques those claims may yet be established.

Comparing this list of the twelve tribes with the names of Jacob's twelve sons reveals some differences. This will not surprise the student of Scripture, for there are many variations of tribes listed throughout the Old Testament, and it is beyond the scope of this discussion to trace all the variations, except to note that in some lists of the twelve tribes the two sons of Joseph, Ephraim and Manasseh, are numbered as separate tribes.

In this list Manasseh is mentioned but Ephraim is not, and in place of Ephraim, the name of Joseph his father is given in verse 8. No explanation is made concerning this substitution. There is also no mention of the tribe of Dan, and the Bible does not tell us why Dan should be omitted. One suggestion made for this omission is that the Antichrist would come from the tribe of Dan (cf. Gen. 49:17).[3] A more common explanation is that the tribe of Dan was one of the first to go into idolatry, was small in number, and probably was thereafter classified with the tribe of Naphtali, another son of Jacob born to the same mother as Dan.

Though a full answer does not present itself for these omissions, the most important issue is that Israel is here divided into the twelve tribes. Representatives of each tribe are selected for the honor of being sealed by the angel.

The fact that the twelve tribes of Israel are singled out for special reference in the tribulation time is another evidence that the term "Israel" as used in the Bible is invariably a reference to the descendants of Jacob, who was given the name Israel. Paul's benediction in Galatians 6:16 to "the Israel of God" is often cited as an example of Israel being used as a term for the church.

But as Donald Campbell points out, "All the 65 other occurrences of the term 'Israel' in the New Testament refer to Jews. It would thus be strange for Paul to use 'Israel' here to mean Gentile Christians." He goes on to note that Paul referred to two kinds of Israelites, unbelieving and believing Jews (cf. Rom. 9:6), and thus in Galatians 6:16 was referring to true Israelites who had come to Christ.[4] Bible scholar S. Lewis Johnson says this distinction is in "complete harmony" with the usage of the terms *Israel* and *the church* in the early chapters of Acts, "for Israel exists there alongside the newly formed church, and the two entities are kept separate in terminology."[5]

The prevalent idea that the church is the true Israel is not sustained by any explicit reference in the Bible, and the word *Israel* is never used of Gentiles and refers only to those who are racially descendants of Israel, or Jacob. The remnant of Israel as portrayed in Revelation should not therefore be taken as meaning the church. It would be rather ridiculous to carry the typology of Israel representing the church to the extent of dividing them into twelve tribes as was done here, if it was the intent of the writer to describe the church. It is instead a clear indication of God's continued purpose for the nation Israel and their preservation through this awful time of trouble.

The mention of the twelve tribes of Israel is likewise a refutation of the idea that the tribes of Israel are lost, as well as of the theory that the lost tribes are perpetuated in the English-speaking people of the world. Obviously none of the tribes are lost as far as God is concerned, and as noted above, the genealogies may yet be traced through modern forensics. But all speculation aside, this vision given to John is prophetic of the fact that God has a future purpose for Israel (cf. Rom. 9–11), and that in spite of satanic persecution a godly remnant will be preserved to be on earth when Christ returns.

The question has also been raised whether the "12,000" in each tribe means literally 12,000. There seems to be indication that more than 12,000 from each tribe actually will be saved. The point of this Scripture is that in any event 12,000 in each tribe are made secure. There will be other Israelites saved besides these 144,000, but many of these will die martyrs' deaths. The 144,000 are those who are delivered from their persecutors and brought safely through this terrible time of tribulation. In chapter 14 they are seen triumphant at the end of the tribulation when Christ returns.

THE MARTYRED DEAD OF
THE GREAT TRIBULATION (7:9–10)

7:9–10 After this I looked, and behold, a great multitude that no one could number, from every nation, from all tribes and peoples and languages, standing before the throne and before the Lamb, clothed in white robes, with palm branches in their hands, and crying out with a loud voice, "Salvation belongs to our God who sits on the throne, and to the Lamb!"

The second half of chapter 7 of Revelation demonstrates that not only will many be saved in Israel, but also many Gentiles will come to Christ in the great tribulation. In his vision, John sees a great multitude beyond human computation coming from all nations, peoples, and languages standing before the throne. In contrast to those coming from the twelve tribes as pictured earlier in the chapter, this throng comes from all nations. The white robes mentioned seem to refer to 6:11, and the palms indicate their triumph. This great multitude is heard in a great symphony of praise as they ascribe salvation to God. The fact that they are martyrs is stated later in the chapter (vv. 13–14).

THE PRAISE OF THE HEAVENLY HOST (7:11–12)

7:11–12 And all the angels were standing around the throne and around the elders and the four living creatures, and they fell on their faces before the throne and worshiped God, saying, "Amen! Blessing and glory and wisdom and thanksgiving and honor and power and might be to our God forever and ever! Amen."

Joining the multitude of the saints, the angels and all those in heaven are described as falling down before the throne to worship God in a sevenfold ascription of praise similar to that in Revelation 5. The point of this introduction, however, is to identify the presence in glory of the great multitude coming from all nations.

THE MARTYRED DEAD
IDENTIFIED AS TRIBULATION SAINTS (7:13–14)

7:13–14 Then one of the elders addressed me, saying, "Who are these, clothed in white robes, and from where have they come?" I said to him, "Sir, you know." And he said to me, "These are the ones coming out of the great tribulation. They have washed their robes and made them white in the blood of the Lamb."

It is clear from the elder's questions that the twenty-four elders of Revelation are representative of a group different from those who are here pictured as the great multitude in white robes. If the elders represent the church, the multitude represents a different body of saints. The elder's answer to his question is very specific in Greek: literally, "These are those who came out of the tribulation, the great one." It is undoubtedly a reference to the specific period of the great tribulation of which Christ spoke (cf. Matt. 24:21).

The common tendency to ignore the definite terminology of the prophecies in the book of Revelation is illustrated in the interpretation that would make this throng refer to all the elect of all ages. But these saints are described as a particular group coming from a particular time, namely, the great tribulation.

This passage clearly teaches that many Gentiles will be saved during the tribulation. The command to preach the gospel to every nation throughout the world (cf. Matt. 24:14; 28:19–20) will have its ultimate fulfillment in this way before Christ comes back to establish His millennial kingdom. The concept sometimes advanced that the rapture cannot occur because all the world has not heard the gospel is a faulty conclusion. The requirement that all the world hear the gospel pertains not to the rapture but to the coming of Christ to set up His kingdom. Though the church should press on with all zeal in presenting the gospel to every creature, it is not necessary for the rapture to wait until this task is completed. In spite of the difficulties, there will be worldwide preaching of the gospel during the tribulation.

The question has been raised concerning the time pictured in this vision. Two explanations are possible; the first is that this chapter is a preview of the beginning of the millennium. But the scene here obviously is in heaven, rather than on earth, and the living tribulation saints are not caught up to heaven.

A preferred interpretation understands the passage to teach that those described here are martyrs who have sealed their testimony with their own blood. Some believe that the majority of saints in the tribulation will die as martyrs. Many will be killed by earthquakes, war, and pestilence. Others will be the object of special persecution by the world ruler. They will be hounded to death much as the Jews were in World War II. Because they will not worship the beast, they will be under a death sentence (cf. Rev. 13:15). Those who accept Christ in that time may be faced with the solemn alternative of either renouncing their faith and worshiping the beast or being slain. The result will be multiplied thousands of martyrs.

This picture of the martyrs as being before the throne and the Lamb is similar to chapters 5 and 6. The great multitude represents an important portion of those mentioned in 6:9–11 who are given white robes as faithful witnesses to the Word of God and to the testimony of the Lamb. The main facts in the case are clear, regardless of which interpretation is followed: During the tribulation, countless people of all nations will come to know Christ. It will be a time of salvation for them in spite of persecution and even martyrdom.

In verse 14 the significant detail is given that the martyrs have washed their robes and made them white in the blood of the Lamb. Normally one cannot make anything white with blood. The passage is talking, however, of spiritual purity. The only way sins can be washed away is through the precious blood of Christ and because of His death and sacrifice.

Both the Old and New Testaments speak often of blood as the symbol of life, as in Leviticus 17:14: "For the life of every creature is its blood: its blood is its life." The spiritual significance of shed blood is given prominence in both testaments. According to Hebrews 9:22, "without the shedding of blood there is no forgiveness of sins." Acts 20:28 proclaims that the church has been purchased by the blood of Christ. In Romans 3:25 Christ is declared to be the propitiation for our sins "by his blood, to be received by faith." In Romans 5:9

we are "justified by his blood," and therefore "much more shall we be saved by him from the wrath of God." Ephesians 1:7 states that "we have redemption through his blood." According to Colossians 1:20, Christ has "[made] peace by the blood of his cross."

The frequent references to blood in Revelation itself begin in 1:5: "To him who loves us and has freed us from our sins by his blood." In the second advent in Revelation 19:13, Christ is described as "clothed in a robe dipped in blood."

All of this points to the necessity of Christ's substitutionary death for the believer's redemption. Though a modern world is offended by substitutionary sacrifice and especially by the reference to sacrificial blood, from God's viewpoint, like the children of Israel in Egypt, there is no safety except for those under the blood. God promised Israel in Exodus 12:13, "The blood shall be a sign for you, on the houses where you are. And when I see the blood, I will pass over you, and no plague will befall you to destroy you, when I strike the land of Egypt."

Though not suited to the sophistication of twenty-first century tastes, the blood of Christ is exceedingly precious in the sight of the Lord and is the only cleansing agent for sin. The blood of the Lamb is the assurance of cleansing and forgiveness for these who have been martyred for their faith in Christ. Even their own death could not atone for their sins. They, like all others, must rest alone in that sacrifice that Christ provided for them. What is true for them is true for the saints of all ages; only the blood of Christ is able to wash away sin.

THE HEAVENLY BLISS OF
THE MARTYRED SAINTS (7:15–17)

7:15–17 "Therefore they are before the throne of God, and serve him day and night in his temple; and he who sits on the throne will shelter them with his presence. They shall hunger no more, neither thirst anymore; the sun shall not strike them, nor any scorching heat. For the Lamb in the midst of the throne will be their shepherd, and he will guide them to springs of living water, and God will wipe away every tear from their eyes."

Here is the wonderful blessing of the martyred saints in the presence of their Lord, enjoying the privilege of His fellowship. They are before the throne of God, that is, in a place of prominence and honor. Their special privilege is further defined as serving the Lord day and night in His temple. This expression is highly significant, for it indicates that heaven is not only a place of rest from earthly toil but also a place of privileged service. Those who have served well on earth will have a ministry in heaven.

The fact that they are declared to serve "day and night" has been taken by some as an indication that this is a millennial scene rather than heaven since there is never any night in the temple of God in heaven. The expression, however, can be understood as meaning simply that they will continually serve the Lord, without needing sleep or restoration. The temple of God is a reference to His immediate presence, not to any earthly temple.

Verse 16 reveals that they will be delivered from the afflictions of life. This may be an oblique reference to some of their sufferings that they endured in the tribulation. According to Revelation 13:17, it may be that they had gone hungry rather than buying food and submitting to the worship of the beast. Thirst is another form of suffering common in times of persecution. The glaring sun and burning heat and the trials that may have attended them as they fled from their enemies are far behind them in glory. Instead, verse 17 pictures the Lamb of God as feeding them and leading them to living fountains of water.

The promise that God "will wipe away every tear from their eyes" pictures the Savior's tender comfort. Some have attempted to draw from this passage that there will be actual tears in heaven and have implied that saints will be shedding tears because of grief over wasted lives and unconfessed sin while on earth. This passage, however, does not even suggest such a situation. The point is that the grief and tears of the past, speaking of their trials in the tribulation, will be over when they get to heaven. The saints in glory will be occupied with the beauty and wonder of heaven and the worship of the Savior. They will not have time for repentance of that which can no longer be changed. Instead, God will wipe away all tears resulting from their suffering on earth.

The juxtaposition of the 144,000 in the first half of this chapter immediately preceding the description of the multitude of martyred dead from among the Gentiles would seem to imply that there is a causal relationship between these two groups. The 144,000 on earth are preserved in safety through the tribulation, as a testimony to the power and grace of God, and as a channel through which the gospel could come to the earth. The scene here suggests that their ministry had its fruit among the Gentiles, even as was true in the apostolic age, with the result that great multitudes of the Gentiles were saved. The use of the 144,000 of Israel as a channel of witness to the earth is in keeping with the general purposes of God in relation to the Jewish nation.

Revelation 7 serves as a review of the situation described in the previous chapters and emphasizes two important facts. First, God is going to judge Israel in the period of great trial, yet 12,000 from each tribe will be protected and sealed from the judgments that will fall upon the world in general. Second, a great multitude of Gentiles from every nation will also be saved, but many of these will be martyred, and a multitude of the martyred dead are found in heaven rejoicing in the presence of the Lamb. It is an indication that even in the tragic closing hours prior to the second coming of Christ, countless souls will find Christ as Savior and be saved by His grace.

NOTES

1. Warren Wiersbe, *Wiersbe's Expository Outlines on the New Testament* (Wheaton, IL: Victor, 1992), 815.

2. William Hendriksen, *More Than Conquerors* (Grand Rapids: Baker, 1967), 111.

3. Robert L. Thomas, *Revelation 1–7: An Exegetical Commentary* (Chicago: Moody, 1992), 480.

4. John F. Walvoord and Roy B. Zuck, eds., *The Bible Knowledge Commentary: New Testament* (Wheaton, IL: Victor, 1983), 611.

5. S. Lewis Johnson Jr., "Paul and 'The Israel of God': A Case-Study," *Essays in Honor of J. Dwight Pentecost*, Stanley D. Toussaint and Charles H. Dyer, eds. (Chicago: Moody, 1986), 189.

The Seventh Seal and the Beginning of the Trumpets

8

THE OPENING OF THE SEVENTH SEAL (8:1)

8:1 When the Lamb opened the seventh seal, there was silence in heaven for about half an hour.

With the opening of the seventh seal the narrative is resumed from the close of chapter 6. Though simply introduced, the seventh seal is obviously the most important development up to this point. This is because all the subsequent developments leading to the second coming of Christ, including the seven trumpets and the seven bowls, are contained in the seventh seal.

In recognition of the seventh seal's importance, John says its opening is followed by a half hour of silence in heaven. Though thirty minutes is not ordinarily considered a long time, in this case it indicates that something tremendous is about to take place. It may be compared to the silence before the foreman of a jury reports a verdict; for a moment there is perfect silence and everyone awaits that which will follow.

INTRODUCTION OF THE SEVEN ANGELS (8:2-6)

8:2-6 Then I saw the seven angels who stand before God, and seven trumpets were given to them. And another angel came and stood at the altar with a golden censer, and he was given much incense to offer with the prayers of all the saints on the golden altar before the throne, and the smoke of the incense, with the prayers of the saints, rose before God from the hand of the angel. Then the angel took the censer and filled it with fire from the altar and threw it on the earth, and there were peals of thunder, rumblings, flashes of lightning, and an earthquake. Now the seven angels who had the seven trumpets prepared to blow them.

Though there has been some speculation about the character of the seven angels standing before God, the best interpretation is to take the revelation in its ordinary sense, which is that these are indeed angels appointed by God to direct the judgments symbolized by the seven trumpets. These angels are to be distinguished from those who pour out the seven bowls and are not to be confused with the seven spirits of God in Revelation 5:6. The number seven is in harmony with the seven seals and the seven bowls. The fact that these angels stand before God indicates a place of prominence such as is given to the angel Gabriel (cf. Luke 1:19). Some have even called these the "presence angels."[1]

THE SEVEN TRUMPET JUDGMENTS

First Trumpet (8:7)	Bloody Hail and Fire: One-Third of Vegetation Destroyed
Second Trumpet (8:8–9)	Fiery Mountain from Heaven: One-Third of Oceans Polluted
Third Trumpet (8:10–11)	Falling Star: One-Third of Fresh Water Polluted
Fourth Trumpet (8:12)	Darkness: One-Third of Sun, Moon, and Stars Darkened
Fifth Trumpet (9:1–12)	Demonic Invasion: Torment
Sixth Trumpet (9:13–21)	Army of 200 Million: One-Third of Mankind Killed
Seventh Trumpet (11:15–19)	The Announcement of Christ's Reign: The Kingdom

The use of trumpets by the angels has considerable background in the Scriptures. Trumpets were used in various phases of Israel's history. They were sounded at times of public assembly, used to direct soldiers in war, and to signal important events on the calendar. Trumpets were used on the occasion of the giving of the Mosaic law, were sounded on the first of the month, and served to announce almost every important occasion (cf. Ex. 19:19; Lev. 23:24; 25:9; Num. 10:2–10; Joel 2:1).

In verse 3 another angel is introduced as standing before the altar with a golden censer. The ESV rendering, "he was given much incense to offer with the prayers of all the saints," could be read to mean that the prayers were offered *in addition to* the incense, which is why this phrase would be better translated, "he was given much incense to offer, consisting of the prayers of all the saints."[2]

This is a beautiful picture of the prayers of the saints as seen from heaven. In the Old Testament order the priests would burn incense upon the altar of incense, and the smoke would fill the temple or the tabernacle and then ascend to heaven. Incense was symbolic of worship and prayer and a reminder that intercession to the Lord has the character of sweet incense. The altar in heaven is referred to seven times in this book (6:9; 8:3 [bis], 5; 9:13; 14:18; 16:7). Commentators differ as to whether the altar is the altar of burnt offering or the altar of incense, although the latter is usually preferred.[3]

Difference of opinion has also been expressed concerning whether the angel mentioned in verse 3 is actually an angel of high rank or an angelic representation of the Lord Jesus Christ. From the fact that the angel has items given to him in order to make his worship possible, some have concluded that this is only an angel designated for this work in heaven. From the nature of his work as a mediator serving in the role of a priest, others have argued that it must be the Lord Jesus Christ because this would not be a proper function of an angel. The fact that Christ frequently appeared in the Old Testament as the Angel of Yahweh lends further support to this point of view (cf. Gen. 16:7; Ex. 3:2; Num. 22:22; Judges 2:1; 1 Kings 19:7; Ps. 34:7; Isa. 37:36). The preponderance of opinion seems to favor regarding the angel as Christ in His work as High Priest.

Though nothing is said about the nature of the incense, it is reasonable to suppose that it fulfills the same function as incense used in Old Testament worship, composed of the four spices mentioned in Exodus 30:34–38 and regarded as so holy that the people of Israel were forbidden to use it for any common purpose. The incense, speaking of the perfections of Christ, is inseparably bound up with any ministry of intercession, and the believers' petitions are coupled with the worthiness of Christ in their presentation at the heavenly altar. This points to the necessity of praying in the name of Christ and to the effectiveness of such prayer when faithfully ministered on earth.

John's attention is directed to the censer (v. 5), apparently corresponding to the instrument used to offer incense in the Old Testament worship. It was made of gold (Ex. 37:25–28; Heb. 9:4) and used to take fire off the altar to be carried into the Holy of Holies, where the incense was added. Here the angel takes the censer filled with fire and throws it to earth, which is followed by thunderings, lightning, and an earthquake. The clear implication is that the censer is a symbol of judgment, apparently in response to the intercession and prayers of the suffering saints in the midst of the great tribulation. The scene, therefore, is set for the judgment symbolized by the seven trumpets about to sound according to verse 6.

THE FIRST TRUMPET:
DEVASTATION ON THE EARTH (8:7)

8:7 The first angel blew his trumpet, and there followed hail and fire, mixed with blood, and these were thrown upon the earth. And a third of the earth was burned up, and a third of the trees were burned up, and all green grass was burned up.

In response to the blowing of the trumpet held by the first angel, a scene of desolation is spread abroad upon the earth, directed at the earth's vegetation. Some expositors see this as a symbol of divine judgment rather than literal hail and fire. The obvious parallel, however, is found in the seventh plague in Exodus 9:18–26, where there was literal hail and fire. Since the result is massive destruction of the earth's vegetation, there is no solid reason for not taking this judgment in its literal sense.

The only problem that seems to remain is the meaning of the term "blood." Here we have another helpful suggestion from the plagues of Egypt. According to Exodus 9:19, 25, the hail destroyed not only vegetation but also people and animals who were caught in it. Thus the result of that hail was bloodshed, whether or not blood was actually included in the hail and fire thrown on the earth. This judgment, great as it is, is only the introduction. Six more trumpets are to sound.

THE SECOND TRUMPET:
DEVASTATION ON THE SEA (8:8–9)

8:8–9 The second angel blew his trumpet, and something like a great mountain, burning with fire, was thrown into the sea, and a third of the sea became blood. A third of the living creatures in the sea died, and a third of the ships were destroyed.

The second trumpet brings another horrific judgment on the earth, this time dealing with the sea. Again, the tendency of interpreters is to give this a symbolic meaning. It is not implausible, however, to suggest a reasonable literal interpretation. It is earlier indicated in the sixth seal that the stars from heaven fall and that there are various disturbances of this character during this period. It may be that the great mountain, instead of being a symbol of a government, as is sometimes the case in Scripture, is actually a large object falling from the heavens.

There seems to be another parallel here to the plagues of Egypt. Just as the Nile River and all other bodies of water in Egypt were turned to blood when Aaron stretched out his rod over them, so this object apparently had a similar effect on the sea. The resulting judgment is devastating. The probability is that all life and all ships are destroyed in one portion of the earth, the area nearest to the impact of the burning mountain.

The interpreter of these and later judgments is constantly faced with the problem of how far to take the literal and the symbolic. The point of view adopted here is that these judgments should be interpreted literally as far as the literal interpretation can be reasonably followed. Though all questions cannot be answered, the unmistakable implication of these judgments is that God is dealing in righteous wrath with the wicked earth.

THE THIRD TRUMPET:
THE WATERS MADE BITTER (8:10–11)

8:10–11 The third angel blew his trumpet, and a great star fell from heaven, blazing like a torch, and it fell on a third of the rivers and on the springs of water. The name of the star is Wormwood. A third of the waters became wormwood, and many people died from the water, because it had been made bitter.

When the third trumpet sounds, John witnesses a great star burning like a torch and falling upon rivers and springs of water. It is aptly named "Wormwood," a bitter plant that grows in waste places and a symbol of calamity.[4] It apparently causes the water to be bitter, resulting in the death of many. Expositors have had a field day in assigning symbolic meaning to the components of this judgment. If the meaning is symbolic, there is no clear indication of its interpretation except that the great star can be assigned to some person such as the Antichrist or Satan himself, and the waters could be regarded as symbolic of the peoples of the earth.

Once again, however, it seems preferable to understand this judgment literally. The star seems to be a heavenly body or a mass from outer space, understandably burning as it enters the atmosphere of earth, and falling with contaminating influence upon the rivers and waters. The reference to wormwood seems parallel to the experience of the children of Israel at the waters of Marah (Ex. 15:23–25). There the tree thrown into the bitter waters made them sweet. Here the wormwood has the opposite effect. Such also is the contrast between Christ on the cross atoning for sin and making that which is bitter sweet, and Christ coming in judgment that turns the vain hopes and ambitions of unbelievers into bitterness and despair.

THE FOURTH TRUMPET:
ONE-THIRD OF THE HEAVENS DARKENED (8:12–13)

8:12–13 The fourth angel blew his trumpet, and a third of the sun was struck, and a third of the moon, and a third of the stars, so that a third of their light might be darkened, and a third of the day might be kept from shining, and likewise a third of the night. Then I looked, and I heard an eagle crying with a loud voice as it flew directly overhead, "Woe, woe, woe to those who dwell on the earth, at the blasts of the other trumpets that the three angels are about to blow!"

In contrast to the first three judgments having to do with land, sea, rivers, and springs of water, the fourth trumpet relates to the heavens themselves. As John witnesses the scene, he sees a disruption of light from heaven as a solemn warning of other judgments that were yet to fall upon the earth.

This interpretation is given support by the next verse, which indicates that the first four trumpets are not only judgments in themselves but warnings of the last three trumpets that will be far more severe in character. John records that he both saw and heard the loud voice of an eagle pronouncing a triple woe as the inhabitants of the earth are warned of judgment to come. The trumpet judgments, which have their beginning in this chapter, confirm the predictions of Christ and the Old Testament prophets of the coming time of tribulation far worse than anything the human race has ever experienced (cf. Matt. 24:22; Dan. 9:26–27; Joel 2:1–2).

The first four trumpets deal with aspects of the physical world that are taken more or less for granted. The beauty and benefit of the trees, and the luxury and growth of green grass are seldom occasions for thanksgiving to the living God. In a similar way, human beings are prone to take for granted the blessings of water. These are all gifts from a loving God to an undeserving world, and they come under the blight and judgment described in the second and third trumpets.

Still another area of blessing from God is the light of the sun, moon, and stars. The handiwork of God in the heavens is mentioned frequently in Scripture as a reminder of God's power, sovereignty, and wisdom. David exclaimed, "The heavens declare the glory of God, and the sky above proclaims his handiwork. Day to day pours out speech, and night to night reveals knowledge" (Ps. 19:1–2). The very presence of these aspects of nature so essential to human life and existence is referred to by Paul in Romans 1:20 as manifesting God in His eternal power. Jeremiah spoke of the sun and moon as tokens of God's faithfulness to His promise to the nation of Israel and as symbols of their continuance as long as the earth endures (Jer. 31:35–36).

These very tokens of blessing and revelation of the glory of God are affected by the fourth trumpet. So dramatic are the judgments and so unmistakably an evidence of the power and sovereignty of God that even blasphemers on earth can no longer ignore the fact that God is dealing with them. Fearful as these judgments are, they are only the beginning of God's dealing with the earth, and as indicated in a special announcement, three great woes are still to fall. Though it is difficult in this day of grace to imagine such catastrophic judgments, the Word of God is clear, and people are called everywhere to avail themselves of grace before it is too late.

NOTES

1. John MacArthur, *The MacArthur New Testament Commentary: Revelation 1–11* (Chicago: Moody, 1999), 238.

2. Robert H. Mounce, *The Book of Revelation*, rev. ed., New International Commentary on the New Testament (Grand Rapids: Eerdmans, 1997), 174.

3. F. F. Bruce, *New International Bible Commentary*, F. F. Bruce, gen. ed. (Grand Rapids: Zondervan, 1979), 1611.

4. Merrill F. Unger, *The New Unger's Bible Dictionary*, R. K. Harrison, ed. (Chicago: Moody, 1988), 1341.

The Fifth and Sixth Trumpets: The First and Second Woes

THE FIFTH TRUMPET: THE FALLEN STAR AND THE OPENING OF THE ABYSS (9:1–2)

9:1–2 And the fifth angel blew his trumpet, and I saw a star fallen from heaven to earth, and he was given the key to the shaft of the bottomless pit. He opened the shaft of the bottomless pit, and from the shaft rose smoke like the smoke of a great furnace, and the sun and the air were darkened with the smoke from the shaft.

The rising crescendo of judgments on the earth now introduces the first woe, a dramatic event described by John in the first twelve verses of this chapter. As the fifth trumpet sounds, John sees a star fallen from heaven having the key to the bottomless pit. Earlier, in connection with the sixth seal (6:12–17) and the fourth trumpet (8:12), we read of unusual disturbances in the starry heavens. In chapter 6, the stars of heaven fall, and heaven itself rolls up like a scroll. In chapter 8, a great star from heaven falls upon rivers and springs of water. In these instances it is probable that reference is made to material stars or fragments of them, and their falling on the earth is a form of divine judgment upon an evil world.

The star mentioned here, however, seems to refer to a person rather than a literal star or meteor. The word *fallen* is in the perfect tense, which signifies completed action. (For the event itself, see Revelation 12.) His fallenness is a clue to this being's identity. In Luke 10:18, Jesus said He saw Satan "fall like lightning from heaven." This being is given the key of the bottomless pit, or "the pit of the abyss," as it is better translated, the abode of demons (Luke

8:31). No explanation is offered in the passage itself concerning the identity of this person, but the occasion may be the aftermath of the warfare in heaven mentioned in Revelation 12:7–9, where the devil is cast out into the earth. Verse 1 does not record the fall itself, but rather the star is seen as already fallen. It seems likely, therefore, that the person referred to as the star is none other than Satan.[1]

To this personage is given the key of the bottomless pit, or pit of the abyss. This is the first instance of this expression in Scripture, mentioned three times in this chapter and four additional times later in Revelation. The Greek word for "bottomless pit" is found seven times in Revelation (9:1, 2, 11; 11:7; 17:8; 20:1, 3).

Satan himself is confined to the abyss for a thousand years during the reign of Christ on earth (20:1–3). The opening verse of this chapter, therefore, presents Satan as having the key to the pit of the abyss with power to release those who are confined there. The second verse records the use of the key. The pit of the abyss is opened, and out of it comes a smoke so great it darkens the sun and the air. This smoke seems to foreshadow the spiritual corruption that will be caused by these demons released from their confinement, and it identifies the judgment of the fifth trumpet as that of demonic and satanic oppression.

THE FIFTH TRUMPET:
DEMONIC TORMENT LOOSED UPON THE EARTH (9:3–6)

9:3–6 Then from the smoke came locusts on the earth, and they were given power like the power of scorpions of the earth. They were told not to harm the grass of the earth or any green plant or any tree, but only those people who do not have the seal of God on their foreheads. They were allowed to torment them for five months, but not to kill them, and their torment was like the torment of a scorpion when it stings someone. And in those days people will seek death and will not find it. They will long to die, but death will flee from them.

This vision of judgment gets more horrific as John sees locusts coming out of the smoke that are likened to scorpions. As is borne out by the description given later, these are not natural locusts, but the hordes of demons loosed upon the earth. The locusts are commanded, probably by God, or perhaps by Satan himself, not to hurt the earth's vegetation, but only those people who do not have the seal of God.

The description of these demons as having the destructive power of locusts and the painful sting of scorpions is most appropriate. In the Old Testament, locusts were a greatly feared plague because they could strip the country of every green leaf and sprout, leaving people and animals alike to die for lack of food. Frequently in the Bible locusts are used by the Lord as a divine judgment upon a wicked world. In the contest of Moses with Pharaoh in Egypt the plagues of locusts quickly caused Pharaoh to be humbled (Ex. 10:12–20). Pharaoh pleaded with Moses and Aaron to "remove this death from me." A similar plague of locusts is mentioned in Joel 1:4–7.

The locusts in Revelation 9 have the specific purpose of executing divine judgment. They do not eat vegetation, as ordinary locusts would do, and their stinging ability is certainly not characteristic of real locusts. They are able to torment people, and apparently the entire unbelieving human race is vulnerable to their attacks. We believe those who are sealed by God, including the 144,000 of Revelation 7, will be protected from this terrible judgment. It seems improbable that any true believer in that day would be subject to the torment of the locusts; the torment is rather a judgment upon those who have rejected Christ.

The torment caused by these demons is compared to the bite of a scorpion. Scorpions in all climates are fearful and harmful creatures. In warm climates, they grow to such size as to make their sting not only painful but dangerous. Small children sometimes die from the sting of a scorpion in tropical countries. Though the affliction here described is not actually a sting of a scorpion, it is compared to the pain and suffering caused by such a sting.

Further, the torment is said to extend for five months. The best interpretation is to take this literally as a period of five months, which is the normal life span of locusts from May to September.[2] Although the time of the suffering is limited, the pain is so intense that people will seek death to escape it—but death will escape them.

This is a horrible picture of domination by demons to such an extent that people lose their ability of free choice and are in agony of body and soul. As is common in demonic affliction as recorded in the Gospels, those in the grip of demons are not free to exercise their own will and therefore are not free to take their own lives. Even the hope of death to deliver them from their present troubles is taken away from them in that dark hour.

The attempts of some commentators to spiritualize this trumpet and work out an elaborate prophetic system, based on the idea that each day in the five months is a year, is totally unjustified. There is no evidence in Scripture that the terms "month" and "year" are ever used in a symbolic way. Though the word *day* frequently refers to a period of time longer than twenty-four hours, and the weeks or sevens of Daniel's prophecy in Daniel 9 are evidently prophetic years rather than twenty-four-hour days, in this instance there is no justification for taking the expression to mean anything other than a literal five months. This also fits in the chronology of the tribulation time as it is elsewhere taught in the Scriptures. The introduction of the time element is to show that the torment is not a passing experience of a few days, but rather a plague that extends over a considerable period of time, making its affliction a fearful experience to contemplate.

THE FIFTH TRUMPET:
THE LOCUSTS DESCRIBED (9:7–11)

9:7–11 In appearance the locusts were like horses prepared for battle: on their heads were what looked like crowns of gold; their faces were like human faces, their hair like women's hair, and their teeth like lions' teeth; they had breastplates like breastplates of iron, and the noise of their wings was like the noise of many chariots with horses rushing into battle. They have tails and stings like scorpions, and their power to hurt people for five months is in their tails. They have as king over them the angel of the bottomless pit. His name in Hebrew is Abaddon, and in Greek he is called Apollyon.

Since demons do not have physical shape, what John is seeing must symbolize demonic possession. The demons' awesome combination of human and animal qualities depicts the fearful character of these instruments of divine judgment. This is in keeping with the general character of the book of Revelation as an unmasking of the true nature of Satan and evil. Wiersbe suggests that the features of these demons are Satan's way of imitating the heavenly creatures described in Revelation 4:7.[3]

These locust-like creatures from the abyss are said to have breastplates of iron, implying that they are immune to destruction. They are also equipped with wings that sound like many chariots going to battle, implying speed and the impossibility of evading their attack. The fact that they have power to hurt people for five months is repeated in verse 10, as if to call special attention to the length of their torment.

Verse 11 adds a new detail, the fact that the locusts have a king who is the angel of the pit of the abyss. The Hebrew name "Abaddon" and the Greek name "Apollyon" both mean "destroyer." Such is the character of Satan (cf. John 10:10a) and those who affiliate with him as fallen angels. Though in the modern world Satan often "disguises himself as an angel of light" (2 Cor. 11:14) in the role of that which is good and religious, here the mask is stripped away and evil is seen in its true character. Satan and the demons are the destroyers of human souls who can only bring affliction. When divine restraint is released, as in this instance, the true character of the evil one is revealed immediately.

ANNOUNCEMENT OF TWO MORE WOES (9:12)

9:12 The first woe has passed; behold, two woes are still to come.

The fearful torment inflicted by the locusts out of the pit of the abyss is only the first of three great judgments, called woes, which conclude the trumpet period. The word *woe* in Scripture refers to some great calamity, usually a judgment from God, such as Christ pronounced upon Chorazin and Bethsaida (Matt. 11:21). This word expresses the desperate situation of those who do not know Christ in these tragic hours preceding His return to judge the world.

The tribulation period also unmasks human evil as well as the true character of Satan. In our modern day while Satan is still restricted it is easy to forget the great conflict that is raging between the forces of God and the forces of Satan referred to in Ephesians 6:12. In the great tribulation and especially with the release of the confined demons, Satan will be exposed. For the first time in history, all those who do not know the Lord Jesus Christ as Savior will come under demonic possession and affliction. This is also true to some degree today, for the only deliverance from the power of Satan and his affliction is salvation in Christ and the power of God.

THE SIXTH TRUMPET:
THE LOOSING OF THE FOUR ANGELS (9:13–15)

9:13–15 Then the sixth angel blew his trumpet, and I heard a voice from the four horns of the golden altar before God, saying to the sixth angel who had the trumpet, "Release the four angels who are bound at the great river Euphrates." So the four angels, who had been prepared for the hour, the day, the month, and the year, were released to kill a third of mankind.

The golden altar is the place where incense is offered, consisting of the prayers of the saints (cf. 8:3). Here in its final mention in Revelation, the altar is related to God's judgment. The inference is that this judgment, like those preceding it, is partially an answer to the prayers of the persecuted saints on earth and a token of divine response and preparation for their deliverance. The four horns seem to indicate that this altar is similar to the design of the altar of incense used in the tabernacle and later in the temple. If the horns have significance, they refer to the sovereignty and judicial government of God.

The voice instructed the sixth angel to loose the four angels who were once bound and continue to be bound (the Greek tense is perfect) in the great river Euphrates.[4] The identification of these four angels and the reason for their being bound are two questions that need to be answered if we are to understand this unusual event.

These apparently are not the same four angels mentioned in 7:1, who are in authority over the winds of the earth. The four angels of chapter 7 are instructed not to inflict their punishment until the 144,000 of Israel are sealed and protected. They seem to be holy angels or instruments of God's divine wrath upon the world. The four angels in chapter 9, however, are obviously of different character. There is no instance in Scripture where holy angels are bound. Some of the evil angels, however, are bound according to Jude 6. Likewise, Satan is later bound for one thousand years and cast into the pit of the abyss (cf. Rev. 20:1–3).

From these parallels, it may be concluded that the four angels bound in the Euphrates are evil angels who are released in order to execute this judgment that takes the lives of multiplied millions of people. They are prepared for their hour of activity much as the great fish was prepared to swallow Jonah and effect divine discipline upon the prophet. We can see the all-powerful hand of God in both of these instances, for Jonah 1:17 says God "appointed" the fish to swallow Jonah, and here in Revelation 9 the evil angels of the sixth trumpet are not released until the moment chosen by God. As Ryrie states, "These demons who had been kept for this hour could not have released themselves or been freed by Satan until God gave the command."[5]

Another question is why these four evil angels were bound in the Euphrates River. The answer seems to be that the vision concerns an invasion from the east (see discussion below).

God's sovereign control over this event is further indicated by the expression "the hour, the day, the month, and the year." This does not refer to the duration of their activity, but the fact that this judgment comes by God's precise appointment. Though God often uses created beings to accomplish His purpose, the time schedule is determined by Him and no one else. Even angels execute God's will in God's time.

The judgment depicted here, the killing of one-third of the earth's people, is one of the most devastating mentioned anywhere in Revelation prior to the second coming. Earlier in the fourth seal, a fourth of mankind is killed. These two judgments alone account for half of the world's population, and it is clear that in addition to these judgments there is widespread destruction of human life in other divine judgments contained in the seals, trumpets, and bowls. Never since Noah has such a substantial proportion of the earth's population come under God's righteous judgment.

THE SIXTH TRUMPET:
THE ARMY OF TWO HUNDRED MILLION (9:16–19)

9:16–19 The number of mounted troops was twice ten thousand times ten thousand; I heard their number. And this is how I saw the horses in my vision and those who rode them: they wore breastplates the color of fire and of sapphire and of sulfur, and the heads of the horses were like lions' heads, and fire and smoke and sulfur came out of their mouths. By these three plagues a third of mankind was killed, by the fire and smoke and sulfur coming out of their mouths. For the power of the horses is in their mouths and in their tails, for their tails are like serpents with heads, and by means of them they wound.

Having declared the purpose of the army, John now gives details. The most staggering statistic is the fact that the number of the army is declared to be two hundred thousand thousands, or two hundred million. Because the number "ten thousand times ten thousand" is often used of an innumerable company (cf. 5:11), some believe this should not be understood as a literal number, especially since never in the history of the human race has there been an army of this size. The total number of men under arms in World War II on both sides of the conflict was never more than fifty million.

Therefore, many have been tempted to spiritualize the number or to regard the army as demonic rather than human. An army of two hundred

164

million horsemen must have been especially astounding to John, for at that time the total world population did not exceed this number. But John seems to emphasize the accuracy of the number, for he says he heard it, showing that this incredible number was a part of his vision,[6] not something he invented.

And with the advent of the twenty-first century, an army of two hundred million from the East is increasingly possible. If such an army is to be raised up, it would be natural to conclude that it would come from China and possibly India, the great population centers of the world, accounting for over two billion of the earth's six billion people. It is fascinating that China alone is reported to have over 314,000,000 men ages 16 to 49 who are "fit for military service," along with over 298,000,000 women in this category![7]

These staggering numbers make it very feasible that the number revealed in verse 16 should be taken literally. If so, this is an imposing statistic of the power and influence of the armies opposing God in the final world war. The deadly character of the army is revealed in their slaughter of one-third of the world's population, a figure mentioned in Revelation 9:15 and again in verse 18.

A similar and later development mentioned in Revelation 16:12 following the outpouring of the sixth bowl also depicts an invasion from the East. Unless the bowls and the trumpets coincide, as some believe, these are two different events, possibly two different phases of the same operation. Chronologically the trumpets involved closely succeed one another and their judgments seem to fall like trip-hammer blows as the great tribulation comes to its close. Whatever the size of this army, it is clearly a massive force of tremendous military power as evidenced in its capacity to kill one-third of the human race. It may be that this army continues to fight until the second coming of Christ, and the number slain is the total number involved in the conflict.

John also gives a graphic description of the horses as well as of the warriors who sit upon them. Some have plausibly interpreted the description as John's understanding of a scene in which modern warfare and its sophisticated weapons is being described. It is an awesome picture of an almost irresistible military force destroying all that opposes it. The terms "horses," "lions," and "serpents" all speak of deadly warfare. As the king of beasts, the lion speaks of victorious conquest.

Verse 18 also seems to picture modern warfare rather than ancient weapons. This indicates that though there may be a disarmament in the early phases of the time period between the rapture and the second coming, toward the close of the tribulation modern means of war are once again being fully used. The world that longs for peace and seeks to attain it by the worship of the beast of Revelation 13 will learn the sad lesson that there can be no peace until the Prince of Peace rules.

THE SIXTH TRUMPET:
MANKIND STILL UNREPENTANT (9:20–21)

9:20–21 The rest of mankind, who were not killed by these plagues, did not repent of the works of their hands nor give up worshiping demons and idols of gold and silver and bronze and stone and wood, which cannot see or hear or walk, nor did they repent of their murders or their sorceries or their sexual immorality or their thefts.

In spite of the dramatic judgment inflicted by this invading military force, those who survive are declared to be unrepentant. Such is the hardness of the human heart even though faced by worldwide destruction and divine judgment. Though the power of satanic false religion is evident in the world, it does not have the transforming, redeeming quality found only in the power and grace of God. Though people can be made to fear God by the demonstration of divine power, they are not brought to the place of repentance apart from faith in Christ and divine grace. These verses present a striking portrait of mankind's total depravity.

NOTES

1. For a presentation of the view that this being is an angel rather than Satan, see Alan F. Johnson, *Revelation*, The Expositor's Bible Commentary, Frank E. Gaebelein, ed., vol. 12 (Grand Rapids: Zondervan, 1981), 492.

2. John MacArthur, *The MacArthur New Testament Commentary: Revelation 1–11* (Chicago: Moody, 1999), 261.

3. Warren Wiersbe, *Wiersbe's Expository Outlines on the New Testament* (Wheaton, IL: Victor Books, 1992), 822.

4. Charles C. Ryrie, *Revelation*, rev. ed. (Chicago: Moody Publishers, 1996), 74.

5. Ibid., 75.

6. Robert L. Thomas, *Revelation 8–22: An Exegetical Commentary* (Chicago: Moody, 1995), 46–47.

7. *CIA World Factbook,* https://www.cia.gov/library/publications/the-world-factbook/geos/ch.html, dated May 27, 2010. The numbers quoted in this chapter regarding China's military capability are also said to be rising at a rate of about ten million people per year!

The Mighty Angel with the Little Scroll

THE ANGEL AND THE SEVEN THUNDERS (10:1–4)

10:1–4 Then I saw another mighty angel coming down from heaven, wrapped in a cloud, with a rainbow over his head, and his face was like the sun, and his legs like pillars of fire. He had a little scroll open in his hand. And he set his right foot on the sea, and his left foot on the land, and called out with a loud voice, like a lion roaring. When he called out, the seven thunders sounded. And when the seven thunders had sounded, I was about to write, but I heard a voice from heaven saying, "Seal up what the seven thunders have said, and do not write it down."

Chapter 10 begins another parenthetical section, which continues through chapter 14. With the exception of 11:15–19, introducing the seventh trumpet, the narrative does not advance in these chapters and various topics are presented. Like chapter 7, this section does not advance the narrative but presents other facts that contribute to the total prophetic scene. The chapter also has the character of reassurance to the faithful, as Thomas notes: "This section . . . consoles believers by reiterating God's role as the sovereign over earthly affairs, who will not only judge the wicked, but also will exalt the suffering faithful in due time."[1]

The word "another" as a description of the mighty angel is the Greek word that means "another of the same kind"—that is, an angel similar to other angels who have been previously introduced. It seems evident from the context that this angel is not the sixth angel mentioned in 9:13, nor the angel who sounds the seventh trumpet in 11:15. As no clear statement is made, the interpreter is led to determine the character of this angel by the description that follows.

Some expositors of Revelation believe that the angel mentioned here, as well as the angel of 8:3, is none other than Christ. This conclusion is based on the description given of the angel as being in a position of great power over the earth and as possessing majesty. In the Old Testament, Christ did frequently appear in His preincarnate state as the Angel of the Lord, the first instance being in Genesis 16:7 where He appeared to Hagar. In the book of Revelation itself, Christ is presented in several symbols, the most frequent of which is the Lamb slain as in chapters 4 through 6.

But as Hendriksen points out, John does not worship this angel as he worshiped Christ (cf. 1:17).[2] Thus the evidence seems to support the idea that the angel of 10:1 is a holy angel to whom has been given great power and authority. This angel is described as "coming down from heaven," and there is no evidence that Christ comes to earth midway in the tribulation.

There are many instances in Revelation where angels are made the ministers of God for both the punishment of the ungodly and the protection of the righteous. In chapter 12, Michael the archangel is mentioned by name as contending against Satan and the evil angels and expelling them from heaven. Some have concluded that the description given in chapter 10 must be a reference to Michael as the chief of all the holy angels. Though the angel is presented as one having great majesty and power, there is no clear evidence that his function or his person is more than that of an angel entrusted with great authority.

This angel is described in graphic terms. John sees him "wrapped in a cloud" with "a rainbow over his head." The angel's face is compared to the brilliance of the sun, and his legs are like pillars of fire. The angel is standing with his right foot upon the sea and his left foot upon the earth, implying a position of power and authority over the entire earth. All of this, however, is introductory to the point of primary importance, which is that in his hand he holds a little scroll or book that is open.

In Revelation 5, the Lamb has in His hands a seven-sealed scroll that is progressively unrolled, revealing the judgments symbolized by the seals. This scroll, by contrast, is already open and specifically described as being small in size. Some have tried to connect this scroll with the scroll of chapters 4 through 6, but there is no clear identification that would make these the same. The Greek words used in each case are different: in 5:1 the scroll is described as a *biblion*, whereas here the diminutive form of this word, *biblaridion*, is used to describe this small scroll.

The contents of the little scroll are nowhere revealed in Revelation, but they seem to represent in this vision the written authority given to the angel to fulfill his mission. As John beholds the vision, this mighty angel calls out with a loud voice that John says is like a lion's roar. "Seven thunders" are heard in answer to the angel's call, and it is apparent from John's intention to write what they said that these thunders spoke with a voice John readily understood. But their message, as well as that of the little scroll, remains a mystery because John is forbidden to write, and the exact contents of the scroll are not revealed. Many commentators link thunder with a pronouncement of judgment by God, citing Psalm 29 in which the voice of God is mentioned seven times.[3]

Although the principal purpose of the vision given to John was to enable him to write the book of Revelation and thus pass on divine revelation to the church, in this instance the revelation is for John's ears and eyes only, and he is not permitted to reveal what he heard. This illustrates a divine principle that while God has revealed much, there are secrets that God has not seen fit to reveal at this time.

ANNOUNCEMENT OF
THE END OF THE AGE (10:5–7)

10:5–7 And the angel whom I saw standing on the sea and on the land raised his right hand to heaven and swore by him who lives forever and ever, who created heaven and what is in it, the earth and what is in it, and the sea and what is in it, that there would be no more delay, but that in the days of the trumpet call to be sounded by the seventh angel, the mystery of God would be fulfilled, just as he announced to his servants the prophets.

One indication that the angel in this vision is not Christ is the fact that he swears by God, implying that God is greater than the angel. It is, however, a very solemn oath. Notice the absolute authority of God to carry out His will on the earth. He is both the ever-living God and the Creator of all that is. As the Creator, God is also the sovereign Ruler who can declare that there will be no more delay in the execution of His plan.

This announcement that the "mystery of God" is about to be fulfilled is in keeping with the nature of what John sees in the vision of the little scroll and what he hears from the seven thunders. Although the contents of the vision are not revealed, it seems clear that the purpose of Revelation 10:1–7 is to signal the final outpouring of God's judgment, the end of the age, and the destruction of Christ's enemies.[4]

Verse 7 declares that the "mystery of God" will be fulfilled when the seventh trumpet is sounded by an angel. In the New Testament, a mystery is not an enigma to be solved, but truth about God previously hidden that is now revealed. Paul wrote that God has made known to us "the mystery of his will, according to his purpose, which he set forth in Christ as a plan for the fullness of time" (Eph. 1:9–10).

Surely the mystery of God referred to in Revelation 10 is included in this "mystery of his will" referred to by Paul. The "mystery of God" is truth about God and His eternal plan that was hidden from all ages until it was revealed in the final book of Scripture. The prediction that this mystery will be "fulfilled" (v. 7) is related to the full manifestation of the divine power, majesty, and holiness of God that will be evident in the glorious return of Christ, the establishment of His millennial kingdom, and the creation of the eternal state that will follow. MacArthur suggests that the mystery of God (10:7) may also include all that is revealed from this point on in Revelation.[5]

This mystery is said to have been "announced to his servants the prophets" (v. 7). Although many of the details were lacking, the mystery of God is unfolded therefore in the Old Testament in the many passages that speak of the establishment of the kingdom of God on earth.

The ignorance of God and the disregard of His majesty that characterize the present age, as well as the great tribulation, will exist no longer when

Christ returns and manifests Himself in glory to the entire earth. In that day all, from the least to the greatest, will know the Lord—that is, know the important facts about Him (cf. Jer. 31:34).

THE EATING OF THE LITTLE SCROLL (10:8–11)

10:8–11 Then the voice that I had heard from heaven spoke to me again, saying, "Go, take the scroll that is open in the hand of the angel who is standing on the sea and on the land." So I went to the angel and told him to give me the little scroll. And he said to me, "Take and eat it; it will make your stomach bitter, but in your mouth it will be sweet as honey." And I took the little scroll from the hand of the angel and ate it. It was sweet as honey in my mouth, but when I had eaten it my stomach was made bitter. And I was told, "You must again prophesy about many peoples and nations and languages and kings."

John then hears a voice from heaven, apparently the same voice he had heard speaking to him earlier (cf. 4:1). John is commanded to eat the little scroll in the angel's hand, and as he obeys he experiences first the sweetness and then the bitterness that the voice from heaven predicted. This incident should be compared to the similar experiences of the prophets Jeremiah (Jer. 15:16–18) and Ezekiel (Ezek. 2:9–10; 3:1–4, 14).

This experience of John naturally raises a question concerning the meaning of his eating the little scroll. No interpretation of the experience is given in the Scriptures, but it is obvious that the symbolism is supposed to convey meaning. By eating the scroll, John partakes of its content and, in his act of obedience, appropriates the statements, promises, and affirmations contained in the scroll. The scroll itself seems to be a symbol of the Word of God as it is delivered to human recipients—that is, divine revelation already given.

This seems to be confirmed by the word of the angel to John in the last verse of the chapter where John is commanded to prophesy to many people. The testimony to which John is called is that of faithfully delivering the Word of God as it is committed to him. John's obedience to his commission produces the twofold effect mentioned. To John, God's Word is sweet because it is a word of promise, a word of grace, and a revelation of the love of God. Though he is an exile on Patmos and experiencing the bitterness of persecution, the Word is a precious assurance of his salvation, a basis for his present fellowship with Christ, and the ground for his hope of glory to be fulfilled in the future.

Partaking of the Word of God is indeed sweet. How precious God's written revelation should be to His child. As David wrote in Psalm 19:9–10, "The fear of the LORD is clean, enduring forever; the rules of the LORD are true, and righteous altogether. More to be desired are they than gold, even much fine gold; sweeter also than honey and drippings of the honeycomb."

The Word of God that is sweet to John's soul also has its bitter aspects. John is experiencing this in his exile and is enduring hardness as a good soldier of Jesus Christ, separated from friends, afflicted by age and discomfort, and tasting somewhat of the suffering of Christ. More particularly, however, the Word of God is bitter in that it not only contains promises of grace, but as Revelation itself abundantly illustrates, it reveals the divine judgments that will be poured out on the earth as God deals in wrath with an unbelieving and Christ-rejecting world. God who created heaven also prepared the lake of fire for the devil and his angels (cf. Matt. 25:41).

Thus it is probable that the little scroll in Revelation 10 is the Word of God itself. Though John will never know the bitterness of being lost or the afflictions of eternal punishment, he knows what it is to be like his Master, despised and rejected.

The invitation to John to eat the scroll is the invitation of God to all who would participate in the blessing of His Word. Though there may be trials and afflictions for the saints of God, like John they have been promised eternal blessing when the Lord comes for His own. The trials during the brief span of the Christian's life in this world are only the prelude to the eternal blessing that will be the fulfillment of God's grace to those who trust in Christ. Like John, believers today should eat with the assurance that the Word will be sweet, whatever sufferings and trials they may endure in this life.

After eating the scroll, John is told that he must continue to prophesy about many peoples, nations, languages, and kings. The succeeding chapters of Revelation record the apostle's fulfillment of this sacred calling.

NOTES

1. Robert L. Thomas, *Revelation 8–22: An Exegetical Commentary* (Chicago: Moody, 1995), 58.

2. William Hendriksen, *More Than Conquerors* (Grand Rapids: Baker, 1967), 124.

3. Robert H. Mounce, *The Book of Revelation*, rev. ed., New International Commentary on the New Testament (Grand Rapids: Eerdmans, 1997), 203.

4. Wilbur M. Smith, *The Wycliffe Bible Commentary*, Charles F. Pfeiffer and Everett F. Harrison, eds. (Chicago: Moody, 1990), 1510.

5. John MacArthur, *The MacArthur New Testament Commentary: Revelation 1–11* (Chicago: Moody, 1999), 286.

11 The Two Witnesses and the Seventh Trumpet

Many students of Revelation believe chapter 11 is one of the most difficult to interpret in the entire book. A comparison of many commentaries reveals a wide disagreement as to the meaning of this chapter. A primary reason for this difference is the issue we have encountered before: the interpretive question of whether the prophecies of Revelation are to be interpreted literally, unless otherwise clearly indicated, or symbolically.

Interpreters who take the symbolic view will indeed encounter difficulties. Wiersbe even states flatly, "If we spiritualize this passage [referring to chapter 11] and apply any of it to the church, we will be in serious trouble."[1] This exposition regards the terms in the prophecy of chapter 11 as real people, places, events, and numbers, not merely as symbolic of other realities. Thus, the great city of 11:8 is identified as the literal city of Jerusalem. The time periods are taken as literal time periods. The two witnesses are interpreted as two individuals. The three-and-a-half days are taken literally. The earthquake is an actual earthquake. The 7,000 people who are slain by the earthquake are 7,000 individuals who die in the catastrophe. The death of the witnesses is literal, as are their resurrection and ascension. These assumptions provide an intelligent understanding of this portion of prophecy even though the possibility of difference of opinion is acknowledged.

As noted in the previous chapter, Revelation 11 continues the parenthetical section begun in chapter 10 and extending through chapter 14. In chapter 15, the chronological developments continue as the contents of the seventh trumpet, the seven bowls, are revealed. In 11:1–14, there is a continuation of the same subject as in chapter 10.

THE MEASURING ROD OF GOD (11:1–2)

11:1–2 Then I was given a measuring rod like a staff, and I was told, "Rise and measure the temple of God and the altar and those who worship there, but do not measure the court outside the temple; leave that out, for it is given over to the nations, and they will trample the holy city for forty-two months."

John is given a measuring rod, a bamboo-like cane that grew abundantly along the banks of the Jordan River and could reach a height of twenty feet.[2] He is told, presumably by an angel, to measure the temple, the altar, and the worshipers, but no more. The term "temple" here refers to the Holy Place and the Holy of Holies, the inner parts of the temple, not to its outer court—called the court of the Gentiles and encompassing about twenty-six acres.[3]

The altar may be a reference to the bronze altar that was in the outer court of the temple, although the altar in chapter 8 seems to be the altar of incense. Only priests could go into the temple, but others could approach the bronze altar with their sacrifices. The voice explains to John that he is not to measure the outer court because it will be trampled by Gentiles—under Gentile domination, in other words. This will be the case for forty-two months.

What is the meaning of this symbolic picture? In Zechariah 2, a man is seen measuring Jerusalem, a scene that evidently portrays God's divine judgment on the city. Another instance is found in Ezekiel 40, where the temple of the future kingdom is carefully measured with a rod. Still another instance is where the new Jerusalem is measured (Rev. 21:15–17). The act of measuring seems to signify that the area belongs to God in some special way. It is an evaluation of His property.

By the time of John's exile and the writing of Revelation, the second temple in Jerusalem had already been destroyed in A.D. 70 by the Romans. And as of this writing, there is no temple in Jerusalem, although many believe that the third temple will yet be built by the nation Israel both for the worship of the Jews and for all nations. The reader can search the Internet and find reams of material related to all the speculation and preparations that surround a third temple in Jerusalem.

The Bible does indeed seem to indicate that a future temple will be in existence during the great tribulation. In fact, this passage and others in Revelation require an earthly temple. Thus Revelation 11 has to do with a temple that apparently will be in existence during the great tribulation. Originally constructed for the worship of the Jews and the renewal of their ancient sacrifices, during the great tribulation it is desecrated and becomes the home of an idol of the world ruler (cf. 2 Thess. 2:4; Rev. 13:14–15; Dan. 9:27; 12:11).

Therefore, it is significant that John is told to measure the worshipers along with the temple and altar. It is saying in effect that God is the judge of our worship and our character, and that we must all give an account to Him. Since the rod is far longer than a human being's height, this also implies that humanity comes far short of the divine standard.

Verse 2 adds further light with the explanation concerning the temple's outer court being trampled by the Gentiles for forty-two months. Here again is the familiar three-and-a-half-year period, or half of the seven-year period predicted by Daniel the prophet (Dan. 9:27) in which Israel's history will be consummated with Christ's return.

Expositors have differed as to whether the forty-two months are the first half of the seven years or the second half. The decision is complicated by the fact that in verse 3 another reference is made to the three-and-a-half years as the period during which the two witnesses give their testimony. On the basis of the evidence, it is not possible to be dogmatic. If, however, the view is adopted that Revelation is primarily concerned with the latter half of Daniel's seventieth week, this would seem to give weight to the conclusion that this is the latter half of Daniel's final week prior to the second coming of Christ. This view is strengthened in light of the details of the judgments portrayed in the seals, trumpets, and bowls.

This conclusion is substantiated in verse 2 by the fact that the Gentiles have control of the outer court and the city. It would seem that under the covenant relationship between the beast and the children of Israel they are given considerable freedom in their worship for the first three-and-a–half years of the tribulation, and this would probably preclude the Gentiles trampling the outer court, even though the holy city as such is under Gentile dominion. Since the Gentiles are said to tread the holy city underfoot only forty-two months, this ill treatment better fits the latter half of Daniel's seventieth week. If the former half were mentioned, Jerusalem would be trodden underfoot for the entire seven-year period rather than for only half of that time. The passage seems to anticipate freedom from Gentile dominion after the three-and-a-half years have run their course, which would mean that the second half of the tribulation is in view.

The statement that the holy city is under Gentile control is borne out by the prophecy of Christ in Luke 21:24. He uses the same Greek word for "trample" that is used in Revelation 11:2. Jesus referred to the "times of the Gentiles," which end at His second coming as Gentile dominion is destroyed and Christ establishes His kingdom. This is predicted in the seventh trumpet revealed later in this chapter. While God permits Gentile dominion and persecution of Israel during the second half of the tribulation, He will be the judge of her persecutors.

THE PROPHECY OF THE TWO WITNESSES (11:3–6)

11:3–6 And I will grant authority to my two witnesses, and they will prophesy for 1,260 days, clothed in sackcloth. These are the two olive trees and the two lampstands that stand before the Lord of the earth. And if anyone would harm them, fire pours from their mouth and consumes their foes. If anyone would harm them, this is how he is doomed to be killed. They have the power to shut the sky, that no rain may fall during the days of their prophesying, and they have power over the waters to turn them into blood and to strike the earth with every kind of plague, as often as they desire.

The 1,260 days during which these two unusual witnesses will prophesy are exactly equivalent to three-and-a-half years or forty-two months of thirty days each. This time period is unquestionably related to the seven years of

Daniel's seventieth week, the only question being, again, which half is in view. The fact that the witnesses pour out divine judgments upon the earth, and need divine protection lest they be killed, implies that they are in the latter half of the seven years when awful persecution will afflict the people of God. Such protection would not be necessary in the first three-and-a-half years. The punishments and judgments the witnesses inflict on the world also seem to fit better in the great tribulation period.

Interpreters have had a field day with the identity of these two witnesses. Some have suggested that these represent Israel and the church, or Israel and the Word of God, as the two principal instruments of witness in the world. But the language suggests that they are specific persons. The actions are those of people, and their resultant death and resurrection, including their bodies lying in the streets of Jerusalem for three-and-a-half days, can hardly refer to Israel, the church, or the Word of God.

One popular view that has biblical support identifies them with Moses and Elijah.[4] It is pointed out that Elijah called down fire from heaven on two companies of soldiers sent to arrest him (cf. 2 Kings 1; Rev. 11:5), and he also stopped the rain for three-and-a-half years (cf. 1 Kings 171–2). Moses turned the waters of Egypt into blood and struck the land with other plagues (cf. Ex. 7:14–11:10). In addition, the Bible predicts that Elijah will be sent "before the great and awesome day of the Lord comes" (Mal. 4:5), and both Moses and Elijah appeared on the mount of transfiguration with Jesus (Matt. 17:3). The dispute of Michael with the devil over the body of Moses (Jude 9) is mentioned preceding a prophecy of the second coming, but no specific connection is made between the two.

Two important objections to this view must be considered. One is that if Moses is one of the witnesses, does this mean he must die a second time (see below on Heb. 9:27)? A second objection is that according to Jesus, Malachi's prophecy about the coming of Elijah was at least partially fulfilled in John the Baptist (cf. Matt. 17:10–13).

A second common view replaces Moses with Enoch. Thomas notes that this view was held by many leaders in the ancient church.[5] The reasoning is that since Elijah and Enoch were both translated to heaven without dying, they must die to fulfill the statement of Hebrews 9:27 that "it is appointed for man to die once." This alone, however, is not compelling evidence since the entire generation of believers alive at the rapture will be translated to heaven without experiencing death.

It seems far preferable to regard these two witnesses as two prophets who will be raised up from among those who turn to Christ in the time following the rapture. What is not in doubt, however, is their incredible power from God to witness for 1,260 days in spite of the antagonism of the world. Their unusual character as prophets of doom is symbolized in the fact that they are clothed in sackcloth (cf. Isa. 37:1–2; Dan. 9:3). It is worth noting that in Satan's attempt to mimic God, the evil one also has his two "witnesses" in the end times, the world ruler and the false prophet.

The two witnesses of Revelation 11 are described as two olive trees and two lampstands, perhaps a reference to Zechariah 4 where a lampstand and two olive trees are mentioned. In answer to the question, "What are these?" the answer is given to Zerubbabel: "This is the word of the LORD to Zerubbabel: Not by might, nor by power, but by my Spirit, says the Lord of hosts" (v. 6). It is evident that a similar meaning is intended in Revelation. The olive oil from the olive trees in Zechariah's image provided fuel for the lampstand that shed light in the darkness. The two witnesses of this period of Israel's history, namely Joshua the high priest and Zerubbabel, were the leaders in Zechariah's time. Just as these two witnesses were raised up to be lampstands or witnesses for God and were empowered by olive oil representing the power of the Holy Spirit, so the two witnesses of Revelation 11 will also execute their prophetic office and shine for God in earth's darkest hour.

Verses 5 and 6 record the miraculous powers given to the two witnesses to destroy anyone who tries to harm them. This is at once a judgment of God upon their enemies and a means of protecting the two witnesses until their ministry is completed. Taking all the facts furnished, it is evident that these witnesses have a combination of the greatest powers ever given prophets on earth. It is only at the end of the great tribulation when their ministry has been accomplished that their enemies temporarily have the upper hand, and this is allowed by sovereign appointment of God.

THE DEATH OF THE TWO WITNESSES (11:7–10)

11:7–10 And when they have finished their testimony, the beast that rises from the bottomless pit will make war on them and conquer them and kill them, and their dead bodies will lie in the street of the great city that symbolically is called Sodom and Egypt, where their Lord was crucified. For three and a half days some from the peoples and tribes and languages and nations will gaze at their dead bodies and refuse to let them be placed in a tomb, and those who dwell on the earth will rejoice over them and make merry and exchange presents, because these two prophets had been a torment to those who dwell on the earth.

As in the case of other great prophets of God, He permits the enemies of these prophets to kill them when their ministry is finished. The beast, who is none other than Satan himself, overcomes the two prophets. This is the first of thirty-eight references in Revelation to a beast; the beast out of the pit referring to Satan, "the beast rising out of the sea" (13:1) to the world dictator, "the beast rising out of the earth" (13:11) to the false religious leader of that day. This unholy trinity is the satanic counterfeit of the divine Trinity, the Father, the Son, and the Holy Spirit. (For further discussion see exposition of 13:11–18; 17:7–8.)

The "victory" over these two witnesses is considered so significant to their enemies that their dead bodies are allowed to lie in the streets of the city, described symbolically as "Sodom and Egypt, where their Lord was crucified." This is unquestionably Jerusalem, where these witnesses had their prophetic ministry and where they die. It appears that Jerusalem will be the center of the world dictator's rule during this time.[6]

There was a time when interpreters wondered how people from every part of the earth would be able to see the prophet's bodies, but of course modern technology has made this completely possible. Anyone with a cell phone can snap a picture and post it on the Internet where it can be viewed instantly.

The people who turn the witnesses' deaths into a giant party are called "those who dwell on the earth" (v. 10), almost a technical term in Revelation for unbelievers who are left on the earth after the church is raptured. This phrase is repeated a dozen times or more in Revelation. The two witnesses' dead bodies will be a symbol of victory for the beast and those who oppose God, certain that their fear of God's wrath and power is no longer justified.

A righteous prophet is always a torment to an evil generation. The two witnesses are an obstacle to evil, unbelief, and satanic power prevalent in that time. If their ministry is in the time of great tribulation, it is all the more a thorn in the side of the world rulers of that day. The Word of God makes it clear that it is often possible to silence a witness to the truth by death, but such action does not destroy the truth that has been announced. The power of God will be ultimately revealed. If this is at the end of the great tribulation, only a few days remain before Christ comes back in power and great glory.

THE TWO WITNESSES RESTORED
TO LIFE AND CAUGHT UP TO HEAVEN (11:11–12)

11:11–12 But after the three and a half days a breath of life from God entered them, and they stood up on their feet, and great fear fell on those who saw them. Then they heard a loud voice from heaven saying to them, "Come up here!" And they went up to heaven in a cloud, and their enemies watched them.

The worldwide merrymaking by the enemies of God is cut short when the two witnesses suddenly come back to life and ascend into heaven. The fear of the observers is understandable given this sight alone, to say nothing of the loud voice from heaven.

Though there are similarities between this event and the rapture of the church, the contrast is also evident. The rapture will take place in a moment, and apparently will not be gradual enough for people to observe. The parallel here is to the ascension of Christ on the Mount of Olives in Acts 1, when the disciples beheld Him ascending into heaven, and, like the two witnesses,

He was received by a cloud. This is a special act of God addressed to those who reject His grace and designed as a final warning of the supreme power of God over all mankind whether in life or in death. This act of resurrection and catching up into heaven is distinct from any other mentioned in the Bible in that it occurs after the rapture and before the resurrection in chapter 20.

Some have attempted to say the three-and-a-half days of 11:11 represent three-and-a-half years as in Daniel's seventieth week (Dan. 9:27). In this view, those who minister on earth as the two witnesses do are on earth the first three-and-a-half years of the seven-year period, are dead for the next three-and-a-half years, and then are raised at the end. Though this is a possible interpretation, it is unlikely. If the 1,260 days of verse 3 are literal days, it would seem strange to have these three-and-a-half days become symbolic. Besides, it seems impossible that the two witnesses' bodies would lie in the streets of Jerusalem for three-and-a-half years, which would be required if the days are not literal. This is another case when taking the Scriptures in their plain sense, when there is no indication to do otherwise, yields the most plausible interpretation.

ANNOUNCEMENT OF THE THIRD WOE (11:13–14)

11:13–14 And at that hour there was a great earthquake, and a tenth of the city fell. Seven thousand people were killed in the earthquake, and the rest were terrified and gave glory to the God of heaven. The second woe has passed; behold, the third woe is soon to come.

The dramatic events of verse 13 bring great fear to those who survive the earthquake in Jerusalem. The reference to "the God of heaven" is one of two in the New Testament (cf. Rev. 16:11). It is a familiar phrase in the Old Testament where it is used to distinguish the true God from pagan deities. Here the significance is that they recognize the true God in contrast to their worship of the beast. Even though they recognize the power of the God of heaven, it does not seem to indicate that they have come to the point of true faith in Christ.

With this event, the second woe is brought to its completion and is evidently regarded as the final phase of the sixth trumpet. The third woe contained in the seventh trumpet is announced as coming quickly. The end of the age is rapidly approaching.

THE SEVENTH TRUMPET SOUNDS (11:15)

11:15 Then the seventh angel blew his trumpet, and there were loud voices in heaven, saying, "The kingdom of the world has become the kingdom of our Lord and of his Christ, and he shall reign forever and ever."

When the seventh trumpet sounds, John hears great voices in heaven. In contrast to previous instances where a single voice makes the announcement, here there is a great symphony of voices chanting the triumph of Christ. The fact that earthly rule will pass into the hands of God is frequently mentioned in Old Testament prophecy (cf. Ezek. 21:26–27; Dan. 2:35, 44; 4:3; 6:26; 7:14, 26–27; Zech. 14:9). The question that remains, however, is how at this point the kingdom of the world can become the kingdom of Christ when the seven bowls of judgment are seemingly still to be poured out. The answer, as indicated previously, seems to be that just as the seven trumpets are contained in the seventh seal, so the seven bowls are contained in the seventh trumpet. The process of destruction of earthly power is therefore already under way.

Christ is declared to reign "forever and ever." This is more than simply announcing His millennial reign on earth, which will extend for only one thousand years. In some sense, Christ's reign continues in the new heaven and the new earth. Never again will the earth be under the control of humans. Even the brief rebellion recorded in Revelation 20 at the close of the millennium is unsuccessful.

THE WORSHIP OF THE
TWENTY-FOUR ELDERS (11:16–17)

11:16–17 And the twenty-four elders who sit on their thrones before God fell on their faces and worshiped God, saying, "We give thanks to you, Lord God Almighty, who is and who was, for you have taken your great power and begun to reign."

The twenty-four elders have previously appeared seven times in Revelation in a similar context. Here they give thanks to God because He has manifested His power and assumed authority over the earth. The event for which they give thanks is the fulfillment of Psalm 2:9, where Christ the Anointed of God reigns supreme over the earth.

EVENTS MARKING THE REIGN OF CHRIST (11:18)

11:18 "The nations raged, but your wrath came, and the time for the dead to be judged, and for rewarding your servants, the prophets and saints, and those who fear your name, both small and great, and for destroying the destroyers of the earth."

This comprehensive statement gives the main features of the transition from the kingdom of earth to the kingdom of God. It begins with the fact that the nations are angry at the time when the wrath of God comes. There is a play on words in the Greek of this verse, for the word in verb form for the rage of God's enemies is used in noun form for God's wrath. The contrast is clear; the wrath of humanity is impotent, but the wrath of God is omnipotent.

Here important events related to the judgment of God are mentioned. The dead are judged at this time. The context seems to indicate that the resurrection of the righteous dead is in view rather than that of the evil dead, who are not raised until after the millennium. The following comment speaks of the reward given to those who serve God, and of the destruction of those living on the earth at that time who rebel against God.

Verse 18 teaches that in general the tribulation is a time of divine wrath, of resurrection of the dead and their reward, and of dealing with those who oppose God. All of these aspects of the second coming of Christ are borne out in later prophecies in Revelation.

THE OPENING OF THE
TEMPLE OF GOD IN HEAVEN (11:19)

11:19 Then God's temple in heaven was opened, and the ark of his covenant was seen within his temple. There were flashes of lightning, rumblings, peals of thunder, an earthquake, and heavy hail.

The opening of the heavenly temple seems to be related to the revelation given in chapter 12 rather than to the seventh trumpet specifically. There may be an antithesis between the temple of God in heaven (v. 19) and the temple of God in Jerusalem during the great tribulation (vv. 1–2). Though the earthly temple may have been desecrated by the beast, its counterpart in heaven reflects the righteousness and majesty of God. The heavenly ark of the covenant speaks of God's righteousness.

The accompanying disturbances seem to indicate that God is now going to deal in summary judgment with the earth. Nineteenth-century Bible teacher J. N. Darby believed that what precedes verse 19 "brings the general history of the ways of God [with mankind] to a termination."[7]

Before the details of the judgment to follow are unfolded in the seven bowls in chapter 16, the revelation turns to other important aspects of this period that chronologically precede the consummation. Apart from the outpourings of the bowls, which occur in rapid succession, there is little narrative movement from this point until chapter 19 and the second coming of Christ. Events and situations are now introduced that are concurrent with the seals and the trumpets. These serve to emphasize the dramatic climax of this period in the second coming of Jesus Christ.

NOTES

1. Warren Wiersbe, *Wiersbe's Expository Outlines on the New Testament* (Wheaton, IL: Victor, 1992), 827. For a presentation of the events of Revelation 11 as symbolic of the "witnessing church," see Robert H. Mounce, *The Book of Revelation*, rev. ed., New International Commentary on the New Testament (Grand Rapids: Eerdmans, 1997), 217.

2. Walter C. Kaiser and Duane Garrett, eds., "Revelation," *The Archaeological Study Bible* (Grand Rapids: Zondervan, 2005), 2059.

3. Walter C. Kaiser and Duane Garrett, eds., "Revelation," *The Archaeological Study Bible*, 2059.

4. Tony Evans, *The Best Is Yet to Come* (Chicago: Moody, 2000), 181–182.

5. Robert L. Thomas, *Revelation 8–22: An Exegetical Commentary* (Chicago: Moody, 1995), 88.

6. John MacArthur, *The MacArthur New Testament Commentary: Revelation 1–11* (Chicago: Moody, 1999), 304.

7. J. N. Darby, *Notes on the Apocalypse* (London: G. Morrish, 1842), 55.

The Conflict in Heaven and on Earth

12

Beginning with Revelation 12:1, we come to another parenthetical section of the book, which ends at 14:20. Within this section seven primary characters are introduced: (1) the woman, representing Israel, (2) the dragon, representing Satan, (3) a male child, referring to Christ, (4) Michael, representing the angels, (5) Israel, the remnant of the woman's seed, (6) the beast out of the sea, the world dictator, and (7) the beast out of the earth, the false prophet and religious leader of the world. Around these main characters swirls the tremendously moving scene of the great tribulation. Chapter 12 is the most symbolic chapter in the Bible's most symbolic book.

THE WOMAN CLOTHED
WITH THE SUN: ISRAEL (12:1–2)

12:1–2 And a great sign appeared in heaven: a woman clothed with the sun, with the moon under her feet, and on her head a crown of twelve stars. She was pregnant and was crying out in birth pains and the agony of giving birth.

The first of the seven personages to be introduced in this section is the woman who is described as a great sign in heaven, clearly indicated to be someone of regal splendor.[1] The word "sign" signifies a symbol of important truth rather than merely a wonder. Subsequently, six other signs are mentioned (12:3; 13:13–14; 15:1; 16:14; 19:20). This sign in verse 1 is distinguished by being called "great." Though the sign is seen in heaven, it apparently portrays a reality on the earth, for the woman pictured is afterward persecuted by Satan in the great tribulation. The woman is pregnant and due to give birth to a son.

Many explanations have been offered for the identity of this woman. She does not represent Christ, nor the church in general because the church did not give birth to Christ. On the contrary, Christ gave birth to the church. Since the woman's child is obviously Christ, some have suggested this is Mary—an implausible identification given that this woman is persecuted in the last half of the tribulation.[2] The Roman Catholic Church insists this is Mary, but the church also teaches that Mary gave birth to Christ without pain, a teaching that is contradicted by Revelation 12.[3]

Rather, the woman is Israel as the matrix from which Christ came. By contrast, other representative women mentioned in Revelation are Jezebel (2:20), representative of false religion as a system; the harlot (17:1–7, 15–18), the apostate church of the future; and the bride, the Lamb's wife (19:7), the church joined to Christ in glory.

The identification of the woman of Revelation 12 as Israel is consistent with Old Testament teaching. There Israel is frequently presented as the wife of Yahweh, often in her character as being unfaithful to her husband (cf. Hosea's prophecy). Here is the godly remnant of Israel standing true to God in the time of the great tribulation.

The regal description of the woman is an allusion to Genesis 37:9–11, where these heavenly bodies represent Jacob and Rachel, thereby identifying the woman with the fulfillment of the Abrahamic covenant. In the same context, the stars represent the patriarchs, the sons of Jacob.[4] The symbolism may extend beyond this to represent in some sense the glory of Israel and her ultimate triumph over her enemies. This identification of the woman as Israel also seems to be supported by the evidence from this chapter. Israel is obviously the source from which have come many of the blessings of God, including the Bible, Christ, and the apostles. According to Isaiah 9:6, Israel is the source of the Messiah. As noted above, the persecution of the woman coincides with the persecution of Israel.

The woman as the nation of Israel is seen in the pain of childbirth, awaiting delivery of her child. Frequently in Scripture, Israel is pictured in the tribulation time as going through great trial and affliction. Though historically the nation gave birth to Christ through the Virgin Mary, the implication of verse 2 is that the references are to the sufferings of Israel as a nation rather than to the historic birth of Christ. It may refer to the sufferings of the nation in general over its entire history. If strictly interpreted, it may signify the pain of Israel at the time of the first coming of Christ as borne out by verses 3 and 4.

THE GREAT RED DRAGON: SATAN (12:3-4)

12:3–4 And another sign appeared in heaven: behold, a great red dragon, with seven heads and ten horns, and on his heads seven diadems. His tail swept down a third of the stars of heaven and cast them to the earth. And the dragon stood before the woman who was about to give birth, so that when she bore her child he might devour it.

The second sign appearing in heaven is a great dragon. From the similar description given in 13:1 and the parallel reference in Daniel 7:7–8, 24, it is clear that the revived Roman Empire is in view. Satan, however, is also called the dragon later in 12:9, and it is clear that the dragon is both the empire and the representation of satanic power. The color red may indicate his murderous characteristics (cf. John 8:44).[5] The seven heads and ten horns refer to the original ten kingdoms of Daniel 7:7–8, of which three were subdued by the little horn who is to be identified with the world ruler of the great tribulation who reigns over the revived Roman Empire.

The tail of the dragon is declared to draw a third part of the stars of heaven and cast them to the earth. This seems to refer to the gathering under his power of those who oppose him politically, and also involves his temporary subjugation of a large portion of the earth.

The dragon is seen awaiting the birth of the child with the intent to destroy it as soon as it is born. The allusion here is unmistakably to the circumstances surrounding the birth of Christ in Bethlehem (the dragon referring to the Roman Empire at that time as dominated by Satan) and the attempts of Herod to destroy the baby Jesus (cf. Matt 2:13–15). It is significant that Herod as an Edomite was a descendant of Esau and of the people who were the traditional enemies of Jacob and his descendants. Whether motivated by his family antipathy to the Jews or by political consideration because he did not want competition in his office as king, Herod nevertheless fulfilled historically this reference to the destruction of children in Bethlehem.

THE CHILD: CHRIST (12:5–6)

12:5–6 She gave birth to a male child, one who is to rule all the nations with a rod of iron, but her child was caught up to God and to his throne, and the woman fled into the wilderness, where she has a place prepared by God, in which she is to be nourished for 1,260 days.

The woman identified as Israel gives birth to a child who is destined to rule all nations with an iron rod (a reference to the Messiah from Ps. 2:9), but who for the time being is caught up to God's throne. A similar expression is found in Revelation 19:15, where it is stated of Christ, "He will rule them with a rod of iron," to be distinguished from His rule over Israel, which is of more benevolent character (cf. Luke 1:32–33).

While many Bible expositors have agreed that the woman is Israel, there has been considerable difference of opinion on the identity of the child. Some have argued that this is the New Testament church destined to reign with Christ and that the act of being caught up to God is the rapture. But the church is not the "child" of Israel, nor is the church's mission to rule the nations. In addition, the child is clearly identified as a male, while the church is referred to in the feminine as the bride of Christ (cf. Rev. 19:6–8).

Though the pregnant woman is to be identified with Israel collectively rather than with the Virgin Mary specifically, the interpretation that the child is Christ Himself is far preferable. His catching up to God and to His throne seems to represent His ascension. An alternative view is that the "catching up" refers to the flight to Egypt after Jesus' birth to protect Him from Herod (cf. Matt. 2:13–15). But as Thomas points out, that incident does not satisfy the conditions of Revelation 12:5, where the catching up is to the throne of God in heaven.[6]

The Greek verb for "caught up" in verse 5 is a form of the word *harpazō*. This word is sometimes used to mean "to seize" or "to catch up," as a wild beast would its prey, as in John 10:12 where the wolf "snatches them and scatters them." The same word is used for the rapture of the church in 1 Thessalonians 4:17 where the church is caught up to heaven, and is likewise used of Paul being caught up to paradise (2 Cor. 12:2, 4), and of the Spirit of God catching up Philip (Acts 8:39).

If the identification of the twenty-four elders is properly to be regarded as the church in heaven, it would seem to mix metaphors to have the church represented as a male child, especially when the church is regarded in chapter 19 as the wife and bride. There is no good reason for not identifying the man-child as Christ and interpreting the drama of verse 5 as describing His ascension, as noted above. The fact that He is caught up not only to God but to "his throne" is another indication that Christ is intended.

In verse 6, the attention is directed back to the child's mother, Israel. Here she is seen in the time of great tribulation fleeing into the wilderness to a place prepared by God where for 1,260 days she is cared for (again, the exact length of three-and-a-half years). There is obviously a tremendous time lapse between verses 5 and 6, but this is not an uncommon occurrence in prophecy; the first and second comings of Christ are frequently spoken of in the same sentence. Since Israel is comparatively tranquil and safe in the first three-and-a-half years of Daniel's seventieth week (Dan. 9:27), the reference must be to the preservation of a portion of the nation Israel through the great tribulation to await the second coming of Christ.

SATAN CAST OUT OF HEAVEN BY MICHAEL (12:7–9)

12:7–9 Now war arose in heaven, Michael and his angels fighting against the dragon. And the dragon and his angels fought

back, but he was defeated and there was no longer any place for
them in heaven. And the great dragon was thrown down, that
ancient serpent, who is called the devil and Satan, the deceiver of
the whole world—he was thrown down to the earth, and his
angels were thrown down with him.

Though the conflict of the end of the age is primarily on earth, there will
also be war in heaven. Michael and his angels (that is, the holy angels) fight
against Satan and the evil angels associated with him, with the result that
Satan and his hordes are thrown out of heaven. The description of Satan in
verse 9 is significant as all of his important titles are given: "the dragon," a term
that also applies to the empire that he dominates in the end time; "that
ancient serpent," a reference to the Garden of Eden and the temptation of
Eve; "devil," which means "defamer" or "slanderer," the master accuser of
believers; and Satan, meaning "adversary." This name is mentioned fourteen
times in the book of Job, and occasionally elsewhere (1 Chron. 21:1; Ps.
109:6; Zech. 3:1–2). Given Satan's all-out opposition to God, it is fitting
that the Greek construction of verse 7 indicates that the dragon will start
this war.[7]

The concept that there is a spiritual warfare in the very presence of God
in heaven has been resisted by some expositors, preferring to regard this war
as being fought in the atmospheric or the starry heaven rather than in the
very presence of God.[8] The event here prophesied was predicted by Daniel
the prophet in Daniel 12:1, where it is recorded that Michael shall "arise" as
the one "who has charge of your people." This event marks the beginning of
the great tribulation described in Daniel 12:1. It is undoubtedly the same
event as in Revelation 12.

It may seem strange to some that Satan should have access to the very
throne of God. Yet this is precisely the picture of Job 1, where Satan along
with other angels presents himself before God and accuses Job of fearing God
because of God's goodness to him. Thus early in biblical revelation, Satan is
cast in the role of "the accuser of our brothers," the title given him in Revelation 12:10.

From this point in Revelation, therefore, Satan and his hosts are excluded from the third heaven, the presence of God, although their temporary dominion over the second heaven (outer space) and the first heaven (the sky) continues. Satan's defeat in heaven, however, is the occasion for him to be cast down to earth and explains the particular virulence of the great tribulation time. Note that even as Satan accuses believers before God day and night prior to his being thrown out of heaven, so the four living creatures of 4:8 do not stop day or night to ascribe holiness to the Lord.

This is another place where we must let the words and events of Scripture speak for themselves and take them at their face value unless compelled to do otherwise. Satan, the deceiver of the whole world (literally, "the inhabited earth"), is now limited in the sphere of his operation. A major step is taken in his ultimate defeat. Believers in this present dispensation, who are now the objects of satanic attack and misrepresentation, can rest assured of the ultimate downfall of Satan and the end of his ability to afflict the people of God. Though the events of this chapter deal in general with the end of the age, it is clear that they do not come chronologically after the seventh trumpet. Rather, the fall of Satan may be predated to the time of the seals in chapter 6, or even before the first seal. His fall begins the great tribulation.

ANNOUNCEMENT OF SATAN'S WRATH
AND THE SAINTS' ULTIMATE VICTORY (12:10–12)

12:10–12 And I heard a loud voice in heaven, saying, "Now the salvation and the power and the kingdom of our God and the authority of his Christ have come, for the accuser of our brothers has been thrown down, who accuses them day and night before our God. And they have conquered him by the blood of the Lamb and by the word of their testimony, for they loved not their lives even unto death. Therefore, rejoice, O heavens and you who dwell in them! But woe to you, O earth and sea, for the devil has come down to you in great wrath, because he knows that his time is short!"

197

The loud voice making this important announcement is not identified and probably cannot be with certainty. Some have ascribed this voice to God Himself, others to the angels, the twenty-four elders, or the martyred saints in heaven mentioned in 6:10, because they also cry with a loud voice. Support for the latter view is given in that in the same verse the loud voice mentions "the accuser of our brothers." This would seem to eliminate angels and indicate believers in heaven.[9] The "loud voice" may very well be the shout of triumph of the tribulation saints longing for and anticipating their ultimate victory.

The salvation mentioned here is not salvation from the guilt of sin but salvation in the sense of deliverance and completion of the divine program. The reference to strength implies that now God is going to strengthen His own and manifest His own power. The kingdom being announced is the millennial kingdom when Christ will reign on the earth. Coupled with this is the power or authority of Christ. The expression "his Christ," also used in 11:15, parallels "his anointed" in Psalm 2:2, a reference to God's Messiah against whom the kings of the earth rebel but under whose authority they are certain to come.

The victory of the saints in that hour is revealed in verse 11 through the use of three strong spiritual weapons. Satan's accusations are nullified by the blood of the Lamb that renders the believer pure and makes possible his spiritual victory. The word of the believers' testimony opposes the deceiving work of Satan in that the preaching of the gospel is the power of God unto salvation. The believers also exhibit total commitment to their task in which many of them die as martyrs. The word for "loved" is a form of the familiar Greek word *agapē*, which describes the love of God. Though these believers do not foolishly seek a martyr's death, they do not regard their lives as more precious than their witness for Christ. They follow the instruction given to the church in Smyrna (2:10) of being faithful unto death, as well as the example of the Savior, who laid down His life for the sheep (John 10:11, 15; cf. Matt. 16:25).

The voice from heaven continues, exhorting those in the heavens to rejoice because of this great victory. At the same time, the voice pronounces a solemn woe upon the inhabitants of the earth and of the sea. The awfulness of the hour ahead is attributed to the fact that the devil has been thrown down to earth and is about to unleash his wrath on the earth's inhabitants. The short time Satan has refers to the great tribulation after which he will be bound for the duration of the millennial kingdom. Though many of the judgments of God inflicted on the earth during the great tribulation originate in divine power rather than satanic influence, the afflictions of the inhabitants of the earth spring largely from the activities of Satan, resulting in the martyrdom of countless saints and in widespread human suffering of every kind.

THE PERSECUTION OF ISRAEL
IN THE GREAT TRIBULATION (12:13–16)

12:13–16 And when the dragon saw that he had been thrown down to the earth, he pursued the woman who had given birth to the male child. But the woman was given the two wings of the great eagle so that she might fly from the serpent into the wilderness, to the place where she is to be nourished for a time, and times, and half a time. The serpent poured water like a river out of his mouth after the woman, to sweep her away with a flood. But the earth came to the help of the woman, and the earth opened its mouth and swallowed the river that the dragon had poured from his mouth.

Satan immediately turns his anger toward Israel. This apparently is the beginning of the great tribulation of which Christ warned Israel in Matthew 24:15–22. This had its foreshadowing in Herod's slaughter of the infants following the birth of Christ (Matt. 2:16). It seems here to refer specifically to the great tribulation that is yet future. The persecution of Israel is a part of the satanic program to thwart and hinder the work of God. As far as Israel is concerned, this had its beginning in the miraculous intervention of God required to bring about the birth of Isaac and fulfill this portion of the promise to Abraham. Satan used other means thereafter to persecute the descendants of Jacob, including the effort in the time of Esther to blot them out completely. Israel is hated by Satan not because of any of its own characteristics, but because she is the chosen of God and essential to the overall purpose of God for time and eternity.

The divine intervention of God thwarts this attempt at satanic persecution. The figure of the "two wings of the great eagle" seems to be derived from Exodus 19:4, Deuteronomy 32:11–12, and similar passages where God uses the strength of an eagle to illustrate His faithfulness in caring for Israel. The same flight is indicated in Matthew 24:16, where Christ warns those in Judea to flee to the mountains.

Some have felt that the reference here is to some specific place such as the rock city of Petra, in the southern part of modern Jordan, as the end-time city of refuge for the Jewish people where at least a portion of Israel might be safe from her persecutors. Fruchtenbaum makes a strong case for Petra, pointing to clues in Matthew 24:16; Revelation 12:6, 14; Isaiah 33:13–16; Micah 2:12; and Daniel 11:41.[10] Benware links this time of tribulation with Jesus' judgment of the sheep and goats in Matthew 25, which relates to the Gentiles' treatment of Israel as the nation undergoes this persecution.[11]

Verse 14 implies that there is some supernatural care of Israel during this period such as that which Elijah experienced by the brook Cherith (cf. 1 Kings 17:5), or that which Israel experienced during the forty years she lived on the manna in the wilderness. Whether natural or supernatural means are used, it is clear that God does preserve a godly remnant, though according to Zechariah 13:8, two-thirds of Israel in the land will perish.

The time element of Israel's suffering is described as "a time, and times, and half a time." This again seems to be a reference to the three-and-a-half years of tribulation. A parallel reference is found in Daniel 7:25 and 12:7 referring to the same period of great tribulation. The dragon is here called a serpent (cf. Matt. 10:16; John 3:14 where the word is used in other contexts; Rev. 12:9, 14–15; 20:2 where "serpent" is used in connection with the devil).

The flood sent by Satan to destroy Israel and God's supernatural protection have been the subject of various interpretations. This may be a literal flood, but the contour of the Holy Land and the fact that Israel's people would probably not all flee in the same direction combine to make such a literal, physical interpretation improbable.

It is more plausible to understand this symbolically. The flood is the total effort of Satan to exterminate Israel, and the resistance of earth is the natural difficulty in executing such a massive program. The terrain of the Middle East provides countless places of refuge for a fleeing people. Though the exact meaning of these two verses cannot be determined with certainty, the implication is that Satan strives with all his power to persecute and exterminate the people of Israel. By divine intervention, both natural and supernatural means are used to thwart the enemy's program and carry a remnant of Israel safely through their time of great tribulation.

THE PERSECUTION OF
THE GODLY REMNANT OF ISRAEL (12:17)

12:17 Then the dragon became furious with the woman and went off to make war on the rest of her offspring, on those who keep the commandments of God and hold to the testimony of Jesus. And he stood on the sand of the sea.

The godly remnant of Israel is identified by their faith in Christ, "all those who name the name of Jesus Christ."[12] While the program of Satan is against the Jewish race as such, anti-Semitism as a whole will reach its peak against Jewish *believers* during this period. There is a double antagonism against those in Israel who turn to Christ as their Messiah and Savior in those critical days and maintain a faithful witness. Undoubtedly, many of them will suffer a martyr's death, but others will survive the period, including the 144,000 sealed in chapter 7.

In some versions of the Bible such as the *New International Version* (NIV) and the *New American Standard Bible* (NASB), the phrase translated here as "and he stood on the sand of the sea" is part of Revelation 13:1, although in the Greek text it is listed as Revelation 12:17. The *English Standard Version* (ESV) better reflects the Greek text, which suggests that the dragon is the subject of the verb "stood," rather than John and also ties the dragon more closely to his origin in the sea. The reading "I stood," meaning John, is found in the majority of the Greek manuscripts, but the reading "he stood," meaning the dragon, is attested by the better manuscripts.[13]

Taken as a whole, chapter 12 is a fitting introduction to the important revelations given in chapter 13. Here are the principal actors of the great tribulation with the historic background that provides so much essential information. Israel, Satan, Christ, the archangel, and the godly remnant figure largely in the closing scenes of the age. Next, the two principal human actors are introduced: the beast out of the sea and the beast out of the earth, the human instruments that Satan will use to direct his program during the great tribulation.

NOTES

1. Charles C. Ryrie, *Revelation*, rev. ed. (Chicago: Moody, 1996), 89.

2. Ibid., 90.

3. Wilbur M. Smith, *The Wycliffe Bible Commentary*, Charles F. Pfeiffer and Everett F. Harrison, eds. (Chicago: Moody, 1990), 1511–1512.

4. Merrill F. Unger, *The New Unger's Bible Handbook*, rev. Gary N. Larson (Chicago: Moody, 1984), 676.

5. Ibid., 677.

6. Robert L. Thomas, *Revelation 8–22: An Exegetical Commentary* (Chicago: Moody, 1995), 126.

7. John MacArthur, *The MacArthur New Testament Commentary: Revelation 12–22* (Chicago: Moody, 2000), 16.

8. For a presentation of the view that the war in heaven is not to be interpreted literally, see William Hendriksen, *More Than Conquerors* (Grand Rapids: Baker, 1967), 141.

9. Mounce argues that the designation "our brothers" does *not* rule out angels, citing Revelation 19:10 where an angel identifies himself as a fellow servant of John and his brothers. See Robert H. Mounce, *The Book of Revelation*, The New International Commentary on the New Testament (Grand Rapids: Eerdmans, 1997), 238.

10. Arnold G. Fruchtenbaum, *The Footsteps of the Messiah: A Study of the Sequence of Prophetic Events*, rev. ed. (Tustin, CA: Ariel Ministries, 2003), 294–297.

11. Paul Benware, *Understanding End Times Prophecy* (Chicago: Moody, 2006), 327.

12. John MacArthur, *Because the Time Is Near* (Chicago: Moody Publishers, 2007), 211.

13. Michael H. Burer, W. Hall Harris III, and Daniel B. Wallace, eds., *New English Translation: Novum Testamentum Graece* (Dallas: NET Bible Press, 2003), 656. For a fuller discussion of this textual issue, see Appendix VI on p. 885.

13 The Two Beasts

THE FIRST BEAST OUT OF THE SEA (13:1–2)

13:1–2 And I saw a beast rising out of the sea, with ten horns and seven heads, with ten diadems on its horns and blasphemous names on its heads. And the beast that I saw was like a leopard; its feet were like a bear's, and its mouth was like a lion's mouth. And to it the dragon gave his power and his throne and great authority.

In the first ten verses of chapter 13, a character is introduced of central importance to the events of the great tribulation. This passage is first of all a revelation of the revived Roman Empire in its period of worldwide dominion, but more especially this paragraph directs attention to the evil character who exercises satanic power as the world dictator (see chart).

TITLES OF THE COMING WORLD RULER

The little horn (Dan. 7:8)

The coming prince (Dan. 9:26)

The willful king (Dan. 11:36)

The man of lawlessness (2 Thess. 2:3)

The son of destruction (2 Thess. 2:3)

The Antichrist (1 John 2:18, 22)

The rider on the white horse (Rev. 6:2)

The beast (Rev. 13:1-10)

This is the beast with ten horns and seven heads that John sees coming up out of the sea. Ten crowns are on the horns, and on the seven heads names of blasphemy are written. The identity of this beast is quite clear in its reference to the revived Roman Empire, since the description is similar to Daniel 7:7–8 and Revelation 12:3 and 17:3, 7. The stage of the empire depicted by the beast is the period after the emergence of the little horn, the future world ruler, displacing three of the horns (Dan. 7:8). The description fits the time of the empire during the great tribulation.

The fact that the beast rises out of the sea is taken by many to indicate that he comes from the Gentile nations.[1] Others take it as a reference to the Mediterranean Sea, specifying a location. Probably both are true in that the beast is a Gentile and does come from the Mediterranean scene. Evans notes that the beast could be of European origin, "because Europe contains the remnants of the old Roman Empire and will be the center of the revived empire."[2]

The monstrosity of seven heads and ten horns probably refers to the remnants of the confederacy that formed the revived Roman Empire in the beginning, the ten nations of which three were overthrown by the little horn of Daniel 7:8. The ten crowns, therefore, refer to the diadems or symbols of governmental authority. The fact that they have names of blasphemy ("names" is properly plural) indicates their blasphemous opposition to God and to Christ. It is worth noting that Roman emperors in the ancient world often assumed titles of deity. Domitian was addressed as *Dominus et Deus noster* ("our Lord and God") and emperor worship was compulsory.[3]

Some consider the seven heads as successive phases of governmental and political history during this period. Others believe that they are simultaneous kings who are sub-rulers under the beast. The successive idea seems to be borne out by Revelation 17:10–12, where the heads are indicated to be successive rulers. The difficulty can be resolved by regarding the heads as successive, referring to kings or emperors, and the horns as kings who will reign while receiving their power from the beast (cf. Rev. 17:12). John may be seeing the beast in both its historic and prophetic characters.

The beast is further described as being comparable to a leopard with the feet of a bear and the mouth of a lion, and as receiving his power, throne, and authority from the dragon, that is, from Satan. The selection of these three animals is similar to the revelation given in Daniel 7, where the successive world empires are described by the lion, referring to Babylon, the bear, referring to Medo-Persia, and the leopard, referring to the Alexandrian Empire of Greece. It is worth noting that in John's vision these three animals are mentioned in reverse order from Daniel's vision. Daniel was looking forward in time and so he saw the three kingdoms in chronological order, while John was looking back in time.[4]

The fourth empire gathers all these elements and characteristics into itself and is far more dreadful in its power and blasphemy than the preceding empires.

As many have pointed out, the beasts selected are typical of the revived Roman Empire in the great tribulation, having the majesty and power of the lion, the strength and tenacity of a bear, and the swiftness of a leopard—so well illustrated in the conquest of Alexander the Great.[5] In addition to these natural symbols of strength is the added factor of power coming from Satan himself.

THE DEADLY WOUND OF THE BEAST (13:3)

13:3 One of its heads seemed to have a mortal wound, but its mortal wound was healed, and the whole earth marveled as they followed the beast.

What is the meaning of the beast's head that received a deadly wound but was healed? The apparent parallelism is to the slain Lamb, described in 5:6, but does this head represent a human being? Certainly a person who was killed and then came to life again would make all the world marvel, and it would fit the devil's character as the great imitator of everything God does. But it is questionable whether Satan has the power to restore to life one who has died, even though his power is great.

Despite this, generations of Bible students have suggested numerous evil rulers or other persons from history as the beast. Those from ancient times have suggested Nero and Judas Iscariot, and in modern times tyrants like Hitler and Stalin have been named—the former especially because of his murder of the Jews. The multiplicity of suggestions seems to be evidence in itself that these explanations are not the meaning of the passage.

The wounding of this head seems instead to indicate that the Roman Empire as such seemingly died and is now going to be revived. It is significant that while one of the heads is wounded to death, the beast itself is not said to be dead. So a far more probable explanation is that this is the Roman Empire, long since dead in history but destined by God to be revived in the end times.

The identification of a head with the government over which he has authority is not unusual. The person is often the symbol of the government, and what is said of the government can be said of him. Although verse 3 will continue to be a subject of controversy, the theological reasons for resisting an actual resurrection of a historical character to head the revived Roman Empire are so great as to render it improbable. The beast is both personal and, in a sense, the empire itself; so also is the wounded head. The revival of the future empire is considered a miracle and a demonstration of the power of Satan.

THE WORSHIP OF SATAN BY THE WORLD (13:4)

13:4 And they worshiped the dragon, for he had given his authority to the beast, and they worshiped the beast, saying, "Who is like the beast, and who can fight against it?"

The final form of apostasy is not simply the worship of some pagan deity but the worship of Satan himself, whose desire since his fall has been to be "like God" (Isa. 14:14). The people who worship Satan and his beast are those in the "whole earth" (v. 3), that is, the unbelieving world of people in the great tribulation. The beast is Satan's substitute for Christ as King of kings and Lord of lords, and the world falls for the deception because the beast's power seems insurmountable. This apparently occurs at the beginning of the great tribulation when the head of the revived Roman Empire is able to assume authority over the entire world.

The basis for this authority is undoubtedly power given to him by Satan, aided by the fact that there is no serious contender for his office. It may be that the battle of Ezekiel 38 and 39, predicting the destruction of the northern confederacy, takes place just before this, thereby removing the threat of eastern and northern powers to the beast's authority and reign and providing the power vacuum for him to fill. Of course, the answer to the question of verse 4 is Christ Himself manifested in His power at His second coming, when He will throw the beast into the lake of fire. Until that time the beast is allowed to reign and fulfill his place in human destiny.

THE BLASPHEMOUS CHARACTER OF THE BEAST (13:5–6)

13:5–6 And the beast was given a mouth uttering haughty and blasphemous words, and it was allowed to exercise authority for forty-two months. It opened its mouth to utter blasphemies against God, blaspheming his name and his dwelling, that is, those who dwell in heaven.

The evil character of the world ruler of that day is shown in his boasting and blasphemy. A similar description of the same character is given in Daniel 7:8, 11, 25. His authority continues for forty-two months, again the familiar three-and-one-half years of the great tribulation. It is probable that the person who heads the revived Roman Empire comes into power before the beginning of the entire seven-year period of Daniel 9:27, and as such enters into covenant with the Jewish people.[6]

His role as world ruler over all nations, however, does not begin until the time of the great tribulation. From that point, he continues for his allotted three-and-one-half years until the second coming of Christ terminates his reign. It is evident that blasphemy is not an incidental feature of his kingdom but one of its main features, and he is described in verse 6 as blaspheming against God and everyone and everything associated with God. As Satan's mouthpiece he utters the ultimate in unbelief and irreverence in relation to God. If the king of Daniel 11:36–45 is the same individual, as some believe, he does so in total disregard of any god because he magnifies himself above all (Dan. 11:37).

THE UNIVERSAL DOMINION OF THE BEAST (13:7)

13:7 Also it was allowed to make war on the saints and to conquer them. And authority was given it over every tribe and people and language and nation.

As is anticipated in Daniel 7:23, where the beast devours "the whole earth, and trample[s] it down, and break[s] it to pieces," here the worldwide extent of his power is indicated. Conquering the world has been the dream of countless rulers in the past, and it is finally achieved by this last Gentile ruler. It is the satanic counterfeit of Christ's millennial reign permitted by God in this final display of the evil of Satan and evil humanity.

Again, the beast's authority is given to him by Satan. Acting as Satan's tool, the beast is able to make war against God's people throughout the globe and overcome them (cf. Dan. 7:25; 9:27; 12:10; Rev. 6:9–11). In the will of God, many believers in Christ among both Jews and Gentiles die as martyrs during this awful time of trial, while others are preserved in spite of all the beast can do.

The time of this universal sway is clearly indicated in verse 5 as being forty-two months, namely the last three-and-one-half years preceding the return of Christ. This period is otherwise described as the great tribulation. It is apparent, however, that as the period moves on to its end a massive world war commences, continuing until the return of Christ. This war is a rebellion against the universal rule of the beast and comes at the very end of the tribulation. Though the beast enjoys tremendous power, he is apparently not able to suppress this eventual uprising against his authority.

THE UNIVERSAL WORSHIP OF THE BEAST (13:8)

13:8 And all who dwell on earth will worship it, everyone whose name has not been written before the foundation of the world in the book of life of the Lamb that was slain.

Just as the entire world is under the political domination of the beast, so all the world except believers in Jesus Christ will worship him. These are described as people among both Jews and Gentiles whose names are not in the book of life, a book frequently mentioned in the Revelation (3:5; 17:8; 20:12, 15; 21:27; 22:19; cf. Luke 10:20; Phil. 4:3). The translation "the Lamb that was slain" follows the order of the Greek. Most expositors have taken the expression "before the foundation of the world" to refer to the writing of the names in the book, rather than to the slaying of the Lamb that occurred on Calvary.

Some Bible references to the book of life seem to indicate that it is the book of everyone born into the world, and that those who do not trust in Christ are blotted from it, leaving only the saved (cf. Rev. 3:5). But the simplest explanation seems the best, which is that the names of those who would be saved were written in the book of life from eternity past. This was made possible by anticipation of the future death of the Lamb on their behalf. The ultimate meaning is that all who are not saved will worship the beast and that those who are saved will not worship him.

EXHORTATION TO HEAR (13:9–10)

13:9–10 If anyone has an ear, let him hear: If anyone is to be taken captive, to captivity he goes; if anyone is to be slain with the sword, with the sword must he be slain. Here is a call for the endurance and faith of the saints.

It is clear from verse 8 that the universal worship of the beast will achieve at long last the characteristics of a world religion in that it will be ecumenical.

In today's post-9/11 world with its fear of religious fanaticism, there is a strong movement to silence the witness of Christians because they insist on proclaiming the truth of the gospel that Jesus is the only Lord and Savior. It is questionable whether this religious uniformity will be achieved prior to the end of the church age. However, in the great tribulation as here described, a world religion will be advanced that will have as its focal point the worship of a man chosen and empowered by Satan himself. In that day, true believers in Christ will be separated from this world religion and will be the objects of its fearful persecution.

The invitation to hear emphasizes the great importance of what is being revealed. Here, as in the Gospels, where a similar expression is frequently found (Matt. 11:15; 13:9, 43; Mark 4:9, 23; 7:16; Luke 8:8; 14:35), the invitation concludes the revelation on which the exhortation is based. The omission of the phrase "to the churches" in 13:9, which is found in Revelation 2 and 3 addressed to the churches, is most significant and tends to support the teaching that the church, the Body of Christ, has previously been raptured and is not in this period. The exhortation in Revelation 13 is much wider, to anyone in the world who will listen.

Reinforcing the exhortation is the warning of the sovereign justice of God that will be brought to bear upon this scene of evil. A number of variations occur in the text of verse 10,[7] but the general meaning is clear. What is described here is the law of divine retribution. Those who persecute the saints and lead them into captivity must in turn suffer the righteous wrath of God. The endurance and faith of the saints in their hour of trial is found in the ultimate triumph and judgment upon evil people. The Scriptures frequently mention this final vindication (Gen. 9:6; Matt. 5:38; 26:52; Rom. 12:19; Gal. 6:7). The same truth that serves as an encouragement to believers is a warning to their persecutors. Their doom is assured at the end of their brief period of power (Rev. 13:5; 16:6; 18:2–3, 5–8, 20; 19:20).

Revelation 13:1–10 predicts a future world government that from God's point of view will be a continuation of the ancient Roman Empire, expanded to cover not only the area of the ancient empire, but the entire world. This government will be empowered by Satan, and its primary objective will be forcing the whole world to worship Satan and his human representative, the world dictator.

Satan's purpose to take the place of God in the great tribulation is the motivating power behind Satan's activities today. Satan's desire to be like God first plunged the universe into sin (Isa. 14:14). His program has never changed, and he is always seeking to lure people to obey him instead of God. In the great tribulation this purpose will be transparently clear, and after its manifestation it will be brought into divine judgment.

THE SECOND BEAST OUT OF THE EARTH (13:11–12)

13:11–12 Then I saw another beast rising out of the earth. It had two horns like a lamb and it spoke like a dragon. It exercises all the authority of the first beast in its presence, and makes the earth and its inhabitants worship the first beast, whose mortal wound was healed.

John now sees a second beast, this one rising from the earth and occupying a secondary role supporting the activities of the first beast. The two beasts are similar in nature; the Greek word for "another" means "one of the same kind." If the sea represents the mass of Gentile humanity, indicating the first beast's racial background, the reference to the second beast indicates that this character, who is later described as a false prophet (Rev. 19:20), is a creature of earth rather than heaven. The land here is not Israel, thus this beast is not a Jew.

He is pictured as having two horns like a lamb, which seems to indicate that he has a religious character, a conclusion supported by his being called a prophet. His speaking as a dragon indicates that he is motivated by the power of Satan, who is "the dragon."

The second beast is a supporting character to the first beast and exercises his authority. There is some evidence for the conclusion that the second beast is the head of the apostate church during the first half of Daniel's seventieth week. With the rise of the first beast to a place of worldwide dominion, the apostate church is destroyed according to Revelation 17:16, and the worship of the whole world is directed to the first beast. The second beast, however, survives the destruction of the church that had been under his control, and he assists the beast in making the transition. Facilitating this change into the final form of apostate religion, the beast out of the earth causes people to worship the first beast. For a brief time, Satan will have the worship he has always craved.

The identification of the second beast as the head of the apostate church is indicated in many ways in Revelation. It is obvious that he is associated with the first beast in a religious way in that his miracles and activities tend to cause people to worship the image of the first beast (cf. 13:13–17). It is also clear that he shares prominence and leadership with the first beast throughout the great tribulation as they both are thrown alive into the lake of fire at its close (19:20).

THE DECEPTIVE MIRACLES
OF THE FALSE PROPHET (13:13–14)

13:13–14 It performs great signs, even making fire come down from heaven to earth in front of people, and by the signs that it is allowed to work in the presence of the beast it deceives those who dwell on earth, telling them to make an image for the beast that was wounded by the sword and yet lived.

The first miracle accomplished by the false prophet is described as one of many signs he is able to perform. The miracle of fire coming down from heaven may be an imitation of Pentecost (Acts 2:3), or similar to Elijah's miracles (2 Kings 1:10–12), or the destructive fire coming out of the mouths of the two witnesses (Rev. 11:5). The Scriptures indicate that the devil does have power to do miracles and that by their use he deceives people into worshiping the beast.

This beast's deceptive power is mentioned specifically in verse 14. The people on earth who see these great signs (the Greek present tense indicates the second beast does this repeatedly) are told to make an image of the first beast, described for the third time in this chapter as one who was wounded. The beast is both the empire and its ruler. As ruler he is the symbol of the empire and the executor of its power. Though the wound by the sword apparently refers to the decline of the historic Roman Empire and its revival is indicated by the expression "yet lived," the man who serves at the head of the empire is the symbol of this miraculous restoration.

The image made to the beast is not necessarily a likeness of him but, like the image of Nebuchadnezzar in Daniel 3, is the symbol of his power and majesty. Whatever its character, the image becomes the center of the false worship of the world ruler. This image, referred to three times in the chapter, is mentioned six more times in the book of Revelation (14:9, 11; 15:2; 16:2; 19:20; 20:4). It is the center of the false worship and the focal point of the final state of apostasy, the acme of the idolatry that has been the false religion of so many generations.

ALL REQUIRED TO
WORSHIP THE BEAST (13:15–17)

13:15–17 And it was allowed to give breath to the image of the beast, so that the image of the beast might even speak and might cause those who would not worship the image of the beast to be slain. Also it causes all, both small and great, both rich and poor, both free and slave, to be marked on the right hand or the forehead, so that no one can buy or sell unless he has the mark, that is, the name of the beast or the number of its name.

As indicated above, most expositors believe that the extraordinary powers given by Satan to the false prophet do not extend to giving life to that which does not possess life, because this is a prerogative of God alone. The intent of the passage seems to be that the image has the appearance of life manifested in breathing, but actually it may be no more than a robot. The image is further described as being able to speak, a faculty easily accomplished by the sophisticated technology of the twenty-first century.

In ancient times, religious ventriloquism was sometimes used to give the impression of supernatural speech, a practice confirmed by archaeological excavations in Corinth. Sometimes, the image of an idol would be hollow, allowing a priest to hide inside and speak for the god.[8] It is, however, also possible that this describes a supernatural event, controlled by Satan. In Acts 16:16 the slave girl possessed by a demon was able to bring gain to her masters by her divination. She also supernaturally recognized Paul and his companions as "servants of the Most High God, who proclaim to you the way of salvation" (Acts 16:17). Her power of speech was under demonic control. Whether completely natural or supernatural power is used to create the impression of life, the image apparently is quite convincing to the mass of humanity and helps to turn them to a worship of the first beast as their god.

The absolute authority of both the first and second beasts is such that those who will not worship the image of the beast are sentenced to be killed. Some expositors insist that the decree to kill nonworshipers of the beast demands that the sentence be carried out on everyone who refuses.[9] This is needless, however, since the decree is one thing and its execution another. A countless multitude will undoubtedly be martyred according to Revelation 7:9–17, but the disorder that attends the latter half of the great tribulation as the world empire begins to break up makes it impossible to fully carry out this decree.

The regulation is issued that all classes of people who worship the beast are to receive a mark on their right hands or on their foreheads and that possession of this identification is necessary to buy or sell. The mark seems to vary according to verse 17, in some cases being the name of the beast and in others the number of his name.

THE NUMBER OF THE BEAST (13:18)

13:18 This calls for wisdom: let the one who has understanding calculate the number of the beast, for it is the number of a man, and his number is 666.

The appeal for wisdom in recognizing the mark of the beast indicates the importance of this issue. The number six in Scripture is the number of mankind, symbolic of how humanity is constantly falling short of God's perfection, which in Scripture is represented by the number seven. Man was to work six days and rest the seventh. The image of Nebuchadnezzar was sixty cubits high and six cubits broad. Whatever may be the deeper meaning of the number, it implies that this title referring to the first beast, Satan's masterpiece, limits him to man's level, which is far short of the deity of Christ.

Many generations of Bible students have sought to match 666 with a figure from history. This is known as *gematria*, a system of assigning numerical values to a word or phrase in the belief that words or phrases with identical numerical values bear some relation to each other, or to things such as a person's name. Roman emperors such as Caesar, Nero, and Caligula have been favorite suggestions. The explanation for this is rather complicated, involving the numerical equivalents of certain letters in Hebrew, Latin, Greek, and Aramaic.[10] Bruce suggests that the identification of the person involved could have been deliberately obscured to avoid a charge of sedition against the ruler in power.[11] The fact that one aspect of the beast is the revived Roman empire makes the idea that the beast-ruler is a former Roman emperor attractive to many people. But as suggested above, it is unlikely that someone would rise from the dead to take this role, and what's more, the Scripture doesn't demand it.

There is no need for a complicated explanation. The mark is simply a token that they are beast worshipers, and it serves as an identification necessary to conduct business and to purchase the necessities of life. It is another device to force all people to worship the beast.

Chapter 13 is one of the great prophetic chapters of Scripture and is the only passage that presents in any detail the two principal evil characters of the end of the age who form with Satan an unholy trinity. Here is clearly presented the fact that the head of the revived Roman Empire ultimately becomes the ruler of the entire world. Dominated by Satan, he is Satan's masterpiece and substitute for Christ, and is aided and supported by the second beast called the false prophet. Satan's evil trinity contrasts with the heavenly Trinity: Satan corresponding to God the Father, the first beast corresponding to Christ, and the second beast corresponding to the Holy Spirit. Again, what we would expect from the devil as the imitator of God.

Expositors have not agreed entirely as to the identity of these two characters as revealed in other passages of Scripture. The preferable view seems to be that the first beast in Revelation 13 is the "little horn" of Daniel 7:8, "the prince who is to come" of Daniel 9:26, the willful king of Daniel 11:36–45, and the man of sin, or the lawless one, of 2 Thessalonians 2:3 who is "uncompromisingly hostile to the rule of law."[12] The term "antichrist" is variously assigned either to the first or second beast, or by some to neither. Among premillennial expositors, the trend seems to be to identify all of these terms with the first beast and relegate the second beast to a subordinate role as a religious rather than a political ruler.

There is no evidence that either of the beasts is a Jew. The expression "the gods of his fathers" in Daniel 11:37 that would seem to make the king in that passage a Jew is better translated "gods" in keeping with the Hebrew *elohim*, which removes any specific Jewish character from the phrase. It is significant that in many cases where the God of Israel is referred to, "LORD" is added to make clear that the God of their fathers is Yahweh (cf. Ex. 3:15, "The LORD, the God of your fathers." Similar expressions are found frequently [cf. Deut. 1:11, 21; 4:1; 6:3; 12:1; 26:7; 27:3; 29:25; Josh. 18:3; Judges 2:12]).

It seems quite unlikely that either of the two beasts of Revelation 13 will be a Jew inasmuch as they both persecute the Jewish people and are the final Roman rulers of the times of the Gentiles. The general character of the great tribulation, however, is graphically portrayed in this chapter. It will be a time of absolute rule, and Satan will have his way. The ultimate in false religion will sweep the entire world in a manifestation of evil never before seen on the earth. The fact will be demonstrated beyond question that mankind is not able to solve his own problems and only God can bring righteousness and peace to the earth. Attempts at the unification of, or at least hand-in-glove alliances between, ecclesiastical and political powers, such as those seen in the medieval world, seem to be the forerunner and preparation for this end-time situation.

NOTES

1. J. Dwight Pentecost, "The Antichrist: Who Is the Next World Ruler?" in *The Road to Armageddon*, Charles R. Swindoll, John F. Walvoord, J. Dwight Pentecost, eds. (Nashville: Word, 1999), 82.

2. Tony Evans, *The Best Is Yet to Come* (Chicago: Moody, 2000), 166.

3. Walter C. Kaiser and Duane Garrett, eds., *The Archaeological Study Bible* (Grand Rapids: Zondervan, 2005), 2052.

4. John MacArthur, *The MacArthur New Testament Commentary: Revelation 12–22* (Chicago: Moody, 200), 44.

5. John MacArthur, *Because the Time Is Near* (Chicago: Moody, 2007), 216.

6. MacArthur, *Revelation 12–22*, 49.

7. Robert H. Mounce, *The Book of Revelation*, The New International Commentary on the New Testament (Grand Rapids: Eerdmans, 1997), 252–53.

8. Kaiser and Garrett, eds., *The Archaeological Study Bible*, 2063.

9. Robert L. Thomas, *Revelation 8–22: An Exegetical Commentary* (Chicago: Moody, 1995), 179.

10. Many scholars who hold to a preterist (past) view of the book of Revelation maintain that the mark of the beast was completely fulfilled during the reign of the Roman ruler Nero (A.D. 54–68).[1] They argue that the Greek form "Neron Caesar" written in Hebrew characters is equivalent to 666. They further bolster their argument by pointing out that some ancient Greek manuscripts contain the variant number 616 instead of 666 and that the Latin form "Nero Caesar" is equivalent to 616.[2] Proponents of the preterist view also point to the fact that the persecution under Nero lasted about 42 months, or 1,260 days, as mentioned in Revelation 13:5.[3]

    However, there are serious difficulties with identifying Nero with the beast out of the sea in Revelation 13. First, the book of Revelation was written in A.D. 95, after the reign of Nero was already over. Therefore, it can't be a prophecy about him.[4] Second, and most importantly, Nero never fulfilled the numerous clear statements in Revelation 13 about worldwide worship, the mark of the beast, and never had a person like the beast out of the earth supporting him. Third, in order for Nero's name to equal 666, one must use the precise title Neron Caesar. No other form of his name will work. Moreover, there is an abbreviated form of the name Domitian (the Roman Caesar from A.D. 81–96) that also equals 666.[5] Fourth, if the relationship of 666 to Nero is so obvious, as preterists claim, why did it take almost five hundred years after Nero's death for anyone to make this connection between his name and 666?[6] All of the early church fathers who wrote after the time of Nero adopted a futurist view of the beast out of the sea and the number 666.[7]

    [1]Gary DeMar, *End Times Fiction* (Nashville: Thomas Nelson, 2001), 142–45; Kenneth Gentry, *The Beast of Revelation* (Tyler, TX: Institute for Christian Economics, 1989).

    [2]Gentry, 35. O. Ruhle says that the 616 variant was an attempt to link Gaius Caesar (Caligula) to the beast out of the sea in Revelation 13. The numerical value of his name in Greek equals 616. Gerhard Kittel, ed., *The Theological Dictionary of the New Testament*, trans. Geoffrey W. Bromiley, vol. 1. (Grand Rapids: Eerdmans, 1964), 462–463.

    [3]Kenneth Gentry, *The Beast of Revelation*. (Tyler, TX: Institute for Christian Economics, 1989), 53–54.

[4]For a thorough discussion of the date of Revelation, see Mark Hitchcock, "The Stake in the Heart: The A.D. 95 Date of Revelation," in *The End Times Controversy* (Eugene, OR: Harvest House, 2003), 123–150.

[5]David E. Aune, *Revelation 6–16*, Word Biblical Commentary, Bruce M. Metzger, gen. ed. (Nashville: Thomas Nelson, 1998), 771.

[6]For a complete refutation of the view that Nero is the beast of Revelation 13, see Andy Woods, "Revelation 13 and the First Beast," *The End Times Controversy* (Eugene, OR: Harvest House, 2003), 237–250.

[7]Irenaeus who wrote in the late second century suggested three names for the total 666: Evanthas, Lateinos, and Teitan (*Against Heresies* 5.30.3). But he never suggested Nero.

11. F. F. Bruce in *New International Bible Commentary*, F. F. Bruce, gen. ed. (Grand Rapids: Zondervan, 1979), 1616.

12. John R. W. Stott, *The Message of 1 & 2 Thessalonians* (Downers Grove, IL: InterVarsity Press, 1999), 159.

14 ▶ The Victory of the Lamb and His Followers

Chapter 14 brings to a conclusion the material found in chapters 12 through 14. Chapter 12 deals with the important characters of the period, chapter 13 with the evil rulers of the period, and chapter 14 with the ultimate triumph of Christ. This material is not chronological, but prepares the way for the climax that begins in chapter 15. Chapter 14 is a series of pronouncements and visions assuring the reader of Christ's ultimate triumph and the judgment of evil. Much of the chapter is prophetic of events that have not yet taken place, but that in the context are now impending.

THE LAMB AND THE
144,000 ON MOUNT ZION (14:1–5)

14:1–5 Then I looked, and behold, on Mount Zion stood the Lamb, and with him 144,000 who had his name and his Father's name written on their foreheads. And I heard a voice from heaven like the roar of many waters and like the sound of loud thunder. The voice I heard was like the sound of harpists playing on their harps, and they were singing a new song before the throne and before the four living creatures and before the elders. No one could learn that song except the 144,000 who had been redeemed from the earth. It is these who have not defiled themselves with women, for they are virgins. It is these who follow the Lamb wherever he goes. These have been redeemed from mankind as firstfruits for God and the Lamb, and in their mouth no lie was found, for they are blameless.

John introduces this portion of Revelation with a vision of the Lamb, Jesus Christ, standing on Mount Zion accompanied by 144,000 people. Chapter 14 presents expositors with a number of challenges, beginning with the meaning of Mount Zion. Identifying it as heaven seems to be a common theme among interpreters. To interpret this as a heavenly city, however, involves numerous problems that must be taken into consideration. If this group is the same as the 144,000 of chapter 7, they are specifically said to be sealed and kept safely through the tribulation. In this case, they move on into the millennial earth without going to the third heaven, since this is the meaning of the seal (cf. 7:3).

Further, the argument that the 144,000 must be in heaven as they hear the song before the throne may be disputed. There is no statement to the effect that they hear the song, only the declaration that they alone can learn it. The reasons for making Mount Zion a heavenly city in this passage are therefore lacking a sure foundation. It is preferable to see this as a prophetic vision of the ultimate triumph of the Lamb following His second coming, when He joins the 144,000 on Mount Zion at the beginning of His millennial reign. Thomas summarizes the case well: "Without some special qualification, Scripture never uses Mount Zion to denote a celestial abode of God or His people. The text does not say the 144,000 are in the same place as the singers."[1]

The question is also raised whether the 144,000 in chapter 14 are the same group as in chapter 7. Ryrie links them and notes several traits of the 144,000 that are true for both the group in chapter 7 and those here.[2] This seems to be the preferable view. In their first mention, the 144,000 are seen at the beginning of the great tribulation. In their second mention in chapter 14, they are still intact, preserved by God through the fearful days of persecution and standing triumphantly with the Lamb at the beginning of the millennial reign. In chapter 7, the seal is mentioned as simply being the seal of God, whereas here we have more detail in that the 144,000 belong to both God the Father and to Christ.

The identification of the 144,000 with Mount Zion and with God the Father is their mark of being saved Jews; their identification with Christ reveals their salvation through faith in Him. They are "the overcomers upon whom the risen Christ has written his own new name (3:12)."[3]

The voice John hears is described in very majestic terms. He describes it as the sound of harpists playing, and he hears the singing of a "new song" before the throne of God, the four living creatures, and the elders. This scene seems reminiscent of chapters 4 and 5, though the expression "from heaven" is not in some manuscripts. The preponderance of evidence seems to indicate that this is indeed a heavenly scene that John is seeing "in the Spirit" while his body is on earth.

If the 144,000 are on earth in Zion, who then are the company in heaven? Though their identity is not clearly stated, the heavenly group are probably the martyred saints of the tribulation, in contrast to the 144,000 who are on earth and do not suffer martyrdom. Both groups, however, experience the trials of the great tribulation and therefore are alone worthy to enter into the song of redemption, recounting their victory over their enemies and praising God for His grace by which they were redeemed.

Chronologically, the song John hears is a hymn of praise in heaven during the time of the great tribulation, but the same song is echoed by the 144,000 who stand triumphantly on Mount Zion after the tribulation. As is true of the rest of the vision in this chapter, the chronological order is not maintained, but rather different subjects are brought into view pertaining to the general theme of God's ultimate triumph. There seems to be a definite connection between the new song that is sung and the ascription of praise (7:10) in which the martyred dead cry out to God, "Salvation belongs to our God who sits on the throne, and to the Lamb!" Different in character, but also a new song is that of the twenty-four elders in 5:9–10. In the reference to the 144,000 as redeemed from the earth, the thought seems to be that both those in heaven and on earth have been redeemed—purchased by the blood of Christ and delivered from their enemies, one group through martyrdom, the other group by divine preservation through the tribulation.

Returning to the subject of the 144,000 in verse 4, John describes them as virgins. This can refer to abstinence from marriage in the critical days of the tribulation when a normal marital life for a person true to God is impossible, or to spiritual purity by not being defiled by love of the world or compromise with evil in a morally filthy world. Israel is referred to frequently in the Bible as "the virgin daughter of Zion" (2 Kings 19:21; Isa. 37:22; Lam. 2:13) and as the "virgin Israel" (Jer. 18:13; 31:4, 21; Amos 5:2). In the New Testament also, the term "virgin" is used of both men and women as in 2 Corinthians 11:2 in reference to the church as a bride.

The possibility that their virgin character signifies their spiritual purity primarily[4] is indicated in the next statement describing them as those "who follow the Lamb wherever he goes." Here again it is obviously in the earthly scene, as the 144,000 of Israel do not ever go to heaven during their natural lifetime. The third statement also introduced by "these," as the two previous affirmations, repeats the thought that these are redeemed from among humanity as the firstfruits to God and to the Lamb. The term "firstfruits" seems to refer to the beginning of a great harvest—here to the beginning of the millennial kingdom. The 144,000 are the godly nucleus of Israel that is the token of the redemption of the nation and the glory of Israel that is to unfold in the kingdom.

The description of the 144,000 closes with the statement that they are without falsehood or blame. The falsehood may refer especially to false religion (cf. use of the Greek word *pseudo* in Rom. 1:25; Rev. 21:27; 22:15). This large number has been kept utterly clean from the false religion of the great tribulation. They are blameless in contrast to apostates who are described as "blots" or "blemishes," as in 2 Peter 2:13. How important this makes the life and testimony of any believer who seeks to emulate these who in this most trying time do not compromise with error or defile themselves with impurity. Christians are exhorted to be "holy and blameless before him" (Eph. 1:4), "holy and without blemish" (Eph. 5:27; 1 Peter 1:19), "holy and blameless" (Col. 1:22), "without blemish" (Heb. 9:14), and "blameless" (Jude 24), all in the sight of God.

THE ANGEL WITH THE EVERLASTING GOSPEL (14:6–7)

14:6–7 Then I saw another angel flying directly overhead, with an eternal gospel to proclaim to those who dwell on earth, to every nation and tribe and language and people. And he said with a loud voice, "Fear God and give him glory, because the hour of his judgment has come, and worship him who made heaven and earth, the sea and the springs of water."

Next John sees another angel, the first of several in this chapter, flying overhead, literally "in mid–heaven," with the everlasting gospel to preach to the entire world. The reference to "another" seems to be to an angel in addition to the seven angels introduced in 8:2, and also in contrast to "another angel" in 8:3 and 10:1.

The expression "an eternal gospel" is an arresting phrase. It is eternal in the sense that it is ageless, not for any specific period. Ordinarily, one would expect this to refer to the gospel of salvation. In verse 7, however, the content of the message is quite different, announcing the hour of God's judgment and the command to worship Him.

Some expositors use the term "gospel" to include all the revelation God has given in Christ and hence conclude that there is only one gospel with various phases of truth belonging to this gospel.[5] There are others who prefer to distinguish various messages in the Bible as gospel or "good news" even though they contain only one aspect of divine revelation: thus the expression "gospel of grace," referring to the goodness of grace, or to the gospel of the kingdom, dealing with the good news of the kingdom of God. The everlasting gospel seems to be neither the gospel of grace nor the gospel of the kingdom, but rather the good news that God at last is about to deal with the world in righteousness and establish His sovereignty over it. This is an ageless gospel in the sense that God's righteousness is ageless. Throughout eternity God will continue to manifest Himself in grace toward the saints and in punishment toward evil. To refer to the gospel of grace as an everlasting gospel is to ignore the context and usage of the term.

PROPHECY OF THE COMING FALL OF BABYLON

14:8 Another angel, a second, followed, saying, "Fallen, fallen is Babylon the great, she who made all nations drink the wine of the passion of her sexual immorality."

The pronouncement against Babylon is made by another angel, apparently also flying in mid-heaven. The repetition of the phrase "fallen" is for emphasis. Prophetically, Babylon sometimes refers to a physical city, sometimes to a religious system, sometimes to a political system, all stemming from the evil character of historic Babylon. The announcement here is prophetic as the actual fall of Babylon probably comes later if the reference is to the physical city. There is some evidence, however, that the woman called "Babylon the great, mother of prostitutes" (17:5), referring to the apostate church that will hold sway in the first half of the seventieth week of Daniel, is actually destroyed at the beginning of the great tribulation in preparation for the worship of the beast. The destruction of the city of Babylon itself, whether a reference to Rome, as some believe, or to a rebuilt city of Babylon on the ancient site of historic Babylon, does not take place until the end of the great tribulation. Since the context here seems to deal primarily with the end of the great tribulation and the beginning of the millennial kingdom, the reference seems to be to the literal city.

The fall of Babylon is due to "the wine of the passion of her sexual immorality." This peculiar expression seems to be a shortened expression of the two phrases "the wine of God's wrath" (14:10) and "the wine of [her] sexual immorality" (17:2). The resultant meaning is that the nations who participate in the spiritual corruption induced by Babylon ultimately share her divine condemnation and judgment. Like the pronouncement of the previous angel and the other prophecies of this chapter, the promise of judgment upon the evil Babylonian system is designed to bring comfort to those in trial in that period.

THE DOOM OF
THE BEAST'S WORSHIPERS (14:9–11)

14:9–11 And another angel, a third, followed them, saying with a loud voice, "If anyone worships the beast and its image and receives a mark on his forehead or on his hand, he also will drink the wine of God's wrath, poured full strength into the cup of his anger, and he will be tormented with fire and sulfur in the presence of the holy angels and in the presence of the Lamb. And the smoke of their torment goes up forever and ever, and they have no rest, day or night, these worshipers of the beast and its image, and whoever receives the mark of its name."

The third angel adds immediately to the pronouncement of the previous angel by proclaiming the sad doom of those who worship the beast. Anyone who receives the mark of the beast as required in 13:17 shall also undergo God's judgment. As unbelievers drink of the wine of spiritual immorality, they will also shall drink the cup of God's wrath. It is described in most dramatic terms as "full strength," that is, untempered by the Lord's mercy and grace, and these worshipers of the beast are to be tormented forever. That their punishment is said to be in the presence of God does not lessen it. On the contrary, as Bruce asks, "Would their anguish not be rendered the more acute by the presence of the one whom they have denied by their apostasy?"[6] The same Scripture that assures all Christians of the love and grace of God extended to those who trust in Christ is unequivocal in its statements of judgment upon evil.

Some want to deny the reality of hell and the idea of eternal punishment for those who reject Christ. Yet Jesus referred to hell (*gehenna*, the lake of fire) in eleven out of its twelve occurrences in the New Testament, and He made twelve out of the nineteen references to hell fire. Our Savior used such expressions more than any other person in the New Testament.[7]

The righteousness of God is as inexorable as the love of God is infinite. The love of God is not free to express itself to those who have spurned Jesus

225

Christ. Their torment is not a momentary one, for it is described in verse 11 as continuing forever, the strongest expression of eternity of which the Greek is capable. To emphasize the idea of continued suffering, they are declared to have no rest day or night. In describing the worshipers of the beast, the word *worship* as well as the word *receive* in verse 11 is in the present tense, emphasizing continued worship of the beast over a long period of time—the worshipers spurning the testimony of the godly remnant and plunging blindly to their doom. The same present tense is used in describing their torment. As the worship of the beast is not interrupted by repentance, so their torment is not interrupted when repentance is too late. How dangerous it is for people to trifle with false religions, which dishonor the incarnate Word and contradict the written Word.

THE BLESSING OF THE SAINTS (14:12–13)

14:12–13 Here is a call for the endurance of the saints, those who keep the commandments of God and their faith in Jesus. And I heard a voice from heaven saying, "Write this: Blessed are the dead who die in the Lord from now on." "Blessed indeed," says the Spirit, "that they may rest from their labors, for their deeds follow them!"

The stern warning addressed to all worshipers of the beast is also an encouragement to those who put their trust in Christ in the time of the great tribulation. Though some will face martyrdom and others will need to go into hiding, they are assured that their lot is far preferable to that of those who accept the easy way out and worship the beast. Verse 12 gives the proper link between works and faith so necessary in all ages, but especially in the great tribulation, which is that works do not save but are evidence of true salvation (cf. Eph. 2:8–10).

In verse 13, John hears a voice from heaven pronouncing a blessing on those who die in the Lord during this period as martyrs of the faith. Four times previously there is a record of a voice from heaven (10:4, 8; 11:12;

14:2). Again in 18:4 and 21:3 a voice is heard—a direct communication from God as contrasted with communication through an angel. The implication is that this is unusually important and a direct divine pronouncement. The blessing is repeated, this time in the voice of none other than the Holy Spirit. This verse is the second in a series of beatitudes in Revelation (cf. 1:3; 16:15; 19:9; 20:6; 22:7, 14).

THE JUDGMENT OF THE SON OF MAN (14:14–16)

14:14–16 Then I looked, and behold, a white cloud, and seated on the cloud one like a son of man, with a golden crown on his head, and a sharp sickle in his hand. And another angel came out of the temple, calling with a loud voice to him who sat on the cloud, "Put in your sickle, and reap, for the hour to reap has come, for the harvest of the earth is fully ripe." So he who sat on the cloud swung his sickle across the earth, and the earth was reaped.

Following the reassurance of the tribulation believers' ultimate reward, a further revelation is graphically given. It is introduced by the familiar phrase, "Then I looked, and behold," indicating another major advance in the revelation. The One described is probably Christ Himself participating in God's judgments on an evil world. This probability is reinforced by the golden crown speaking of His glorified state and His royal dignity. As Unger points out, "Son of Man [is] the title under which Christ deals with the earth and earth dwellers (Mt. 25:31; Jn. 5:27 and claims universal dominion [Dan. 7:13 & 14; Rev. 1:13–14])."[8] His sharp sickle indicates this is the time of harvest, referring to the climactic judgments relating to the second coming.

If the reaper is Christ, it is remarkable that an angel would issue a command to the Savior. But this should be regarded as an entreaty of a holy angel to Christ as the Son of Man in His position as judge of mankind (cf. John 5:22, 27). The fact that the angel comes from the temple seems to allude to this judgment as proceeding from the very presence and righteousness of God. Further, the angel urges judgment at this time because, in God's sovereign

227

plan, it is the time for judgment. The full ripeness of the earth seems to imply that judgment is overdue. Interestingly, the verb "is fully ripe" means "to become dry or withered," which is a negative connotation (cf. Matt. 21:19–20; Mark 3:1, 3; 11:20; Luke 8:6; Rev. 16:12). The picture is of a fruit or vegetable that has become so ripe that it has begun to dry up and wither. The rotten moral condition of the world is dealt with now with a sharp sickle. Verse 16 indicates that Christ does as the angel requests, possibly using angelic means to accomplish this end (cf. Matt. 13:30, 39–42).

Some Bible commentators distinguish between the reaping in verses 14–16 and the reaping that follows. They believe the first harvest is that of believers, in contrast to the second harvest, which obviously deals with evil people. But there is no distinct event in this sequence of prophecies that clearly presents a harvest of believers, and it is preferable to consider the first harvest as the judgments in general that characterize the period and the second harvest as the final, climactic one.

THE ANGEL WITH THE SHARP SICKLE (14:17–20)

14:17–20 Then another angel came out of the temple in heaven, and he too had a sharp sickle. And another angel came out from the altar, the angel who has authority over the fire, and he called with a loud voice to the one who had the sharp sickle, "Put in your sickle and gather the clusters from the vine of the earth, for its grapes are ripe." So the angel swung his sickle across the earth and gathered the grape harvest of the earth and threw it into the great winepress of the wrath of God. And the winepress was trodden outside the city, and blood flowed from the winepress, as high as a horse's bridle, for 1,600 stadia.

The use of angels to assist in the harvest of the earth is now stated explicitly. Though not enumerated, the angel of verse 17 is the fifth to appear in this chapter and, like the angel of verse 15, comes from the temple in heaven. This angel also has a sharp sickle indicating the severity of the judgment, and is exhorted by another angel, the sixth in the chapter, to begin reaping. The sixth angel is said to have power over fire, perhaps indicating that he is acting in response to the prayers of God's people for judgment on the evil of earth. Power over fire also indicates the purging judgment of which he is capable.

The sharp sickle is mentioned twice in verse 18, and the grape clusters are described as "ripe." This a different term for ripeness than that used in verse 15. Here it pictures grapes fully grown in their prime, almost bursting with juice. Though the figure is somewhat different, the spiritual meaning is the same. The time has come for the final harvest. The figurative use of a vine, frequently found in the Bible in relation to Israel (Ps. 80:8, 14–15; Isa. 5:2–7; Jer. 2:21; Ezek. 17:5–8; Hosea 10:1), is also used of the church in John 15:1–6. In contrast to how Israel and the church were to bear righteous fruit to the Lord, here we have the vine producing the fruit of evil and corruption.

The angel swings his sickle across the earth and throws the harvested clusters into "the great winepress of the wrath of God." This action is actually fulfilled in Revelation 19:15, where the same figure of speech is used. This is obviously a picture of ultimate judgment of unbelievers at the second coming of Christ, when they will be judged "everlastingly," as Hendriksen rightly observes.[9] This passage speaks prophetically of that which will chronologically follow the return of Christ to the earth.

The spurting of the grape juice from under the bare feet of those treading the grapes in the winepress is compared to the spurting of blood and speaks of the awful human carnage of Revelation 19:17–19, 21. The unusual expression in verse 20 that the blood flows "as high as a horse's bridle, for 1,600 stadia" has intrigued expositors. The scene of this event is apparently the city of Jerusalem, outside which the judgment takes place. It seems quite impossible that the blood will flow in depth as high as the horses' bridles, and it is better to understand this simply as a heavy shedding of blood as part of a tremendous outpouring of God's final judgment on evil mankind.

This interpretation is confirmed by the parallel in Isaiah 63:3. The area described (1,600 stadia) is approximately two hundred miles, and specifies that the area within a two-hundred-mile radius from Jerusalem will be the center of the final carnage where the armies of the world will be gathered at

Christ's second coming. There is no significant problem here in taking the distance literally. The terrible picture of the bloodletting that will mark the end of the age may include various phases of the battle taking place in the great tribulation and the climax of Christ's victory when He judges the nations at its end.

Revelation 14 emphasizes first that the 144,000 of Israel seen at the beginning of the great tribulation will be preserved triumphantly through it. Second, the rest of the chapter is devoted to various pronouncements of divine judgment upon an evil world, reassuring tribulation believers that, though they may suffer and even be martyred, God's ultimate justice will triumph, evil will be judged, and they will be rewarded. The implications of the message for today are only too plain. Today is a day of grace; but what is true of the tribulation is also true today, that God will ultimately judge all people. Today, however, the invitation is still open to those who will receive the grace of God by trusting in Christ and being saved from entering this awful period that may be impending for this present generation.

NOTES

1. Robert L. Thomas, *Revelation 8–22: An Exegetical Commentary* (Chicago: Moody, 1995), 190.

2. Charles C. Ryrie, *Revelation*, rev. ed. (Chicago: Moody, 1996), 101. See also Paul Benware, *Understanding End Times Prophecy* (Chicago: Moody, 2006), 302–303.

3. Robert H. Mounce, *The Book of Revelation*, The New International Commentary on the New Testament (Grand Rapids: Eerdmans, 1997), 265.

4. Wilbur M. Smith, *The Wycliffe Bible Commentary*, Charles F. Pfeiffer and Everett F. Harrison, eds. (Chicago: Moody, 1990), 1513–14.

5. For a presentation of this view, see John MacArthur, *The MacArthur New Testament Commentary: Revelation 12–22* (Chicago: Moody, 2000), 68.

6. F. F. Bruce, *New International Bible Commentary*, F. F. Bruce, gen. ed. (Grand Rapids: Zondervan, 1979), 1618.

7. J. B. Smith, *A Revelation of Jesus Christ* (Scottdale, PA: Herald Press, 1961), 216.

8. Merrill F. Unger, *The New Unger's Bible Handbook*, rev. Gary N. Larson (Chicago: Moody, 1984), 679.

9. William Hendriksen, *More Than Conquerors* (Grand Rapids: Baker, 1967), 155.

The Vision of the Seven Last Plagues

THE SIGN OF THE SEVEN ANGELS
WITH THE PLAGUES (15:1–2)

15:1–2 Then I saw another sign in heaven, great and amazing, seven angels with seven plagues, which are the last, for with them the wrath of God is finished. And I saw what appeared to be a sea of glass mingled with fire—and also those who had conquered the beast and its image and the number of its name, standing beside the sea of glass with harps of God in their hands.

Chapters 15 and 16 bring to consummation the chronologically ordered events leading up to the second coming of Christ described in chapter 19. These events are "the seven last plagues" preceding the second coming of Christ. As previously indicated, the chronological order of events in Revelation is presented basically in the seven seals (6:1–17; 8:1). The seventh seal includes all of the seven trumpets (8:1–9:21; 11:15–19). The seven bowls of divine judgment are included in the seventh trumpet. The order of events forms a dramatic crescendo, the seventh seal being all-inclusive of the end-time events including the seven trumpets, and the seventh trumpet including the events described in the seven bowls. Christ then returns immediately after the seventh bowl. The intervening sections such as 10:1–11:14; 13–14; 17–18 do not advance the narrative chronologically. Chapter 19 follows immediately after chapter 16 in the chronological development.

John introduces this vision as "another sign in heaven." The word *another* refers to the two preceding signs of chapter 12—the woman who appeared in heaven (12:1) and the "great red dragon" (12:3), signifying the empire of the beast under Satan's control. The three signs taken together represent important elements in the prophetic scene: (1) Israel, that is, the woman; (2) the final world empire under the control of Satan and the beast, that is, the great red dragon; and (3) the seven angels having the seven last plagues, that is, the divine judgment upon the satanic system and political power of the beast.

This sign is described as "great and amazing," which along with verse 3 are the only two times these two Greek words appear together in the New Testament, though they appear separately elsewhere. The seven angels are central to the vision, being apparently another group of seven angels not to be confused with any other group of seven, since the article is not used with the expression. These seven angels have the seven last plagues. As in the trumpets and seals, the number of completion, seven, is used. It is most significant that they are described as "last," even more emphatic in the Greek (literally "having seven plagues, the last ones"). This implies that the previous judgments unfolding in the breaking of the seals and the blowing of the trumpets were also plagues, that is, divine judgments of God pouring out affliction upon an evil world (cf. other divine judgments in 9:18, 20; 11:6; 13:3, 12, 14; cf. also 16:7–9; 18:8; 19:2; 22:18). These are the final judgments preceding the second coming itself.

The seven plagues are further described as acts of judgment that finish God's wrath against an evil world. The finality of this pronouncement is evident in the Greek verb translated "finished," which means to bring to the ultimate goal, that is, a fulfillment of divine purpose. Jesus used this word on the cross when He cried out, "It is finished" (John 19:30). God did not leave His work of redemption half completed, and He will not leave His work of judgment half completed either.

The word for "wrath" is worth noting. The Greek word *thymos* can be defined as "anger, wrath, rage."[1] It does not denote divine wrath as an attitude, but divine judgment as the expression of God's wrath. The other word translated "wrath" in Revelation is *orgē*, used in Revelation 16:19 in the final judgment upon Babylon extending from the seventh bowl. In fact, both words are used in that verse, translated as "the fury of his wrath." As Bauer observes, the combination of *thymos* and *orgē* in 16:19 connotes a heightening of the outpouring of divine judgment. It may be concluded, therefore, that the anger of God is the preliminary expression of divine righteousness, while the wrath of God is its final expression.[2]

The "sea of glass" seems to be an allusion to the same situation as in 4:6 where "a sea of glass, like crystal" is seen in front of the throne in heaven. The sea is designed to reflect the glory of God, and in chapter 4 its description "like crystal" speaks of His holiness. Unlike the previous occurrence, here is the sea is mixed with fire, which speaks of divine judgment proceeding from God's holiness. Thomas calls this mixed sea "a mighty reservoir of just judgments about to become realities."[3]

John sees a company of people standing on the sea. They are specifically said to have overcome the beast of Revelation 13:1–10 and his image, which means they unmistakably are the martyred dead, destroyed by the beast whose number is given in 13:18. Their triumph consists in the fact that they remained faithful to death instead of yielding to the blasphemous demand of the beast. Their resurrection and reward are described in 20:4–6.

These saints have "harps of God." The harp or lyre and the trumpet are the only musical instruments mentioned in Revelation. Though possessed by this group of triumphant believers, the harps apparently are not given to all the martyred dead (cf. the absence of harps in 7:9–17). The harpers' privileged position before the throne is their reward for refusing to worship the beast, receive his mark, bow to his image, or be identified with his number. They belong to saints martyred during the time of great tribulation, confirming that the time schedule is near the end of the period and contrasting them to believers of other ages. The fact that they are able to stand on the sea of glass reflects God's faithfulness in upholding His own in keeping with His divine character.

THE SONG OF MOSES AND
THE SONG OF THE LAMB (15:3–4)

15:3–4 And they sing the song of Moses, the servant of God, and the song of the Lamb, saying, "Great and amazing are your deeds, O Lord God the Almighty! Just and true are your ways, O King of the nations! Who will not fear, O Lord, and glorify your name? For you alone are holy. All nations will come and worship you, for your righteous acts have been revealed."

The fact that the word "song" is repeated with a definite article in both cases would lead to the conclusion that two songs are in view rather than one, both being sung by the martyred throng. The former recounts the faithfulness of God to Israel as a nation in recognition that a large number of Israelites are among these martyred dead. The song of the Lamb speaks of redemption from sin made possible by the sacrifice of the Lamb of God and would include all the believers in Christ.

There has been difference of opinion as to what song is meant by "the song of Moses." The traditional interpretation identifies it as the song of Exodus 15 sung by Moses and the children of Israel following their victory over Pharaoh and his army at the Red Sea. An alternative view, advanced by Smith, has much to commend it, however.[4] He suggests the song of Deuteronomy 32, which was written and spoken to the children of Israel by Moses himself at the close of his career. It is a comprehensive picture of God's faithfulness to Israel and His ultimate purpose to defeat their enemies. This latter song more nearly corresponds to the situation in Revelation 15. Both passages, however, ascribe praise to God and are similar in many ways to the hymn recorded by John.

The hymn begins with a repetition of the words "great and amazing," as noted above. Here it is the works of God that arouse wonder or astonishment. This could apply to God's works in the past, but more probably anticipates the great work just ahead. The verb ("are your deeds") is omitted in the Greek text and could be past, present, or future, though the thought seems to be the present tense with a futuristic intent. God is also described as "just and true" in His ways, a God who is perfectly righteous and keeps His promises. He is also the "King of the nations," the sovereign ruler of all who is about to manifest His sovereignty and divine judgment to an evil world.

The futuristic view of the passage is indicated by the question of verse 4,

"Who will not fear, O Lord, and glorify your name?" Though the nations neither fear God nor glorify Him in their mad unbelief during the great tribulation, the day is to come soon when they will both fear Him and be forced to acknowledge Him as God. A similar question is found in Jeremiah 10:7: "Who would not fear you, O King of the nations?" (cf. also Rev. 14:7). The prospect of all nations worshiping the Lord, a familiar theme of the prophets, is brought out in the statement: "For you alone are holy. All nations will come and worship you, for your righteous acts have been revealed" (cf. Ps. 2:8–9; 24:1–10; 66:1–4; 72:8–11; 86:9; Isa. 2:2–4; 9:6–7; 66:18–23; Dan. 7:14; Zeph. 2:11; Zech. 14:9).

THE TABERNACLE OF THE
TESTIMONY IN HEAVEN OPENED (15:5–6)

15:5–6 After this I looked, and the sanctuary of the tent of witness in heaven was opened, and out of the sanctuary came the seven angels with the seven plagues, clothed in pure, bright linen, with golden sashes around their chests.

This is a later vision that John sees, marked by the familiar phrase "I looked," which always introduces something dramatically new. Here the new element is the introduction of the judgments represented in the seven bowls. John sees the Holy of Holies in the heavenly tabernacle being opened. We know the location because the word "sanctuary" refers to the inner holy place of the tabernacle, the design of which God gave to Israel during the wilderness wandering. The "tent of witness" refers to the whole tent-like structure, a portion of which contained the Holy of Holies. In turn, the Holy of Holies contained the ark of the covenant in which were the stone tablets containing the Ten Commandments (cf. Ex. 32:15; Acts 7:44). This is mentioned frequently in the Old Testament (Ex. 38:21; Num. 1:50, 53; 10:11; 17:7–8; 18:2).

As John looks intently on the scene, the curtain separating the Holy of Holies from the outer portion of the heavenly tabernacle is parted, and he sees seven angels coming out of the sanctuary. The holy place, into which the high priests alone could go, and only after proper sacrifices, does not exclude holy angels who have no sin. Each of the angels is carrying one of the bowls containing the seven plagues, and each is clothed in pure white linen and a golden sash, which befits these holy and majestic creatures.[5] Linen here, as in the garment of the wife of the Lamb (19:8), represents righteousness in action, also certainly proper for holy angels. If gold reflects the glory of God, it would point to the conclusion that these angels pouring out righteous judgments on the earth thereby bring glory to God.

The whole scene is very symbolic of what is about to happen. The angels coming out of the sanctuary indicate that the judgments to be poured out stem from the holiness of God and are properly required of God, who must do all things right.

SEVEN GOLDEN BOWLS
GIVEN TO THE ANGELS (15:7–8)

15:7–8 And one of the four living creatures gave to the seven angels seven golden bowls full of the wrath of God who lives forever and ever, and the sanctuary was filled with smoke from the glory of God and from his power, and no one could enter the sanctuary until the seven plagues of the seven angels were finished.

The seven angels who already have the seven plagues are given seven golden bowls described as "full of the wrath of God." The reference to plagues in verse 6 may be prophetic, or the bestowal of the bowls may be the authorization to use them. The extent of the divine judgment is indicated by the word "full," describing the devastating character of this judgment. The word for "wrath" is *thymos*, "anger," rather than *orgē*, properly "wrath" (see discussion above). The reminder that God lives forever gives a solemn finality to the wrath that is to be poured out, which will be inflicted forever upon those who perish.

As the angels emerge from the sanctuary, it is filled with smoke proceeding from the glory of God and His power, a pointed reminder of God's unapproachable holiness. The scene can be compared to that when the cloud filled the tabernacle in Exodus 40:34–35. Access into the sanctuary is made impossible by the smoke until the judgments contained in the seven plagues are fulfilled. It is an ominous sign of impending doom for those who persist in their blasphemous disregard of the sovereignty and holiness of God.

NOTES

1. Walter Bauer, *A Greek-English Lexicon of the New Testament*, Theodore Danker, William F. Arndt, and F. Wilbur Gingrich, translators and revisers, 3rd ed. (Chicago: University of Chicago Press, 2000), 461.

2. Walter Bauer, *A Greek-English Lexicon of the New Testament*, 461.

3. Robert L. Thomas, *Revelation 8–22: An Exegetical Commentary* (Chicago: Moody, 1995), 232.

4. J. B. Smith, *A Revelation of Jesus Christ* (Scottdale, PA: Herald Press, 1961), 224–26.

5. John MacArthur, *The MacArthur New Testament Commentary: Revelation 12–22* (Chicago: Moody, 2000), 132.

16 The Bowls of God's Wrath

THE COMMAND TO POUR OUT THE BOWLS (16:1)

16:1 Then I heard a loud voice from the temple telling the seven angels, "Go and pour out on the earth the seven bowls of the wrath of God."

The seven angels to whom were given the plagues symbolized in the seven bowls are now commanded to pour out their divine judgment upon the earth. The voice is undoubtedly the voice of God, which is described as "loud," a form of the Greek word *mega*, which has been brought over into English as a prefix meaning "great." This word occurs throughout the chapter, variously translated as "fierce" heat (v. 9), the "great" river Euphrates (v. 12), the "great" day of God Almighty (v. 14), a "loud" voice (v. 17), a "great" earthquake (v. 18), the "great" city and Babylon the "great" (v. 19), "great" hailstones (v. 21), and the plague that was "severe" (v. 21). As J. B. Smith expresses it, "This is the *great* chapter of the Bible."[1]

The seven bowls have often been compared to the seven seals and to the seven trumpets, especially the latter. One interpretation has been to view the bowls as merely an enlargement on the trumpet judgments, corresponding numerically to them. There are undoubtedly many similarities between the trumpet judgments and the judgments inflicted by the pouring out of the bowls. In both the trumpets and the bowls, the first in the series deals with the earth, the second with the sea, the third with rivers and fountains of water, the fourth with the sun, the fifth with darkness, the sixth with the Euphrates River, and the seventh with lightning, thunder, and a great earthquake.

The principle is often overlooked, however, that similarities do not prove identity. A careful study of the seven bowls as compared to the seven trumpets will reveal numerous differences. The first four trumpet judgments deal only with one-third of the earth, while the bowl judgments seem to be universal in their application and greater in intensity. Therefore, this exposition understands the bowl judgments as being subsequent to the trumpet judgments, proceeding out of and constituting the seventh trumpet. The bowls "gather together all the horrors and terrors from all the previous judgments of God."[2]

The judgments described in the trumpet and bowl pronouncements fall in rapid succession like trip-hammer blows, and they all will be consummated within a short period of time toward the close of the great tribulation. The bowl judgments, the climax of God's divine dealings with a blasphemous earth, lead up to the second coming of the Lord and Savior Jesus Christ.

SEVEN BOWL JUDGMENTS

Revelation 16:1–21

1. First Bowl (16:2) upon the Earth: Sores on the Worshipers of the Antichrist

2. Second Bowl (16:3) upon the Seas: Turned to Blood

3. Third Bowl (16:4–7) upon the Fresh Water: Turned to Blood

4. Fourth Bowl (16:8–9) upon the Sun: Intense, Scorching Heat

5. Fifth Bowl (16:10–11) upon the Antichrist's Kingdom: Darkness and Pain

6. Sixth Bowl (16:12–16) upon the River Euphrates: Armageddon

7. Seventh Bowl (16:17–21) upon the Air: Earthquakes and Hail

THE FIRST BOWL (16:2)

16:2 So the first angel went and poured out his bowl on the earth, and harmful and painful sores came upon the people who bore the mark of the beast and worshiped its image.

With the pouring out of the first bowl, a terrible judgment falls upon those who have the mark of the beast. There is a notable contrast between the first bowl and the first trumpet, in that the first trumpet (8:7) burns up one-third of the trees and all the green grass. Here the judgment is upon a particular group of humans, the beast worshipers who have received his mark. The judgment is in the form of a terrible sore or ulcer that brings widespread suffering. These sores recall the sixth plague of boils that God inflicted on Egypt (Ex. 9:9–11).[3] The Greek word for "sores" here is the same word used by the translators of the Old Testament into Greek (the Septuagint) for the boils inflicted on the Egyptians.[4]

Confirmation that the bowl judgments occur late in the great tribulation is here in that this judgment falls on those who worship the beast's image. This image apparently is established in the early part of the great tribulation, the last half of the seven-year period preceding the second coming (13:14–17). Almost everyone seems to comply with the demand that all people worship the beast and receive his mark. The bowl judgment, therefore, follows this edict. The only ones who escape the judgment are those who have refused to obey the edict, the few individuals who trust in Christ in those evil days. From 13:8, it would appear that only a small fraction of the earth's population resists the beast. The warning given in 14:9–11 is now reinforced in a preliminary judgment that anticipates the ultimate doom of the beast worshipers.

THE SECOND BOWL (16:3)

16:3 The second angel poured out his bowl into the sea, and it became like the blood of a corpse, and every living thing died that was in the sea.

The judgment of the second bowl results in death to every living creature in the sea. Whether the reference here is limited to the Mediterranean, the "great sea" of Scripture, or includes all major bodies of water on earth, the effect is beyond imagination. The stench alone would be unbearable.

This judgment is similar to both the second trumpet in Revelation 8:8 and the first of the ten plagues on Egypt (Ex. 7:20–25), which killed all the fish in the Nile River and made the water unfit to drink. Only one-third of the sea is turned to blood and one-third of its creatures die in the second trumpet judgment. But here the judgment is universal. MacArthur states the situation and its spiritual significance in stark terms: "The transforming of the world's seas into putrid pools of stinking death will be graphic testimony to the wickedness of man."[5]

THE THIRD BOWL (16:4–7)

16:4–7 The third angel poured out his bowl into the rivers and the springs of water, and they became blood. And I heard the angel in charge of the waters say, "Just are you, O Holy One, who is and who was, for you brought these judgments. For they have shed the blood of saints and prophets, and you have given them blood to drink. It is what they deserve!" And I heard the altar saying, "Yes, Lord God the Almighty, true and just are your judgments!"

The third bowl judgment extends the turning of water into blood to rivers and fountains, apparently with the same devastating effect, though the results of the judgment are not mentioned. Though some understand rivers and fountains to be symbolic, there is no reason for not taking this in the literal sense, as the sea in the second bowl and the people in the first bowl. The physical affliction stems from spiritual apostasy.

At this point John hears an angel with authority over waters pronounce God's justice in this judgment. There is a remarkable variety of ministries assigned to angels in Revelation. The angel declares that because evil unbelievers have killed God's people, He is righteous in cursing them with blood to drink. Even as believers are worthy of rest and reward, so the evil are worthy of divine chastening and judgment. The bloodletting during the great tribulation, with believers slaughtered by the thousands, is without parallel in the history of the human race. Christ Himself declares it will be a time of trouble without precedent (Matt. 24:21). The multitude of martyrs in heaven is revealed in chapter 7. The eternal God, though awaiting the proper time, is inexorable in His judgment of those who persecuted His people.

The statement of the angel of the waters is confirmed by another voice that declares that God is "true and just" in His judgments. The phrase, "I heard the altar saying," in verse 7 is a personification that Mounce suggests reflects the testimony of the martyrs of 6:9 and the prayers of believers in 8:3–5.[6] Combining the judgment of the second and third bowls, it appears that all water is turned into blood, constituting a universal testimony to all humanity that God will avenge his martyred saints. This is further evidence that these final plagues must be poured out just before Christ returns, because the earth could not sustain life very long in this condition.

THE FOURTH BOWL (16:8–9)

16:8–9 The fourth angel poured out his bowl on the sun, and it was allowed to scorch people with fire. They were scorched by the fierce heat, and they cursed the name of God who had power over these plagues. They did not repent and give him glory.

Like the fourth trumpet, the fourth bowl is a judgment that affects the starry heavens, specifically the sun. In the fourth trumpet, the judgment extends to one-third of the sun, moon, and stars, resulting in the darkening of one-third of the day and of the night. By contrast, the fourth bowl relates only to the sun and increases rather than decreases the sun's intensity, with scorching results for earth dwellers. Neither the judgment inflicted here nor those of the fifth and seventh bowls cause unbelievers on earth during the great tribulation to repent of their evil and turn to God, even though they recognize Him as the source of their anguish. Instead, they increase their hatred and blasphemy of God.

The Greek text of 16:8 uses the definite article with "people," literally, "the people," suggesting the same class of people as in verses 2, 5, and 6. It also occurs this way in verse 9 where the English text begins with the word "they." The implication is that those in this awful period who are true believers in Christ will not suffer from this plague, and possibly creatures other than evil humans may also escape. The wishful thinking of some that people would repent if they only knew the power and righteous judgment of God is shattered by frequent mention in this chapter of the hardness of the human heart in the face of the most stringent and evident divine discipline (cf. vv. 11, 21).

THE FIFTH BOWL (16:10–11)

16:10–11 The fifth angel poured out his bowl on the throne of the beast, and its kingdom was plunged into darkness. People gnawed their tongues in anguish and cursed the God of heaven for their pain and sores. They did not repent of their deeds.

The result of the fifth bowl judgment no doubt includes the effect of the preceding judgment when sores were inflicted in the first bowl. The beast is probably the first beast of Revelation 13. As in the fifth trumpet and in the ninth plague of Egypt (Ex. 10:21–23), there is darkness over the earth, but this is only part of the divine judgment. As in both trumpet and bowl judgments, there is also pain and torment. The evil in their suffering are declared to gnaw their tongues in pain, a description of severe agony. The sores inflicted in the first bowl are aggravated and increased in this judgment. Again, we have the sad note that they blasphemed God as the author of these judgments and did not repent of their deeds. Though they are declared once more in verse 21 to have blasphemed God, this is the last reference to their failure to repent (cf. 2:21; 9:20–21; 16:9). Again, the Scriptures plainly refute the notion that evil people will quickly repent when faced with catastrophic warnings of judgment. When confronted with the righteous judgment of God, their blasphemy is deepened and their evil purpose is only accentuated.

THE SIXTH BOWL (16:12–16)

16:12–16 The sixth angel poured out his bowl on the great river Euphrates, and its water was dried up, to prepare the way for the kings from the east. And I saw, coming out of the mouth of the dragon and out of the mouth of the beast and out of the mouth of the false prophet, three unclean spirits like frogs. For they are demonic spirits, performing signs, who go abroad to the kings of the whole world, to assemble them for battle on the great day of God the Almighty. ("Behold, I am coming like a thief! Blessed is the one who stays awake, keeping his garments on, that he may not go about naked and be seen exposed!") And they assembled them at the place that in Hebrew is called Armageddon.

Numerous interpretations have been offered for this bowl judgment. Some have been farfetched, and the historical school has in the past attempted to identify this battle with a previous major world conflict. But the most natural explanation is the best, which is that this judgment actually dries up the great Euphrates River, thereby preparing for an invasion from the East.

The River Euphrates, here called "the great," is one of the prominent rivers of the world. It formed the eastern boundary of the ancient Roman Empire as well as the prophesied eastern boundary of the land that God promised to the seed of Abraham (Gen. 15:18; Deut. 1:7; 11:24; Josh. 1:4). In Genesis 15:18, Deuteronomy 1:7, and Joshua 1:4, it is called "the great river . . . Euphrates," as here. These references seem to establish unmistakably the geographic usage in this passage. In Isaiah 11:15 and Zechariah 10:11 there is a similar prediction of the drying up of the Euphrates River, though the name of the river is not mentioned.

Who are "the kings from the east"? As many as fifty different interpretations have been advanced over the years.[7] But the very number of these interpretations is their refutation. The passage is best understood as referring to kings from, literally, the "sun rising," referring to Oriental rulers who will descend upon the Middle East in connection with the final world conflict described a few verses later. The massive specter of communist China alone, with its population of more than 1.3 billion people, makes such an invasion a reasonable prediction. As Wiersbe points out, there is biblical precedent for a river being dried up to let people out. God did this when He dried up the Red Sea during the exodus of Israel from Egypt.[8]

This final world conflict is clearly the work of Satan, since it is against God. We know this from the parenthetical section of verses 13–16, in which John has an additional vision of three unclean spirits that is related to the sixth bowl. Their source is the counterfeit trinity of the world ruler specified as the beast, his associate who is the false prophet, and the dragon himself, Satan (cf. 12:9; 13:1–8, 11–18). These spirits are specified as demonic, and should be so interpreted. They are able (cf. 13:12–15) and commissioned to gather the kings of the entire earth to do battle against "God the Almighty"— meaning they are doomed to defeat! In the battle the omnipotence of God will be fully demonstrated.

While many commentators have agreed that this is the prelude for the great battle climaxing in the second coming of Christ, some have been confused as to the details. The battle is probably better translated "war," for this is not merely an isolated military engagement but a major war. The evidence, however, seems to point to the conclusion that this is a climax of a series of military events described in Daniel 11:40–45, where the reference to the "news from the east" (11:44) may have this invasion in view.

The major problem is how a war is possible when there is a world government under the control of Satan and the beast. It probably reflects a conflict among the nations themselves in the latter portion of the great tribulation as the world empire so hastily put together begins to disintegrate. The armies of the world contending for honors on the battlefield at the very time of the second coming of Christ do all turn, however, and combine their efforts against Christ and His army from heaven when He appears. It will be the final challenge to divine sovereignty and power as the military might of the world of that day will be engaged in fighting on the very day Christ returns (cf. Zech. 14:1–3).

Verse 15 is apparently spoken by Christ. The example is used of a thief who comes suddenly and unexpectedly to inflict loss on the part of the person surprised. Jesus compared His second coming to a thief (Matt. 24:43; Luke 12:39) who will overtake those who are not alert. A similar warning is given to the church in Sardis (Rev. 3:3). In 2 Peter 3:10 and in 1 Thessalonians 5:2, 4, the day of the Lord is said to come as a thief. All of these passages teach that the coming results in loss for those not ready.

The contrast between those who are overtaken by Christ at His coming and those who are prepared by faith in Him is expressed in the beatitude of 16:15b. (For previous beatitudes in Revelation, see 1:3 and 14:13.) The symbolism of preservation of garments is not entirely clear from the passage. Some have construed this symbolism as the garments of salvation, but more probably the righteousness of the saints is symbolized, as expressed in their life and testimony (cf. 19:8). Believers will thus be protected from spiritual nakedness (cf. the spiritual nakedness of the Laodiceans in 3:18)[9] at the coming of the Lord. The believers here are evidently those still on earth who have been able to escape martyrdom even though they remain true to their Lord. It is probable that the beast will not be able to enforce his edict of death on those who are located in the outer reaches of his empire, and that he will not find all those who are in hiding (cf. Matt. 24:16).

The conclusion of the combined action of the sixth bowl and the entice-ment of the demons is that the armies of the earth are gathered in the Middle East in a place described as Armageddon. Though the armies are lured by the demons under the direction of Satan, they nevertheless fulfill the Word of God.

There has been considerable discussion of the meaning of "Armaged-don," taken by some to mean "Mount of Slaughter." Geographically, it relates to the Mount of Megiddo located adjacent to the plain of Megiddo to the west and the large plain of Esdraelon to the northeast.

Megiddo is the Hebrew term corresponding to the Greek word *Armaged-don.* The history of the city of Megiddo lends weight to the idea that this is the location intended. As one source notes, "Many critical battles took place at Megiddo, one of the most strategic cities in the region now called Palestine."[10] For example, this area was the scene of many of the great battles of the Old Testament such as that of Barak and the Canaanites in Judges 4 and the victory of Gideon over the Midianites in Judges 7. Here also occurred the deaths of Saul and Josiah. The area, though it is a large one, is not sufficient for the armies of all the world, though the valley of Esdraelon is fourteen miles wide and twenty miles long. What this Scripture seems to indicate is that this area is the central point for the military conflict that ensues. The armies are actually deployed over a two-hundred-mile area up and down from this central location (cf. 14:20). At the time of the second coming, some of the armies are in Jerusalem itself (Zech. 14:1–3).

The difficulty of the historical interpretation of the book of Revelation is illustrated in the identification of Armageddon with various world conflicts of the past. History alone has proven countless theories of the historical school to be in error. In view of the fact that the second coming that brings this battle to a climax is still future, it is far better to regard this entire conflict as part of the latter stages of the great tribulation.

The relationship between the drying up of the Euphrates and the battle that follows has sometimes been connected with the sixth trumpet in 9:13–21. In the sixth trumpet, an army of two hundred million is loosed to slay one-third of humanity (9:15). This army is related to the Euphrates River, even as the army of the kings of the East. Probably the best explanation is that the seven bowls follow very rapidly after the trumpets, and that the events such as a great invasion are pictured in their early stages in the sixth trumpet with a statement of their ultimate purpose that is actually realized in the sixth bowl. The time sequence here may be in terms of days rather than months or years.

THE SEVENTH BOWL (16:17–21)

16:17–21 The seventh angel poured out his bowl into the air, and a loud voice came out of the temple, from the throne, saying,

"It is done!" And there were flashes of lightning, rumblings, peals of thunder, and a great earthquake such as there had never been since man was on the earth, so great was that earthquake. The great city was split into three parts, and the cities of the nations fell, and God remembered Babylon the great, to make her drain the cup of the wine of the fury of his wrath. And every island fled away, and no mountains were to be found. And great hailstones, about one hundred pounds each, fell from heaven on [the] people; and they cursed God for the plague of the hail, because the plague was so severe.

With both the seal and the trumpet judgments, there was an interlude in time before the execution of the sixth and seventh judgments. But there is no such break with the bowls. They are relentless in their outpouring.

The bowl of the seventh angel also results in catastrophic destruction on the earth. It is accompanied by a great voice in heaven stating an ominous introduction to this final judgment in emphatic terms, "It is done!" The statement is one word in Greek, in the perfect tense, indicating action accomplished. It is the final act of God preceding the second coming of Christ.

There has been speculation as to why this bowl should be poured into the air, since Satan as "the prince of the power of the air" (Eph. 2:2) has already been thrown down from heaven. MacArthur suggests that by this action God is cleansing the earth's atmosphere as the former domain of Satan.[11] The fact that Satan has been cast out of the third heaven, however, does not mean that he still does not have great power in the atmospheric heavens that are here in view. It is also clear that the control of the air as well as space has become increasingly important in military matters. Undoubtedly air and space travel will continue to increase rather than decrease as the end of the age comes upon the world.

Some have compared this prophecy to Ezekiel 38:9, 16, where the host from the north is described as "coming on like a storm" and "like a cloud covering the land." While this may imply an air attack, it is perhaps reading too much into the passage to assume this. In any event the seventh bowl, which is poured out in the air, has its principal result on the earth.

As in the case of the final seal and the seventh trumpet (8:5; 11:19), the final bowl is introduced by the sound of voices, thundering, lightning, and an earthquake greater than any previous one. The earth literally convulses as the times of the Gentiles come to an end. Verse 19 declares that "the great city" is split into "three parts" and that the other cities of the Gentile world fall. It is a picture of awesome destruction.

The identity of "the great city" has been questioned, since Babylon is mentioned later in the verse. Some take this to indicate Babylon, while others have identified it as Jerusalem (cf. 11:8). It is also clear that great topographical changes will take place around Jerusalem in connection with the judgments at the end of the age (cf. Zech. 14:4). There is therefore justification for considering Jerusalem as a possible interpretation.

However, there does not seem to be any clear evidence that Jerusalem is destroyed with these judgments at the end of the great tribulation. Babylon, however, according to Scripture, is destined to be destroyed. Whether this refers to Rome, which is spiritual Babylon, or to a rebuilt city of Babylon on the Euphrates, it is clear that Babylon is the special object of divine judgment. Charles Dyer notes, "God says in Isaiah and Jeremiah and Zechariah, that . . . Babylon, the place where evils started, is going to be around and be judged by God."[12] This is the final judgment of this evil city. The fact that the judgment is an earthquake seems to indicate that a literal city is in view, and that the judgment results in its physical destruction just prior to Christ's second coming.

Every city of the world will come under terrible judgment as a result of the great earthquake, which leaves all monuments of human ingenuity in shambles. The Scriptures also indicate great changes in the topography of the world. The sweeping statement is made in verse 20 that every island is affected and mountains disappear. The fierceness of God's wrath is visible in the entire earth. The movement of the islands and mountains mentioned in 6:14 as stemming from the sixth seal is here carried to a more violent conclusion when the earth radically changes its appearance. Such a judgment undoubtedly causes great loss of life and disruption of whatever world organization may remain up to this time. This judgment comes at the climax of the great tribulation and the return of Christ, when other Scriptures indicate changes in topography, including an entirely new appearance of the Holy Land itself (cf. Zech. 14:4; Luke 3:5).

Verse 21 records a great hailstorm, with every stone weighing about a hundred pounds. Such a hailstorm would have a devastating effect and destroy much that was still left standing by the earthquake. It is a judgment compared to the destruction of Sodom and Gomorrah, but here extending over the whole earth. Although the judgment and its demonstration of the power and sovereignty of God are great, unbelievers [literally, "the people"] are still unrepentant, continuing to curse God. Chronologically the next event is that prophesied in 19:11, where Christ Himself descends from heaven to take over His kingdom on earth.

Though we are not able to immediately understand all the details of these dramatic judgments, the unmistakable impression of the Scriptures is that the whole world is being brought to the bar of justice before Christ as King of kings and Lord of lords. There is no escape from divine judgment except for those who receive the grace of God in that day by faith in Jesus Christ. The utter perversity and depravity of human nature, which will reject the sovereignty of God in the face of such overwhelming evidence, confirms that even the lake of fire will not produce repentance on the part of those who have hardened their hearts against the grace of God.

NOTES

1. J. B. Smith, *A Revelation of Jesus Christ* (Scottdale, PA: Herald Press, 1961), 228.

2. John MacArthur, *The MacArthur New Testament Commentary: Revelation 12–22* (Chicago: Moody, 2000), 138.

3. Alan F. Johnson, *Revelation*, The Expositor's Bible Commentary, Frank E. Gaebelein, ed., vol. 12 (Grand Rapids: Zondervan, 1981), 549.

4. Smith, *A Revelation of Jesus Christ*, 229.

5. John MacArthur, *Because the Time Is Near* (Chicago: Moody, 2007), 250.

6. Robert H. Mounce, *The Book of Revelation*, The New International Commentary on the New Testament (Grand Rapids: Eerdmans, 1997), 296.

7. This conclusion is based on a survey of one hundred commentaries on the book of Revelation.

8. Warren Wiersbe, *Wiersbe's Expository Outlines on the New Testament* (Wheaton, IL: Victor Books, 1992), 843.

9. Robert L. Thomas, *Revelation 8–22: An Exegetical Commentary* (Chicago: Moody, 1995), 267.

10. Walter C. Kaiser and Duane Garrett, eds., *The Archaeological Study Bible* (Grand Rapids: Zondervan, 2005), 1541.

11. MacArthur, *Revelation 12–22*, 151.

12. Charles Dyer, "Babylon: Iraq and the Coming Middle East Crisis," *The Road to Armageddon*, Charles R. Swindoll, John F. Walvoord, J. Dwight Pentecost, eds. (Nashville: Word, 1999), 133.

17

The Destruction of Ecclesiastical Babylon

THE INVITATION TO VIEW THE GREAT PROSTITUTE'S JUDGMENT (17:1–2)

17:1–2 Then one of the seven angels who had the seven bowls came and said to me, "Come, I will show you the judgment of the great prostitute who is seated on many waters, with whom the kings of the earth have committed sexual immorality, and with the wine of whose sexual immorality the dwellers on earth have become drunk."

Chapters 17 and 18 are dedicated to the description of the final destruction of Babylon in both its ecclesiastical and political forms. It is evident from these chapters that the events described precede the events represented in the seven bowls by a considerable period of time. In fact, it is probable that the events of chapter 17 occur at the beginning of the great tribulation. The revelation is given to John, however, subsequent to the revelation of the bowls. It pleased God to reveal various aspects of future events in other than their chronological order.

Expositors have widely differing views of Revelation 17 and 18. In general, however, it is helpful to consider chapter 17 as dealing with Babylon as an ecclesiastical or spiritual entity and chapter 18 as dealing with Babylon as a political entity. It is also helpful in chapter 17 to distinguish the vision in verses 1–6 from the interpretation in verses 7–18.

John is invited by one of the seven bowl angels to view the destruction of Babylon, representing false religion, and also to view the judgment of a woman, the symbol of Babylon, described as "the great prostitute," who is seen sitting on many waters—the many nations ruled by Babylon. The earth dwellers are said to have become drunk with the wine of her immorality. The picture of the woman as utterly evil signifies the spiritual adultery of those who outwardly and religiously seem to be joined to the true God, but who are untrue to Him.

The symbolism of spiritual adultery is not ordinarily used in Scripture of pagan nations that do not know God; two exceptions are Nineveh in Nahum 3:4 and Tyre in Isaiah 23:17. The term is most often used of people who outwardly carry the name of God while actually worshiping and serving other gods. The apostate people of Israel were frequently spiritual adulterers (cf. Ezek. 16 and 23; all of Hosea). In the Old Testament, Yahweh is declared to be Israel's husband (cf. Isa. 54:1–8; Jer. 3:14; 31:32). In the New Testament, the church is viewed as a virgin destined to be joined to her husband, Jesus Christ, in the future (2 Cor. 11:2), but she too is warned against spiritual adultery (James 4:4).

The alliance of the apostate church with the political powers of the world during this future period not only debauches the true spiritual character of the church and compromises her testimony in every way, it also has the devastating effect of inducing religious drunkenness on the part of earth's inhabitants. False religion is always the worst enemy of true religion, and the moral evil involved in the union of the church with the world imposes a stupefying drunkenness as far as spiritual things are concerned. The hardest to win to Christ and the most difficult to instruct in spiritual truth are those who have previously embraced false religion with its outward show of a worship of God.

The concept presented here, enlarging on the previous revelation in 14:8, makes plain that the apostate church has eagerly sought and solicited the adulterous relation with the world political powers and therefore is primarily to be blamed. She will reap the penalty of her sin. As Evans notes, "Organized religion will do the Antichrist's will, until such time as he turns on this false system and destroys it."[1]

THE VISION OF
THE WOMAN ON THE BEAST (17:3–4)

17:3–4 And he carried me away in the Spirit into a wilderness, and I saw a woman sitting on a scarlet beast that was full of blasphemous names, and it had seven heads and ten horns. The woman was arrayed in purple and scarlet, and adorned with gold and jewels and pearls, holding in her hand a golden cup full of abominations and the impurities of her sexual immorality.

John is carried away to a place described as a wilderness. From this vantage point, John is able to see this woman seated on a scarlet-colored beast bearing blasphemous names along with seven heads and ten horns. This is the same beast described in 13:1, where it is described as the revived Roman Empire, the center of the world government of Gentile power in that day. The fact that the woman is riding the beast, and is not the beast itself, signifies that she represents ecclesiastical power as distinct from the beast, which is the political power. Her position as a rider indicates on the one hand that she is supported by the political power of the beast, and on the other that she is in a dominant role and at least outwardly controls and directs the beast.

The situation described here is apparently prior in time to that described in Revelation 13, where the beast has already assumed all power and has demanded that the world worship its ruler as God. This would seem to indicate we are in the first half of Daniel's seventieth week before the time of the great tribulation, which is the second half. While such a relationship has many parallels in the history of the Roman church in relation to political power, the implication is that this is a future situation that will take place in the end time.

The significance of the seven heads and ten horns is revealed subsequently in this chapter—the seven heads apparently referring to forms of government that are successive, and the ten horns to kings who reign simultaneously in the end time. That the woman, representing the apostate church, is in such close association with the beast, which is guilty of utter blasphemy, indicates the depth to which apostasy will ultimately descend. The only form of a world church recognized in the Bible is this apostate form destined to come into power after the true church has been raptured.

The woman's regalia of gold, scarlet, and gems is all too familiar to anyone acquainted with the trappings of ecclesiastical pomp today, especially of high officials in certain branches of Christendom. Purple and scarlet, symbolically rich in their meaning when connected with true spiritual values, are here prostituted to this false religious system and designed to glorify it with religious garb, in contrast to the simplicity of pious adornment (cf. 1 Tim. 2:9–10). The most striking aspect of her presentation, however, is that she has a golden cup in her hand full of the filth of her immorality. The Word of God does not spare words in describing the utter debauchery of this adulterous relationship in the sight of God. Few crimes in Scripture are spoken of in more unsparing terms than that of spiritual adultery of which this woman is the epitome. As alliance with the world and showy pomp increase, so spiritual truth and purity decline.

THE WOMAN'S NAME (17:5)

17:5 And on her forehead was written a name of mystery: "Babylon the great, mother of prostitutes and of earth's abominations."

It has been commonly held that the title assigned to this woman is not a reference to Babylon as a city or to Babylonia as a nation, but is instead a religious designation implying that the woman corresponds religiously to what Babylon was religiously. The meaning is made clear by her description as "mother of prostitutes and of earth's abomination." It has been noted by many writers that the iniquitous and pagan rites of Babylon crept into the early church and were largely responsible for the corruptions incorporated in Roman Catholicism from which Protestantism separated itself in the Middle Ages.[2]

The subject of Babylon in the Scripture is one of the prominent themes of the Bible beginning in Genesis 10, where the city of Babel is first mentioned, with continued references throughout the Scriptures climaxing here in the book of Revelation. From these various passages, it becomes clear that Babylon in Scripture is the name for a great system of religious error. Babylon is a counterfeit religion that plagued Israel in the Old Testament as well as the church in the New Testament, and which, after the apostolic days, has had a tremendous influence in moving the church from biblical simplicity to apostate confusion. In keeping with the satanic principle of offering a poor substitute for God's perfect plan, Babylon is the source of counterfeit religion sometimes in the form of false Christianity, and sometimes in the form of pagan religion.

Nimrod was the founder of Babel, later called Babylon, and leader of the rebellion against God in attempting to make a city and a tower that would reach to heaven (Genesis 10–11). In the ancient world it was a common practice to build huge mounds (ziggurats) of sun-dried bricks, of which the most ancient illustration was discovered at Erech, a place mentioned in Genesis 10:10 and dated more than 3,000 years before Christ. The tower of Babel was apparently a forerunner of later towers dedicated to various heathen deities. This tower was a monument to human pride and an express act of rebellion against the true God.

In judging this act, God confounded the language of the people and the city was named "Babel," meaning "confusion" (Gen. 11:9). The city, later named Babylon, had a long history. It became prominent under Hammurabi (1728–1686 B.C.) who was the guiding light to the empire during the Old Babylonian period. Babylon's greatest glory was achieved under Nebuchadnezzar, who lived during the Neo-Babylonian period about six hundred years before Christ. Daniel the prophet wrote his book at that time. The story of the city and empire has been deciphered from thousands of cuneiform tablets unearthed by archaeologists.

Of primary importance in the study of Babylon is its relation to religion as unfolded in Revelation 17. In addition to information in the Bible itself, ancient accounts indicate that the wife of Nimrod, who founded the city of Babylon, became the head of the so-called Babylonian mysteries that consisted of secret religious rites developed as a part of idol worship. She was known by the name of Semiramis and was a high priestess of the idol worship. According to extrabiblical records, Semiramis gave birth to a son who she claimed was conceived miraculously.

This son, named Tammuz, was considered a savior of his people and was, in effect, a false messiah, purported to be the fulfillment of the promise given to Eve. The legend of the mother and child was incorporated into the religious rites and is repeated in various pagan religions.[3] Idols picturing the mother as the queen of heaven with the baby in her arms are found throughout the ancient world, and countless religious rites were introduced promising supposed cleansing from sin.

Though the rites observed in Babylonian false religion differed greatly in various localities, there usually was a priestly order that furthered the worship of the mother and child cult, practiced the sprinkling of holy water, and established an order of virgins dedicated to religious prostitution. Tammuz, the son, was said to have been killed by a wild animal and then brought back to life—apparently a satanic anticipation of the resurrection of Christ.

In the Scriptures themselves, though many of these facts are not mentioned, there are a number of allusions to the conflict of the true faith with this pseudoreligion. Ezekiel protests against the ceremony of weeping for Tammuz (8:14). Jeremiah mentions the heathen practices of making cakes for the queen of heaven (Jer. 7:18) and offering incense to the queen of heaven (44:17–19, 25). Baal worship, characteristic of pagan religion in Canaan, was another form of this same mystery religion originating in Babylon. Baal is considered identical to Tammuz. The doctrines of the mystery religions of Babylon seem to have permeated the ancient world, giving rise to countless offshoots, each with its cult and individual beliefs offering a counterfeit religion and a counterfeit god in opposition to the true God. Babylon as an evil woman is portrayed in the prophecy of Zechariah 5:1–11, where the woman of verse 7 is described as personifying evil in verse 8.

The Babylonian cult eventually made its way to other cities, including Pergamum, the site of one of the seven churches of Asia. The chief priests of the Babylonian cult wore crowns in the form of the head of a fish, in recognition of Dagon the fish god, with the title "Keeper of the Bridge"—that is, the "bridge" between man and Satan—imprinted on the crowns. The Roman equivalent of the title, *Pontifex Maximus*, was used by the Caesars and later Roman emperors, and was also adopted as the title for the bishop of Rome. In the early centuries of the church in Rome, incredible confusion arose. Attempts were made to combine some features of the mystery religion of Babylon with the Christian faith—the results of which are still present in the Roman church today. In Revelation 17, the last stage of counterfeit religion is revealed as it will be in existence in the period before Christ's return to earth.

Spiritual apostasy, which is seen in its latent form today, will flower in its ultimate form in this future "superchurch" that will apparently engulf all Christendom in the period after the rapture of the church.

THE WOMAN DRUNK WITH
THE BLOOD OF MARTYRS (17:6–7)

17:6–7 And I saw the woman, drunk with the blood of the saints, the blood of the martyrs of Jesus. When I saw her, I marveled greatly. But the angel said to me, "Why do you marvel? I will tell you the mystery of the woman, and of the beast with seven heads and ten horns that carries her."

The woman is pictured not only as the source of all evil in apostate Christendom, but also as actively engaged to the point of drunkenness in the persecution of the true saints. Here the primary reference is not to ancient Babylon, but to Babylon perpetuated in apostate Christendom, especially in its future form. The history of the church has demonstrated that apostate Christendom is unsparing in its persecution of those who attempt to maintain a true faith in Jesus Christ. What has been true in the past will be brought to its climax in this future time when the martyrs will be beyond number from every nation and language. The blood shed by the apostate church is exceeded only by that of the martyrs who refuse to worship the beast in the great tribulation.

The vision of this woman causes John to wonder, and the angel announces the nature of the woman and the beast. Few passages in Revelation have been the subject of more dispute among scholars than the explanation of the beast in the following verses. Great care, therefore, must be taken to determine as much as possible the precise meaning of the revelation given here.

THE BEAST'S ORIGIN (17:8)

17:8 "The beast that you saw was, and is not, and is about to rise from the bottomless pit and go to destruction. And the dwellers on earth whose names have not been written in the book of life from the foundation of the world will marvel to see the beast, because it was and is not and is to come."

The angel explains the beast to John by its chronology. The "bottomless pit" (Gr., *abyssos*, meaning "bottomless" or "the abyss") is the home of Satan and demons, and indicates that the power of the political empire is satanic in its origin, as is plainly stated in 13:4. The beast's destruction refers to eternal damnation. The power of the political empire in the last days is going to cause wonder as indicated in the questions in 13:4: "Who is like the beast, and who can fight against it?" The overwhelming satanic power of the world's final political empire will be most convincing to great masses of mankind.

There is a confusing similarity among the descriptions of Satan, who was apparently described as "the angel of the bottomless pit" (9:11), "the beast that rises from the bottomless pit" (11:7), the beast who "seemed to have a mortal wound, but its mortal wound was healed" (13:3), and the beast of 17:8. The solution to this intricate problem is that there is an identification to some extent of Satan with the future world ruler and identification of the world ruler with his world government. Each of the three entities is described as a beast. Only Satan himself actually comes from the abyss. The world government that he promotes is entirely satanic in its power and to this extent is identified with Satan. It is the beast as the world government that is revived.

The man who is the world ruler, however, has power and great authority given to him by Satan. The fact that Satan and the world ruler are referred to in such similar terms indicates their close relationship to each other.

While many have attempted to demonstrate from this verse that the final world ruler is some resurrected being such as Judas Iscariot, Nero, or one of the more recent world rulers (see the extended discussion on Nero in the endnotes to chapter 13), it is preferable to regard the "eighth" beast (cf. v. 11) as the political power of the world government rather than its human ruler. What is revived is imperial government, not an imperial ruler (cf. Rev. 13:3). That which seemingly went out of existence in history never to be revived is miraculously resuscitated at the end of the age.

THE BEAST'S SEVEN HEADS (17:9–11)

17:9–11 "This calls for a mind with wisdom: the seven heads are seven mountains on which the woman is seated; they are also seven kings, five of whom have fallen, one is, the other has not yet come, and when he does come he must remain only a little while. As for the beast that was and is not, it is an eighth but it belongs to the seven, and it goes to destruction."

The explanation of the beast anticipates the complexity of the revelation to follow. The reader is warned that spiritual wisdom is required to understand that which is unfolded. The first key is the meaning of the seven mountains on which the woman is seated. Many expositors believe this refers to Rome because seven mountains formed the nucleus of the ancient city on the left bank of the Tiber.[4] This passage in Revelation is taken, therefore, to indicate that the seat of the false ecclesiastical power will be in Rome geographically rather than in Babylon. Throughout its history, Rome has been described as the city of seven mountains as indicated in coins that refer to it in this way and in countless allusions in Roman literature.

The seven heads of the beast, however, are also said to be symbolic of seven kings as described in verse 10. Five of these are said to have fallen, one is in existence in John's lifetime, the seventh is yet to come and will be followed by another described as the eighth, which is the beast itself. The seven heads are best explained as referring to seven kings who represent seven successive kingdoms. Because the seven heads are identified with kings in verse 10, some prefer to divorce the meaning from the city of Rome entirely. Thomas's treatment of this subject is worthy of extended quotation here.

> A preferable view of the seven heads and mountains is that they are seven successive empires, with the seven kings of v. 10 as heads and personifications of those empires (Seiss, Ladd). This view agrees with a common meaning of "mountain" or "hill" in the Bible (e.g., Pss. 30:7; 68:15–16; Isa. 2:2; 41:15; Jer. 51:25; Dan. 2:35; Hab. 3:6; Zech 4:7) (Lee, Bullinger, Seiss, Ladd, Johnson). This is sensible because the next phrase says the heads are also seven kings (v. 10). This double identification is probable especially in light of Daniel 7 where at one point Daniel identifies the four beast-kingdoms as four kings (v. 17) (Ladd). The principal weakness of this viewpoint is that it involves a double symbolism, a rare if not impossible hermeneutical principle (Dusterdieck). Yet the view that identifies the seven hills with the city of Rome entails a double symbolism of a different and even more unusual type. This view gives the heads a geographical and political meaning, which is probably unprecedented. Giving the mountains a double meaning of kingdoms and kings is a much better choice. The call for special wisdom in v. 9a probably has in view the ability to grasp this double meaning of the mountains. Rome as one of the seven world empires is indirectly in view. It is probably the sixth empire, referred to as "one is," in v. 10, but the seven mountains or hills is not a reference to the city's topography.
>
> In Dan. 7:17, 23 kings and kingdoms are interchangeable, showing that a king can stand for the kingdom ruled by that king (Swete, Lee). The seven kingdoms are the seven that dominate [the] world scene throughout human history: Egypt (or Neo-Babylonia, Gen. 10:8–11), Assyria, Babylon, Persia, Greece, Rome, and the future kingdom of the beast.[5]

The final form of world government, symbolized by the eighth beast itself, is the world empire of the great tribulation. The revived Roman Empire that will be in power immediately after the rapture of the church is apparently indicated by the seventh head, while the beast, described in verse 11 as the eighth, is the world empire, which is destroyed by Jesus Christ at His second coming. Thus verses 8–11 describe the final form of Gentile world power in alliance with apostate religion symbolized by the prostitute.

GENTILE EMPIRES OF THE EARTH

Revelation 17:9–11

1. Egypt
2. Assyria
3. Babylon
4. Medo-Persia
5. Greece
6. Historical Roman Empire
7. Revived Roman Empire (Revelation)
8. The Eighth Kingdom: Antichrist

THE BEAST'S TEN HORNS (17:12–14)

17:12–14 "And the ten horns that you saw are ten kings who have not yet received royal power, but they are to receive authority as kings for one hour, together with the beast. These are of one mind and hand over their power and authority to the beast. They will make war on the Lamb, and the Lamb will conquer them, for he is Lord of lords and King of kings, and those with him are called and chosen and faithful."

The final stage of this world empire has a nucleus of ten kings apparently joined in a confederacy represented by the ten horns. In contrast to the seven heads of the beast, these kings do not rule in succession but simultaneously at the end time. A comparison with chapter 13 will show that this is the form of the Roman Empire just preceding the world empire. The ten horns' rule as kings is subject to the beast, and their time in power is brief. They are a phase of the transmission of power from the various kingdoms to that of the beast itself.

This is shown by verse 13 where the kings yield their power to the beast. They are further described as making war with the Lamb, a reference to the Lord Jesus Christ, and their ultimate subjugation under Him will be fulfilled at His second coming. This triumph is anticipated in verse 14 with its description of Christ and His faithful followers.

THE EXPLANATION OF THE WATERS (17:15)

17:15 And the angel said to me, "The waters that you saw, where the prostitute is seated, are peoples and multitudes and nations and languages."

In verse 1 the prostitute is seen sitting upon many waters. Here the description and the symbolic meaning of the waters are given. Generally speaking, when water is mentioned in Revelation, it should be taken literally. The fact that a symbolic meaning is assigned to it here is the exception to the usual rule. The situation described here is one of great political power on the part of the beast, but a sharing of rule with the woman who controls the multitudes of the world.

THE WOMAN'S DESTRUCTION (17:16–18)

17:16–18 "And the ten horns that you saw, they and the beast will hate the prostitute. They will make her desolate and naked, and devour her flesh and burn her up with fire, for God has put it into their hearts to carry out his purpose by being of one mind and handing over their royal power to the beast, until the words of God are fulfilled. And the woman that you saw is the great city that has dominion over the kings of the earth."

Verse 16 reveals a most remarkable development in the vision, which is also the climax and the purpose of the preceding description. The ten horns or ten kings destroy the woman riding the beast in a very graphic way. The best reading indicates that the ten horns and the beast combine in this effort. The action of this verse is cast in the future tense that must be understood as future from John's point of view. The prostitute is stripped of all her finery, her flesh is eaten, and she is burned with fire. These graphic words clearly picture the downfall of the apostate world church of the future.

By comparison with other Scriptures, the time of this event may be placed approximately at the midpoint of the seven years of Daniel's seventieth week, which leads up to and climaxes in the second coming of Christ. During the first half of the seven years, apostate Christendom flowers and establishes its power over all the world. During this period there is a measure of religious freedom as indicated by the fact that the Jews are allowed to worship and renew their sacrifices (Dan. 9:27). There may even be widespread preaching of the gospel in this same period, as it would hardly seem possible to extend religious freedom to the Jews without doing the same for all.

However, false religion triumphs here. All religions of the world, apart from the true faith of Christ, gather in one great church. Only those who are truly saved, whose names are written in the Lamb's book of life and who know Christ as Savior, seem to escape this unification. The climax of this series of events is seen in the early portion of chapter 17 where the woman in all her pomp and wickedness is riding the beast.

However, with the beginning of the second half of the week, the ruler of the revived Roman Empire, who is the political head of the world empire and is himself designated also as "the beast," is able to proclaim himself dictator of the whole world. He no longer needs the help and power of the church, which he destroys and replaces with the worship of himself. According to 13:8, all people will worship the beast except true believers in Christ. Many find a parallel revelation in Daniel 11:36–39 where the willful king likewise puts aside all other deities in favor of the worship of himself.

The divine judgment inflicted upon apostate Christendom follows a pattern that can be observed in other judgments upon evil nations and ungodly rulers. Ancient Babylon was used to bring affliction upon the people of Israel, as were also the governments of Assyria and Egypt. But in due time, the same nations that inflicted divine judgment were themselves the objects of God's wrath. The principle involved is plainly stated in verse 17. Their action, though inspired by a blasphemous attempt to institute a world religion, nevertheless fulfills God's will that the kingdoms of the world come under the domain of the beast in fulfillment of prophecy until the end of the age. Thus the plan of the ages unfolds majestically, and Scripture indicates that God sovereignly permits the growth of evil until its cup of sin overflows.

At the close of the chapter, the woman is again identified with the great city that reigns over the kings of the earth. This refers to the ecclesiastical power and control of the political powers that has characterized portions of church history and will have its climax in this future period. The "great city" is obviously a reference to Babylon in its religious rather than its historical significance. The influence of Babylon on Roman Christianity was partly responsible for the assumption by Rome of political power, namely, the authority of the church over the state. Just as ancient Babylon conquered kings in a political way, so its religious counterpart would dominate political states during the period of Roman papal power.

The interpretation that this is a reference to pagan political Rome, as advanced by the historical school of interpretation, or that it refers to a future literal city of Babylon, is wrong. According to verse 5, the city is a mystery, not a literal city. The entire context of chapter 17 supports this interpretation, distinguishing between the city identified with the woman and the political power referred to as the beast and the ten horns.

After the disposal of Babylon in its religious form by its destruction at the hands of the beast, the prophetic revelation in chapter 18 then deals with Babylon as a political force, also destined for destruction at a later date.

NOTES

1. Tony Evans, *The Best Is Yet to Come* (Chicago: Moody, 2000), 186.

2. Wilbur M. Smith, *The Wycliffe Bible Commentary*, Charles F. Pfeiffer and Everett F. Harrison, eds. (Chicago: Moody, 1990), 1517.

3. H. M. Carson, "Roman Catholicism," in *The Dictionary of the Christian Church*, J. D. Douglass, gen. ed. (Grand Rapids: Zondervan, 1978), 855.

4. Robert H. Mounce, *The Book of Revelation*, The New International Commentary on the New Testament (Grand Rapids: Eerdmans, 1997), 315.

5. Robert L. Thomas, *Revelation 8–22: An Exegetical Commentary* (Chicago: Moody, 1995), 296–297. Seiss marshals a convincing array of evidence that the seven mountains of 17:9 refer not to the seven mountains of Rome but rather to successive imperial governments. See Joseph A. Seiss, *The Apocalypse* (Grand Rapids: Zondervan, 1957), 391–94.

18 The Fall of Babylon

THE FALL ANNOUNCED (18:1–3)

18:1–3 After this I saw another angel coming down from heaven, having great authority, and the earth was made bright with his glory. And he called out with a mighty voice, "Fallen, fallen is Babylon the great! She has become a dwelling place for demons, a haunt for every unclean spirit, a haunt for every unclean bird, a haunt for every unclean and detestable beast. For all nations have drunk the wine of the passion of her sexual immorality, and the kings of the earth have committed immorality with her, and the merchants of the earth have grown rich from the power of her luxurious living."

The words "after this" mark chapter 18 as a later revelation than that given in chapter 17. The words "another angel" make it clear that the angel of 18:1 is different than the angel of 17:1, even though the word "another" means "one of the same kind." MacArthur suggests the angel may be the same one who announced Babylon's judgment in 14:8.[1] The majestic description of this angel indicates that he is delegated to do a great work on behalf of God—to announce Babylon's fall. The aorist tense of the Greek verb translated "fallen" indicates a sudden event viewed as completed, though the context would indicate a future event.

THE TWO BABYLONS OF REVELATION 17–18

	Revelation 17 Religious Babylon	Revelation 18 Political/Commercial Babylon
Focus:	Babylon as a System	Babylon as a City
Timing:	Falls at the Beginning of the Great Tribulation	Falls at the End of the Great Tribulation
Destroyer:	The Beast and the Ten Kings	Jesus Christ at His Second Coming
Result:	No Mourning	Great Mourning

As the accompanying chart illustrates, there are a number of reasons to believe the judgment of chapter 18 is subsequent to that of chapter 17, and not two parts of the same event—although the two are described in similar terms. The woman who is destroyed in chapter 17 is made desolate, naked, and burned by the beast with the ten horns. From this we have concluded that the woman in chapter 17 is Babylon in its ecclesiastical or religious sense, and that her destruction probably occurs when the beast assumes the role of God at the beginning of the great tribulation. The world church is destroyed in favor of a world religion honoring the political dictator, the beast out of the sea of chapter 13.

In chapter 18, the context seems to indicate that Babylon is being viewed in its political and economic character rather than in its religious aspect. The term "Babylon" in Scripture is more than a reference to the false religious system that stemmed from the pagan religion of ancient Babylon. Out of ancient Babylon also came the political power represented in Nebuchadnezzar and fulfilled in the first world empire. In some sense this is continued in the commercial system that arises in Revelation from both the religious and the political Babylons. It seems that chapter 17 deals with the religious aspect and chapter 18 with the political and economic aspects of Babylon.[2]

The kings and merchants of the earth will mourn the passing of economic Babylon (v. 9; there is no mourning indicated with the destruction of religious Babylon in chapter 17). The destruction of economic Babylon should be compared with the preceding announcement in 16:19 where the great city is divided and the Gentile cities fall. This event comes late in the great tribulation, just prior to the second coming of Christ, in contrast to the destruction of the woman of chapter 17, which seems to precede the great tribulation and paves the way for the worship of the beast (13:8).

The downfall of the city of Babylon in 18:2 is followed by its becoming the habitation of "detestable creatures and evil spirits."[3] The threefold description of these creatures is a reference to fallen angels in their various characteristics as demons and evil spirits, symbolized by the bird (cf. "birds," Isa. 34:11–15; Matt. 13:32). This abandonment of destroyed Babylon to demons is a divine judgment stemming from the utter corruption of its inhabitants described in verse 3. Political Babylon has had evil, immoral relationships with all the nations of earth and their leaders. The resulting association has made the world's merchants rich. Just as the church of chapter 17 had grown rich in proportion to its evil, so the nations have prospered as they have abandoned God and sought to accumulate worldly wealth. The wealth originally collected through the influence of the apostate church is taken over by the political system in the great tribulation, which has the power to exploit to the full its accumulation of wealth.

A CALL TO SEPARATION FROM BABYLON (18:4–5)

18:4–5 Then I heard another voice from heaven saying, "Come out of her, my people, lest you take part in her sins, lest you share in her plagues; for her sins are heaped high as heaven, and God has remembered her iniquities."

As John contemplates the announcement of Babylon's fall, he hears another voice from heaven calling God's people to flee the doomed city, just as His people were urged to leave Babylon in ancient days (Jer. 51:45). The children of Israel were urged to "Flee from the midst of Babylon" (Jer. 50:8), and commanded again, "Flee from the midst of Babylon; let every one save his life!" (Jer. 51:6). MacArthur compares the command to come out of Babylon to the warning to Lot to leave Sodom (Gen. 19:12–13).[4]

The purpose of leaving Babylon is twofold: First, by separation from her they will not partake of her sin, and second, they will not have her plagues inflicted on them. The plagues refer to the bowls of chapter 16, especially the seventh bowl that falls upon Babylon itself (16:17–21). This is further evidence that chapter 18 is subsequent to the seventh bowl and therefore in contrast to the destruction of the woman in chapter 17.

In verse 5, Babylon's sins are declared to reach to the heavens with the result that God remembers, that is, judges her (cf. Jer. 51:9). The Greek word for "heaped" (*kollaō*) can suggest something piled up like bricks in a building, an allusion to the tower of Babel that began the evil career of ancient Babylon (Gen. 11:5–9). Though God permits the heaping up of sin, its ultimate divine judgment is inescapable. As Wiersbe notes, "There is a lesson here for God's people today: 'Do not share in other people's sins' (see 1 Tim. 5:22; also Jer. 51:9)."[5]

THE INDICTMENT AGAINST BABYLON (18:6–8)

18:6–8 "Pay her back as she herself has paid back others, and repay her double for her deeds; mix a double portion for her in the cup she mixed. As she glorified herself and lived in luxury, so give her a like measure of torment and mourning, since in her heart she says, 'I sit as a queen, I am no widow, and mourning I shall never see.' For this reason her plagues will come in a single day, death and mourning and famine, and she will be burned up with fire; for mighty is the Lord God who has judged her."

The enormity of Babylon's sin now brings the enormity of God's judgment. The Greek verb here means literally "to pay a debt" or "to give back that which is due." It is the law of retribution sometimes called *lex talionis*. Divine justice exacts the "eye for an eye" and the "tooth for a tooth."

But the voice John hears demands that the law of retribution be doubled in payment of Babylon's hideous sins. She mixes a "cup" of sin that the nations will drink down to the full, so she is given a double cup of divine judgment to drink (cf. 14:10).

The same law of retribution is indicated in verse 7 where the standard of her judgment is compared to her luxurious living in which she was given to self-glorification. The expression "lived in luxury" means "to be wanton" or "to revel" and comes from a word meaning "hardheaded" or "willful." Her willful sin against God is now to be rewarded with torment and sorrow. The picture of judgment here is to trial by torture with its resultant mental anguish and grief. Babylon's wishful thinking is going to be rewarded by sudden destruction from the Lord, "in a single day" (v. 8). Then her vaunted strength will be as nothing compared to the power of God.

Like the church at Laodicea, Babylon's wealth has brought a sense of false security (3:17). Her claim to not being a widow has only the faulty foundation of her illicit love affairs with the earth's kings (17:2). The fact that her judgment comes in one day, emphasized in the Greek by being placed first in the sentence, is reminiscent of the fall of Babylon in Daniel 5, which fell in the same hour that the finger traced its condemning words on the wall. Before morning, the ancient power of Babylon had been destroyed. In a similar way, the rich fool of Luke 12:16–20 lost his barns and his soul in one night. When it is time for God's judgment, it descends with unwavering directness.

THE LAMENT OF THE EARTH'S KINGS (18:9–10)

18:9–10 And the kings of the earth, who committed sexual immorality and lived in luxury with her, will weep and wail over her when they see the smoke of her burning. They will stand far off, in fear of her torment, and say, "Alas! Alas! You great city, you mighty city, Babylon! For in a single hour your judgment has come."

The destruction of political and economic Babylon is lamented by her kingly lovers. These kings are a wider designation than the ten kings of 17:12, 16, who participated in the destruction of the prostitute. The time is the second coming of Christ at the end of the great tribulation. The lament over Babylon is most emphatic in the Greek by repetition: literally, "You great city, you mighty city, Babylon!" It was great in its extent of power and accomplishment, and mighty in the strength of its rule. In spite of its greatness and strength, it nevertheless falls in one hour.

Some believe that ancient Babylon is to be rebuilt as the capital of the world empire in the great tribulation and that Babylon in this chapter refers to ancient Babylon rather than to Rome.[6] According to Isaiah 13:19–22, Babylon was to be completely destroyed and not inhabited. This seems also the teaching of Jeremiah 51:24–26, 61–64. It is argued that ancient Babylon as a city was not destroyed for hundreds of years after the fall of the empire, and therefore these prophecies have not been literally fulfilled.

The destruction of Babylon according to Jeremiah 51:8 was to be sudden. This is confirmed in Revelation 18. This was not true of ancient Babylon, as it continued for many years after its political downfall. Further, it is pointed out that the prophecy of Isaiah 13:6, 9–11, which forms the context of verses 19–22, indicates that the destruction of Babylon would be in the day of the Lord. Thus, some expositors believe that Babylon will be rebuilt and then destroyed by Christ at His second coming.[7]

Others identify Babylon as Rome,[8] the seat of the apostate church as described by the seven mountains of 17:9, and also the political city as elsewhere described. It is possible that Rome might be the ecclesiastical capital, and rebuilt Babylon the political and commercial capital. It is also conceivable that Rome might be the capital in the first half of the last seven years and Babylon in the second half in the world empire phase.

Those who deny that Babylon will be rebuilt do so on the principle that the prophecy of destruction refers to ecclesiastical and political power symbolized in Babylon but not embodied in an actual city. The city of Babylon politically, therefore, is now destroyed historically. The power and religious character of Babylon are destroyed at the second coming. The ultimate decision depends upon the judgment of the expositor, but in many respects it is simpler to postulate a rebuilt Babylon as fulfilling literally the Old Testament prophecies as well as those embodied in this chapter.

Regardless of its location, the burning city is a symbol of the fall of its political and economic might, and the kings marvel at the destruction of the seemingly infinite power of the world empire's capital. Their lament involves both words and, possibly, beating their breasts, a common act of distress. "Alas! Alas!" is probably better translated "Woe! Woe!" because it is much more emphatic. The word is mournful in both its sound and meaning and is reminiscent of the hopeless wailing of those who mourn the passing of loved ones. Their mourning is also characterized by fear lest they encounter the same judgment that has overcome the city, and for this reason they stand far off. How sad is the hour of judgment when it is too late for mercy.

THE LAMENT OF THE
MERCHANTS OF THE EARTH (18:11–19)

18:11–19 And the merchants of the earth weep and mourn for her, since no one buys their cargo anymore, cargo of gold, silver, jewels, pearls, fine linen, purple cloth, silk, scarlet cloth, all kinds of scented wood, all kinds of articles of ivory, all kinds of articles of costly wood, bronze, iron and marble, cinnamon, spice, incense, myrrh, frankincense, wine, oil, fine flour, wheat, cattle and sheep, horses and chariots, and slaves, that is, human souls. "The fruit for which your soul longed has gone from you, and all your delicacies and your splendors are lost to you, never to be found again!" The merchants of these wares, who gained wealth from her, will stand far off, in fear of her torment, weeping and mourning aloud, "Alas, alas, for the great city that was clothed in fine linen, in purple and scarlet, adorned with gold, with jewels, and with pearls! For in a single hour all this wealth has been laid waste." And all shipmasters and seafaring men, sailors and all whose trade is on the sea, stood far off and cried out as they saw the smoke of her burning, "What city was like the great city?" And they threw dust on their heads as they wept and mourned, crying out, "Alas, alas, for the great city where all who had ships at sea grew rich by her wealth! For in a single hour she has been laid waste."

That Babylon is a commercial power is evident from the lament of the world's merchants, wailing over the loss of their trade with the city. Everything that indicated the wealth of the ancient world is itemized as the treasure of Babylon in her hour of destruction. Like the kings who stood far off and watched the ascending smoke of Babylon's burning, so the world's merchants also fear to go near the city and they repeat the kings' lament.

Those in ships, apparently standing off from shore on the sea, likewise witness the scene and join in the mourning for Babylon, their partner in trade. For the third time the mourning cry is heard: "Alas, alas." Their mourning is not for the city, however, but because their wealth derived from trade in shipping is now at an end. Christ warned against coveting the wealth of this world in Matthew 6:19–21, where He told us, "Lay up for yourselves treasures in heaven."

In contrast to the transitory wealth and glory of this world, which are here consumed by a great judgment from God, the true riches of faith, devotion, and service for God are safely stored in heaven beyond the destructive hands of man and protected by the righteous power of God. The destruction of Babylon also ends the nefarious control of human souls mentioned last in the list of commodities in verse 13. No longer can ancient Babylon control the world religiously, politically, or economically.

REJOICING IN HEAVEN
OVER BABYLON'S FALL (18:20)

18:20 "Rejoice over her, O heaven, and you saints and apostles and prophets, for God has given judgment for you against her!"

In contrast to the grief overtaking worldly rulers and merchants by the destruction of Babylon, those in heaven, who are mentioned later in 19:1, are called upon to rejoice at God's righteous judgment. The expression "has given judgment for you" is literally "God has judged your judgment on them," that is, "God has inflicted your judgment on them," thus bringing to bear upon Babylon the righteous recompense for her martyrdom of the saints. As Ryrie states, "Babylon had slain the saints; now, God slays Babylon."[9] It is another case where the righteous ultimately triumph as victory follows suffering.

THE UTTER DESTRUCTION OF BABYLON (18:21–24)

18:21–24 Then a mighty angel took up a stone like a great millstone and threw it into the sea, saying, "So will Babylon the great city be thrown down with violence, and will be found no more; and the sound of harpists and musicians, of flute players and trumpeters, will be heard in you no more, and a craftsman of any craft will be found in you no more, and the sound of the mill will be heard in you no more, and the light of a lamp will shine in you no more, and the voice of bridegroom and bride will be heard in you no more, for your merchants were the great ones of the earth, and all nations were deceived by your sorcery. And in her was found the blood of prophets and of saints, and of all who have been slain on earth."

In John's vision he sees a "mighty angel" (cf. 5:2; 10:1) throw a huge stone into the sea, portraying Babylon's violent downfall. A similar instance is found in Jeremiah 51:61–64, where Seraiah, a prince who accompanied Zedekiah into Babylon, is instructed after reading the book of Jeremiah to tie a stone to it and throw it into the midst of the Euphrates with the words, "Thus shall Babylon sink, to rise no more, because of the disaster that I am bringing upon her, and they shall become exhausted."

The symbolism is the same here in Revelation 18, for the angel's action represents the destruction of the great city, which like a stone sinking into the sea will disappear. The ultimate end of Babylon in all its forms will be accomplished by God's judgment at the end of the great tribulation. Babylon will be found "no more" (cf. vv. 14, 22–23). The expression occurs seven times with minor variations.

The angel now expounds on the cessation of Babylon's activity. The vocal and instrumental music that characterized the city's life and luxurious existence is now silent. Similarly, the craftsmen who produced the ultimate in luxurious goods are no longer to be found. The sound of the millstone grinding out the grain is silent. In like manner, the light of the candle is now out, the city cold and dead, and no longer do its streets ring with the voices of the bridegroom and the bride. Of the nine different features mentioned, seven are described by the Greek word *phōnē*, literally "sound." The very silence of the city is a testimony to God's devastating judgment.

Verses 23 and 24 provide another brief summary of the extent of Babylon's sins and greatness. Her merchants were "great ones of the earth." All nations were deceived by Babylon's sorceries. Here too was the martyred blood of prophets and saints. The greatness that was the secret of her rise in power and influence makes her downfall all the more impressive. Babylon is declared to be guilty of the blood of prophets and saints, referring in part to the martyrs of the great tribulation.

There are obvious parallels in the rise and fall of Babylon in its various forms in Scripture. As introduced in Genesis 11:1–9, Babylon, historically symbolized by the tower reaching to heaven, proposed to maintain the union of the world through a common worship and a common language. God defeated this purpose by confusing the language and scattering the people. Ecclesiastically, Babylon is symbolized by the woman in Revelation 17, who proposes a common worship and a common religion through uniting in a world church. This is destroyed by the beast in Revelation 17:16 who thus fulfills the will of God (Rev. 17:17).

Politically, Babylon is symbolized by the great city of Revelation 18, which attempts to achieve its domination of the world by a world common market and a world government. These are destroyed by Christ at His second coming (Rev. 19:11–21). The triumph of God is therefore witnessed historically in the scattering of the people and the unfinished tower of Genesis 11, and prophetically in the destruction of the world church by the killing of the prostitute of Revelation 17 and the destruction of the city of Revelation 18. With the graphic description of Babylon's fall contained in chapters 17 and 18, the way is cleared for the presentation of the major theme of the book of Revelation, the second coming of Christ and the establishment of His glorious kingdom.

NOTES

1. John MacArthur, *Because the Time Is Near* (Chicago: Moody, 2007), 273.

2. Robert L. Thomas, *Revelation 8–22: An Exegetical Commentary* (Chicago: Moody, 1995, 313–14.

3. Alan F. Johnson, *Revelation*, The Expositor's Bible Commentary, Frank E. Gaebelein, ed., vol. 12 (Grand Rapids: Zondervan, 1981), 566.

4. John MacArthur, *The MacArthur New Testament Commentary: Revelation 12–22* (Chicago: Moody, 2000), 181.

5. Warren Wiersbe, *Wiersbe's Expository Outlines on the New Testament* (Wheaton, IL: Victor, 1992), 848.

6. Alan F. Johnson argues that the reference is not to any earthly city, but to the "great satanic system" that has corrupted the earth. See Johnson, *Revelation*, 565.

7. Charles Dyer, "Babylon: Iraq and the Coming Middle East Crisis," in *The Road to Armageddon*, Charles R. Swindoll, John F. Walvoord, J. Dwight Pentecost, eds. (Nashville: Word, 1999), 136–37. See also Charles Dyer, "The Identity of Babylon in Revelation 17–18," two articles in *Bibliotheca Sacra*, vol. 144, no. 575 (July–Sep 1987), 305–16; vol. 144, no. 576 (Oct–Dec 1987), 433–49.

8. Robert H. Mounce, *The Book of Revelation*, The New International Commentary on the New Testament (Grand Rapids: Eerdmans, 1997), 331ff.

9. Charles C. Ryrie, *Revelation*, rev. ed. (Chicago: Moody, 1996), 125.

19 The Second Coming of Christ

THE SHOUT OF THE SAINTS IN HEAVEN (19:1–3)

19:1–3 After this I heard what seemed to be the loud voice of a great multitude in heaven, crying out, "Hallelujah! Salvation and glory and power belong to our God, for his judgments are true and just; for he has judged the great prostitute who corrupted the earth with her immorality, and has avenged on her the blood of his servants." Once more they cried out, "Hallelujah! The smoke from her goes up forever and ever."

This multitude in heaven is rejoicing over the destruction of Babylon in all its forms. The time, therefore, must be just before the second coming of Christ. The multitude is the same group as in Revelation 7:9. Though the general reference may be to all people in heaven, the allusion seems to be to the martyred dead of the great tribulation. The word "hallelujah" appears only four times in the New Testament, all in this chapter (vv. 1, 3, 4, 6). It is a transliteration of the Greek term, which in turn is the equivalent of the Hebrew word. As MacArthur points out, "It is a word often associated both with the judgment of the ungodly and the salvation of God's people."[1] Poellot appropriately calls 19:1–6 "the New Testament Hallelujah Chorus."[2]

The saints here speak with a "loud voice" (cf. 7:10), expressing praise to God in three great words: "salvation," "glory," and "power." The uniqueness of God's possession of these attributes is emphasized by the definite article that occurs in Greek before each word: *the* salvation, *the* glory, and *the* power of God. God is praised for having judged the great prostitute and having avenged the blood of His servants shed by her hand. This includes both the punishment of the guilty and the vindication of the innocent.[3] The ascription of praise is followed by a second hallelujah and the statement that the smoke of Babylon will continue to rise forever. This cannot refer to the city itself, but will be fulfilled by a perpetual judgment of the people who engaged in her wicked deeds. Thus is answered the appeal of the martyred saints in 6:10 for God's righteous judgment on those who shed their blood.

THE HALLELUJAH OF
THE TWENTY-FOUR ELDERS (19:4)

19:4 And the twenty-four elders and the four living creatures fell down and worshiped God who was seated on the throne, saying, "Amen. Hallelujah!"

The twenty-four elders first introduced in chapter 4 along with the four living creatures add their praise and worship of God to this scene. The fact that these beings are worshiping God in a separate way from the great multitude seems to confirm the earlier suggestion that the great multitude is the martyred dead of the great tribulation who suffered immediately from the evil of Babylon in its form just prior to the second coming of Christ. If the twenty-four elders represent the church, they are witnesses of these events from heaven even though they have not participated in quite the same way.

THE FINAL HALLELUJAH OF
THE GREAT MULTITUDE (19:5–6)

19:5–6 And from the throne came a voice saying, "Praise our God, all you his servants, you who fear him, small and great." Then I heard what seemed to be the voice of a great multitude, like the roar of many waters and like the sound of mighty peals of thunder, crying out, "Hallelujah! For the Lord our God the Almighty reigns."

Another voice is now heard from the throne, calling God's servants to praise the Lord. It is probable that this is a voice of an angel rather than the voice of God or the voice of the saints. The occasion for this praise is God's judgment against evil people who have oppressed His people, and all of God's servants are invited to join the praise. The verb "praise" is in the present tense and is therefore a command to "keep on praising" the Lord.

In antiphonal response to this call to praise, John hears the voice of the great multitude of verse 1, speaking with a majestic sound that he compared to those of roaring waters and thunder, saying for the fourth time in this passage, "Hallelujah! For the Lord our God the Almighty reigns." Bruce calls this expression "the keynote of the whole book."[4]

THE MARRIAGE SUPPER OF
THE LAMB ANNOUNCED (19:7–8)

19:7–8 "Let us rejoice and exult and give him the glory, for the marriage of the Lamb has come, and his Bride has made herself ready; it was granted her to clothe herself with fine linen, bright and pure"—for the fine linen is the righteous deeds of the saints.

Continuing the praise of the Lord their God, the great multitude now announces a major feature of the Lord's reign upon earth—His marriage to His bride. In verse 7, the great multitude expresses its joy that the marriage of the Lamb has come and that His wife has made herself ready. Some expositors place this marriage in heaven, but the text does not say where it takes place.[5] This event is obviously subsequent to the destruction of Babylon. If this occurs at the end of the great tribulation, which is immediately climaxed and succeeded by the second coming of Christ, the more natural presumption is that the marriage supper takes place on earth in connection with Christ's second coming to earth.

It is most significant, and in keeping with the concept of a pretribulational rapture, that those in the great multitude of tribulation saints should thus regard the Lamb's Bride as an entity other than themselves.

Though marriage customs varied in the ancient world, usually there were three major aspects: (1) The marriage contract was often consummated by the parents when the future spouses were still children. The payment of a suitable dowry was often a feature of the contract. When consummated, the contract meant that the couple was legally married. (2) When a couple had reached a suitable age, the second step in the wedding took place. This was a ceremony in which the bridegroom, accompanied by his friends, would go to the bride's house to escort her to his home. This is the background of the parable of the virgins in Matthew 25:1–13. (3) Then the bridegroom would bring his bride to his home, and the marriage supper, to which guests were invited, would take place. It was such a wedding feast that Christ attended at Cana (John 2:1–11).

The marriage symbolism is beautifully fulfilled in the relationship of Christ to His church. The wedding contract is consummated at the time the church is redeemed. Every true Christian is joined to Christ in a legal marriage. When Christ comes for His church at the rapture, the second phase of the wedding is fulfilled: the Bridegroom goes to receive His bride. The third phase then follows, the wedding feast. Here it is significant to note that the bride is already the wife of the Lamb, for the bridegroom has already come for His bride prior to His second coming described in 19:11–16. Therefore, the wedding feast and not the wedding union is being announced here. The third phase of the wedding is about to take place, the feast, which presumes the earlier rapture of the bride.

A problem of interpretation surrounds the term "bride." In the biblical use of the figure of marriage, variations can be observed in both the Old and New Testaments. Frequently in the Old Testament, as for instance in the book of Hosea, Israel is described as the unfaithful wife of God to be restored to her position as a faithful wife in the future millennial reign. While marriage is often used as an illustration of various truths, the norm is that Israel is already married to God and has proved unfaithful to her responsibility as a wife.

By contrast, in the New Testament, the church is pictured as a virgin waiting for the coming of her bridegroom (2 Cor. 11:2). In this case the wedding union and feast are still future. The dispensational distinction between the saints of the present age belonging to the church, the Body of Christ, and saints of other ages, such as those in the Old Testament or in the future tribulation, therefore seems to be observed in this passage. The bride is distinguished from the great multitude identified in chapter 7 as martyrs out of the great tribulation. The "marriage of the Lamb" (v. 7) is properly the marriage supper of the Lamb, the final aspect of the marriage relationship between Christ and His church.

In verse 8, a beautiful picture is drawn of the holiness and righteousness of the church in that hour, for the bride is described as arrayed in "fine linen, bright and pure," which is explained as "the righteous deeds of the saints." The reference seems to be not to the believer's justification by faith, but rather to the work of God in the believer to bring his spiritual state up to the level of his position in Christ (cf. Eph. 5:26). This seems to be the meaning of the unusual phrase "his Bride has made herself ready." Thus the fine linen may, in some sense, be a part of the reward given at the judgment seat of Christ to those who have served Him, here seen collectively as the bride of the Lamb.

THE BLESSEDNESS OF THOSE CALLED
TO THE MARRIAGE SUPPER (19:9–10)

19:9–10 And the angel said to me, "Write this: Blessed are those who are invited to the marriage supper of the Lamb." And he said to me, "These are the true words of God." Then I fell down at his feet to worship him, but he said to me, "You must not do that! I am a fellow servant with you and your brothers who hold to the testimony of Jesus. Worship God." For the testimony of Jesus is the spirit of prophecy.

Here is the fourth beatitude in Revelation, this time announcing the blessedness of those who are invited to the marriage supper of the Lamb. In this verse, as in verses 7–8, the wife is distinguished from the attendants at the wedding, the wife apparently being the church, and the attendants at the wedding the saints of past and future ages. The unfounded notion that God treats all saints of all ages exactly alike is not a biblical concept. The fact that the divine purpose is not the same for Israel, the Gentile believers, or the church of the present age is plainly written in the Word of God. Each has its peculiar advantages and particular place in the divine program. Just as no two individuals have exactly the same destiny, so no two nations or groups in God's program are treated exactly alike. In all these relationships God is completely sovereign, righteous, and wise.

The angel speaking in verse 9 is apparently the same one who on other occasions has informed John that he should write (cf. 14:13, but contrast 21:5 where the command is from God). So awesome is the revelation that, according to verse 10, John falls at the feet of the angel in an attitude of worship. Such a reaction, however, is not appropriate for an angel, and John is rebuked with the statement that the one speaking is "a fellow servant with you and your brothers who hold to the testimony of Jesus." The word for "fellow servant" (Gk., *sundoulos*) could be translated "fellow slave." The NET Bible notes that "[t]he lowliness of a slave is emphasized in the Greek text with the emphatic position of *sundoulos*.[6] It is significant that not only people who are redeemed are slaves of Jesus Christ, but even the angels have a similar obligation of implicit obedience to Him. Together they form the body that bears testimony to Jesus. The command, "Worship God," means that God alone should be worshiped.

The concluding phrase of verse 10, "The testimony of Jesus is the spirit of prophecy," means that prophecy at its very heart is designed to unfold the beauty and loveliness of our Lord and Savior, Jesus Christ. In the present age, therefore, the Spirit of God is not only to glorify Christ but to show believers things to come as they relate to His person and majesty (cf. John 16:13–15). Christ is not only the major theme of the Scriptures but also the central theme of prophecy. The phrase is an apt introduction to Christ's second coming in glory to the earth (v. 11). In keeping with the subject of the book itself, "the revelation of Jesus Christ" (1:1), all that precedes Revelation 19:11 is in some sense introductory, and that which follows is an epilogue.

The revelation of Christ is in contrast to the Christ of the Gospels, where

He is revealed in rejection, humiliation, suffering, and death. His return is to be one of triumph, glory, sovereignty, and majesty. This is anticipated in the judgment upon Babylon in chapters 17 and 18, and in the dramatic introduction of the second coming in 19:1–10. In many respects, Christ's second coming is not only the high point of Revelation, but the high point of all history. Here is the manifestation of the Son of God in glory, the demonstration of the sovereignty of God, and the beginning of the end of human rebellion. How poverty-stricken is any theology that minimizes the second coming of Christ, and how limited the hope that does not include this glorious climax to God's program of exalting His Son and putting all creation under His control (cf. Ps. 2).

THE REVELATION OF
THE KING OF KINGS (19:11–13)

19:11–13 Then I saw heaven opened, and behold, a white horse! The one sitting on it is called Faithful and True, and in righteousness he judges and makes war. His eyes are like a flame of fire, and on his head are many diadems, and he has a name written that no one knows but himself. He is clothed in a robe dipped in blood, and the name by which he is called is The Word of God.

For the second time in Revelation, John sees heaven open. As MacArthur observes, "Heaven opens this time not to let John in, but to let Jesus out."[7] This passage contains one of the most graphic pictures of the second coming of Christ to be found anywhere in Scripture. Even a casual study should make evident the remarkable contrast between this event and the rapture of the church. At the rapture, Christ meets His own in the air, and there is no evidence of immediate judgment upon the earth. By contrast, Christ here is coming to the earth with the specific purpose of bringing divine judgment and establishing His righteous rule.

Many Scriptures in both the Old and New Testaments anticipate this scene. Zechariah 14:3–4 revealed the event in these words:

> Then the Lord will go out and fight against those nations as when he fights on a day of battle. On that day his feet shall stand on the Mount of Olives that lies before Jerusalem on the east, and the Mount of Olives shall be split in two from east to west by a very wide valley, so that one half of the Mount shall move northward, and the other half southward.

According to Zechariah, when Christ returns He will come to the Mount of Olives, the point from which He ascended into heaven in Acts 1. His return will be dramatic, with the mountain splitting in half in evidence of His power and authority. The Mount of Olives today has two high points, and what seems to be a natural division between them will be transformed into a great valley stretching toward the east from Jerusalem and extending down to Jericho at the Jordan River. No such event will take place at the rapture of the church.

The second coming of Christ is also described in Matthew 24:27–31.

> "For as the lightning comes from the east and shines as far as the west, so will be the coming of the Son of Man. Wherever the corpse is, there the vultures will gather. Immediately after the tribulation of those days the sun will be darkened, and the moon will not give its light, and the stars will fall from heaven, and the powers of the heavens will be shaken. Then will appear in heaven the sign of the Son of Man, and then all the tribes of the earth will mourn, and they will see the Son of Man coming on the clouds of heaven with power and great glory. And he will send out his angels with a loud trumpet call, and they will gather his elect from the four winds, from one end of heaven to the other."

The Bible makes it clear that Christ's second coming will be a glorious event that all the world will see, both believers and unbelievers. It is compared to lightning that shines from the east to the west, in other words, illuminating the whole heaven. The second coming will be preceded by phenomena in the heavens that Jesus mentioned in Matthew 24 and that are vividly revealed in Revelation. The climax to all these events will be the return of Christ Himself in the clouds of heaven with power and great glory and accompanied by the saints. The final revelation of this event is found in these verses.

In John's vision he sees a person who can be no other than the Lord Jesus Christ on a white horse. In contrast to the pseudo ruler of the world (6:2), Christ is presented here as the true ruler. The plea of Isaiah as recorded in 64:1–2 is now fulfilled:

> Oh that you would rend the heavens and come down, that the mountains might quake at your presence—as when fire kindles brushwood and the fire causes water to boil—to make your name known to your adversaries, and that the nations might tremble at your presence!

Added to the drama of heaven opening is the symbolism of a rider on a white horse, drawn from the custom of conquerors riding on a white horse as a sign of victory or triumph. The rider on the white horse in Revelation 6 is described as one who "came out conquering, and to conquer." Now the true King of kings and Lord of lords is going to triumph over those who blasphemously assumed control over the world. The titles given here to Christ are in keeping with the divine judgment that follows. He is declared to be faithful and true, and to judge and make war in righteousness. This is to be the demonstration of the sovereignty and righteousness of God even as Christ in His first coming demonstrated grace and truth. The titles here ascribed to Christ are previously given in Revelation 1:5 and 3:7, and were anticipated in the prophecies of Isaiah 11:3–4. His title as "Faithful and True" is particularly sweet to believers, for it reminds us that God is faithful to His promises and will vindicate the faith of all who trust in Him.[8]

These attributes are demonstrated in the appearance of Christ as described in the following verses. In verse 12, His eyes are as a flame of fire, a term previously used to describe Christ in 1:14 and 2:18. This speaks of His righteous judgment upon sin. His head is crowned with many crowns, or diadems, the symbol of sovereignty. He possesses a name that no one knows, as yet unrevealed. His robe is "dipped in blood," as if anticipating the bloodshed to come (cf. Isa. 63:2–3; Rev. 14:20). Christ as the slain Lamb in Revelation speaks of redemption by blood; here blood represents divine judgment upon evil people. The name given to Christ in verse 13 is "The Word of God," who according to John 1:1–3 is the Creator of all. He is also the judge of all.

THE COMING OF THE KING OF KINGS (19:14–16)

19:14–16 And the armies of heaven, arrayed in fine linen, white and pure, were following him on white horses. From his mouth comes a sharp sword with which to strike down the nations, and he will rule them with a rod of iron. He will tread the winepress of the fury of the wrath of God the Almighty. On his robe and on his thigh he has a name written, King of kings and Lord of lords.

Accompanying Christ on His second coming are those described as "the armies of heaven." Some expositors limit this army to the church, the Bride of Christ, on the basis that it is described as clothed in fine linen, white and clean. There is, however, no reason to limit this to the church, though the church is arrayed in fine linen. The church is not alone in having righteousness in the form of righteous deeds, and it is more probable that here not only the saints but also the holy angels are meant.[9] It is well not to impose limitations upon a Scripture text that are not implicit in the text itself. This scene is a demonstration that now at long last the filthy, blasphemous situation on earth is going to be wiped clean with a divine judgment of tremendous character.

A further description is given of Christ, adding to the picture of divine judgment. Out of His mouth goes a sharp sword, which according to the text will be used to smite the nations and bring them under His rule. The word for "sword" indicates one unusually large and longer than most swords. The same word is sometimes used to describe a javelin, a sword sufficiently light and long to be thrown as a spear. Here the word is used symbolically to represent a sharp instrument of war with which Christ will strike the nations and establish His absolute rule. The expression of ruling "with a rod of iron" is also found in Psalm 2:9 and Revelation 2:27, with a similar expression, "the rod of his mouth," in Isaiah 11:4. It represents unyielding, absolute government under which everyone is required to conform to the righteous standards of God.

The picture of divine judgment as the treading of a winepress also appears in 14:19–20 and is anticipated in Isaiah 63:1–6. All of these passages point to the sad conclusion that in the day of judgment it is too late for anyone to expect the mercy of God. There is nothing more inflexible than divine judgment where grace has been spurned. The scene of awful judgment that comes from this background is in flat contradiction of the modern idea that God is dominated entirely by His attribute of love.

Finally, Christ wears the title "King of kings and Lord of lords." Here at last has come One who has a right to rule the earth, whose power and majesty will demonstrate His authority as He brings to bear His sovereign judgment on a wicked world. It is in anticipation of this ultimate triumph that God the Father holds the nations of the world in derision in their rebellion against the Lord's Anointed (Ps. 2:1–4). God will indeed break the nations with a rod of iron and dash them in pieces and give the uttermost parts of the earth to His Son as His rightful possession. In view of this consummation, how pertinent is the invitation of Psalm 2:10–12 to serve the Lord and kiss the Son while there is yet time to claim the blessing of those who put their trust in Him.

THE BATTLE OF THE GREAT
DAY OF GOD ALMIGHTY (19:17–19)

19:17–19 Then I saw an angel standing in the sun, and with a loud voice he called to all the birds that fly directly overhead,

291

"Come, gather for the great supper of God, to eat the flesh of
kings, the flesh of captains, the flesh of mighty men, the flesh of
horses and their riders, and the flesh of all men, both free and
slave, both small and great." And I saw the beast and the kings of
the earth with their armies gathered to make war against him who
was sitting on the horse and against his army.

John now sees an angel standing in the light of the sun, with the angel
himself possibly shining with even greater brilliance. The angel cries with a
loud voice, signifying that something important is about to happen (cf. 6:10;
7:2, 10; 10:3; 14:15; 18:2). The angel's message is addressed to the birds flying
overhead, inviting them to the supper of God. The contrast to this is found
in 19:9, where the saints other than the church are invited to the marriage
supper of the Lamb. The same word is used for both verses, but the events are
in sharp contrast. The birds are invited to eat the flesh of those killed in the
battle, the army of the beast—people of all classes and even their horses. The
divine judgment upon evil is no respecter of persons or station, and is the
great equalizer of all.

There is an evident parallel in this passage to the prediction of Ezekiel
39:17–20 as far as the description is concerned. However, the Ezekiel passage
seems to refer to an earlier battle, when the army from the North invaded
Israel, whereas in this battle God is contending with the armies of the entire
world. The resultant destruction of human flesh and its consumption by
birds are similar. The actual parallel to the scene in Revelation is found in
Matthew 24:28, where reference is made to the carcasses of those who fall in
battle and the gathering of the birds to eat them. Care must be exercised in
interpreting passages so similar by following the rule that similarities do not
necessarily prove identity. Birds of prey are always in evidence where there is
death.

The destruction of the beast's armies is the prelude to the destruction of
the beast himself and his associates. John in his vision sees not only the carnage but also the beast, referring to the world ruler, and those gathered with
him to make war against Christ and His army from heaven. The beast is to

be identified with the one of Revelation 13:1–10, and the kings with the ten kings immediately associated with the beast as well as others who participate in this final battle. There is evidence that a struggle is going on between the various segments of the world empire at the time of Christ's second coming; but with the appearance of the Lord in glory and His armies, these armies of earth forget their differences and join in battle against the King of kings and Lord of lords.

Evans draws a strong lesson from this scene: "If you refuse to repent, you will fall into the hands of the living God—and that, as the Bible says, is 'a terrifying thing' (Hebrews 10:31)."[10]

THE DOOM OF THE BEAST
AND THE FALSE PROPHET (19:20)

19:20 And the beast was captured, and with it the false prophet who in its presence had done the signs by which he deceived those who had received the mark of the beast and those who worshiped its image. These two were thrown alive into the lake of fire that burns with sulfur.

Utterly defeated, the world ruler is taken, and with him the false prophet, the second beast of Revelation 13:11–16. They are "thrown alive" into the lake of fire burning with sulfur. By comparison with other Scriptures, it seems that the beast and the false prophet are the first to inhabit the lake, which is eternal hell itself. Unsaved people who die prior to this time are cast into Hades, a place of torment, but not into the lake of fire, which is reserved for those who have been finally judged as unworthy of eternal life in God's presence.

These who were Satan's masterpieces precede Satan himself to this final place of everlasting punishment into which he is thrown a thousand years later (20:10). The rest of the evil dead, after being judged at the great white throne, will follow the beast, the false prophet, and the devil into this eternal doom.

THE DOOM OF THE
ARMY OF THE BEAST (19:21)

19:21 And the rest were slain by the sword that came from the mouth of him who was sitting on the horse, and all the birds were gorged with their flesh.

Those not killed in the first stage of the battle are now put to death. It seems that the entire army of the beast is killed. These who are killed are specifically said to be killed by the sword that came from Christ's mouth. This act of judgment seems to be exercised by the immediate power of Christ rather than by the armies that accompany Him. The slaughter is so great that the birds are able to gorge on the flesh of the dead.

The Word of God makes plain that God so loved the world that He gave His Son, and that all who avail themselves of the grace of God are immeasurably blessed in time and eternity. On the other hand, the same Word of God states plainly that those who spurn God's mercy must experience His judgment without mercy. How foolish it is to rest in the portions of the Word of God that speak of the love of God and reject the portions that deal with His righteous judgment. The present age reveals the grace of God and suspended judgment. The age to come, while continuing to be a revelation of the grace of God, will give conclusive evidence that God brings every evil work into judgment and that those who spurn His grace must experience His wrath.

NOTES

1. John MacArthur, *The MacArthur New Testament Commentary: Revelation 12–22* (Chicago: Moody, 2000), 197.

2. Luther Poellot, *Revelation* (St. Louis: Concordia Publishing House, 1962). 240.

3. Michael H. Burer, W. Hall Harris III, and Daniel B. Wallace, eds., *New English Translation: Novum Testamentum Graece* (Dallas: NET Bible Press, 2003), 671.

4. F. F. Bruce, *New International Bible Commentary*, F. F. Bruce, gen. ed. (Grand Rapids: Zondervan, 1979), 1623.

5. Paul Benware, *Understanding End Times Prophecy* (Chicago: Moody, 2006), 233.

6. Burer, Harris, and Wallace, *New English Translation*, 672.

7. MacArthur, *Revelation 12–22*, 214.

8. Robert H. Mounce, *The Book of Revelation*, The New International Commentary on the New Testament (Grand Rapids: Eerdmans, 1997), 352.

9. It should be noted that a number of expositors rule out angels as part of this army. For this argument, see Robert L. Thomas, *Revelation 8–22: An Exegetical Commentary* (Chicago: Moody, 1995), 388; Alan F. Johnson, *Revelation*, The Expositor's Bible Commentary, Frank E. Gaebelein, ed., vol. 12 (Grand Rapids: Zondervan, 1981), 575; and MacArthur, *The MacArthur New Testament Commentary: Revelation 12–22* (Chicago: Moody, 2000), 218–19.

10. Tony Evans, *The Best Is Yet to Come* (Chicago: Moody, 2000), 209.

20 The Reign of Christ

This is one of the great chapters of the Bible. It presents in summary the tremendous series of events that relate to the millennial reign of Christ on earth. In this future period of a thousand years, many expositors believe that hundreds of Old Testament prophecies will be fulfilled, such as Jeremiah 23:5–6:

> "Behold, the days are coming, declares the LORD, when I will raise for David a righteous Branch, and he shall reign as king and deal wisely, and shall execute justice and righteousness in the land. In his days Judah will be saved, and Israel will dwell securely. And this is his name by which he will be called: 'The Lord is our righteousness.'"

However, an often bewildering array of interpretations has been set forth concerning the teaching of the millennium in Revelation 20. Smith calls 20:1–6 "one of the most debated passages in the Word of God."[1] Generally speaking, major views of the millennium fall into three categories, which must be understood in order to arrive at a proper interpretation of this chapter. These are (1) the literal and premillennial interpretation, which this exposition reflects, that the thousand-year reign of Christ in the earth is a literal period of time preceded and followed by resurrection and judgment. Smith also notes that "the early church was unanimous in holding this view"[2]; (2) the amillennial view which, as the name suggests, denies the literal nature of an earthly millennial kingdom over which Christ reigns for a thousand years; and (3) the postmillennial view, which basically states that Christ will return at the end of the millennium, seen as a "golden age" of ever-increasing righteousness and victory for the church. In this view, Christ's triumphant return is the capstone to this glorious period.

These divisions of thought arise from differing interpretations of the thousand years spoken of here in Revelation 20. All premillennial interpreters consider the second advent of Christ as preceding His thousand-year reign on the earth. They differ, however, in their interpretation of preceding passages in Revelation as well as in their concept of the millennium itself.

Premillennial interpretation. Johnson notes that one view held by some premillenarians is called the "end-historical" view, which he says is the early church's basic view and which he summarizes in this way: "Parousia—defeat of Antichrist—binding of Satan—resurrection—Millennium—release of Satan—final judgment—new heavens and earth."[3]

Another form of premillennialism emphasizes the soteriological character of the millennium. This point of view is usually advocated by covenant theologians who are premillennial. The millennium is considered by them as primarily an aspect of God's soteriological program, and the political character of the kingdom and the prominence of the nation Israel are subordinated. For this reason, some attempt a synthesis of the amillennial and premillennial points of view by finding some prophecies relating to the future kingdom as being fulfilled in the present age.

The most popular form of premillennialism is supported by premillenarians who consider the millennium an aspect of God's theocratic program, a fulfillment of the promise given to David that his kingdom and throne would continue forever over the house of Israel. Advocates of this view believe that the millennium is a period in which Christ will literally reign on earth as its supreme political leader. Also, the many promises of the Old Testament relating to a kingdom on earth in which Israel will be prominent and Gentiles will be blessed will have complete and literal fulfillment. Because the distinctive character of Christ's millennial reign is maintained in contrast to the present age, this view is sometimes designated as the *dispensational* interpretation. These interpreters consider all material from 4:1 as future, and are often called futurists. (See exposition at 4:1.)

Amillennial interpretation. This is essentially a denial that there will be a thousand-year reign of Christ on earth after His second advent. There are a great variety of amillennial interpretations, and adherents of this view also form several subdivisions.

(1) The historic Augustinian form of amillennialism is based on Augustine's work *The City of God*. In his discussion of the millennium, Augustine advanced the theory that the thousand years are a reference to the period between the first and second advents of Christ—that is, the church age. As MacArthur points out, Augustine's position as the pre-eminent theologian of the early church ensured that amillennialism would dominate the church for centuries.[4] Because this denied a future millennium after the second advent, Augustine's interpretation has in modern times been called amillennial.

Augustine was an advocate of the view, common in his day, that human history would be completed in six thousand years. Unlike some early premillenarians who held the same point of view but believed that the millennium would be the seventh millennium of history, Augustine felt that the seventh millennium was the eternal state. Because Augustine also believed that the six millennia of history began several centuries before Christ, he considered that the final millennium was well along at the time of his writing in the fifth century A.D. Augustine tended to interpret the thousand years as literal, but he was not emphatic on this point and left the question somewhat open. Augustinian amillennialism is very important because most schools of thought that oppose premillennialism are derived in some measure from Augustinian theology. Many modern scholars hold with some minor variations to Augustinian amillennialism.

Buis, an amillenarian belonging to the preterist school of interpretation, believes that the thousand years describe the period between the first and second advents of Christ. His reasons for holding this position are typical of the amillennial position:

1. No other passage of Scripture mentions such a thousand-year period. Obscure passages are to be interpreted in the light of less obscure passages, and not vice versa. 2. The entire book [of Revelation] is one filled with symbolism; therefore any doctrine based on insisting upon a literal

thousand-year period is building on a weak foundation. 3. The amillennial position agrees most fully with the interpretation that the primary application of the beast was the Roman Empire. 4. The creeds of the church such as the Apostles' Creed make no mention of such a literal period between this age and the eternal kingdom. The greatest Bible scholars of all times, the Reformers, were not premillenarian.[5]

Premillenarians have objected to these types of arguments as being inconclusive. The six mentions of "a thousand years" in Revelation 20 are sufficient to establish the doctrine as scriptural. Amillennarians base much of their position on the argument that numbers in Revelation, such as the thousand years, are symbolic and thus not to be understood literally. Thomas ably refutes this presupposition,[6] and MacArthur adds, "It is highly doubtful that any symbolic number would be repeated six times in a text, as a thousand is here."[7] Hoehner notes, "Whenever the number one thousand is used in Revelation, it refers to something definite."[7] Examples are the 144,000 (Rev. 4:7; 14:1, 3); the 1,260 days (Rev. 11:3; 12:6); the 1,600 stadia (Rev. 14:20); and the 12,000 stadia (Rev. 21:16).

A THREE-FOLD CASE FOR PREMILLENNIALISM

1. **Chronology:** "And I saw" or "Then I saw" used repeatedly throughout Revelation.

2. **Context:** The repeated use of 1,000 in Revelation 20 (six times), whereas indefinite terms for time and other measurements are used in other places in the same chapter: "little while" (v. 3), a number "like the sand of the sea" (v. 8).

3. **Church History:** Papias, Justin Martyr, Irenaeus, Victorinus, and other early church fathers held a literal view of the thousand years (called "chialism" in their time, from the Greek word for "thousand"). This view prevailed for the first three hundred years of the church.

Hoehner also asks the question, "If Satan is released for a short time [Rev. 20:3], why didn't John say 'a long time' [in reference to the millennium]? John uses in the same verse definite terms for definite periods of time and indefinite terms for indefinite periods of time. There, the one thousand years have to be taken literally."[8]

(2) A modified Augustinian interpretation of the millennium is probably the most popular amillennial viewpoint today. Like Augustine, these expositors believe that Revelation 20 parallels the earlier chapters of the book of Revelation. Unlike Augustine, however, they believe the millennium refers to the saints reigning in heaven with Christ, and they do not attempt to make the thousand years a literal period. As this was made impossible after A.D. 1000 had come to pass, their "millennium" accordingly runs from the death of Christ to His second coming. The binding of Satan is considered to be partial, consisting in Christ's triumph over him, first in His temptations and later in every triumph that stems from Christ. The first resurrection occurs when the Christian's soul is taken from earth to heaven at death. The second resurrection relates to the resurrection of all people.

Still another variation within amillennialism is a form of preterist interpretation. It is advanced by H. B. Swete in his older work, *The Apocalypse of Saint John*, in which he argues that the millennium started with the triumph of Christianity at the time of Constantine when Christianity began to be a major force in opposing paganism. This view combines various views of amillennialism, premillennialism, and postmillennialism. Like the amillennialists, these interpreters view the millennium as being in the present age and of indeterminate length, following Augustine. Like postmillennialism, this approach is optimistic in viewing the church as moving triumphantly to victory. Like premillennialism, it recognizes the continuity of chapters 19 and 20 of Revelation in that the binding of Satan, the first resurrection, and the thousand years are chronologically subsequent to chapter 19. This and other forms of amillennialism also recognize that the destruction of the beast is the downfall of Rome as a pagan power.

One major flaw of amillennialism is its failure to recognize that when the Bible speaks of "a thousand years" as in Psalm 90:4, a literal thousand years is meant. A thousand years with us is only a moment with God, but this does not deny that it is actually a thousand years with us. Again, when 2 Peter 3:8 states that one day is with the Lord as a thousand years, the meaning is clear that one day with God is as a literal thousand years with mankind.[9] When the verse goes on to say a thousand years are as one day, it is speaking of a literal thousand years. In none of these references is the literalness of a thousand years questioned.

Some consider the millennial teaching of Revelation 20 a complete enigma and are therefore amillennial to the extreme. The amillennial scholar William Hendriksen summarizes this position by stating, "It is clear that the theory of the premillennialists is at variance with the facts [in Revelation 20]."[10]

Postmillennialism. From the standpoint of church history, postmillennialism has to be considered a relatively recent view. Its adherents regard the thousand-year reign of Christ as being completed prior to His second coming. It is very similar to amillennial interpretations in that it views the millennium as the final triumph of the gospel in the present age. MacArthur summarizes the view well: "Postmillennialism teaches that before [Christ's] return will come the best period in history, so that Christ will return at the end of a long golden age of peace and harmony."[11] These interpreters see the gospel as achieving greater and greater triumph until Christ returns.

With the twentieth century now behind us, it is hard to imagine that the world is becoming a better and brighter place, with the gospel triumphing more and more. Two world wars dashed a lot of the optimism of earlier postmillennialists, and we can safely say that little has happened in the secular world in the decades since to lead serious Bible students to believe we are in a golden age of Christian ascendancy and triumph. On the contrary, the witness of Scripture is, "In the last days there will come times of difficulty" (2 Tim. 3:1).

With the great variety of interpretations of Revelation 20 and their corresponding influence on eschatology, the task of giving an exposition of this chapter is greatly complicated. The confusion of so many interpretations, however, is dispelled if the events of this chapter are allowed to follow in their natural chronological sequence, with the return of Christ and the conquest of the beast and the false prophet serving as the introduction to the millennium. The opening events of the twentieth chapter then become a natural outgrowth of the battle in which the beast and the false prophet and his armies are destroyed, leading to the next step, the judgment of Satan himself. The repeated phrases "Then I saw" or "And I saw" (cf. 19:11, 17, 19; 20:1, 4, 11, 12) mark the major steps of the progress of the revelation.

The sequence of events is supported not only by the chronological order itself (note the "when" of 20:7) but by the logical dependence of one event upon the preceding event. This is strong evidence for chronological order in this section, and if this is granted, the millennial kingdom follows the second coming as described in 19:11–16. The only reason for denying such a conclusion would be to avoid premillennialism. There is no evidence in the passage at all that would cause us to question that from 19:1 to 21:8 a strict chronological order is observed. Chapters 19 and 20 constitute a unit and form one continued prophetic strain.

THE BINDING OF SATAN (20:1–3)

20:1–3 Then I saw an angel coming down from heaven, holding in his hand the key to the bottomless pit and a great chain. And he seized the dragon, that ancient serpent, who is the devil and Satan, and bound him for a thousand years, and threw him into the pit, and shut it and sealed it over him, so that he might not deceive the nations any longer, until the thousand years were ended. After that he must be released for a little while.

The next phase of God's prophetic program is introduced by another vision of an angel (cf. 7:2; 10:1; 14:6, 8, 9, 15, 17, 18; 17:1; 18:1; 19:17). This angel possesses the key of "the bottomless pit," (cf. 9:1, 2, 11; also "the abyss," Luke 8:31; Rom. 10:7), the home of demons and unclean spirits. The angel is also seen with a great chain in his hands with which to bind Satan for a thousand years. A seal is also placed on the pit, making it impossible for Satan to deceive until the thousand years have elapsed.

Although the dramatic prophecy of these three verses has been the subject of endless dispute, as noted above, the passage yields to patient exegesis, and there is no solid reason for taking it in other than its ordinary sense. According to the prediction, the angel is empowered for six functions: (1) to lay hold of the dragon; (2) to bind him for a thousand years; (3) to throw him into the bottomless pit; (4) to shut him up, that is, to use the key that will lock up the pit; (5) to seal the pit to render Satan inactive in his work; and (6) to release him after the thousand years. At every point, however, the prediction has been disputed.

As noted earlier, many Bible interpreters over the centuries have identified the binding of Satan as the work of Christ in believers' lives. In this sense, Satan is "bound" for believers but "released" to deceive unbelievers. But as Johnson points out, this does not account for the severity of the language in these verses concerning Satan's binding, nor does it account for his release at the end of the thousand years.[12]

The word *chain* used here is the same as in Mark 5:3 of the demon-possessed man who had been bound with chains. It is also used for the chains that fell off Peter (Acts 12:7) and for Paul's chains (Acts 28:20; 2 Tim. 1:16). Different words, however, are used in 2 Peter 2:4 referring to the chains of darkness binding the wicked angel and for the everlasting chains of Jude 6. These are more general terms for being bound. The four instances in Scripture of the word for "chain" in Revelation 20:1 give no reason for interpreting the word in other than its ordinary sense.

Whatever the physical character of the chain, the obvious teaching of the passage is that Satan is not merely restricted, but rendered completely inactive. The bottomless pit by its character is a place of confinement. If God wanted to show that Satan was totally inactive and out of touch with the world, how could He have rendered it more specifically than He has done in this passage? The fact that Satan is bound for a thousand years is confirmed by the multitude of passages dealing with the kingdom period in which Satan is never found working in the world.

Of major importance, of course, is whether this scene refers to the future millennium or to the present age, as is taught by amillenarians. If the millennium is the present age between Christ's first and second advents, then Satan must be bound now. But there are few theories of Scripture that are less warranted than the idea that Satan was bound at the first coming of Christ. Amillenarians often refer to Luke 10:18, as does Augustine, where Christ said to the seventy witnesses returning in triumph from their period of witness and miracles, "I saw Satan fall like lightning from heaven." From this it has been inferred that Satan's fall occurred at Christ's first coming.

However, the New Testament consistently teaches that Satan is very active today. If anything, he is more active than in preceding ages and continues in unrelenting opposition to all that God purposes to do in the present age. In Luke 22:3, Satan entered into Judas with the result that Judas went out to betray Christ. Satan also attempted to dominate Peter as recorded in the Lord's saying in Luke 22:31: "Simon, Simon, behold, Satan demanded to have you, that he might sift you like wheat." It was only the prayer of Jesus, not Satan's binding, that prevented Peter's defeat.

Throughout the rest of the New Testament, similar references are found. In Acts 5:3, Ananias and Sapphira are said to be filled with Satan and motivated to lie to the Holy Spirit regarding the extent of their gift to the church. In 2 Corinthians 4:3–4, Paul records that Satan is active in blinding the minds of those who hear the gospel. In 2 Corinthians 11:14, Satan is declared to be transformed into an angel of light, thereby deceiving the church through false teachers. The unsaved, according to Ephesians 2:2, live "following the course of this world, following the prince of the power of the air, the spirit that is now at work in the sons of disobedience." Paul writes in 1 Thessalonians 2:18 that Satan had hindered his coming to them. More dramatically, in 2 Timothy 2:26, unsaved people are said to be taken captive by the devil at his will and are rescued only by the grace of God.

The capstone of these references to the activity of Satan is found in 1 Peter 5:8, which should settle the matter beyond dispute. In this passage Christians are told, "Be sober-minded; be watchful. Your adversary the devil prowls around like a roaring lion, seeking someone to devour." Instead of being bound, Satan is like a lion on the loose, seeking prey to devour. That Satan is hindered by the protective power of God is evident throughout the

Scriptures, as in the case of Job. There is no evidence whatever that Satan is bound today, but rather the mounting evil in the world and in the church seems to demonstrate that he is more active than ever. The nations are being deceived today and saints are being opposed by the ceaseless activity and deceptive power of Satan.

Much has been made of the fact that these verses are found in a book largely given to symbolic presentation and visions. It is true that John is seeing a vision in these early verses of chapter 20. The passage reveals, however, something more than what he saw. John visually saw the angel bind Satan and cast him into the pit. But John could not see how long Satan was to be bound, or the purpose of the binding. This was given to John by divine revelation that constituted the interpretation of the vision. Therefore, with the vision recorded as it is, accompanied by the divine interpretation, expositors are not free to inject their own preconceived ideas but must accept the plain statements and interpretations of the passage as given. They must accept the interpretation in its ordinary and literal meaning.

If this is done, there is no other alternative than the premillennial interpretation that holds that at the second coming of Christ, Satan will be bound for a thousand years.[13] This will constitute one of the major features of Christ's righteous rule upon the earth and in fact will make possible the peace and tranquility and absence of spiritual warfare predicted for the millennial kingdom. The period before Satan is bound, which is the great tribulation, and the period at the close of the millennium, when Satan is again loosed, stand in sharp contrast to the tranquility of the thousand years in between. The fact is that the only period in all human history in which Satan will not execute his work of deception will be the thousand years in which Christ will reign.

This passage introduces, for the first time in Scripture, the exact length of Christ's earthly kingdom. Six times in this passage the fact is stated that the period is a thousand years or a millennium.

As discussed above, much of the opposition to the futurist interpretation has been leveled at this concept of a literal thousand years. Some amillennial scholars argue that it is obvious that the thousand years should be interpreted nonliterally, based on the argument that Revelation is apocalyptic literature. But Benware demonstrates that the vast majority of the numbers used in the book of Revelation are to interpreted in the normal way, meaning as expressions of a quantity.[14]

In addition, while Scripture sometimes uses the term "day" in other than a literal sense, never in the Bible is "month" or "year" used in other than its literal sense. Even the word *day*, used for a period of time in reference to "the day of the Lord," is used literally throughout the book of Revelation. It may also be faithfully held that all numbers in the Revelation are literal. Certainly there is nothing inherently impossible in a thousand-year period in which Christ will reign upon the earth. So it must be stated again that there is no good exegetical reason for taking the thousand years of Revelation 20 in other than their literal sense.

THE JUDGMENT AND RESURRECTION
OF TRIBULATION SAINTS (20:4)

20:4 Then I saw thrones, and seated on them were those to whom the authority to judge was committed. Also I saw the souls of those who had been beheaded for the testimony of Jesus and for the word of God, and who had not worshiped the beast or its image and had not received its mark on their foreheads or their hands. They came to life and reigned with Christ for a thousand years.

The interpretation of verse 4 is complicated by a lack of specificity. John refers to the ones sitting on the thrones as "those" (the subject being supplied by the translator as implied in the third person plural of the verb). Who are these sitting on thrones, and what is meant by the judgment given to them? One possibility is that the subject of the verb "seated" includes Christ and all the saints related to Him, including both the church and Israel. Possible confirmation of this is found in 22:5 where the servants of the Lord are said to reign with Christ.

The most probable interpretation is that they are the twenty-four elders who are said to reign on earth (5:10). This correlates with Christ's prophecy recorded in Luke 22:29–30: "And I assign to you, as my Father assigned to me, a kingdom, that you may eat and drink at my table in my kingdom and sit on thrones judging the twelve tribes of Israel." These words addressed to the twelve disciples indicate that they will share with Christ in His rule over the world and especially will judge Israel at the beginning of the kingdom. Inasmuch as the twelve apostles are members of the church, the Body of Christ, they represent the church as such. A parallel passage is found in Matthew 19:28.

The judgment here predicted may be considered as general, involving several phases of divine judgment at this stage in world history. According to Matthew 25:31–46, the nations or the Gentiles will be judged following the return of Christ. In a similar manner, the house of Israel is judged according to Ezekiel 20:33–38. The implication in the latter part of verse 4 is that the tribulation saints resurrected from the dead are also judged and rewarded. If the saints of the Old Testament are also raised at this time, they too may be the objects of divine judgment and reward.

However, the detailed description in verse 4 of those who were resurrected fits only one class of saints, the tribulation saints who in refusing to worship the beast are martyred. Here we learn that they are beheaded, first, for their positive witness for Christ and the Word of God, and second, because they refused to worship the beast and receive his mark. The background of this experience is found in Revelation 13:15–17. Included in the number of tribulation saints are the two witnesses of chapter 11, "the souls of those who had been slain for the word of God and for the witness they had borne" (6:9), and the martyrs referred to in 12:11. The group as a whole is seen in heaven in 7:9–17.

These who were the special objects of Satan's hatred and the beast's persecution are now exalted, rewarded, and blessed by being resurrected and reigning with Christ for a thousand years. The verbs are in the past tense but are obviously prophetic from John's perspective because he is looking at these events from the viewpoint of eternity future as if already accomplished. The expression "came to life" implies that they are resurrected and alive again, similar to the meaning of Christ's statement in John 11:25: "I am the resurrection and the life. Whoever believes in me, though he die, yet shall he live, and everyone who lives and believes in me shall never die." It is the resurrection of life mentioned in John 5:29.

The revelation that the tribulation saints are declared to reign with Christ in His millennial kingdom has troubled some who consider the church as properly reigning with Christ, which implies that saints of other ages will be the subjects of the kingdom. It should be evident from this passage that others will share places of prominent rule with the church as the Body of Christ in His kingdom, as is also revealed in verse 6. There is a sense, of course, in which saints participate in the present spiritual kingdom of God. But the order is that we suffer now and reign in the future (2 Tim. 2:12). Believers are not now reigning with Christ, which would require Christ to be in the present earth in a physical way, participating directly in the government of the world.

Amillenarians who equate the resurrection of verse 4 with a spiritual resurrection or regeneration point out that the verb does not actually mean to be resurrected, but only *to live*. While the word itself is not specific, it is the context that designates it as a bodily resurrection. For example, the resurrection at the end of the millennium is obviously bodily since it includes the unsaved (v. 5). The context therefore invests the word with the necessary content of bodily resurrection. This is confirmed by the fact that the same verb is used of Christ in 1:18, where He states, "I died, and behold I am alive forevermore." The same expression is found also in 2:8. The most important truth introduced in verse 4 is the evident fact that a thousand years separate the resurrection of the martyred dead from the resurrection of the wicked dead. This is borne out in the passage that follows.

THE FIRST RESURRECTION (20:5–6)

20:5–6 The rest of the dead did not come to life until the thousand years were ended. This is the first resurrection. Blessed and holy is the one who shares in the first resurrection! Over such the second death has no power, but they will be priests of God and of Christ, and they will reign with him for a thousand years.

The resurrection at the beginning of the millennium is characterized as "the first resurrection." In what sense can the tribulation saints in their resurrection be labeled "the first resurrection"?

It is obvious that Christ was the first one raised from the dead with a resurrection body as the firstfruits from the dead (1 Cor. 15:20). Matthew records that a number of believers were also resurrected at this time (Matt. 27:52–53). This difficult passage is best explained as an actual resurrection of a token number of believers in keeping with the symbolism of the feast of the firstfruits, when a handful of grain, not just one stalk, was presented to the priest. There is no evidence that the resurrection of Matthew 27 included all the righteous saints up to that time, as Daniel 12:2 seems to place the resurrection of the Old Testament saints immediately after the great tribulation described in Daniel 12:1. In any event, there was a genuine resurrection of some at Christ's resurrection.

The familiar New Testament word for "resurrection" is used in verses 5–6, occurring about forty times in the New Testament. This word is almost always used of bodily resurrection. The only exception seems to be in Luke 2:34. The fact that practically all instances of this word refer to physical resurrection makes it improbable that it means here what amillenarians frequently interpret it to mean, a spiritual resurrection or regeneration. It is just as unnatural to deny that it means bodily resurrection here as in the case of Christ's own resurrection. So we may conclude that the resurrection referred to as "the first resurrection" is also a bodily resurrection.

At the end of the church age the rapture of the church will take place, and the dead in Christ will be raised. At the end of the great tribulation, the tribulation saints will also be raised from the dead. It would seem clear from these facts that the term "the first resurrection" is not an event but an order of resurrection including all the righteous who are raised from the dead before the millennial kingdom begins. They are "first" in contrast to those who are raised last, after the millennium, when the wicked dead are raised and judged. Just as there are two kinds of physical death, the first death that results in burial, and the second death that is described as being cast into the lake of fire (20:14), so there are two kinds of resurrection, a first resurrection of the righteous and a second resurrection of the evil. They are separated by at least a thousand years. Just as the first death did not occur to all in one moment but is experienced individually by those who die over a long period of time, so the first resurrection is fulfilled according to the groups that are in view.

A further question can be raised concerning the special mention of the martyred dead of the tribulation. In view of the fact that they are publicly humiliated and suffer as no preceding generation of saints has suffered, so God selects them for public triumph at the establishment of His kingdom on the earth.

Those who take part in the first resurrection, regardless of classification, are called "blessed and holy" (v. 6). They are delivered from the power of the second death, given the special status of priests of God and of Christ, and are privileged to reign with Him for the thousand years. As previously indicated in verse 4, the privilege of reigning with Christ is not exclusively the reward of the church, but the righteous in general are given privileged places of service. The classifications of believers is not ignored, but each believer is rewarded according to his individual relationship to the sovereign will of God.

If the church is afforded the special place of being the Bride of Christ and reigning in this sense, other resurrected people will also reign and enjoy privileges and rewards. They will apparently not only share in the political aspects of the kingdom but also in its religious life. They are declared to be "priests of God and of Christ," a designation of a privileged rank similar to that which the church enjoys in this present age under Christ our High Priest. Since this is future in relationship to the martyrs who die in the tribulation and are raised in the second advent, it provides added proof for the premillennial interpretation.

The main burden of this passage, however, is to demonstrate beyond any question that there will be a thousand-year period between the resurrections of the righteous and the evil. Passages such as Daniel 12:2 and John 5:28–29, which refer in general to the resurrection of both the righteous and the unrighteous, must be interpreted as declaring the fact of resurrection rather than that the two events take place at the same time. The significance seems to be that the time will come when both the righteous and the wicked will be raised without designating exactly when it will occur. The main facts of this passage are clear when the general rule is applied that that which is plain should interpret that which is obscure.

In considering Revelation 20:1–6 as a whole, there is much to commend its normal and literal interpretation. In arguing for a literal interpretation of the thousand years, Mounce states, "[There is no] particular reason to suppose that in the mind of John the one thousand years represented a period of time of some other duration."[15]

THE RELEASING OF SATAN
AND THE FINAL REVOLT (20:7–9)

20:7–9 And when the thousand years are ended, Satan will be released from his prison and will come out to deceive the nations that are at the four corners of the earth, Gog and Magog, to gather them for battle; their number is like the sand of the sea. And they marched up over the broad plain of the earth and surrounded the camp of the saints and the beloved city, but fire came down from heaven and consumed them.

Before considering the climax of the thousand years, a brief survey of Scripture bearing upon the millennial kingdom described here will serve to emphasize and justify the literal interpretation of the thousand years. John in his vision occupies himself only with the fact and duration of the millennial kingdom. The character of Christ's reign on earth is fully described in many Old Testament passages such as Psalm 72, Isaiah 2:2–4; 11:4–9, and many others. From these Scriptures it may be seen that Jerusalem will be the capital of the millennial kingdom (Isa. 2:3) and that war will be no more (Isa.

2:4). Isaiah 11 describes the righteous reign of Christ and the peace and tranquility of His kingdom. There will be justice for all, the ungodly will be punished, and even the natural ferocity of animals will be abated. The character and extent of the kingdom are summarized in Isaiah 11:9: "They shall not hurt or destroy in all my holy mountain; for the earth shall be full of the knowledge of the Lord as the waters cover the sea." In the latter portion of Isaiah 11, Israel is revealed to be regathered from the various parts of the earth and brought back to her ancient land, rejoicing in the fulfillment of God's prophetic word.

Psalm 72 gives a similar picture of the righteous reign of Christ, describing righteousness as flourishing and abundance of peace as continuing as long as the moon endures. Christ's dominion is stated to be from sea to sea with all kings bowing down before Him, all nations serving Him, and the earth being filled with the glory of the Lord. Then will be fulfilled the desire of the nations for peace and righteousness, for the knowledge of the Lord, for economic justice, and for deliverance from satanic oppression and evil. For the whole period of a thousand years the earth will revel in the immediate presence of the Lord and His perfect divine government. Israel will be exalted and Gentiles also will be blessed. The major factors of the millennium, therefore, include a perfect and righteous government with Christ reigning in absolute power over the entire earth. Every nation will be under His sway, and God's purpose in originally placing man in charge of the Garden of Eden will have its ultimate fulfillment in the Last Adam, the Lord Jesus Christ, who will reign over the earth.

The prominence of Israel in the millennial scene is evidenced in many Old Testament passages. After the purging experience of the great tribulation, those who survive become the citizens of the kingdom after the rebels are purged out (Ezek. 20:34–38). Israel is then rejoined to God in the symbol of marriage, being transformed from an unfaithful wife to one who reciprocates the love of Yahweh. Gentiles who share in the kingdom blessings have unparalleled spiritual and economic benefits, and the thousand-year reign of Christ is a time of joy, peace, and blessing for the entire earth. Though problems in understanding this period persist due to the fact that there is not a complete revelation on all details, the major facts are sufficiently clear for anyone who is willing to accept the authority and accuracy of Scripture and interpret language in its ordinary sense.

John passes quickly over all these details as if it is unnecessary to repeat them at this point and takes us directly to the conclusion of the millennial kingdom when Satan again is released from his prison. The word "ended" means "brought to the goal or the end," thus "finished." The same word is used in verses 3 and 5.

On being relieved from his confinement, Satan loses no time in resuming his evil activities and plunges into his campaign to deceive the nations of the entire earth. These who are tempted are the descendants of the tribulation saints who survive the tribulation and enter the millennium in their natural bodies. Undoubtedly the earth is teeming with inhabitants at the conclusion of the millennium, and yet despite the personal rule of Christ and a perfect moral society, there will be those who choose to rebel against the Lord. We must remember that unlike the resurrected believers who go into the kingdom, those born during this time will still have their sinful Adamic nature and need salvation.[16] Due to their inexperience of real temptation, they are easy victims of Satan's wiles.

The release of Satan serves to reveal once more his "incurable bent toward evil."[17] It also reveals the incurable evil of the human heart that does not experience the saving grace of Christ. And perhaps most important of all, Satan's release shows the power and necessity of the righteous judgment of God.

In describing the nations, the term "Gog and Magog" is used without any explanation. From the context it would seem that this is not the same event as that described in Ezekiel 38 and 39, where Gog and Magog are prominent, and the battle that follows is entirely different and separated by at least a thousand years from that of Ezekiel's prophecy.[18]

While many explanations have been made, one of the intriguing ones is that Gog refers to the ruler and Magog to the people as in Ezekiel 38. Hence, what the passage means is that the nations of the world follow Satan, including the rulers (Gog) and the people (Magog) under the rulers. Another plausible explanation is that the expression is used much as we use the term

"Waterloo" to express a disastrous battle, but one not related to the historic origination of the term.

Many contrasts can be observed between this battle and that of Ezekiel. Satan is prominent in this, whereas he is not mentioned in Ezekiel 38–39. The invasion of Ezekiel comes from the north, whereas this invasion comes from all directions. Ezekiel's battle probably occurs previous to the battle of the great day of God Almighty before the millennium, whereas this occurs after the thousand years have been finished. The number of those who rebel against God and follow Satan is described as innumerable "like the sand of the sea." Thus the last gigantic rebellion of man develops against God's sovereign rule in which the ungodly meet their Waterloo.

As the battle is joined in verse 9, Satan and his armies surround the camp of the saints. The word for "camp" refers to those engaged in battle and who are in battle array, hence a "fortress" or "citadel." Here the term seems to refer to the city of Jerusalem itself, which is described as "the beloved city" (cf. Ps. 78:68; 87:2). Apparently Christ permits the army to assemble and encircle His capital city. No sooner has Satan's army been assembled, however, than fire comes down from God out of heaven, and the besiegers are destroyed, like the destruction of Sodom and Gomorrah. Thus is shattered the last vain attempt of Satan to overthrow the throne of God and usurp His prerogatives. This also ends the false theory that human beings in a perfect environment will willingly serve the God who created and redeemed them. Even in the ideal situation of the millennium, innumerable people respond to the first temptation to rebel. This is the end of the road for the nations who rebel against God as well as for the career of Satan.

THE DOOM OF SATAN (20:10)

20:10 and the devil who had deceived them was thrown into the lake of fire and sulfur where the beast and the false prophet were, and they will be tormented day and night forever and ever.

As Unger notes, "Satan's predestined judgment (Gen. 3:15) is now executed."[19] Attention is called to Satan's nature as the deceiver. He was first self-deceived in trying to be like God (Isa. 14:14) and then began his career by deceiving Eve in the garden. Nothing has changed at his final judgment. There is no sanctifying grace for fallen angels. In the divine act of judgment that throws Satan into the lake of fire, he joins the beast and the false prophet who preceded him by a thousand years, and who with Satan will experience eternal torment. Thus the Word of God plainly declares that death is not annihilation and that the ungodly wicked exist forever, though in torment. There would be no way possible in the Greek language to state more emphatically the everlasting punishment of the lost than that used here in mentioning both day and night and the expression "forever and ever," literally "to the ages of ages." The lake of fire prepared for the devil and the evil angels is also the destiny of all who follow Satan.

THE GREAT WHITE THRONE JUDGMENT (20:11)

20:11 Then I saw a great white throne and him who was seated on it. From his presence earth and sky fled away, and no place was found for them.

The One John sees on the great white throne is of such great majesty that earth and sky flee away from before Him. In 4:2, John had beheld "a throne . . . in heaven" with a description of the One sitting on the throne. Thereafter in the book of Revelation "the throne" is mentioned more than thirty times. But this throne is probably to be distinguished from any previously mentioned in the book. The white may represent God's unchanging holiness.[20]

It is proper to assume that it is God on the throne and, more specifically, Christ Himself, as in 3:21. This is according to John 5:22: "The Father judges no one, but has given all judgment to the Son." Other passages speak of Christ judging (cf. Matt. 19:28; 25:31–32; 2 Cor. 5:10). The time is clearly at the end of the millennium in contrast to the other judgments that precede the millennium.

The most natural interpretation of the fact that earth and sky flee away is that the present earth and sky are destroyed and will be replaced by the new heaven and new earth. This is also confirmed by the additional statement in 21:1, where John sees a new heaven and a new earth replacing the first heaven and the first earth. Frequent references in the Bible seem to anticipate this future time when the present world will be destroyed (Matt. 24:35; Mark 13:31; Luke 16:17; 21:33; 2 Pet. 3:10). According to this last reference, "The day of the Lord will come like a thief, and then the heavens will pass away with a roar, and the heavenly bodies will be burned up and dissolved, and the earth and the works that are done on it will be exposed."

Passages such as Revelation 20:11 and 2 Peter 3:10 state explicitly that this destruction is literal and physical. It would be most natural that the present earth and heaven, the scene of the struggle with Satan and sin, should be displaced by an entirely new order suited for eternity. The whole structure of the universe is operating on the principle of a clock that is running down. What could be simpler than for God to create a new heaven and a new earth by divine decree in keeping with His purposes for eternity?

THE RESURRECTION OF THE EVIL DEAD (20:12–13)

20:12–13 And I saw the dead, great and small, standing before the throne, and books were opened. Then another book was opened, which is the book of life. And the dead were judged by what was written in the books, according to what they had done. And the sea gave up the dead who were in it, Death and Hades gave up the dead who were in them, and they were judged, each one of them, according to what they had done.

John sees the dead standing before God awaiting their judgment. From the context it may be assumed that these are the evil dead, who are not raised in the first resurrection (cf. Dan. 12:2; John 5:29; Acts 24:15; Rev. 20:5).

317

The phrase "great and small" used previously in Revelation (11:18; 13:16; 19:5, 18) indicates that those appearing before the throne come from all walks of life and degrees of greatness. Their standing posture means that they are now about to be sentenced. This is a fulfillment of the principle of Hebrews 9:27: "It is appointed for man to die once, and after that comes judgment."

Their judgment is made on the basis of the books that are opened, being in two classifications. This shows that God's judgment is not arbitrary, but based on evidence from the person's life.[21] The book of life evidently refers to the roll of those who are saved and have eternal life. The other books mentioned as plural are the divine records of their works. The dead are judged on the basis of the records, and as in other final judgments, the sum of their works is now examined. It is noteworthy that all the final judgments are judgments of works. At the judgment seat of Christ (2 Cor. 5:10–11), believers are judged according to their works and rewarded. In Matthew 25:31–46, the Gentiles are judged according to their works in the sense that the works distinguish those who are saved, that is, the sheep, from those who are lost, the goats. Here the works evidently are such that salvation is not the issue but rather the degree of punishment, as there is no indication that any righteous are found in this judgment.

It is clear that the unsaved who die in the millennium are included in this judgment. The Scriptures are silent, however, concerning any rapture or translation of saints who survive the millennium and concerning the resurrection of saints who may die in the millennium. Both events may be safely assumed, but they are not the subject of divine revelation, probably on the principle that this truth is of no practical application to saints now living.

The absolute justice of God is revealed in this judgment. Even for those who have spurned the Lord Jesus Christ there is differentiation in degrees of evil and apparently variation in punishment. While works are never a ground of salvation, they are considered important before God. Though the ungodly are judged according to their works, the book of life is introduced as the deciding factor as to where they will spend eternity.

In verse 13, the resurrection of the evil dead is described, with special mention of those who are raised from the sea where they did not have normal burial. Those who died normal deaths and went to Hades, the intermediate abode of the evil dead, are also presented at this judgment. Careful distinction, therefore, must be made between Hades as the intermediate state in which the unsaved suffer prior to the judgment of the great white throne, and the eternal punishment that follows the great white throne, the lake of fire (cf. Matt. 5:22, 29–30; 10:28; 18:9; etc.).

A special problem is introduced by the resurrection of those who were thrown into the sea with the presumption that their bodies have disintegrated and have been scattered over a wide area. The mention of the sea is occasioned by the fact that resurrection usually implies resurrection from the grave. The resurrection of the dead from the sea merely reaffirms that all the dead will be raised regardless of the condition of their bodies. The expression is, however, somewhat unusual in that bodily resurrection is referred to in relation to the sea, whereas the delivering of the spirits of the unsaved dead is in view in deliverance from Hades, unless "the dead" from Hades are also resurrected with bodies. Any obscurity that this passage may have does not alter the fact of the universal resurrection of all people in their order.

The resurrection of the evil dead is in sharp contrast to the resurrection of the righteous dead. Although the passage does not state so explicitly, the implication in this judgment is that no one is saved. Nothing is said here of the reward of the righteous. Apparently there is a separate resurrection of any righteous who may have died in the millennium, although this teaching is not presented anywhere in the Word of God. The righteous are given bodies like the holy, immortal, and incorruptible body of Christ in His resurrection. The evil dead are given resurrection bodies suited for eternal punishment.

Every person who is judged according to his works thus becomes subject to the perfect righteousness of God. The peculiar construction of the closing clause of verse 13, "they were judged, each one of them," uses a third person plural for the verb, but a first person singular in the masculine for the term "each one." The meaning is that while they are judged as a group, the resulting judgment, nevertheless, is individual.

THE LAKE OF FIRE (20:14–15)

20:14–15 Then Death and Hades were thrown into the lake of fire. This is the second death, the lake of fire. And if anyone's name was not found written in the book of life, he was thrown into the lake of fire.

The summary judgment is pronounced in verse 14. In a word, this means that all who died physically and were in Hades, the intermediate state, are here found unworthy and cast into the lake of fire. This is then described as "the second death," which stands in antithesis to the first resurrection, or the eternal state of bliss, enjoyed by the saved. Both the evil and the righteous in the eternal state are thus permanently assigned to their respective destinies. The basis for the judgment is declared in verse 15 to be whether their names were found written in the book of life.

If the point of view be adopted that the book of life was originally the book of all living from which have been expunged the names of those who departed from life on earth without salvation, it presents a sad picture of a blank space where their names could have been written for all eternity as the objects of divine grace. Though they are judged by their works, it is evident that their destiny is determined primarily by their lack of spiritual life. When the fact is contemplated that Jesus Christ in His death reconciled the world to Himself (2 Cor. 5:19) and that He died for the reprobate as well as for the elect, it is all the more poignant that these now raised from the dead are cast into the lake of fire. Their ultimate destiny of eternal punishment is not, in the last analysis, because God wished it, but because they would not come to God for the grace that He freely offered.

Many attempts have been made to escape the obvious meaning of this passage by spiritualizing the lake of fire as a mere symbol that is not as bad as it seems or, on the other hand, to represent it as the annihilation of the evil rather than the beginning of their eternal punishment. It may be conceded that the lake of fire is a symbol, but the symbol corresponds to reality. The rich man in Luke 16 gave his testimony: "I am in anguish in this flame" (Luke

16:24). If unsaved souls in Hades are tormented by flames, it is reasonable to assume that the lake of fire connotes the same type of punishment. It cannot safely be assumed that there is any important difference between the physical and the spiritual reality embodied in this term. It is an awful destiny.

One further note on verse 15 is worth observing. The English word "if" may imply doubt that there were people at the judgment who were found unworthy of eternal life and were thrown into the lake of fire. But the Greek construction does not allow for such doubt. This is a first-class condition in which the reality of the first clause is assumed and its consequences stated in the second clause.[22] The word "if" could be translated "since."

It also seems very clear, according to Revelation 20:10 as well as other passages, that those thrown into the lake of fire are not annihilated. The beast and the false prophet are still alive and still tormented a thousand years after they are cast into it, and the Scriptures make plain that along with Satan they will be tormented forever. Not only is no termination of eternal punishment recognized in the Bible, but explicit statements are made to the contrary in the strongest possible language. It is difficult for creatures of earth, born in sin and never completely extricated from it even though experiencing God's grace, to enter into the fact of God's inexorable righteousness and inflexible justice that insist that judgment be administered when the grace of God has been spurned.

Even Bible-believing Christians have tended to tone down the awfulness of eternal death for the unsaved. A thorough appreciation of eternal punishment, however, will in the end enhance the doctrine of God's grace and make His love all the more wonderful for those who enter into its truth. The fact of eternal punishment is not limited to this passage of Scripture, for Christ Himself speaks of the destiny of the evil in many passages (Matt. 13:42; 25:41, 46; etc.). Earlier in Revelation itself (14:11) eternal punishment is predicted for those who receive the mark of the beast. A confirming note is also added in Revelation 21:8. The only revelation that has been given concerning the eternal state recognizes two destinies only: one of blessedness in the presence of the Lord, the other of eternal punishment.

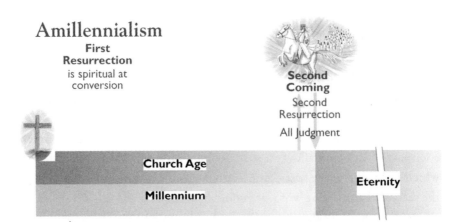

Amillennialism

First Resurrection is spiritual at conversion

Second Coming

Second Resurrection

All Judgment

Church Age

Millennium

Eternity

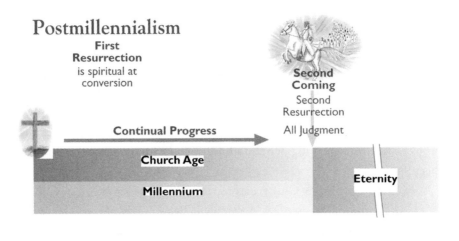

Postmillennialism

First Resurrection is spiritual at conversion

Continual Progress

Second Coming

Second Resurrection

All Judgment

Church Age

Millennium

Eternity

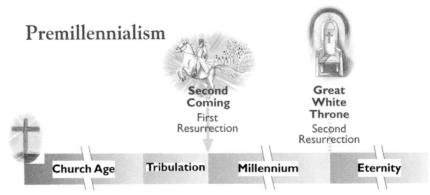

Premillennialism

Second Coming

First Resurrection

Great White Throne

Second Resurrection

Church Age

Tribulation

Millennium

Eternity

Key Events of the Millennium

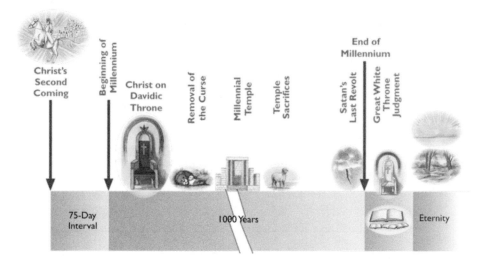

NOTES

1. Wilbur M. Smith, "Revelation," *The Wycliffe Bible Commentary*, Charles F. Pfeiffer and Everett F. Harrison, eds. (Chicago: Moody, 1990), 1519. See also Alan F. Johnson, *Revelation*, The Expositor's Bible Commentary, Frank E. Gaebelein, ed., vol. 12 (Grand Rapids: Zondervan, 1981), 578.

2. Smith, "Revelation," 1520. The demise of chiliastic interpretation in the Western church came with Jerome (347–42) and Augustine (354–430).

3. Johnson, *Revelation*, 580.

4. John MacArthur, *The MacArthur New Testament Commentary: Revelation 12–22* (Chicago: Moody, 2000), 231.

5. Harry Buis, *The Book of Revelation* (Philadelphia: Presbyterian and Reformed, 1960), 107–108.

6. Robert L. Thomas, *Revelation 8–22: An Exegetical Commentary* (Chicago: Moody, 1995), 407–409.

7. Harold W. Hoehner, "Evidence from Revelation 20," *A Case for Premillennialism*, Donald K. Campbell and Jeffrey L. Townsend, gen. eds. (Chicago: Moody, 1992), 249.

8. Ibid.

9. Thomas, *Revelation 8–22*, 407.

10. William Hendriksen, *More Than Conquerors* (Grand Rapids: Baker, 1967), 185.

11. MacArthur, *Revelation 12–22*, 229.

12. Johnson, *Revelation*, 581.

13. Charles C. Ryrie, *Basic Theology* (Chicago: Moody, 1999), 593.

14. Paul Benware, *Understanding End Times Prophecy* (Chicago: Moody, 2006), 134–35.

15. Robert H. Mounce, *The Book of Revelation*, rev. ed., The New International Commentary on the New Testament (Grand Rapids: Eerdmans, 1997), 368.

16. MacArthur, *Revelation 12–22*, 239–40.

17. Thomas, *Revelation 8–22*, 423.

18. Merrill F. Unger, *The New Unger's Bible Handbook*, rev. Gary N. Larson (Chicago: Moody, 1984), 686.

19. Ibid.

20. Warren Wiersbe, *Wiersbe's Expository Outlines on the New Testament* (Wheaton, IL: Victor Books, 1992), 854.

21. Mounce, *The Book of Revelation*, 376.

22. Johnson, *Revelation*, 590.

21 The New Heaven and the New Earth

THE NEW HEAVEN AND
THE NEW EARTH PRESENTED (21:1)

21:1 Then I saw a new heaven and a new earth, for the first heaven and the first earth had passed away, and the sea was no more.

John's attention is now directed to the new heaven and the new earth that replace the old heaven and the old earth that fled away (20:11). These are evidently not simply the old heaven and earth renovated, but an act of new creation. There is remarkably little revealed in the Bible concerning the character of the new heaven and the new earth, but it is evidently quite different from their present form of existence. Most of the earth is now covered with water, but the new earth apparently will have no bodies of water except for the river mentioned in 22:2.

Only a few other passages in the Bible deal with the subject of the new heaven and the new earth, and these are often in a context dealing with the millennium (cf. Isa. 65:17; 66:22; 2 Pet. 3:13). The fact that millennial truths are mentioned in the same context in all three of these major references has often confused expositors. However, it is a common principle in prophecy to bring together events that are distantly related chronologically, such as frequent reference to the first and second comings of Christ, actually separated by thousands of years (Isa. 61:1–2; cf. Luke 4:17–19).

In a similar way, there is mention of the resurrection of the righteous and of the wicked in the same verse, as in Daniel 12:2, events also separated by a thousand years. Malachi 4:5 speaks of the second coming of the Lord, followed by verse 6, referring to His first coming. Second Peter 3:10–13 refers to the day of the Lord beginning before the millennium, as well as to the destruction of the heavens and the earth with fire at the end of the millennium. If all the passages are put together, the sequence of events becomes plain, and the allusions to the new heaven and the new earth are clearly set forth in Revelation as following the millennial kingdom. The eternal state is clearly indicated in the absence of the sea, for frequent mention of bodies of water occur in millennial passages (cf. Ps. 72:8; Isa. 11:9, 11; Ezek. 47:10, 15, 17, 18, 20; 48:28; Zech. 9:10; 14:8). The evidence of Revelation 21:1 is so specific that most commentators do not question that the eternal state is here in view.[1]

FIRST VISION OF THE NEW JERUSALEM (21:2)

21:2 And I saw the holy city, New Jerusalem, coming down out of heaven from God, prepared as a bride adorned for her husband.

John's attention is immediately directed to that which is central in the vision, "the holy city, New Jerusalem" (cf. 3:12). This expression is in contrast to the earthly Jerusalem, which spiritually was referred to as Sodom in 11:8, although it is called holy in Matthew 4:5 and 27:53.

Most important, however, is the fact that the city is declared to come down from God. Nothing is said about the New Jerusalem being created at this point and the language seems to imply that it has been in existence in heaven prior to this event. Nothing is revealed concerning this in Scripture unless the expression of John 14:2, "I go to prepare a place for you," refers to this. If the New Jerusalem is in existence throughout the millennium, it could be a satellite city suspended over the earth during the thousand years as the dwelling place of resurrected and translated believers who also have access to the earthly scene. This would help explain an otherwise difficult problem of where these resurrected believers would dwell during a period in which people are still in their natural bodies and living ordinary lives. If so, the New Jerusalem is withdrawn from the earthly scene at the destruction of the old earth, and later comes down to the new earth.

As presented in Revelation 21 and 22, however, the New Jerusalem is not seen as it may have existed in the past, but as it will be seen in eternity future. The possibility of Jerusalem being a satellite city over the earth during the millennium is not specifically taught in any Scripture and at best is an inference based on the implication that it has been in existence prior to its introduction in Revelation 21. Its characteristics as presented here, however, are related to the eternal state rather than to the millennial kingdom.

The only description of the New Jerusalem is given in verse 2, which says it is "prepared as a bride adorned for her husband." Because a bride is used in the New Testament as a symbol of the church, some have attempted to limit the New Jerusalem as having reference only to the church. Mounce argues that rather than a literal, physical city, the New Jerusalem represents the church as the people of God.[2]

The use of the marriage figure, however, in both the Old and New Testaments is sufficiently frequent so that we cannot arbitrarily insist that figures are always used in precisely the same connotation. The subsequent description of the New Jerusalem in this chapter makes plain that saints of all ages are involved[3] and that what we have here is not the church per se, but a city or dwelling place having the freshness and beauty of a bride.

GOD TO DWELL WITH MEN (21:3-4)

21:3-4 And I heard a loud voice from the throne saying, "Behold, the dwelling place of God is with man. He will dwell with them, and they will be his people, and God himself will be with them as their God. He will wipe away every tear from their eyes, and death shall be no more, neither shall there be mourning nor crying nor pain anymore, for the former things have passed away."

John next heard a loud voice from heaven giving the spiritual significance of this scene. This is the last of twenty-one times that "a great voice" or "a loud voice" is mentioned in Revelation. The loudness of the voice signals that what follows is important and authoritative. This "dwelling place" ("tabernacle," KJV) is in contrast to the tabernacle in the wilderness in which God dwelt and also to the tabernacle in heaven (13:6; 15:5). It symbolizes that God is now present with humanity in the new earth and in the New Jerusalem. The verse itself explains the meaning of God's dwelling with us. The word for "dwell" is the verb form for the noun translated "dwelling place" (cf. John 1:14; Rev. 7:15; 12:12; 13:6). The presence of God in Scripture frequently connotes fellowship and blessing. Here it is stated that the inhabitants of the New Jerusalem will be the people of God and that God will not only be with them but will also be their God, a thought that is often repeated in the Scripture.

God's presence assures an entirely new state for those who inhabit the New Jerusalem. In contrast to their former suffering that included going through the tribulation for many of these saints, God will wipe away each of their tears. There is no just ground for assuming from this text that believers will shed tears in heaven concerning the failures of their former life on earth. The emphasis here is on the comfort of God, not on the remorse of His people.

Instead, the tears seem to refer to tears shed on earth as the faithful endured suffering for Christ's sake. This is in keeping with the rest of the passage that goes on to say that other aspects of human sorrow will also cease to exist. "Crying" is the vocal response to sorrow, in contrast to tears, which are a silent response. The new situation is the consummation of divine grace and the assurance of the estate of endless blessedness for those who were once lost sinners. The Scriptures make plain that not only the old earth and heaven pass away, but also all the details and associations that belong to it that would mar the joy of the new heaven and the new earth.

ALL THINGS MADE NEW (21:5–6)

21:5–6 And he who was seated on the throne said, "Behold, I am making all things new." Also he said, "Write this down, for these words are trustworthy and true." And he said to me, "It is done! I am the Alpha and the Omega, the beginning and the end.

To the thirsty I will give from the spring of the water of life without payment."

It is probably too much to infer from the use of the singular "he" that God the Father is specifically meant here and not Christ the Son. Christ will share the throne in this situation, much as He has done in the past. The special character of His rule over the earth and His contest with the wicked, however, ended at the close of the millennium. The verb "make" means "to make, form, or construct" and is a common verb occurring many times in the New Testament for a work of accomplishment. To argue as some have done, however, that this proves that there is no new heaven or earth created at this time, because the specific word *create* is not used is building too much on too little. The same word is used in Matthew 19:4 where God is said to have "made" Adam and Eve, using both the word "create" and the word "made" for the same act. Everything, of course, is not created here, but all things are made new in the same sense that Eve was made a new creature though formed from the rib of Adam. The word "new" means to be both new in character and in the sense of recently made. It connotes a drastic change.

The message from the throne in verse 6 refers to the work accomplished through the whole drama of human history prior to the eternal state. "It is done!" does not mean that there are no future works of God, but that a major work has been brought to completion and that the works now relating to the eternal state are beginning. The speaker now introduces Himself as the "Alpha and Omega, the beginning and the end." It is by this precise title that Christ is introduced in 1:8, and the phrase is again found in 22:13.

While the expression is also appropriate for God the Father, the fact that it is given to Christ in 1:8 seems to confirm the idea that Christ is also in view in this passage. With the beginning of the eternal state, there is a difference in the divine undertaking but not a difference in the divine majesty of the Second Person. The first of three promises made in verses 6 and 7 then follows, where water from the fountain of the water of life is promised in abundance to the one who is thirsty. "Nothing is required except to come and drink."[4] A similar assurance is given to the martyred throng of tribulation saints in 7:17. It refers to the abundant character of eternal life and the blessings that flow from it and is a fulfillment of the invitation of Isaiah 55:1 as well as that of Christ in John 4:10, 13–14.

THE BLESSINGS OF THE OVERCOMER (21:7–8)

21:7–8 "The one who conquers will have this heritage, and I will be his God and he will be my son. But as for the cowardly, the faithless, the detestable, as for murderers, the sexually immoral, sorcerers, idolaters, and all liars, their portion will be in the lake that burns with fire and sulfur, which is the second death."

Here is another promise to glorified believers, described as overcomers. "This heritage" entails that God will be their God and that in glory each shall be "my son." Frequently in Scripture, particular promises are given those who triumph in faith, but here the generous provision is made that they shall receive a full heritage rather than some particular aspect of the divine provision (cf. Matt. 5:5; 19:29; 25:34; 1 Cor. 6:9–10; Heb. 1:14; 9:15; 1 Pet. 1:4; 3:9; 1 John 5:5). Promises to overcomers are included in the messages to the seven churches and are anticipated in 1 Corinthians 3:21–23.

In sharp contrast, the sad inheritance of unbelief is outlined in verse 8, where the unsaved, pictured in their principal characteristics, are destined to be burned with fire and brimstone, the second death. Similar lists are found in 21:27 and 22:15. Some of the saved were guilty of similar offenses but received the grace of God through faith in Christ (cf. 1 Cor. 6:11). No true believer could be categorized by this list of sins. While there is further mention of the fate of the unsaved later in Revelation, this is the last mention of the lake of fire and of the second death specifically.

THE NEW JERUSALEM AS THE BRIDE (21:9–11)

21:9–11 Then came one of the seven angels who had the seven bowls full of the seven last plagues and spoke to me,

saying, "Come, I will show you the Bride, the wife of the Lamb."
And he carried me away in the Spirit to a great, high mountain,
and showed me the holy city Jerusalem coming down out of
heaven from God, having the glory of God, its radiance like a most
rare jewel, like a jasper, clear as crystal.

With this survey of the eternal state and its blessings before him, John is now invited by one of the seven angels who had poured out the seven bowls of divine wrath of God to behold the Lamb's wife. This angel may have been the one mentioned in 17:1 who showed John the vision of Babylon, but it is impossible to prove that it is the same one of the seven. In keeping with the earlier revelation of 21:2, the holy city, the New Jerusalem, is here characterized as a bride. Since a city is not a bride, the truth here represented is that the city, the residence of the saints of eternity future, is to be compared to a bride for beauty and is intimately related to Christ the Lamb. The city is obviously seen as it will appear in the eternal state in the entire passage beginning with 21:1.

In interpreting the description of the heavenly city, the problem of symbolic interpretation comes to the fore perhaps more than in any other section of Revelation. Even the most conservative scholars are not necessarily in agreement on the extent to which this description should be taken literally. The decision depends ultimately upon the considered judgment of the expositor. Certain guidelines, however, can be laid down.

John actually saw what he recorded, and what he saw is to some extent interpreted for him. Obviously what he saw transcended any earthly experience, and it was necessary for him to describe what he saw in terms that were meaningful to him. This must not be construed, however, as an inaccurate description because John was guided by the Holy Spirit when he wrote, and the description must be viewed as accurate insofar as it was possible to communicate what he saw. The passage itself, however, as in the description of the gold that is transparent (21:21), suggests strongly that the material substances were different from what exists on this present earth.

Of major importance are the facts that John actually saw a city that was inhabited by believers of all ages, and that God Himself was present in it. Until further light is given, it is probably a safe procedure to accept the description of this city as corresponding to the physical characteristics attributed to it.

Responding to the angel's invitation, John is carried away in the Spirit to a mountain. The inference is that he is not actually transported, but only experiences what follows as if he had been taken to a vantage point where he could see the entire scene. He had a similar experience in 17:3. As John watches, he sees the New Jerusalem coming down from heaven. The contrast is evident between this city and Babylon of Revelation 17 and 18. A similar description is given in 21:2, where the city is declared to be holy and to have come from God. It is to be distinguished both from Babylon[5] and from the earthly city of Jerusalem, which in its history had also fallen into evil ways.

In verse 11, a general description of the New Jerusalem is given. The city is characterized as having "the glory of God." It should be noted that the heavenly city is introduced in verses 1 and 2 as "holy," then as "new," "out of heaven," and "from God." Most of these details are repeated in verse 10, and in verse 11 the city is said to have the glory of God, and to have a brilliant light. As the glory of God is the sum of His infinite perfections in their manifestations, so the New Jerusalem reflects all that God is.

The city is ablaze with light compared to the brightness of a precious stone. The word "jasper" is a transliteration of a similar word in Greek used for stones of various colors. The mention of this stone that is costly on earth but used lavishly in the New Jerusalem (cf. 21:19) is designed to manifest the glory of God. Later in the passage (v. 23), the fact is revealed that the city does not originate its light or radiance, but all illumination comes from the Lamb. The believer in Christ does not generate the light of Christ, but should both reflect and transmit its glory without blurring the beauty and loveliness of Christ.

THE WALL AND THE
GATES OF THE CITY (21:12–14)

21:12–14 It had a great, high wall, with twelve gates, and at the gates twelve angels, and on the gates the names of the twelve tribes of the sons of Israel were inscribed—on the east three gates, on the north three gates, on the south three gates, and on the west three gates. And the wall of the city had twelve foundations, and on them were the twelve names of the twelve apostles of the Lamb.

This is a tremendously impressive scene. As Bruce comments, "John ransacks the resources of language and metaphor—jewels, gold and pearls—to describe the indescribable glory which the holy city reflects."[6] Expositors have differed as to the degree in which this description should be taken literally, some believing that the city is actually nonexistent and presented only as a symbolic presentation of the blessings of the saints in eternity future. Such a view, however, is difficult to harmonize with the specific details given that are nowhere explained in other than the literal sense in the Bible. There does not seem to be any solid objection to the concept that believers in the new heaven and the new earth will have such a city as their home, glorious in every aspect, reaching to tremendous heights into the new heaven, and embodying characteristics to remind them of their spiritual heritage.

The height of the city's wall (v. 12) is an obvious symbol of exclusion of all that is unworthy to enter. Only those who are qualified by virtue of faith in Christ may enter. The wall contains twelve gates, guarded by twelve angels and bearing the names of the twelve tribes of Israel. In the description of the New Jerusalem, the number twelve is very prominent as seen in the twelve gates and twelve angels in this passage, the twelve tribes of Israel (21:12), twelve foundations (21:14), twelve apostles (21:14), twelve pearls (21:21), and twelve kinds of fruit (22:2). The height, length, and width of the city are described as "12,000 stadia," or 1,342 miles (21:16), and the wall's height is said to measure twelve times twelve cubits, that is, 144 cubits, or over two hundred feet (21:17).

The name and location of each particular gate is not stated. In the description of the Jerusalem that will be on earth during the millennium, Ezekiel names the twelve tribes inscribed on the gates of the city at that time (cf. Ezek. 48:31–34), along with each gate's position. The New Jerusalem that descends from heaven, however, is an entirely different and much larger city.

It may be, however, that names are assigned to the gates of the New Jerusalem in a similar way to those on the gates of the earthly city of Jerusalem in the millennium. The implication of the fact of gates on each side of the city is that its inhabitants will have freedom to go and come. It is implied that the residents of the New Jerusalem will be able to travel elsewhere on the new earth and possibly also in the new heaven.

Also prominent here are the twelve foundations, mentioned in verse 14, inscribed with the names of the twelve apostles. There has been much speculation as to why the apostles' names are used here, but the most obvious answer is that they have a prominent place in the program of God in relation to the New Jerusalem. The twelve apostles were of Israel and were called out of Israel to be leaders in the church. They are, in some sense, representative of both Israel and the church, though the primary significance of their names seems to be the indication that the believers of the church age are included in this eternal city.

The inclusion of Israel's twelve tribes should settle beyond any question the matter of the inclusion of Old Testament saints. The divine intent is evidently to show that the New Jerusalem will have among its citizens not only believers of the present church age, but also Israel, or the faithful of other ages, whether in the Old Testament or in the tribulation. Later on there is mention also of Gentiles. The careful expositor, therefore, will not confuse Israel and the church as if one were the other, nor deny to both their respective places of privilege in God's program. The anticipation of Hebrews 12:22–24 is specifically that the heavenly Jerusalem will include God and an innumerable company of angels, but also the church and all other saints. Even here the distinction between Israel and the church is maintained

THE DIMENSIONS OF THE CITY (21:15–17)

21:15–17 And the one who spoke with me had a measuring rod of gold to measure the city and its gates and walls. The city lies foursquare; its length the same as its width. And he measured the city with his rod, 12,000 stadia. Its length and width and height are equal. He also measured its wall, 144 cubits by human measurement, which is also an angel's measurement.

The measuring rod the angel uses is a reed about ten feet long, the unit of measure common among the Jews. The measured distance is equivalent to 1,342 miles, often spoken of roughly as 1,500 miles.

The city's shape is not mentioned, but judging from its square dimensions some have assumed it to be a cube.[7] Inspiration, however, does not indicate the shape; it also could be in the form of a pyramid with sides sloping to a peak at the height indicated. This would have certain advantages, not necessarily because it is smaller, but because this shape provides a vehicle for the river of life to proceed out of the throne of God, which seems to be at the top, to find its way to the bottom, assuming our experience of gravity will be somewhat normal also in the new earth.

Whatever its shape, a city of large dimensions would be proper if it is to be the residence of the saved of all ages, including infants who died before reaching the age of accountability. It is not necessary, however, to hold that everyone will live continually within its walls throughout eternity. The implications are that there is plenty of room for everyone and that this city provides a residence for the saints of all ages.

In addition to measuring the city itself, the angel measures the wall that by comparison is much smaller at about 216 feet. However, some expositors believe this is the thickness of the wall, not its height. The city is pictured as descending from heaven to the new earth, and the fact that it has foundations and comes from heaven to the earth seems to imply that it rests on the new earth itself. This also is implied in the fact that people go in and out of the gates, which is difficult to visualize unless the gates themselves rest upon the earth.

THE BEAUTY OF THE CITY (21:18–21)

21:18–21 The wall was built of jasper, while the city was pure gold, clear as glass. The foundations of the wall of the city were adorned with every kind of jewel. The first was jasper, the second sapphire, the third agate, the fourth emerald, the fifth onyx, the sixth carnelian, the seventh chrysolite, the eighth beryl, the ninth topaz, the tenth chrysoprase, the eleventh jacinth, the twelfth amethyst. And the twelve gates were twelve pearls, each of the gates made of a single pearl, and the street of the city was pure gold, transparent as glass.

The glory of the New Jerusalem is as awe-inspiring as its dimensions. The wall is said to be of jasper, in keeping with the general description of verse 11, and probably clear as crystal also. The city as a whole is portrayed as made of pure gold like clear glass. This description would indicate that it is gold in appearance but like clear glass in substance—glass with a gold cast to it. John is endeavoring to describe a scene that in most respects transcends earthly experience. The constant mention of transparency indicates that the city is designed to transmit the glory of God.

The precious stones that garnish the city's foundation make for a sight of indescribable beauty with the light of the city playing upon the multicolored stones. The city's first foundation is again the familiar jasper stone mentioned twice previously. The various foundations are represented as layers built upon each other, each layer extending around all four sides of the city. On top of the jasper stone is a second foundation, the brilliant sapphire, a stone similar to a diamond in hardness and blue in color. The third foundation is agate, a stone thought to be sky-blue with stripes of other colors running through it. The fourth foundation, an emerald, introduces a bright green color. The fifth, the onyx, is a red and white stone. The sixth foundation, the carnelian, refers to a common jewel of reddish color, also found in honey color, that was considered less valuable. The carnelian is used with the jasper in Revelation 4:3 to describe the glory of God on His throne.

The seventh foundation is formed of chrysolyte, a transparent stone golden in color and therefore somewhat different from the modern pale-green chrysolyte stone. The eighth foundation, the beryl, is sea-green. The topaz, the ninth foundation, is yellow-green and transparent. The tenth foundation, the chrysoprase, introduces another shade of green. The eleventh foundation, the jacinth, is a violet color. The last stone, the amethyst, is commonly purple.

Though the precise colors of these stones in some cases are not certain, the general picture here is one of unmistakable beauty, designed to reflect the glory of God in a spectrum of brilliant color. The light of the city within shining through these various colors in the foundation topped by the wall, itself composed of the crystal-clear jasper forms a scene of dazzling beauty in keeping with the glory of God and the beauty of His holiness. The city is undoubtedly far more beautiful to the eye than anything that humans have ever been able to create, and it reflects not only the infinite wisdom and power of God but also His grace as extended to the objects of His salvation.

Built in the walls are the twelve gates described as each being made of one huge pearl, leading to the streets of the city described as pure gold transparent as glass, that is, golden in color and appearance but having the transparency of glass.

THE TEMPLE OF THE CITY (21:22)

21:22 And I saw no temple in the city, for its temple is the Lord God the Almighty and the Lamb.

The next phase of the vision begins with the familiar clause, "and I saw," indicating a new and important phase of the revelation. John finds no temple in the New Jerusalem. This is in contrast to the Old Testament, where Israel first had the tabernacle and then the temple. This is also a sharp contrast to the millennial city where a temple is built for the worship of God. Here the shadows are dispelled and, as the Scripture indicates, the Lord God Himself and the Lamb are the temple of the new city. No longer is a structure necessary, for believers are in the immediate presence of the Lord with no need for an earthly mediator or shadows of things eternal. The word for "temple" is the sanctuary, or God's dwelling place, the Holy of Holies, in the temple of Israel. Believers now have access to the most sacred, intimate fellowship with the Lord their God in fulfillment of the many promises given to the saints.

THE LIGHT OF THE CITY (21:23–24)

21:23–24 And the city has no need of sun or moon to shine on it, for the glory of God gives it light, and its lamp is the Lamb. By its light will the nations walk, and the kings of the earth will bring their glory into it.

In contrast to the millennial earth and all preceding human history, the New Jerusalem does not need the light of the sun nor the moon, for they can add nothing to God's radiance.[8] The city is distinguished by the things that are missing, such as natural light, a temple, and darkness.[9] This is another indication that this is the eternal state rather than the millennium, because if the sun or the moon were in existence, they would shine upon the city. The form of expression would not make impossible the existence of the sun and the moon, as this Scripture merely says there is no need of them. But the position of the city on the new earth in the dimensions indicated is impossible to accommodate with the millennial scene, and as pictured here, the city is portrayed in its eternal character rather than in its existence in time.

That God Himself is the city's light is entirely in keeping with many passages in the Old Testament comparing God to light, and this new situation correlates with Jesus Christ being the light of the world (cf. John 1:7–9; 3:19; 8:12; 12:35). Because God is light and there is no darkness in Him, believers are exhorted to walk in the light in their present existence on this earth in keeping with their future in heaven (1 John 1:5–7).

In verse 24, the nations of the saved as well as the earth's rulers are said to walk in the light of the city and bring their glory and honor into it. Some have arbitrarily assumed that because the nations are mentioned this must be a millennial situation and not the eternal state. This is an unwarranted assumption, however, for the text specifies the nations of them that are saved (21:25–27). The word "nations" here is the word for Gentiles. The meaning is not that political entities will enter into the New Jerusalem, but rather that those who are saved Gentiles, of non-Jewish races, will be in the new city.

In the eternal state, therefore, not only saved Israelites and the church will be present but also saved Gentiles who are not numbered among either Israel or the church. That the kings of the earth bring their glory and honor into the city means that those among the saved who have honored positions on earth will ascribe the glory and honor that once were theirs to their Lord and God. These kings are saved and have access to the city even as others.

ACCESS TO THE CITY (21:25–27)

21:25–27 and its gates will never be shut by day—and there will be no night there. They will bring into it the glory and the honor of the nations. But nothing unclean will ever enter it, nor anyone who does what is detestable or false, but only those who are written in the Lamb's book of life.

The city's gates are never shut, because in the city there is continuous day. Here again is a contrast to the millennial situation in which day and night continue as the norm for the entire earth. The brilliant light of the city, however, dispels any possible darkness. Believers in their glorified bodies do not need rest, and their lives are full of continuous activity even like the holy angels.

Verse 26 indicates that the glory and honor of the nations themselves come into the city. Here again the word "nations" should be translated "Gentiles," referring to the Gentile glory in contrast to the glory of Israel or of the church. Expositors too often have forgotten that God has a purpose for the Gentiles as well as for Israel, and He glorifies Himself through them also. Whatever among the Gentiles can be used to bring honor and glory to the Lord is here also brought into the eternal state.

Verse 27 indicates plainly that nothing will ever enter the city that is in any sense evil, as only those whose names are written in the Lamb's book of life are eligible for entrance. This is another reminder that all who are there have entered the city as the objects of God's grace, otherwise they too would be excluded. This will be a perfect environment in contrast to the centuries of human sin, and the believers will enjoy this perfect situation through all eternity to come. The inhabitants of the city will be characterized by eternal life and absolute moral purity.

NOTES

1. Tony Evans, *The Best Is Yet to Come* (Chicago: Moody, 2000), 232.

2. Robert H. Mounce, *The Book of Revelation*, rev. ed., The New International Commentary on the New Testament (Grand Rapids: Eerdmans, 1997), 382.

3. Paul Benware, *Understanding End Times Prophecy* (Chicago: Moody, 2006), 340–41.

4. Alan F. Johnson, *Revelation*, The Expositor's Bible Commentary, Frank E. Gaebelein, ed., vol. 12 (Grand Rapids: Zondervan, 1981), 594.

5. William Hendriksen, *More Than Conquerors* (Grand Rapids: Baker, 1967), 201.

6. F. F. Bruce, *New International Bible Commentary*, F. F. Bruce, gen. ed. (Grand Rapids: Zondervan, 1979), 1626.

7. See John MacArthur, *The MacArthur New Testament Commentary: Revelation 12–22* (Chicago: Moody, 2000), 281, where he also quotes the late scientist and Bible commentator Henry Morris.

8. Robert L. Thomas, *Revelation 8–22: An Exegetical Commentary* (Chicago: Moody, 1995) 475.

9. Warren Wiersbe, *Wiersbe's Expository Outlines on the New Testament* (Wheaton, IL: Victor, 1992), 856.

22 Concluding Revelations and Exhortations

THE RIVER OF THE WATER OF LIFE (22:1)

22:1 Then the angel showed me the river of the water of life, bright as crystal, flowing from the throne of God and of the Lamb

Here begins the description of the triumph and joy of God's people in His eternal kingdom. Many expositors see Revelation 22 as the restoration of all that was lost in the Garden of Eden, and more.[1] As a provision for believers and in keeping with the complete holiness and purity of the heavenly city, John sees a pure river of the water of life coming out of the throne. This is not to be confused with the river flowing from the millennial sanctuary (Ezek. 47:1, 12) nor with the living waters going forth from Jerusalem (Zech. 14:8), also in the millennial scene. These millennial streams anticipate, however, this future river that is in the New Jerusalem. This river corresponds to the present believer's experience of the outflow of the Spirit. The throne is that of both God and the Lamb; this confirms that Christ is still on the throne in the eternal state, though the throne has a different character than during His mediatorial rule over the earth.

Paradise Lost	Paradise Regained
Eden	*New Heavens and New Earth*
1. River (Gen. 2:10)	River of Life (Rev. 22:1)
2. Tree of Life (Gen. 2:9)	Tree of Life (Rev. 22:2)
3. Human Innocence (Gen. 2:25)	Redeemed Humanity (Rev. 22:4)
4. Spoiled by Sin (Gen. 3:6)	No Sin Allowed to Enter (Rev. 22:3)
5. Sun and Moon (Gen. 1:16)	No Need of Sun (Rev. 22:5)
6. Redemption Promised (Gen. 3:15)	Redemption Realized (Rev. 22:4)
7. Banishment (Gen 3:23)	Eternal Residence (Rev. 22:5)

THE TREE OF LIFE (22:2)

22:2 through the middle of the street of the city; also, on either side of the river, the tree of life with its twelve kinds of fruit, yielding its fruit each month. The leaves of the tree were for the healing of the nations.

Verse 2, because of its somewhat obscure presentation, has caused some difficulty to expositors.[2] The picture is that the river flows through the middle of the city, and the tree is large enough to span the river, so that the river is in the midst of the street, and the tree is on both sides of the river. It would appear that the river is not a broad body of water, but a clear stream sufficiently narrow to allow for this arrangement.

The tree of life seems to have reference to a similar tree in the Garden of Eden (Gen. 3:22, 24). If Adam and Eve had eaten of the tree of life, physical death would apparently have been impossible. The tree in the New Jerusalem seems to have a similar quality and intent. Although it is difficult to distinguish between the literal and the symbolic, the tree is said to bear fruit that apparently can be eaten, and also to provide leaves "for the healing of the nations." Those who believe that this is a millennial scene rather than the eternal state put much weight upon this statement as they ask the natural question, "Why should healing be necessary in eternity to come?"

The answer is in the Greek word for "healing," *therapeian*, from which the English word *therapeutic* is derived. Rather than specifically meaning "healing," it should be understood as "health-giving," as the word in its root meaning has the idea of serving or ministering. In other words, the leaves of the tree promote the enjoyment of life in the New Jerusalem and are not for correcting ills that do not exist.[3] This is confirmed by the fact that there is no more curse, as indicated in verse 3.

The word *nations* is to be understood as "Gentiles" as in 21:24 and 21:26, or possibly "peoples" more generally. The intimation of this passage is that while it is not necessary for believers in the eternal state to sustain life in any way by physical means, they can enjoy that which the tree provides.

THE THRONE OF GOD (22:3)

22:3 No longer will there be anything accursed, but the throne of God and of the Lamb will be in it, and his servants will worship him.

In the millennium there is a lifting of the curse upon the earth, but not a total deliverance from the world's travail brought in by sin, for in the millennium it is still possible for a "sinner" to be "accursed" (Isa. 65:20) with resulting physical death. In the new heaven and the new earth, however, there will be no curse at all and no possibility or need of such divine punishment. God's throne will be in the New Jerusalem, and His servants will give themselves to serve Him unceasingly.

There is no greater privilege believers can have in the eternal state than being servants of the Lord. Who would want to live in eternal idleness and uselessness? This is a picture of blessedness in service rather than of arduous toil, even though John uses the word for "slaves."[4]

THE BLESSEDNESS OF FELLOWSHIP (22:4–5)

22:4–5 They will see his face, and his name will be on their foreheads. And night will be no more. They will need no light of lamp or sun, for the Lord God will be their light, and they will reign forever and ever.

Immediate access to the glory of God will characterize believers in the eternal state. The earlier statement that nothing unclean will enter the city has a parallel in ancient times, when criminals were banished from the king's presence.[5] Further, God's name is on their foreheads, indicating that they belong to Him (cf. 7:3; 14:1; also 2:17; 3:12). The fact that they shall see His face demonstrates beyond question that these are glorified saints (1 John 3:2).

Once again in verse 5, John repeats the fact that there will be no night or need for light other than God's glory. Those who are His servants have the blessed privilege of reigning forever. The eternal character of their reign is another indication that this is the eternal state. The concept that the reign of Christ must cease at the millennium, based on 1 Corinthians 15:24-25, is a misunderstanding. It is the character of His reign that changes. Christ continues for all eternity as King of kings and Lord of lords, even though the scene of His mediatorial and millennial rule over the earth is changed to the new heaven and the new earth. There is no contradiction, therefore, in calling these believers servants and at the same time recognizing them as reigning with Christ.

THE CERTAINTY OF THE BLESSED HOPE (22:6–7)

22:6–7 And he said to me, "These words are trustworthy and true. And the Lord, the God of the spirits of the prophets, has sent his angel to show his servants what must soon take place. And behold, I am coming soon. Blessed is the one who keeps the words of the prophecy of this book."

The angel goes on to remind John, in words similar to Revelation 1:1, that the God of the holy prophets has sent him to show His servants through the apostle John the events that will happen soon. The noun phrase "what must soon take place" literally translated is "what it is necessary to do quickly." In verse 7, the adverb of the same root is also translated "soon." The thought seems to be that when the action comes, it will be sudden. A further indication is that Christ's return is also imminent,[6] meaning it could occur at any moment. Thus verse 7 is a message of warning that those who believe should be alert.

Here John seems to be referring to Christ's coming for the church rather than His second coming to the earth, though both are in the larger context. A special blessing is then pronounced on those who heed the words of this book. This is the sixth of seven beatitudes in Revelation.[7] Compare this to Revelation 1:3, where the note of imminence is emphasized in the expression "for the time is near." How ironic that this final book of the Bible, more neg-

344

lected and misinterpreted than any other book, should carry these special blessings to those who properly regard its promises and divine revelation. The reason is not that this book contains more or varied revelations, but rather that this book above all others honors and exalts the Lord Jesus Christ.

JOHN WORSHIPS BEFORE THE ANGEL (22:8–9)

22:8–9 I, John, am the one who heard and saw these things. And when I heard and saw them, I fell down to worship at the feet of the angel who showed them to me, but he said to me, "You must not do that! I am a fellow servant with you and your brothers the prophets, and with those who keep the words of this book. Worship God."

John is once again overwhelmed by the revelations given to him (cf. 19:10). His response is natural, but he is rebuked by the angel who informs him, as he did previously, that he is John's fellow servant. It should be noted here, as in 19:10, that the one speaking, though an angel, is declared to be a fellow servant and related to human servants of the Lord. The angel's command is direct and to the point: "Worship God."

COMMAND TO PROCLAIM
THE PROPHECY (22:10–11)

22:10–11 And he said to me, "Do not seal up the words of the prophecy of this book, for the time is near. Let the evildoer still do evil, and the filthy still be filthy, and the righteous still do right, and the holy still be holy."

The justification for this urgent command is that the time is at hand. As the prophecy of Revelation was unfolded, it was intended to be revealed; now at its end, John is especially commanded not to seal it up because the consummation of the ages is near. The indeterminate period assigned to the church is the last dispensation before end-time events and, in John's day as in ours, the end is always impending because of the imminent return of Christ at the rapture.

In view of this, verse 11 contains a seemingly strange command. In effect, the angel advocates the status quo for both the evil and the righteous. By this he does not mean that people should remain unmoved by the prophecies of this book, but rather that if the prophecies are rejected, there is no other message that will work. If the warnings of the book are not sufficient, there is no more that God has to say. The evil must continue in their evil way and be judged by the Lord when He comes. The same rule, however, applies to the righteous. Their reaction to the prophecy, of course, will be different, but the exhortation in their case is to continue in righteousness and holiness. It is an either/or proposition with no neutrality possible. There is a sense also in which present choices fix character; a time is coming when change will be impossible. Present choices will become permanent in character.

THE BLESSED HOPE AND
ASSURANCE OF REWARD (22:12)

22:12 "Behold, I am coming soon, bringing my recompense with me, to repay everyone for what he has done."

The second announcement alerting the reader concerning the Lord's coming is found here. The verb is in the present tense, connoting futuristic but impending action. Added here is the promise that the Lord is bringing His reward when He comes. This verse has in view the judgment seat of Christ as it relates to the Christian (2 Cor. 5:10–11). The same standard is established for reward here, which is that of works. As noted earlier, all final judgments relate to works, whether of Christians being rewarded or the unsaved being punished. God, the righteous judge, will deal with every person's works in the proper time and order.

THE MAJESTY OF
THE ETERNAL CHRIST (22:13–16)

22:13–16 "I am the Alpha and the Omega, the first and the last, the beginning and the end." Blessed are those who wash their robes, so that they may have the right to the tree of life and that they may enter the city by the gates. Outside are the dogs and sorcerers and the sexually immoral and murderers and idolaters, and everyone who loves and practices falsehood. "I, Jesus, have sent my angel to testify to you about these things for the churches. I am the root and the descendant of David, the bright morning star."

Though the means of communication seems to be the angel, it is Christ who is speaking, and here as in 22:7 and 12, the first person pronoun is used. Christ again repeats that He is the Alpha and Omega (the first and last letters of the Greek alphabet), which is interpreted as meaning the beginning and the end. For various combinations of these phrases, see 1:8, 17; 2:8; 21:6. When the One who exists from all eternity states, "I am coming soon," it means that from the divine point of view, end-time events are impending. The three pairs of titles given in verse 13 all connote the same truth, that Christ is the beginning and source of all things, as well as the goal and consummation of all; in a word, the eternal God.

Here is the seventh and last beatitude of Revelation. It is somewhat obscured by a debate on the text, since some of the best manuscripts read "that do his commandments" in place of "who wash their robes," as reflected in the King James Version.[8] In either reading, the reference is to those who qualify for entrance, and the resultant meaning is much the same.

By contrast, unbelievers are characterized as being excluded and are described in the most unflattering terms. This is the third description of unsaved people in this general passage (cf. 21:8, 27). The main emphasis in each of them is on the deceitfulness and lying of those who are unsaved. The reference to dogs refers not to the animal but to people of low character (cf. Phil. 3:2). As in the former description of the unsaved, the issue is not that they have at some time committed sins of this character, but rather that these are the settled characteristics of their lives from which they were never delivered, although the grace of God made possible that deliverance.

In verse 16 the unusual term "I, Jesus" is used to indicate that the Lord Jesus Christ had sent His angel to testify to the truth of this book to John for delivery to the churches. Additional titles ascribed to Christ are "the root and descendant of David" (cf. Isa. 11:1) and "the bright morning star" (cf. Num. 24:17; Rev. 2:28). Christ, as the morning star, heralds the coming day in His role of the One who comes for the church in the rapture. It is also true that His coming precedes the millennial kingdom. The reference to the churches of Asia is also significant. This is their first mention since Revelation 3:22.

THE INVITATION OF
THE SPIRIT AND THE BRIDE (22:17)

22:17 The Spirit and the Bride say, "Come." And let the one who hears say, "Come." And let the one who is thirsty come; let the one who desires take the water of life without price.

The Holy Spirit and Christ's bride, the church, now issue a wonderful invitation to eternal life. John is reporting the relevance and practical meaning of his prophecy for the age of which he is a part. In the light of the prophetic word, there is a threefold invitation to all, addressed first to the one who hears, then to the one who is thirsty, then to anyone who will. For all willing to accept the invitation, there is a proffer of the water of life without cost. A similar invitation is extended in Isaiah 55:1. Here it is an urgent command, for the day will arrive when it is too late to come. Now is the day of grace. The hour of judgment is impending.

THE FINAL TESTIMONY OF CHRIST (22:18–20)

22:18–20 I warn everyone who hears the words of the prophecy of this book: if anyone adds to them, God will add to

him the plagues described in this book, and if anyone takes away
from the words of the book of this prophecy, God will take away
his share in the tree of life and in the holy city, which are described
in this book. He who testifies to these things says, "Surely I am
coming soon." Amen. Come, Lord Jesus!

The urgency of the final command is supported by the solemn testimony
of Christ Himself concerning the sacred character of the prophecy given,
with a very sober warning attached. Though frequently in the Bible there are
other warnings against tampering with the Word of God, this is among the
most solemn (cf. Deut. 4:2; 12:32; Prov. 30:6; Rev. 1:3). No one can dare
add to the Word of God except in blatant unbelief and in denial that the
Word is indeed God's own message to humanity. Likewise, no one should
dare take away from the words of this Revelation, which is also an insult to
the inspired Word of God. What a solemn warning this is to critics who have
tampered with this book and other portions of Scripture in arrogant self-
confidence that they are equipped intellectually and spiritually to determine
what is true and what is not true in Scripture. Though not stated in detail, the
point of these two verses is that a child of God who reveres Him will recognize at once that this is the Word of God.

To use these verses, however, as a proof that a child of God once saved and
born into the family of God can lose his salvation is, of course, applying this
passage out of context. Rather, their tampering is proof that those who would
do this deserve to be excluded from the New Jerusalem.[9] This passage assumes
that a child of God will not tamper with these Scriptures. It is the contrast of
unbelief with faith, the blinded, fallen intellect of man in contrast to the
enlightened Spirit-taught believer. Although the true child of God may not
comprehend the meaning of the entire book of Revelation, he will recognize
in it a declaration of his hope and that which has been assured to him in
grace by his salvation in Christ.

The final testimony of the book is yet another repetition of the promise of Christ's soon return. In contrast to the other announcements in this
chapter (vv. 7, 12), this adds the word "surely," a particle used to enforce an

affirmation. It is followed by the word "amen," often translated "truly." Thus the announcement of Christ's coming is wrapped in words that emphasize its certainty. With the word "amen," John begins his own prayer of response: "Come, Lord Jesus!" Though Revelation concerns itself with a broad expanse of divine dealing with humanity, including the tribulation, the millennium, and the eternal state, for John the important event is the Lord's coming for him at the rapture of the church. For this his heart longs, not only because he is on the bleak island of Patmos in suffering and exile, but because of the glorious future he has seen and heard.

BENEDICTION (22:21)

22:21 The grace of the Lord Jesus be with all. Amen.

John closes this remarkable book with a phrase so familiar in Paul's epistles, a benediction that the Lord's grace will be upon his readers. This is only the second of two uses of the word "grace" in Revelation, 1:4 being the other. We could say that Revelation is "bookended" by God's grace, which encompasses all. This final book of the Scriptures, which began with the revelation of Jesus Christ, ends with a prayer that His grace might be with those who have witnessed the scene. Probably no book in the Bible presents in more stark contrast the grace of God as seen in the lives and destinies of the saints as compared to the righteous judgment of God on evil. In no other book are the issues made more specific. The Revelation is the presentation in the Word of God of what the saints will witness and experience in the glorious consummation of the ages.

With John we can pray, "Come, Lord Jesus!"

NOTES

1. Merrill F. Unger, *The New Unger's Bible Handbook*, rev. Gary N. Larson (Chicago: Moody, 2005), 688. See also Robert H. Mounce, *The Book of Revelation*, rev. ed., The New International Commentary on the New Testament (Grand Rapids: Eerdmans, 1997), 397–98.

2. Mounce, *The Book of Revelation*, 399.

3. John MacArthur, *The MacArthur New Testament Commentary: Revelation 12–22* (Chicago: Moody, 2000), 287.

4. Mounce, *The Book of Revelation*, 486.

5. Walter C. Kaiser and Duane Garrett, eds., *The Archaeological Study Bible* (Grand Rapids: Zondervan, 2005), 2074.

6. Charles C. Ryrie, *Revelation*, rev. ed. (Chicago: Moody, 1996), 145.

7. MacArthur, *Revelation 12–22*, 294.

8. F. F. Bruce, "Revelation," *New International Bible Commentary*, F. F. Bruce, gen. ed. (Grand Rapids: Zondervan, 1979), 1628.

9. Ryrie, *Revelation*, 147.

Bibliography

Bauer, Walter. *A Greek-English Lexicon of the New Testament.* William F. Arndt, Theodore Danker, and F. Wilbur Gingrich, trans. and rev., 3rd ed. Chicago: University of Chicago Press, 2000.

Benware, Paul. *Understanding End Times Prophecy.* Chicago: Moody, 2006.

Bruce, F. F., gen. ed. *New International Bible Commentary.* Grand Rapids: Zondervan, 1979.

Burer, Michael H., W. Hall Harris III, and Daniel B. Wallace, eds. *New English Translation: Novum Testamentum Graece.* Dallas: NET Bible Press, 2003.

Campbell, Donald K. and Jeffrey L. Townsend, gen. eds. *A Case for Premillennialism.* Chicago: Moody, 1992.

Evans, Tony. *The Best Is Yet to Come.* Chicago: Moody, 2000.

Fruchtenbaum, Arnold G. *The Footsteps of the Messiah: A Study of the Sequence of Prophetic Events.* Tustin, CA: Ariel Ministries, 2003.

Hendriksen, William. *More Than Conquerors.* Grand Rapids: Baker, 1967.

Johnson, Alan F. *Revelation.* The Expositor's Bible Commentary. Frank E. Gaebelein, ed. vol. 12. Grand Rapids: Zondervan, 1981.

Kaiser, Walter C. and Duane Garrett, eds. *The Archaeological Study Bible.* Grand Rapids: Zondervan, 2005.

MacArthur, John. *Because the Time Is Near.* Chicago: Moody, 2007.

_____. *The MacArthur New Testament Commentary: Revelation 1–11.* Chicago: Moody, 1999.

_____. *The MacArthur New Testament Commentary: Revelation 12–22.* Chicago: Moody, 2000.

Mounce, Robert H. *The Book of Revelation*. rev. ed. The New International Commentary on the New Testament. Grand Rapids, MI: Eerdmans, 1997.

Renatus, Flavius Vegetius. *The Military Institutions of the Romans*. Lt. John Clark, trans. Westport, CT: Greenwood Press Publishers, 1985.

Ryrie, Charles C. *Basic Theology*. Chicago: Moody, 1999.

_____. *Revelation*. rev ed. Chicago: Moody, 1996.

Smith, Wilbur M. *The Wycliffe Bible Commentary*. Charles F. Pfeiffer and Everett F. Harrison, eds. Chicago: Moody, 1990.

Swindoll, Charles R., John F. Walvoord, and J. Dwight Pentecost, eds. *The Road to Armageddon*. Nashville: Word Publishing, 1999.

Thomas, Robert L. *Revelation 1–7: An Exegetical Commentary*. Chicago: Moody, 1992.

_____. *Revelation 8–22: An Exegetical Commentary*. Chicago: Moody, 1995.

Unger, Merrill F. *The New Unger's Bible Dictionary*. R. K. Harrison, ed. Chicago: Moody, 1988.

_____. *The New Unger's Bible Handbook*. Gary N. Larson, rev. Chicago: Moody, 2005.

Walvoord, John F. and Roy B. Zuck, eds. *The Bible Knowledge Commentary: New Testament*. Wheaton, IL: Victor, 1983.

Wiersbe, Warren. *Wiersbe's Expository Outlines on the New Testament*. Wheaton, IL: Victor, 1992.

Subject Index

Abaddon, 161
Abraham, 47, 192, 199
abyss, the, 157–58, 260, 303
accuser, Satan as the, 196, 197
Adam, the last, 313
adultery, spiritual, 71–72, 254, 256, 259
"after this," 98
agapaō, 92
agapē, 198
agapēn, 56
Ages in Revelation, Four, 39
air, judgment on the, 249–51
Alcazar, Luis de, 22
Alexandrian school of theology, 13–14, 21
allegorical approach in scholarship, 21–22
Almighty, the, 43
Alpha and the Omega, the, 42–43, 88, 329, 347
altar, bronze, 178
altar, golden, 162
altars in heaven, 151
altars of incense, 162
amen, 41, 350
Amen, Jesus Christ as the, 87
amillennial interpretation, 25, 297, 298–302, 309, 310, 322
angelology, 34
angels
    angel and the seven thunders, 169–71

Angel of the Lord, 170
Angel of Yahweh, 138, 151
    announcing the fall of Babylon, 269
    authority over waters, 242
    fallen, 161, 271, 316
    as fellow servant, 286, 345
    final hallelujah and, 283
    four angels, loosing of the, 162–64
    four living creatures as, 105
    gospel, with the everlasting, 223
    holy *vs.* evil, 163
    identity of priestly, 151
    key to bottomless pit and, 303–4
    meaning of, 46
    mighty angel, the, 169–71
    ministries assigned to, 242
    pit of the abyss, 161
    power over fire, 229
    presence, the, 150
    revelation to John and, 38
    roles of, 34, 170
    seals and, 139–40
    seven, 149–52
    seven bowls and, 235–36, 331
    of the seven churches, 46
    seven with the plagues, 231–33
    with sharp sickle, 228–30
    singing of, 114
    stone and destruction of Babylon, 277–78
    strong, 109–10
    the term, 54

twenty-four elders as, 114
vision of the four, 138–39
worship of the, 114–15
anger, the term, 232–33
animals and symbolism, 28, 127
Annals, 18
another, the term, 169, 211, 223
anthropology and Revelation, 33–34
antichiliasm, 14
Antichrist, the, 123–124, 125, 127,
      203, 216, 263
Antipas, 65
apocalypse, the term, 37
Apocalypse of Saint John, The, 301
apocalyptic literature, biblical *vs.* non-
      biblical, 20, 26–27
Apollyon, 161
apostasy
      prostitute as symbol of, 24, 31
      Rome as seat of, 274
      in seven churches, 52–53, 68, 69–74
apostate church, the
      as Babylon, 224
      head of, 211–12
      persecution of true believers, 259
      rise and fall of, 265–66
      spiritual adultery and, 254
      true church *vs.,* 256
      woman on the beast as, 255–56
apostles, twelve apostles, 308, 333–34
Archippus, 88
ark of the covenant, 188, 235
Armageddon, 247–48
armies from the East, 164–65
armies of heaven, 290
army of the beast, doom of, 294
army of two hundred million, 150,
      164–66
ascension of Jesus Christ, 184–85,
      194–95

Asia, churches of, 348
Assyria, 262, 263
Augustine, 21, 299, 301, 305
Augustinian form of amillennialism,
      299–300
authorship of Revelation, 13–15, 37

Baal worship, 258
Babel, 256–57, 272, 278
Babylon
      destruction of, 253–54, 266, 269–
            72, 274, 276–78
      as "the great city," 250
      as Gentile empire, 262, 263
      greatness of, 278
      indictment against, 272–73
      influence on Roman church of, 256,
            266
      as Jerusalem, 22
      judgment upon, 34
      political/commercial/religious, 270
      prophecy of coming fall of, 224
      prostitutes, mother of, 256–59
      religious error and, 246
      as seat of Satan's new world empire,
            274
      spiritual, 250
      a woman, 224
Babylonian mysteries, 257–58
Bailey, Mark L., 84
Balaam, 66–67
banishment as punishment, 19
banishment from Garden of Eden, 341
Barclay, William, 78–79
battle of the great day of God
            Almighty, 291–94
Bauer, Walter, 232
bear, symbolism of, 205
beast, scarlet colored, 255
beast, the eighth, 261, 262

beast out of the earth, the
    identity of, 31, 211–12, 215–16
    miracles of, 212–13
    unholy trinity and, 215–16
beast out of the pit, 183, 260
beast out of the sea, the
    authority of, 205–6, 214
    blasphemous character of, 207
    described, 203–5
    destruction of, 260, 293
    dominion of, 208
    final battle and, 292–93
    identity of, 22, 31, 124, 183, 204,
        215–16
    lake of fire and, 316
    number of, 30
    origin of, 260–61
    revived Roman Empire as, 213
    as substitute for Jesus Christ, 108,
        206
    unholy trinity and, 215–16
    woman riding on, vision of, 255
    world ruler as, 213, 265, 270
    worship of, 134, 146, 166, 209,
        213–14, 225–26, 241, 308
    wound of, 205–6, 213
"beasts of the earth, wild," 127
beatitudes in Revelation, 38–39, 227,
    247, 285, 344, 347
believers
    in eternal state, 343
    forgivenss and eternal life for, 135
    light of Jesus Christ and, 332
    martyrdom of, 243
    overcomers, 221, 330
    priesthood and kingdom of, 41
    readiness of, 344
    reassurance for, 169
    resurrected/translated existence,
        326

Revelation and, the book of, 349
benediction, the, 350
Benjamin, the name, 100
Benware, Paul, 119, 200, 307
Bible, relation of Revelation to, 35
bibliology and Revelation, 32
bird, the, 271
birds of prey, 292
birth, new, 89–90
bishop of Rome, 259
black, the color, 126
blameless, the term, 222
blasphemy, names of, 204
blasphemy and the first beast, 207–8
blemish, without, 222
"blessed and holy," those who are, 311
blessings from God, 155–56
blessings in Revelation, 39
blood, hail and fire, 152, 153
blood, symbolism of, 144–45, 153, 290
blood, water turned to, 153, 240
blood of the Lamb, 144–45, 198
bodies and resurrection, 319
bodies of saints in heaven, 132
book, little, 170–71
book, seven-sealed, 109–10, 111
book of Life, 80, 209, 265, 318, 320
books of works, 318
bore witness, the term, 38
born again, 89–90, 92
botanical world and symbolism, 28
bottomless pit, 157–58, 260, 303–4
bow and arrows, 124–25
bowls, the seven
    angels and, 150, 235–36, 236–37
    chart, 240
    command to pour out, 239–40
    fifth, 240, 244–45
    first, 240, 241
    fourth, 240, 243–44

general discussion, 239–40

second, 240

seventh, 240, 248–51

seventh trumpet and, 186

similarities to the seven trumpets, 239–40

sixth, 240, 245–48

symbolism of, 22, 24, 31, 112, 122

third, 240, 242–43

bowls of incense, 112–13

bride, New Jerusalem as a, 327

bride, the Lamb's wife, 192, 283–87

bride, the term, 284–85

bride of Christ, 348

bridge between man and Satan, 258–59

bronze feet, 46, 69, 70

Bruce, F. F., 215, 225, 283, 333

Buis, Harry, 299–300

calf, a, 104

camp, the term, 315

Campbell, Donald K., 140

canon, Revelation and inclusion in the, 27–28

carnelian, 100–1, 336

"catching up," 194–95

censers, 152

chain, the term, 304

character based on present choices, 346

charts

Four Ages in Revelation, 39

Gentile Empires of the Earth, 263

Jesus Christ Is the Central Figure of Revelation 1:1–8. He Is:, 42

Key Events of the Millennium, 323

major views of the millennium, 322

Paradise Lost, Paradise Regained, 341

Parallels Between Matthew 24 and Revelation 6–7, 120

Scenes of Revelation, 121

Seven Bowl Judgments, 240

Seven Churches, The, 51

Seven Seal Judgments, The, 123

Seven Trumpet Judgments, The, 150

Structure of Letters to the Seven Churches, 53

Summary of the External Evidence (dates), 16

symbols and meanings in Revelation, 39

Three-Fold Case for Premillennialism, A, 300

Titles of the Coming World Ruler, 203

Two Babylons of Revelation, The, 270

child of the woman (Israel), birth of the, 194–95

chiliasm, doctrine of, 14, 19, 20, 21

Christological, Revelation as, 32

chronological structure of Revelation, 97–98, 302–3

chronos, 39

church, the

apostate church (*See* apostate church, the)

as bride of Christ, 194, 222, 284–85, 311, 348

future of, 84

in glory, 101–2

in heaven, 98–99

history of, 67, 93

Israel distinguished from, 334

as Israel of God, 140–41

lessons from letters to seven churches, 95

in Middle Ages, 72–73

New Jerusalem as, 327

organization of early, 67–68

problems in, 51–52

rapture and, the, 53, 119, 137, 210, 345–46, 348, 350

reign of Christ and, 311

in Revelation, 99, 119

state in modern times, 78–79, 95

theologies of, 34

tribulation and, the great, 119

the true, 53

twenty-four elders as, 113–14

as the vine, 229

as wife of the Lamb, 34–35, 99

church age, the, 98, 299, 310, 322, 334

church history, Revelation as, 52–53

church in heaven, the, 98

churches of Asia Minor, 16–19, 51

churchianity, 90

cities of the world, judgments and, 250

city, the great, 31, 250

City of God, 21, 299

Clement of Alexndria, 14, 15, 21, 43

"cloud coming" of Jesus, 22

clouds and smoke, 237

"come," 348

"Come, Lord Jesus!", 350

"come up here," 98

command to proclaim the prophecy, 345–46

command to worship God, 345

commissioning to write Revelation, 48–49

compromise and faithfulness, 66–67

Constantine, 64, 67, 301

Council of Nicea, 67

covenant theologians, 298

creation, a new, 325

creation, worship of all, 115–17

creature, the term, 104

creatures, the living, 31, 105–7, 282

creatures and fallen angels, 271

crowns

casting down of, 106

of life, 61, 62, 63

symbolism of, 290

ten, 204

types of, 102, 125

crucifixion of Christ, 34

curse, removal of, 323, 342

damnation, eternal, 260

Dan, tribe of, 140

Daniel, writing of book of, 257

Darby, J. N., 188

darkness and pain, plague of, 240, 244–45

date of composition, 15–20, 19

David, the key of, 31, 82

David, the Root of, 110–11

day, the term, 160, 163, 307

day in New Jerusalem, 339

day of divine wrath, the, 132–35

day of grace, today is, 230

day of the Lord, 44

dead, judgment of the, 187

death

described, 316

as escape, 134

eternal, 321

faithfulness to, 63, 131, 198

first *vs.* second, 311

fourth seal and, 126–30

second, 63, 320, 330

Word of God and, 65

Death, rider of the fourth horse, 127

deceiver, the, 197

"deep things" of Satan, 73

deliverance from the great tribulation, 84–85

demonic invasion, 150, 158–60

demonic possession, 162, 214
demons, shape of, 161
denarius, value of, 126
destroyers of human souls, 161
destruction of earth and heaven, 317
devastation and upheaval, universal,
    123, 152–53, 153–54
devil, the, 196, 200, 212–13
diadem, the term, 102
dictator, the world, 183, 203, 211,
    265–66. *See also* ruler of the
    world, coming
Dionysius of Alexandria, 13
disciples, revelation of God to, 47
discipline, the term, 92
dispensational interpretation, 298
divisions of the book of Revelation, 40,
    48, 49, 51
doctrines
    of Balaam, 66–67
    of chiliasm, 14
    of God, 33
    God's grace, 321
    judgment of sin, 35
    of man, 33–34
    of millennial kingdom, 13–14
    of mystery religions, 258
    of Nicolaitans, 66–67
    rapture, the, 35, 99
    of redemption, 34
    resurrection, 35
    reward, 35
    right living and, 82
    of Scripture, 32
    of sin, 33–34
    sovereignty of God, 62
    a thousand years, 300–2
Domitian, 15, 19, 28, 43, 204, 217n10
done, the term, 329
door, open, 83, 93

doxology, 41
dragon, great
    authority of, 205, 211
    cast out of heaven, 196–97
    described, 193–94, 201–2
    identity of, 31
    as serpent, 200
dragon, great red, 231–32
dragon, the term, 196
drunk with the blood of martyrs, 259–
    60
dwell, the term, 328
dwelling place of God, 328
Dyer, Charles, 8, 250

eagle, 104, 155, 200
earth
    devastation of, 152–53
    human control of, 186
    new, 317, 325–26
    Satan cast down to, 197, 199
    the term, 128
"earth, on," the phrase, 114
earthquake and sixth seal, 132–34
earthquake in Laodicea, 18–19
earthquakes and final judgment, 250
earthquakes and plague, 240
East, armies from the, 164–65
eastern boundary, invasion across, 245–
    46
eat, the term, 93–94, 173
eating of the little scroll, 173–75
ecclesiastical power, 255, 266, 274
ecclesiology, 34
Eden, Garden of, 313, 316, 341, 342
Egypt as Gentile empire, 262, 263
Egypt as Jerusalem, 31
eighth beast, the, 261, 262
eighth kingdom (Antichrist), the, 263
ekklēsia, 35

elders, the twenty-four
  as the church, 101–2, 282
  hallelujah of, 282
  identity of, 113–14, 143
  judgment and resurrection of,
    307–9
  reign on earth of, 308
  worship of, 105–7, 187
elect of all ages, 143
Eliakim, 82
Elijah, 180, 200
empires, successive world, 205
end-historical view, 298
end of the age, announcement of,
    171–73
end-time events. *See* rapture, the
ended, the term, 314
Enoch, 181–82
Ephesus, church of, 16–17, 51, 54–59,
    95
Ephesus, the city, 54, 58
Ephraim, tribe of, 140
eschatology and Revelation, 32, 35
Esdraelon, valley of, 247–48
eternal life, invitation to, 348
eternal residence in paradise, 341
eternal states, 321, 343
eternity, 317, 322, 323
Euphrates River, 163, 240, 245–48
Eusebius, 14–15, 43
Evans, Tony, 204, 254
Eve, 329
events, order of, 98, 122–23, 128–29
everlasting gospel, the, 223
evil, 266, 339, 346
evil dead, resurrection of, 317–19
exhortations, personal, 52
exhortations to hear, 209–11
"eye for an eye," 272
eyes, symbolism of, 104

eyes, the seven, 31, 33, 111
Ezekiel, 44, 47

faith and works, 226
faithful, the suffering, 169
faithfulness to death, 63, 198
false prophet, the, 34, 211–13, 215–
    16, 293, 316
false religion, 254
famine, 120, 126
Father in Revelation, the, 33
fathers of the church, beliefs of, 24–25
fear of God, 235
feet of bronze, 46, 69, 70
fellowship, blessedness of, 343–44
fellowship with Christ, 93–94
female prophetess, 72
final battle, 291–94, 314–15
finished, the term, 232, 314
Fiora, Joachim de, 23
fire
  blood and hail, 152, 153
  coming down from heaven, 212
  power over, 229
  symbolism of, 46, 233
first and the last, the, 47, 60
firstborn from the dead/of all creation,
    88
firstfruits, 41, 222, 310
flood sent by Satan, 200–1
food sacrificed to idols, eating, 71
"forever and ever," 186
forgiveness and blood of the Lamb, 145
forty-two month period, 120, 128,
    132, 179, 180–81, 207
foundation of the world, 208
foundations of New Jerusalem, 336–37
fountain of water of life, 329
four, the number, 30
four angels, the, 162–64

four living creatures, the, 31, 103–5, 197, 282
free will and demonic affliction, 160
Fruchtenbaum, Arnold G., 200
fulfillment of Revelation's prophecies, 97
futurist interpretations, 23–25, 97–98, 122–23, 217n10, 234–35
futuristic character of Revelation, 26–27

Gabriel, the angel, 38, 101, 110, 150
Garden of Eden. *See* Eden, Garden of
garments, preservation of, 247
garments, white, 80, 91, 142
garments of salvation, 247
gates and walls of New Jerusalem, 332–34, 335, 337, 339
gematria, 215
geneology of Israel, 139–40, 141
Gentiles
    beast out of the sea and, 204, 211
    end of times of, 250
    Gentile Empires of the Earth, 263
    God's purpose for, 339
    as Israel, 140–41
    millennial kingdom and, 313
    new converts, 137
    New Jerusalem and, 338–39, 342
    program of, 35
    saved and the great tribulation, 142, 143, 147
    temple in Jerusalem and, 179–80
geography and symbolism, 28–29
Gideon, 47
glory, the term, 281
glory of God, effects of, 47
goats *vs.* sheep, 74, 318
God
    attributes and character of, 33, 40, 104, 281–82, 291

as Creator, 107, 172
execution of judgments by, 163
the Father, 101
fear of, 235
glory of, 332
as light of New Jerusalem, 336–37, 338
love of, 198, 291
measuring rod of, 178–80
in New Jerusalem, 331–32
as omnipotent and omnipresent, 100, 137–38
purposes of, 106
redemption of, 34
secrets of, 171
seven Spirits of, 111
sovereignty of, 62, 104, 106–7, 172
throne of, 99–101, 329, 335, 341, 343
Word of, 65
"God in heaven, the," 185–86
Gog and Magog, 314–15
gold, symbolism of, 45, 91, 102, 236
golden age, 298–99, 302
gospel, the, 198, 223
Gospels, four living creatures and the, 105
government, Satan's new world, 210–11, 261, 262–63
governments, changes in human, 133–34
grace, salvation by, 80
grace, the day of, 135, 348
grace, the term, 39–40, 350
great, the term, 239
"great and small," 318
great city, the, 31, 250
Greece as Gentile empire, 262, 263
green, the color, 127
green horse, pale, 127

greeting of Revelation, 39–43

Hades, 47, 127, 293, 319, 320
Hagar, 170
hagios, 35
hail, plague of, 240, 251
hail and fire, bloody, 150, 152–53
hallelujah, 281, 282–83
hamartiology and Revelation, 33–34
harlot, the, 192
harps, 112, 233
harvest, the, 228–30
hate and Christians, 58, 67
heads, seven, 193, 204, 255, 261–63
healing in paradise, 342
heaping, the term, 272
"heard" and "I looked, I," 115
heaven
    for believers, 116
    the church and, 119
    first, second and third, 98, 197
    John translated to, 98
    ministry of saints in, 146
    new, 317, 325–26
    translated to, 119, 137, 181–82
    two witnesses ascend to, 184–85
    warfare in, 158
heavenly host, praise of, 142
heavens departing as a scroll, 133, 134, 157
hell, 63, 225–26, 293. *See also* lake of fire
Hendriksen, William, 23, 170, 229, 302
Herod, 194, 199
hill, the term, 262
"his Christ," 198
historical interpretation, 23, 122–23, 248
history, Augustine on human, 299

Hitchcock, Mark, 10
Hoehner, Harold W., 300–1
hold, the term, 55
holy, the term, 222
Holy of Holies, 235
Holy Spirit, the
    allusions to, 40
    in the book of Revelation, 33
    invitation to eternal life, 348
    as omnipresent, 138
    purposes of, 286
    seven Spirits of God and, 103, 111
    sevenfold character of, 78, 111
    tribulation and, the great, 137–38
hope, certainty of, 344–45, 346, 349
hope and book of Revelation, 35
hōra, 39
horn, the little, 203, 216
horns, four, 162
horns, seven, 33, 111
horns, ten, 31, 193, 204, 255, 263–64
horns like a lamb, two, 211
horses
    black, 123, 126
    pale, 123, 127
    red, 123, 125
    rider of the white, 31, 123–24, 129, 136n2, 289
    riders of the four, 31, 124
    the term, 165
    white, 123, 289
host, the heavenly, 142
hour, the term, 163
hour of trial, 84
human control of earth, 186
human nature and hardness of heart, 226, 244–45, 251, 315
humanity, redeemed, 341
hunger, 146
hymns of Moses and the Lamb, 234

"I am the resurrection and the life," 309
"I looked" and "I heard," 115
idolatry, 66–68, 71, 213–14, 257–58
if, the term, 321
image to the beast, 213–14
incarnation of Jesus Christ, 138
incense, 112–13, 151, 152
indifference as sin, 90
infants as saved, 335
innocence, human, 341
inspired, Revelation as divinely, 21
intermarriage, 66–68
interpretation of Revelation
    approaches to, 20–26, 97–98
    basis for, 119
    considerations in, 120–21
    futurist, 122–23
    historical, 122–23
    issues in, 21, 153–54, 292, 306, 331
    symbolism and, 27–32, 177
invitation and promise of God
    to eternal life, 348
    from heaven, 97–99
    little scroll and, 174
    to seven churches, 59, 68, 73–74,
        80–81, 86, 93–94
inviting Jesus Christ in, 93–94
Irenaeus, 15, 43
Isaiah, 47
Israel
    church and, the, 140–41, 334
    as descendants of Jacob, 140
    geneology of, 139–40
    God's purpose for, 141, 147
    lost tribes of, 139–40, 141
    millennial kingdom and, 313
    persecution of, 199–201, 201–2
    preservation through tribulation,
        195
    program of events in Revelation
        and, 35, 120, 128
    remnant of, godly, 137
    as source of the Messiah, 192–93
    supernatural care of, 200, 201
    the term, 140
    tribes of, 100, 139–41, 333–34
    as unfaithful wife, 284
    as the vine, 229
    as "virgin daughter of Zion," 222
    as the woman, 232
    as woman clothed with the sun,
        191–93

Jacob, 140, 192
jasper, 100–1, 332, 336
Jerome, 21
Jerusalem, 22, 183, 250, 312, 315,
    333–34
Jerusalem, the New
    access to, 339–40
    as the bride, 330–32
    described, 331–32, 333, 336–37
    dimensions of, 334–35
    first vision of, 326–27
    gates and walls of, 332–34
    inhabitants of, 327–28, 331, 334,
        335, 339–40
    Jerusalem of the millennium and,
        333–34
    light of the city, 336–37, 338–39
    during the millennium, 326–27
    temple of, 337
    the term, 86, 101
Jesus Christ
    as Adam, 313
    as Almighty God, 42, 43
    as Alpha and the Omega, 42–43,
        88, 329, 347
    as the Amen, 87

as Angel of the Lord, 170
as Angel of Yahweh, 138, 151
as the Anointed, 187
appearance and attributes of, 45–46, 289–90
as author of truth, 82
authority of, 47–48, 198
as the beginning, 87–88
in book of Revelation, 33, 37–39, 42
as child of the woman, 192–95
church, coming for the, 344
as Creator and Judge of all, 290
as deity, 33
as the eternal One, 60
on eternal punishment, 321
as faithful Witness, 40, 42, 87–88
fellowship with, 93–94
first and second coming of, 195
as first and the last, 47
as firstborn, 40–41, 41, 42, 88
as firstfruits, 41, 310
Hagar and, 170
on hell, 225
as High Priest (angel), 151
as Holy One, 69–70, 73, 82
incarnation of, 138
inviting in of, 93–94
as Judge, 54–55, 64, 70, 78, 94, 111
King of kings and Lord of lords, 30, 251, 289, 290–91
as the Lamb (*See* Lamb, the)
as light, 332, 338
as the Lion, 110, 111
majesty of eternal, 347–48
as omnipresent and omniscient, 78, 138
as Possessor of the Spirit, 78–79
power and authority of, 47–48, 198
prophecy and Scripture, as central theme of, 286

on the prophecy in Revelation, 349–50
rapture and seeing, the, 41–42
as the reaper, 227–28
as redeemer, 34
reign of, 74, 186–91, 198
return of, beliefs about, 22, 24
revelation of, 286–87
as Root of David, 30, 110–11
as Ruler, 41, 42, 306
sacrifice of, 72–73, 145
second coming of, 34, 35, 39, 41, 93
as Son of God, 70
as Son of Man, 45
sovereignty of, 47, 54, 82, 87, 100, 290
substitutionary death of, 145
symbols in Revelation for, 170
testimony of, final, 348–50
thief, coming as a, 247
throne, great white, 316
titles of, 289–90, 291, 348
transfiguration of, 47
victory of, 111
as Word of God, 290
Jewish believers and Satan, 201–2
Jewish nation, God's purpose for, 141, 147
Jewish war, 22
Jews, identity of beasts as, 216
Jews, saved, 137, 220–21
Jezebel, 70–73, 192
Job, 47
John, gospel of, 37
John, the apostle
  as author of Revelation, 13–15, 37
  banishment to Patmos, 14–15, 19–20, 43
  commissioning to write Revelation, 48–49

in Ephesus, 55
instructions from Jesus Christ, 44
in the presence of God, 99–100
purposes of, 173–74
revelation of God to, 47
suffering of, 174
John Mark, 14
John the Baptist, 181
John the Elder, 14
John the Presbyter, 14
Johnson, Alan F., 298, 304
Johnson, S. Lewis, 140–41
Joseph, tribe of, 140
Joshua, 182
Judah, tribe of, 110
Judas and Satan, 305
judgment
    of all people, 230
    answer to persecuted saints and,
        162
    chart, 322
    directness of God's, 273
    of earth, 188
    elements of, 134
    evil dead and, 317–19
    given to the Son, 316
    God's love vs., 291
    great white throne, 323
    impending, 348
    means of administering, 163
    mercy and, 294
    of nonbelievers, 135
    protection by angelic seal and, 139
    rejoicing and God's, 276
    sickles and, 228–29
    of son of man, 227–28
    time of divine, 120, 135
    of tribulation saints, 307–9
    of wicked, 135
    on worshipers of the beast, 225–26

kairos, 39
key of David, the, 31, 82
key to bottomless pit, 157–58, 303–4
keys of Death and Hades, 82
killing of mankind, 128–29, 164–66
king, the willful, 203, 216
King of kings and Lord of lords, 287,
    290–91, 291, 344
king of the locusts, 161
king vs. kingdom, the terms, 262
kingdom, establishment of His, 42
kingdom (Antichrist), the eighth, 262,
    263
kingdom of believers, 41
kingdoms, seven, 262
kingdoms, ten, 193
kings
    of earth, 273–75, 339
    from the east, 245–46
    seven, 261–62
    of the world empire, ten, 31, 263,
        264

lake of fire
    beasts thrown into, 207, 212, 316
    Hades compared to, 47, 319
    Jesus on, 225
    meanings of, 30, 320–21
    Satan and, 225, 293, 316
    second death, 311
    unsaved, the, 330
Lamb, the
    144,000 on Mount Zion and,
        219–22
    Christ as, 29, 30, 33, 34
    marriage supper of, 283–87
    seven attributes of, 115
    as slain, 111, 205, 209
    song of, 233–35
    the term, 111

throne of, 341
wife of, 192, 236, 331
worship of, 112–14
lament, the term, 275
laments of kings and merchants of
    earth, 273–75, 275–76
lamps of fire, the seven, 31
lampstands, the seven, 31, 45, 48, 55
lampstands, two witnesses as, 182
Laodicea, church of, 18–19, 51, 86–94,
    95, 273
Laodicea, the city, 86–87, 91
law of divine retribution, 210, 272–73
leopard, 205
letters to the seven churches
    to Laodicea, 86–94
    lessons from, 95
    overcomers in, 330
    Pergamum, 64–69
    Philadelphia, 81–86
    to Sardis, 77–81
    Smyrna, 59–64
    structure of, 53–54
    Thyatira, 69–74
lex talionis, 272
life, the power to give, 213
light, symbolism of bright, 46
light of New Jerusalem, 336–37, 338–
    39, 339, 343
light of the Lamb, 332
light of the world, 338
linen, fine, 31, 236, 285
lion, a, 104, 165, 205
literal interpretation, 29, 97–98, 177,
    297, 312–13
literal interpretation of numbers, 307
living creatures, the four, 31, 103–5,
    197, 282
locusts as demons, 159–61
"looked" and "I heard, I," 115

Lord's day, the, 44
Lord's Supper, the, 72–73
lost tribes of Israel, 139–40, 141
loud *(mega),* the term, 239
love, judgment vs. God's, 291
love, the term, 56, 92, 198
love for God, fading, 56–57
lukewarm, spiritual state of, 88–91, 92
Lydia, 69–70, 71
lyres, 233. *See also* harps

MacArthur, John, 80, 101, 113, 172,
    242, 249, 260, 271–72, 281,
    287, 299, 300, 302
Magog and Gog, 314–15
make, the term, 329
"making all things new," 328–30
Malachi, prophecy of, 181
man, symbolism of, 104
man of lawlessness, the, 203, 216
man of sin, 216
Manasseh, tribe of, 140
mankind, Jesus Christ as judge of,
    227–28
mankind, killing of, 128–29, 164–66
mankind, symbol for, 215
manna, the hidden, 31, 68
Manoah, revelation of God to, 47
Marah, waters of, 154
mark of the beast, 214–16, 217n10,
    225, 308, 321
marriage, symbolism of, 284–85
marriage customs, ancient, 284
marriage supper of the Lamb, 80, 283–
    87, 285–86
martyrdom of Polycarp, 63
martyrs
    appeals for judgment by, 130–31,
    282
    bliss of saints, heavenly, 146

classes of, 132
described, 132, 137
godly remnant, 201
of the great tribulation, 131–32,
142, 233, 281, 282
in heaven, 131–32, 221
Israelites among, 141, 234
new song and, 221
symbolism of, 123
tribulation saints, 137, 143–45,
233, 308
victory of the saints and, 198
Mary, mother of our Lord, 67–68, 72,
73, 192–93
material wealth, 90–91, 276
measuring, the term, 178
measuring rod and New Jerusalem, 335
measuring rod of God, 178–80
Medo-Persia, 262, 263
Megiddo, 247–48
messiah, false, 258
Messiah, Israel as source of, 192–93
Michael, the angel, 110, 170, 181,
195–97
Michael, the prince, 128–29
Middle Ages, the church in, 72–73
millennial kingdom
announcement of, 198
born during, those, 314
Christ now vs. Christ and, 94
Christians and, 74
described, 35, 306, 312–14
length of, 306
mystery fulfilled and, 172–73
preaching the gospel and, 143
rebellion in, 314–15
second coming of Jesus Christ and,
303
millennium, the
events introducing, 302–3

Key Events of the Millennium
(chart), 323
major views of, 297, 322
reign of Christ, 74, 114
resurrection and, 41
Satan and, 304–5
month, the term, 160, 163, 307
moon darkened, 120, 132, 150, 155
moon in Garden of Eden, 341
morning star, the, 74, 348
morning stars, 114
Moses, 181
Moses, song of, 233–34
mother and child, legend of (cult), 258
Mounce, Robert H., 83, 243, 312, 327
Mount Zion, 220
mountain, the term, 262
mountain from heaven, fiery, 150, 153
mountains, seven, 261–63
musical instruments and symbolism,
28, 233
myrrh, 60
"mystery of God," 172–73
mystery religions of Babylon, 257–59

nakedness, spiritual, 247
names
of blasphemy, 204
of God on forehead, 343
new, 69, 86, 221
numerical values of, 215
pseudonyms vs. genuine, 14
Naphtali, tribe of, 140
nations, the term, 338, 339, 342
nature and symbolism, 28
nature as manifestation of God, 156
Nebuchadnezzar, 213, 215, 257, 270
Nero, 15, 19, 22, 217n10
"new, making all things," 328–30
new, the term, 329

new birth, 89–90

New Jerusalem. *See* Jerusalem, the New

new names for believers, 69, 86, 221

new songs, 113, 114, 221

Nicolaitans, 58, 66–67

Nicolaus, the proselyte of Antioch, 58

Nile River turned to blood, 153

Nimrod, 257

Noah, 128, 129, 139, 164

nonliteral approach in scholarship, 21–22

number of the beast, 214–16

numbers
    666, 30

numbers, interpretation of, 29–30, 300, 307

numerical values and names, 215

Old Testament references, 28–29, 32

olive oil, 45

olive trees, 182

omnipresence and omniscience of God, 104

"on earth," the phrase, 114

144,000, 120, 137, 139, 141, 147, 219–22, 300

1,600 stadia, 229, 300

1,260 days, 180, 300

oral tradition in the early church, 38

Origen, 15, 21

overcomers, 221, 330

palm branches, 142

Papias, 14

Paradise Lost, Paradise Regained, 341

Parallels Between Matthew 24 and Revelation 6-7, 120

Patmos, banishment of John to, 14–15, 19–20, 43

Paul

blinding of, 46

churches and, seven, 16–18, 54, 56–57, 87, 88

execution of, 19

on fading love for God, 57

greetings in letters of, 39

on Israel of God, 140–41

Jews' hostility toward, 61

revelations to, 44

on Satan, 305

spiritual state of, 89

suffering of, 62

on "the mystery of his will," 172

peace, existence of, 166

peace, the term, 39–40

peace of the dead, 78

people and symbolism, 28

perfection, symbol for, 215

Pergamum, church of, 51, 64–69, 95, 258

Pergamum, the city, 64

persecution, retribution for, 210

persecution of the early church, 64

Persia, 262, 263

Peter, 19, 44, 47, 305

Petra, 200

Philadelphia, church of, 51, 81–86, 95

Philadelphia, the city, 81–82, 86

Philadelphia, the word, 81

phileō, 92

Phrygian powder, 91

pit, bottomless, 157–58, 260, 303–4

plagues
    of bowls, 231–32, 239, 272
    described, 232
    of the tribulation and Egypt, 152–53, 158–61, 181, 241, 242, 244

Poellot, Luther, 281

political power, 274

Polycarp, 17, 61, 63
pomp, ecclesiatical, 256
Pontifex Maximus, 259
poor, the term, 90
pope and papacy, the, 23
population centers on earth, 165
postmillennial interpretation, 23, 25,
    297, 302–3, 322
poverty, spiritual, 90
"power, little," 83
power, the term, 281
praise, command to, 283
praises by saints to God, 282, 283
prayer, effectiveness of, 152
prayer, importance of, 113
prayer in the name of Christ, 152
prayers of the saints, 112, 113, 162
premillennial interpretation, 25, 297–
    98, 300, 306, 311, 322
Premillennialism, A Three-Fold Case
    for, 300
presence of God, the term, 328
preterist approach in scholarship,
    22–23, 98, 217n10, 301
priesthood in Israel, 101–2
priesthood of believers, 41
priests of Babylonian cults, 258–59
priests of God and of Christ, 311
prince, the coming, 203
"prince who is to come," 124, 129, 216
promise of God to seven churches, 59,
    93–94
prophecies
    chronology of events in, 325–26
    fulfillment of Old Testament, 297
    interpretation of, 121
    John instructed to make, 173–74
    Revelation as book of, 39
    themes of, 26, 35, 286
    time lapses in, 195

of two witnesses, 180–82
    understanding of, 25
prophets
    deaths of, 183–84
    of doom, 182
    the false, 34, 211–13, 215–16, 293,
        316
    female, 72
    John compared to other, 173
    two witnesses as, 181–82
prostitute, the, 31, 35, 253–54, 264–
    66, 278–79
protection of God's own, 139
Protestant Reformation, 23, 81
pseudepigrapha, 26–27
punishment, eternal, 320–21
purple dye and cloth, 69

queen of heaven, 258

Rachel, 192
Rahab, protection of, 139
rapture, the
    announcement of, 41
    believers and, 53, 116, 182
    church age and, the, 310
    described, 184
    doctrine of, 35, 99
    John entering heaven and, 98
    as next great event, 39
    saved people on earth after, 119,
        137–38, 210, 345–46, 348,
        350
    second coming of Christ *vs.,* 287
    timing of, 84–85, 98–99, 143
    who will *see* Jesus Christ and, 41–42
reaping by Jesus Christ, 227–28
red, the color, 193
redemption, 34, 290, 341
Reformation, the Protestant, 23, 81

refuge from persecutors, 200, 201
reign of believers, 343–44
reign of Christ
    announcement of, 150
    character of, 344
    church and, the, 309, 311
    described, 312–14
    earthly, 114
    event marking the, 187–88
    general description, 297–303
    Satan and, 306
religion, false, 254
religion, world, 209
religious freedom, 265
remnant, godly
    bride of the Lamb, 192
    identification of, 201
    invitation and promise to, 80–81
    of Israel in the great tribulation,
        137, 139, 140–41
    persecution of, 201–2
    preservation of, 200, 208, 221
    responsibilities of, 73
repentance
    call to, 68, 92
    described, 166
    hardness of human heart and, 226,
        244–45, 251
    of saints in heaven, 146–47
reprove, the term, 92
resurrection
    bodily *vs.* spiritual, 309, 310
    body condition and, 319
    of evil dead, 317–19
    first, 41, 301, 309–12, 320, 322
    "I am the resurrection and the life,"
        309
    Jesus Christ and, 40–41, 44
    of others with Christ, 310
    of the righteous dead, 187

satanic anticipation of, 258
from the sea, 319
second, 301, 322
the term, 310
thousand years between first and
    second, 312
of tribulation saints, 307–9
two witnesses and, the, 184–85
universal, 319
of the wicked, 309, 311
retribution, law of divine, 210, 272–73
retribution for martyred saints, 277
retribution in present time, 135
Reuben, the name, 100
Revelation, the book of
    acceptance as Scripture, 20, 49n1
    all churches and, 51–52
    apocalyptic character of, 26–27
    author of, 37
    chronological structure of, 40,
        97–98
    command to proclaim the
        prophecy, 345–46
    described, 345, 350
    divisions of, 39, 40, 48, 49, 51
    early church history and, 13–14
    fulfillment of prophecies of, 97
    interpretations of, 48
    Jesus Christ on, 349–50
    objectives of, 32
    outline of, 48–49, 97
    prophetic character of, 37
    purposes of, 26, 49, 99, 106
    recipients of, 39, 44, 51
    scenes of, shifting, 121–22
    source of, 37
    symbols in, 49
    as Word of God, 349
revelation, the term, 37
revelation of Jesus Christ, 286–87

revolt, final, 312, 314–15, 323
reward of believers, 135, 346
riches, material, 90–91, 276
riches, true, 276
rider of the beast, 255
rider of the white horse, 125, 203
ripe, the term, 228, 229
river of life, 325, 335, 341, 342
"robes, who wash their," 347
robes of martyrs, white, 131, 142, 144
rod, New Jerusalem and the measuring,
    335
rod, rule all nations with an iron, 194,
    291
rod of God, measuring, 178–80
"rod of his mouth," 291
Roman church
    influence of Babylon on, 256, 266
    on Mary, mother of our Lord, 192–
        93
    mystery religion of Babylon and,
        258–59
    political power and, 255
    state of, 81
Roman Empire, historical, 262, 263
Roman Empire, revived
    as beast, 203–4, 255, 263
    beast out of the sea as, 213
    as dragon, 193
    form of, 264
    as Gentile empire, 262, 263
    wounded head of beast and, 206
Rome, 250, 261, 262, 274, 301
Root of David, Jesus Christ as the,
    110–11, 348
rule, the term, 74
rule all nations with an iron rod, 194
rule by Christ's faithful ones, 74
ruler of the world, coming, 125, 203,

    213, 215, 260–61. See also dic-
        tator, the world
Ryrie, Charles C., 23, 44, 61, 78, 125,
    163, 220, 277

sackcloth, 182
sacrifice of Christ, finished vs. contin-
    ual, 72–73
sacrifice of Christ, substitutionary, 145
sacrifices, temple, 323
saints
    of all ages and their treatment, 286,
        335
    believers as servants and, 344
    blessing of the, 226–27
    bodies in heaven of, 131–32
    the church, 307
    classes of, 132
    death of in the millennium, 318,
        319
    descendants of tribulation, 314
    described, 137
    glorified, 343
    godly remnant, 80–81
    groups in tribulation, 137
    heavenly bliss of martyred, 145–47
    Israel as, 307
    ministry in heaven of, 146
    Old Testament, 334
    persecution by apostate church, 259
    resurrection of, 310
    retribution for persecution of, 210
    in Revelation, 99
    righteous deeds of the, 285
    shouts in heaven of, 281–82
    songs of martyred, 234–35
    tribulation saints, 143–45, 221,
        307–9, 330–31
    victory of, 197–99, 198
salutation of Revelation, 39–43

salvation, 34, 65, 80, 198, 281
salve, 91
sanctuary, 235–36
Sardis, church of, 51, 77–81, 95
Sardis, the city, 77, 78, 79
Satan
    as accuser, 196, 197
    air and the domain of, 249
    as the beast, 183
    binding up of, 158, 163, 298, 301,
        303–7
    body of Moses and, 181
    bottomless pit and, 183, 260
    cast out of heaven, 195–97, 199,
        249
    character of, 161–62
    death, authority over, 47–48, 205
    deep things of, 73
    descriptions of, 260
    doom of, 315–16
    as dragon, 193–94, 211, 246
    fall of, 305
    as fallen star, 157–58
    forces of, 83–84
    in Garden of Eden, 316
    government powered by, 210–11
    as great red dragon, 193–94
    hell and, 293
    home of, 260
    as imitator of God, 182, 216
    Israel and, 199–201
    Jewish believers and, 201–2
    key to pit of the abyss, 158
    meaning of, 196
    Michael and, 170
    in New Testament, 305
    power of, 47–48, 205–6
    purposes of, 206, 211, 314
    release of, 312, 314–15
    revolt of, 323

    symbols of, 31
    synagogue of, 83
    titles of, 196
    today, 305–6
    witnesses belonging to, 182
    worship by world of, 206–7, 210–
        12
    wrath of, 197–99
saved people after the rapture, 137–38,
    142
scorpions, 159
Scripture, central theme of, 286
Scripture, Revelation and acceptance
    as, 20, 49n1
Scripture, Revelation and connections
    to rest of, 32
scroll, little, 170–71, 173–75
scroll, seven-sealed, 109–10, 111, 170–
    71
sea, devastation on the, 153–54
sea, resurrection from the, 319
sea of brass in the temple, 104
sea of glass, 104, 233
seal of God the Father and Christ,
    219–20
seal with God's name, 343
seals, angelic, 139–40
seals, seven
    described, purposes of, 122
    fifth, 123, 130–32
    first, 122–25, 123, 125, 129–30
    fourth, 123, 126–30
    interpretation of, 122–23
    as judgment, 22, 24
    order of events in, 231
    second, 123, 125
    seventh, 123, 149, 231
    sixth, 123, 132–35
    symbolism of, 109
    third, 123

unfolding of, 122
seas turned to blood, judgment of, 240, 241–42
second coming of Jesus Christ
  angels and, 34
  announcement of, 41
  anticipation of, 264
  events prior to, 35
  introduction of, 281–87
  millennial kingdom and, 303
  mystery fulfilled and, 172–73
  Old and New Testament anticipation of, 288–89
  parallels between Revelation and Matthew, 120
  rapture *vs.,* the, 287
  seven seals and, 122
  seven years of Israel's program and, 120
  as a thief, 247
  timing of, 37–38, 39, 85, 93, 231, 322, 323
secrets of God, 171
Semiramis, 258
seraphim, 105
serpent, the term, 165, 196, 200
servant, apostle as, 38
servants of Christ, 286
servants of God and New Jerusalem, 343
seven, the number, 29–30, 52, 150, 215, 232
Seven Bowl Judgments, 240
seven churches, as foreshadow of later churches, 81
seven churches, chart of the, 51
seven churches, significance of, 52
Seven Seal Judgments, The (chart), 123
seven years, 24, 120, 128, 132

seventieth week of Daniel, 120, 128–29, 132, 180–81, 265
sexual immoralities, 70–71
sheep *vs.* goats, 74, 200, 318
sickle of Jesus Christ, 227–28
sign, the term, 191
signs of divine judgment, 232
silence, 149, 278
sin, blood of the Lamb and, 145
sin, Garden of Eden and, 341
sin, man of, 216
sin, paradise regained and, 341
sin, sharing in others', 272
666, 30, 217n10
six, the number, 30, 215
slaves of Christ, 286
Smith, J. B., 234, 239
Smith, Wilbur M., 297
smoke, 237
Smyrna, church of, 17–18, 51, 95
Smyrna, the city, 59–60
Sodom, 31, 183, 251, 326
Son, the, 33
son of destruction, the, 203
Son of God, Jesus Christ as, 70
Son of Man, Jesus as, 45
Son of Man, judgment of, 227–28
song of redemption, 221
songs, new, 113, 114, 221
sons of God, believers as, 330
soon, the term, 37–38, 85, 344
sores on worshipers of the Antichrist, judgment of, 240, 241
soteriology, 34
speech, supernatural, 213–14
Spirit, the Holy. *See* Holy Spirit, the
spirit, the term, 40
spirits of God, the seven, 33, 40, 77–78, 102–3, 150
spiritual adultery, 254, 256, 259

spiritual interpretation, 21
spiritual poverty *vs.* material wealth, 90
spiritual purity, 222
spiritual states, 88–91, 92
spiritual weapons, 198
spiritual wisdom, 261
Sproul, R. C., 22
stadia, 1600, 229
star, falling, 150, 154, 157
star, morning, 31, 74, 348
star, the fallen, 31, 157–58
stars
    crown of, 192
    darkened, 150, 155
    falling, 120, 132–33, 157
    morning, 114
    the seven, 31, 46, 48, 55, 77–78
    of the sky, 31
stephanos, the term, 102
stone, white, 68–69
stone as symbol of Babylon's destruc-
        tion, 277–78
stones, precious, 100, 336–37
substitutionary death of Jesus Christ,
        145
suffering and judgment of God
        vs.satanic influence, 199
suffering of Christians, 62–64, 116,
        169, 174, 309
sun, the
    darkened, 120, 132, 134, 150, 158
    in Garden of Eden, 341
    judgments and, 155, 243–44
    in paradise regained, 341
    scorcing heat and, plague of, 240
surely, the term, 349–50
Swete, H. B., 301
swords
    of christ, 46, 65
    from Christ's mouth, 290–91, 294

rider of red horse and, 125
    symbolism of, 125, 290–91
symbolism in the book of Revelation
    double, 262
    explanations of, 27–32
    list of meanings and, 31
    literal interpretation and, 177
    purposes of, 49
    references to other Scripture and,
        30
    symbolism *vs.* literal interpretation,
        29
synagogue of Satan, 83

tabernacle, 45, 235
Tacitus, 18
Tammuz, 258
tears in heaven, 146, 328
temple, the
    destruction of, 139–40
    Gentile control of, 179–80
    of God in heaven and Jerusalem,
        146, 188
    during the great tribulation, 178–79
    millennial, 323
    in New Jerusalem, 337
    sacrifices, 323
    the term, 178
ten, the number, 30
Ten Commandments, 235
ten days, 62
ten kingdoms, 193
"ten thousand times ten thousand," 164
tent of witness, 235
Tertullian, 15
textual problems, 113
theology and Revelation, 32–35
thief, come as a, 79–80, 317
thirst, promise of water for those who,
        329

thirst, symbolism of, 146

Thomas, Robert L., 93, 127, 169, 181, 195, 220, 233, 262, 300

"those who dwell on earth," 184

thousand years, a. *See also* millennial kingdom; reign of Christ

  binding up of Satan and, 303, 306

  chart, 323

  doctrine of, 300–2

  length of, 306–7

  reign of Christ, 297–98

  resurrections and, 312

three-and-a-half year period

  authority of the first beast and, 207

  events pictured in the seals, trumpets and bowls, 120

  Gentile domination of the temple, 179

  Israel's program, 128

  martyrs and, 132

  prophecies of two witnesses, 180–81

thrones

  of David, 94, 323

  in eternal kingdom, 341

  of God, 99–101, 329, 335, 341, 343

  great white, 316, 322, 323

  twenty-four, 101

thunder, 122

thunders, seven, 171

Thyatira, church of, 51, 69–74, 95

Thyatira, city of, 69–70

Timothy and Ephesus, 17, 54–55

Titles of the Coming World Ruler, 203

tools and symbolism, 28

"tooth for a tooth," 272

torches, seven, 103

transfiguration of Jesus Christ, 47

translation to heaven, 119, 137, 181–82

tree of life, 341, 342

trial, hour of, 84

tribes of Israel, 100, 139–41, 333–34

tribulation, the great

  chart, 322

  the church and, 53, 119

  covenant with Israel and, 101

  day of wrath and, 134

  deliverance from, 84

  description of, 30, 128–30, 188, 216

  events prior to, 35

  martyred dead and, 142, 143–45, 281

  persecution of Israel in, 199–201

  preaching the gospel and, 143

  predictions of, 155

  purposes of, 84

  resurrection of the saints, 310

  saints and, 143–45

  Satan and, 197, 199

  timing of, 128–29, 134, 208

  world ruler of, 124–25

Trinity, the Holy, 103

trinity, unholy, 183, 215–16, 246

truly, the term, 350

trumpets, 122, 123, 150, 151, 233

trumpets, the seven

  chart, 150

  fifth, the, 157–61

  first, 152–53

  fourth, 155–56

  judgments and, 22, 24, 150

  second, the, 153

  seventh, 186–89, 231

  similarities to the seven bowls, 239–40

  sixth, 162–66, 248

  third, the, 154–55

truth, the, 82, 184

twelve, the number, 30, 333
12,000, 139, 141, 147
12,000 stadia, 300

unbelievers, 184, 228–30, 347–48
Unger, Merrill F., 60, 227, 316
universal resurrection, 319
upheaval and devastation, universal,
    123

Vegetius, 46
ventriloquism, religious, 214
Victorinus, 14, 43
victory of Jesus Christ on the cross, 111
victory over the world, 94
vine, the term, 229
virgin, the term, 221–22
voices from heaven
    of God, 170–71, 173, 184, 221, 239
    of Holy Spirit, 226–27
    identities of, 163, 178, 186, 198–99
    last loud/great voice, 327–28

walls and gates of New Jerusalem, 332–
    34, 335, 337, 339
Walvoord, John E., 10
Walvoord, John F., 10–12
war
    final, 245–47
    in heaven, 196
    millennial kingdom and, 312–13,
        314–15
    symbols of, 165
    world war at end of tribulation, 208
warning regarding the Word of God,
    349
wars and the seven seals, 120, 123, 125,
    126
"wash their robes, who," 347
washstands, 104

water of life, 329, 341, 348
water on the new earth, 325–26
water turned to blood, fresh, 240, 242–
    43
waters, the living, 341
waters made bitter, 154–55
waters on which the woman sits, 31,
    264
wealth, material, 90–91, 271, 276
wealth, true, 276
week, the term, 160
white, the color, 80, 316
white garments, 80, 131
white stone, 68–69
"who can stand," 135
wicked, judgment of, 316, 346
Wiersbe, Warren, 32, 161, 177, 246,
    272
wife of the Lamb, 192, 236, 331
wild animals (beasts), 127
wills in Roman world, 109
winepress, 229, 291
"wipe away every tear from their eyes,"
    146
wisdom, spiritual, 261
witnesses, God's use of, 137
witnesses, the two, 180–85, 308
woes, 157–61, 162, 185–91, 198–99
woman and the child (clothed with the
    sun), the, 31, 191–93, 195
woman on the beast, the, 255–60, 270,
    278–79
Word of God
    character of, 65, 173–74
    as Jesus Christ, 290
    little scroll and, 173
    sanctifying power of, 104
    warning regarding the, 349
works, judgment based on, 226, 318,
    346

world, changes in topography of, 250–51

world empire, capital of, 274

world empires, successive, 205

world government, 261, 263–64

world religion, 209

Wormwood, the star, 154

worship
    of all creation, 115–17
    of the angels, 114–15
    Baal, 258
    of the beast out of the sea, 134, 146, 166, 209, 213–14, 225–26, 241, 308
    children of Israel and, 179–80
    command to worship God, 345
    of image of the beast, 213–14
    of the Lamb, 112–14
    of Satan, 206–7, 210–12
    trumpets and, 113
    twenty-four elders and, 105–7, 187
    of the world dictator, 265–66

worshipers, measuring of, 179

worshipers of the beast, doom of, 225–26

worshipers of the beast and judgment, 225–26

wounded head of the beast, 205–6

wrath, the day of divine, 132–35

"wrath, the great day of their," 130

wrath, the term, 232–33

wrath of God, seven gold bowls and, 236–37

wrath of God *vs.* wrath of humanity, 187

wretched, the term, 90

Yahweh, Angel of, 138, 151

Yahweh, wife of, 192

year, the term, 160, 163, 307

Zacharias, 47

Zechariah, father of John the Baptist, 101

Zerubbabel, 182

ziggurats, 257

Scripture Index

OLD TESTAMENT

Genesis

1:16	341
2:9	41
2:10	341
2:25	341
3:6	341
3:15	341
3:16	316
3:22	59
3:22–24	342
3:23	341
7:1	39
9:6	210
10	256
10:8–11	262
10:10	257
10–11	257
11:1–9	278
11:5–9	272
11:9	257
15:18	245
16:7	151, 170
17:3	47
19:12–13	272
24:55	62
37:9–11	192
49:17	140

Exodus

3:2	151

3:15	216
7:14–11:10	181
7:20–25	242
9:9–11	241
9:18–26	152
9:19 25	153
10:12–20	159
10:21–23	244
12:13	145
15	234
15:23–25	154
16:33–34	31
19:4	200
19:16	103
19:19	151
24:10	104
28:17–21	100
30:23	60
30:34–38	152
32:15	235
37:25–28	152
38:21	235
38:30	46
40:34–35	237

Leviticus

17:14	144
23:24	151
25:9	151

Numbers

1:50 53	235
10:2–10	151
10:11	235
17:7–8	235
18:2	235
22:22	151
22–25	66
24:17	348
31:8	66
31:15–16	66

Deuteronomy

1:7	245
1:11 21	216
4:1	216
4:2	349
6:3	216
11:24	245
12:1	216
12:32	349
26:7	216
27:3	216
29:25	216
32	234
32:11–12	200

Joshua

1:4	245
5:13–15	138
6:22–23	139
18:3	216

Judges

2:1	151
2:12	216
4	248
6:22–23	47
7	248
13:20	47

1 Kings

16:33	71
17:1–2	181
17:5	200
19:7	151

2 Kings

1	181
1:10–12	212
19:21	222

1 Chronicles

21:1	196

Job

1	196
38:7	114
42:5–6	47
book of	196

Psalm

2	287
2:1–4	291
2:2	198
2:8–9	235
2:9	109, 187, 194, 291
2:10–12	291
19:1–2	156
19:9–10	174
24:1–10	235
29	171
30:7	262
34:7	151
45:8	60
66:1–4	235
68:15–16	262
72	312–13
72:8	326
72:8–11	235
72:11	41

78:68	315	14:3	206
80:8, 14–15	229	14:14	206, 211, 316
86:9	235	22:22	31, 82
87:2	315	23:17	254
90:4	301	33:13–16	200
109:6	196	34:4	134
139:21–22	58	34:11–15	271
141:2	113	37:1–2	182
		37:22	222
Proverbs		37:36	151
30:6	349	41:15	262
		54:1–8	254
Song of Solomon		55:1	330, 348
3:6	60	61:1–2	325
5	93	63:1–6	291
		63:2–3	290
Isaiah		63:3	229
2:2	262	64:1–2	289
2:2–4	235, 312	65:17	325
2:3	312	65:20	343
5:2–7	229	66:18–23	235
6:2–3	105	66:22	325
6:3	105	book of	27
6:5	47		
9:6	192	**Jeremiah**	
9:6–7	41, 235	2:21	229
11	40, 313	3:14	254
11:1	110	7:18	258
11:2–3	40	10:7	235
11:2–5	78	15:16–18	173
11:3–4	289	18:13	222
11:4	291	23:5–6	297
11:4–9	312	30:7	129
11:9	313	31:4, 21	222
11:9 11	326	31:32	254
11:10	110–11	31:34	173
11:15	245	31:35–36	156
13:6 9–11	274	44:7–19, 25	258
13:6–13	134	50:8	271
13:19–22	274	51:6	271

51:8	274	2:35	262
51:9	272	2:35, 44	186
51:24–26, 61–64	274	3	213
51:25	262	4:3	186
51:45	271	5	273
		6:26	186
Lamentations		7	205
2:13	222	7:7–8	193, 204
5:10	126	7:7–8, 24	193
		7:8	203, 204, 216
Ezekiel		7:8, 11, 25	207
2:2	44	7:9	45–46
2:9–10	173	7:13–14	111–12, 227
3:1–4, 14	173	7:14	235
3:12 14	44	7:14, 26–27	186
3:23	47	7:17, 23	262
8:14	258	7:23	129, 208
16	254	7:24	111
17:5–8	229	7:25	200, 208
20:33–38	308	8:16	38
20:34–38	313	8:17	47
21:26–27	186	9	160
23	254	9:2, 21–22	38
38	207	9:3	182
38:9, 16	249	9:25–27	84
38–39	314, 315	9:26	124, 128, 129, 203, 216
39	207	9:26–27	155
39:17–20	292	9:27	30, 120, 128, 132, 179,
40	178		185, 195, 207, 208, 265
43:3	47	10:8–9, 15–17	47
44:4	47	11:36	203
47:1, 12	341	11:36–39	266
47:10, 15, 17, 18, 20	326	11:36–45	208, 216
48:28	326	11:37	208, 216
48:31–34	333	11:40–45	246
book of	27, 28, 29	11:41	200
		11:44	246
Daniel		12:1	128, 196, 310
2:28	37	12:2	310, 317, 325
2:28–29, 45	37	12:4, 9	25

12:7	200	**Habakkuk**	
12:10	208	3:6	262
12:11	179		
book of	24, 27, 28, 29	**Zephaniah**	
		2:11	235
Hosea			
10:1	229	**Zechariah**	
book of	254	2	178
		3:1–2	196
Joel		4:7	262
1:4–7	159	5:1–11	258
2:1	151	9:10	326
2:1–2	155	10:11	245
2:1–3	129	12:10	42
2:2, 10, 30–31	134	13:8	200
book of	27	14:1–3	247, 248
		14:3–4	288
Amos		14:4	250, 251
5:2	222	14:8	326, 341
		14:9	41, 186, 235
Jonah		book of	27, 28 ,29
1:17	163		
		Malachi	
Micah		4:5	181
2:12	200	4:5–6	325–26
Nahum			
3:4	254		

NEW TESTAMENT

Matthew		10:16	200
2:13–15	194, 195	10:28	319
2:16	199	10:37	57
3:16	103	11:10	54
4:5	326	11:15	210
5:5	330	11:21	162
5:22, 29–30	319	13:9, 43	210
5:38	210	13:30, 39–42	228
6:1–21	276	13:32	271

13:42	321	25:41, 46	321
16:25	198	26:42	210
17:3	181	26:64	41
17:6	47	27:52–53	310
17:10–13	181	27:53	326
18:9	319	28:1	44
19:4	329	28:19–20	143
19:28	308, 316	28:20	138
19:29	330	24:6–7a	120
21:19–20	228	24:7b	120
24	289		
24:4–5	120	**Mark**	
24:4–31	120	1:2	54
24:6	125	3:1, 3	228
24:6–7	120	4:9, 23	210
24:7	120, 134	5:3	304
24:7–9	120	6:39	127
24:9–10	120	7:16	210
24:9–10, 16–22	120	8:12	40
24:14	120, 143	11:20	228
24:15–22	199	13:26	41
24:15–25	128	13:31	317
24:16	200, 247	14:62	41
24:21	143, 243	16:2, 9	44
24:21–22	129		
24:22	155	**Luke**	
24:27–31	288	1:8–20	101
24:28	292	1:12	47
24:29	120	1:19	150
24:30	41	1:26–31	38
24:32–25:26	120	1:32–33	194
24:35	317	2:13–14	114
24:43	247	2:34	310
25	200	2:35	65
25:1–13	284	3:5	251
25:31	94, 227	4:17–19	325
25:31–32	316	5:8	47
25:31–46	74, 308, 318	7:24, 27	54
25:34	330	8:6	228
25:41	174	8:8	210

8:31	157–58, 303
9:52	54
10:18	157, 305
10:20	209
12:16–20	273
12:35–36	93
12:39	247
14:35	210
16:17	317
16:24	320–21
18:8	38
21:11	120
21:24	180
21:27	41
21:33	317
22:3	305
22:29–30	308
22:31	305
24:1	44

John

1:1–3	290
1:14	328
1:29	111
2:1–11	284
3:14	200
3:18, 36	135
3:34–35	37
4:10, 13–14	330
5:20–24	37
5:22	74, 316
5:22, 27	227
5:27	227
5:29	309, 317
7:16	37
8:28	37
8:44	193
10:11, 15	198
10:12	195
10:28–29	55, 63

11:25	309
12:49	37
14:2	326
14:10, 24	37
15:1–6	229
16:7	111
16:13–15	286
16:15	37
17	37
18:37	40
19:30	232
20:1 19	44
10:10a	161

Acts

1	184
1:9	41
2:3	103, 212
5:3	305
6:5	58
7:44	235
8:39	195
9:16	62
10:10–11	44
11:5	44
12:7	38, 304
16:14–15	69
16:16	214
16:17	214
19	54
19:28–41	54
20:7	44
20:28	144
20:29–30	17
22:17–18	44
22:18	38
24:15	317
25:4	38
25:6	62
26:23	40–41

28:20	304	11:14	161, 305
		12:2, 4	195
Romans		12:2–4	98
1:1	38	12:7	62
1:20	156		
1:25	222	**Galatians**	
2:28–29	61	1:6	17
3:25	144	6:7	210
5:3–5	62	6:9	56
5:9	144–45	6:16	140
7:24	90		
9:6	140	**Ephesians**	
9–11	141	1:4	222
10:7	303	1:7	145
12:10	81	1:9–10	172
12:19	210	1:15–16	56
16:20	38	2:2	249, 305
		2:8–10	226
1 Corinthians		5:26	285
2:10	73	5:27	222
3:21–23	330	6:12	162
6:9–10	330	6:24	56–57
6:11	330		
11:20	44	**Philippians**	
11:30–32	62	1:1	38
11:31–32	92	1:21–23	63
15:19	90	2:9–11	106
15:20	41, 310	3:2	347
15:24–25	344	4:3	209
16:2	44		
16:9	83	**Colossians**	
		1:13	41
2 Corinthians		1:15	41, 88
1:20	87	1:16	114
2:12	83	1:18	88
4:3–4	305	1:20	145
5:10	316	1:22	222
5:10–11	318, 346	2:1	18, 87
5:19	320	4:3	83
11:2	222, 254, 284	4:13	18

4:13, 16	18	**Titus**	
4:15	87, 88	1:1	38
4:16	38		
4:17	88	**Hebrews**	
		1:7, 14	40
1 Thessalonians		1:14	330
1:10	119	2:14–15	47
2:18	305	5:8	62
4:9	81	9:4	31, 152
4:13–17	85	9:14	222
4:16–18	41	9:15	330
4:17	42, 195	9:22	144
5:2, 4	247	9:27	181–82, 318
5:2–4	79	12:3–11	92
5:9	84	12:3–13	62
5:9–10	119	12:22–24	334
5:27	38	13:1	81
2 Thessalonians		**James**	
2:3	203, 216	1:1	38
2:4	179	2:5	61
2:7	137	4:4	254
1 Timothy		**1 Peter**	
1:3–7	17	1:4	330
2:9–10	256	1:10–12	25
4:13	38	1:15	82
5:22	272	1:19	222
6:10	57	1:22	81
		2:9	41, 113
2 Timothy		3:9	330
1:16	304	5:8	305
2:12	309		
2:17–18	17	**2 Peter**	
2:19	92	1:1	38
2:26	305	1:7	81
3:1	302	1:19	31
3:1–5	53	2:4	304
4:6–8	63	2:15	66
		3:8	302

3:10	247, 317	1:9–18	43–48
3:10–12	24	1:10	33, 98, 99
3:10–13	326	1:10–11	44
3:13	325	1:12	45
3:14	24	1:13	31
		1:13–14	227
1 John		1:13–15	70
2:15	57	1:13–16	45
2:18, 22	203	1:14	289
3:2	46, 343	1:16	31, 65
5:4	94	1:17	170
5:5	59, 330	1:17–18	47
5:21	57	1:18	82, 309
		1:19	40, 48, 51, 97, 119
Jude		1:19–20	48–49
1	38	1:20	31, 46
6	163, 304	2 3	25, 48, 49, 210
9	181	2:1	54, 78
11	66	2:1–7	16, 17, 54–59
24	222	2:2	17
		2:2–3	55
Revelation	151	2:3	204
1	48, 49, 60	2:4	95
1:1	14, 37, 38, 42, 286, 344	2:4–5	56
1:1 4, 9	14	2:6	58, 67
1:1–8	42	2:7	59
1:2	32, 38, 42	2:8	60, 309, 347
1:3	32, 38, 39, 227, 247, 344, 349	2:9	61
1–3	121	2:10	95, 198
1:4	33, 39, 42–43, 78, 103, 350	2:10–11	61
1:4, 9	37	2:12	64
1:5	34, 42, 87, 145, 289	2:12, 16	46, 65
1:5 6	42	2:12–17	64
1:5–6	40	2:13	65
1:6	113	2:14–15	66, 95
1:6–7	74	2:16	38, 68
1:7	34, 41, 42	2:17	31, 68, 343
1:8	40, 42, 43, 44, 329	2:18	69, 70, 289
1:8, 17	347	2:18–29	69–74
1:9	14, 19	2:19	70

2:20	95, 192	4:4	101, 113
2:20–23	70–71	4:5	31, 33, 40, 102
2:21	244	4–5	121
2:24–25	73	4:6	233
2:25	35	4–6	170
2:26–29	73	4:6–8	103
2:27	291	4:7	31, 161, 300
2:28	31, 348	4:8	40, 197
3:1	33, 40, 77, 103	4:9–11	105–7
3:1–2	95	4–18	34
3:1–6	77–81	4–19	24, 35
3:2	79	4–20	22
3:2–3	79	4–22	48
3:3	247	5	34, 57–58, 101,
3:4–6	80		142, 144, 170
3:5	209	5:1	171
3:7	31, 82, 87, 289	5:1 7	33
3:7–13	81–86	5:1–4	109–10
3:8–9	82–83	5:2–8	124
3:10	84	5:5–7	110–12
3:10–11	35, 84	5:6	31, 33, 40, 78, 150, 205
3:11	38, 95	5:8	31
3:12	221, 326, 343	5:8–10	112–14
3:12–13	85–86	5:9	34
3:14	40, 42, 87	5:9–10	113, 221
3:14–22	19, 78, 86–94	5:10	41, 113, 308
3:14–22:16	35	5:11	164
3:15–16	88, 95	5:11–12	114–15
3:17	273	5:13–14	115–17
3:17–18	90	6	28, 120, 135, 144, 157
3:19	91	6:1	124
3:20–22	93	6:1–2	23, 120, 122
3:21	111, 316	6:1–8	121
3:22	348	6:1–17	231
4	30, 34, 105	6:1ff	31
4 5	97, 221	6:2	124, 203, 289
4:1	37, 97, 98, 173	6:3–4	23, 120, 126
4:2	316	6:5–6	23, 120, 126
4:2–3	33, 99	6–7	120
4:3	336	6:7–8	23, 120, 126–7

6:8	46, 65, 127	8:3	151, 162, 170, 223
6:9	151, 243, 308	8:3 5	151
6:9–11	23, 120, 121,	8:3–5	243
	130, 144, 208	8:5	152, 250
6:10	198, 282, 292	8:6	152
6:11	132	8:7	127, 150, 152, 241
6:12–14	120	8:7–11:14	121
6:12–16	121	8:8–9	150, 153
6:12–17	23, 120, 132–33, 157	8:10–11	150, 154
6:14	250	8–11	34
6:15–17	120	8:12	150, 157
6:17	130	8:12–13	155
6–19	85, 119, 120	9	163
7	131, 137, 147, 243	9:1	31
7:1	163	9:1, 2, 11	158, 303
7:1–3	138	9:1–2	157
7:1–8	120	9:1–12	150
7:1–8:6	121	9:3–6	158
7:2	303	9:4	127
7:2, 10	292	9:7–11	160–61
7:3	220, 343	9:11	31, 260
7:4	85	9:12	161
7:4–8	139	9:13	151, 169
7:8	140	9:13–15	162
7:9–10	142	9:13–21	150, 248
7:9–17	214, 233, 308	9:15	165, 248
7:10	34, 221, 281	9:16	165
7:11–12	142	9:16–19	164
7:13–14	142, 143	9:18	165, 166
7:14	34, 144	9:18 20	232
7:15	328	9:20–21	166, 244
7:15–17	145–46	10	161
7:16	146	10:1	110, 170, 223, 303
7:17	330	10:1–4	169
8	135, 157	10:1–7	172
8:1	149, 231	10:1–11:14	231
8:1–2	23	10:3	292
8:1–9:21	231	10:4	44
8:2	223	10:4, 8	226–27
8:2–6	149–50	10:5–7	171

10:7	172	12:9, 14–15	200
10:8–11	173	12:10	34, 196
11	161, 177, 308	12:10–12	197
11:1–2	178, 188	12:11	198, 308
11:1–14	177	12:12	328, 333
11:2	179, 180	12:13–16	199
11:3	179, 300	12:14	31 200
11:3–6	180	12:17	201
11:5	181, 212	13	24, 28, 124, 131, 166, 202,
11:5 6	182		210, 215, 244, 255
11:6	182, 232	13:1	31, 111, 183, 193, 201, 255
11:7	158, 260	13:1–2	203
11:7–10	183	13:1–8, 11–18	246
11:8	31, 177, 250, 326	13:1–10	31, 203, 210, 233
11:11	185	13:3	205, 260, 261
11:11–12	184	13:3, 12 ,14	232
11:12	226–27	13:4	206, 260
11:13–14	185	13:5	208, 210
11:14	38	13:5–6	207–8
11:15	169, 186, 198	13:6	328
11:15–12:4	121	13:7	129, 208
11:15–19	150, 169, 231	13:8	209, 241, 265–66, 271
11:16–17	187	13:9	210
11:17	40	13:9–10	209–11
11:18	187, 318	13:10	210
11:19	188, 250	13:11	183
12	28, 29, 34, 170, 202	13:11–12	211
12:1	231	13:11–16	293
12:1–2	31, 191	13:11–17	31
12:1–14:20	191	13:11–18	183
12:3	191, 231	13:12–15	246
12:3–4	193	13:13–14	191, 212
12:4	31	13:14	212
12:5	195	13–14	231
12:5–6	31, 194	13:14–15	179
12:5–14:20	121	13:14–17	241
12:6	31, 300	13:15	144
12:6, 14	200	13:15–17	213, 308
12:7–9	158, 195–96	13:16	318
12:9	31, 193, 246	13:17	146, 214

13:18	30, 214, 233, 247	16:4–7	240, 242
14	219, 230	16:5	40
14:1	343	16:6	210
14:1, 3 300		16:7	151, 243
14:1–5	219	16:7–9	232
14:2	226–27	16:8	244
14:4	221	16:8–9	240, 243
14:6, 8, 9, 15, 17, 18	303	16:9	239, 244, 271
14:6–7	223	16:10–11	240, 244
14:7	223, 235	16:11	185
14:8	224, 254, 269	16:11 21	244
14:9, 11	213	16:12	165, 228, 239
14:9–11	225–26, 241	16:12–16	240, 245–48
14:10	224, 273	16:13–16	246
14:11	321	16:14	191, 239
14:12–13	226–27	16:15	39, 227, 247
14:13	39, 247, 286	16:15b	247
14:14	45	16:17	239
14:14–16	227–28	16:17–21	240, 248–49, 272
14:15	229, 292	16:18	239
14:17–20	228	16–18	121
14:18	151	16:19	232, 239
14:19–20	291	16:20	250
14:20	229, 248, 290, 300	16:21	239, 244, 251
15	34 234	17	24, 28, 29, 35, 257, 270
15, 16	231	17 18	253, 287, 332
15:1	191	17:1	31, 264, 269, 303, 331
15:1–2	231	17:1–2	253
15:1–8	121	17:1–7, 15–18	192
15:2	213	17:2	224, 273
15:3–4	233–34	17:3	332
15:5	328	17:3 7	204
15:5–6	235	17:3, 7–8, 11–13 ,16–17	31
15:7–8	236	17:3–4	255
16	34, 46, 231	17:5	31, 224, 256, 266
16:1	239	17:6–7	259
16:1–21	240	17:7–8	183
16:2	213, 240, 241	17:8	158, 209, 260–61
16:2, 5, 6	244	17:8–11	263
16:3	240, 241	17:9	31, 270, 274

17:9–11	261, 263	19:1–21:8	303
17:9a	262	19:2	232
17:10	261–62	19:4	282
17:10–12	204	19:5 18	318
17:11	261	19:5–6	282
17:12	31, 204	19:6–8	194
17:12, 16	273	19:7	99, 192, 285
17:12–14	263	19:7–8	34, 283, 285
17:13	264	19:7–9	80
17:14	30, 264	19:8	31, 236, 247, 285
17:15	31, 264	19:9	39, 227, 286 ,292
17:16	212, 265	19:9–10	285
17:16–18	264–65	19:10	286, 345
17:18	31	19:11	251, 286
17–18	22, 231	19:11, 17, 19	303
18	270	19:11–13	287
18:1	303	19:11–16	284, 303
18:1–3	269	19:11–16 19	31
18:2	271, 292	19:11–20:10	121
18:2–3, 5–8 20	210	19:12	289
18:3	271	19:13	145, 290
18:4	226	19:14–16	290
18:4–5	271	19:15	46, 194, 229
18:5	272	19:15, 21	46, 65
18:6–8	272	19:17	303
18:8	232, 273	19:17–19	291–92
18:9–10	273	19:17–19 21	229
18:11–19	275	19:20	31, 191, 210, 211,
18:19–22	274		212, 213, 293
18:20	276	19:21	294
18:21	110	20	24, 46, 301, 302
18:44 22–23	278	20:1	304
19	22, 24, 28, 33, 34,	20:1, 3	158
	41, 49, 231, 301	20:1, 4, 11, 12	303
19 20	303	20:1–3	158, 163, 303
19:1	34, 276	20:1–6	297
19:1, 3, 4, 6	281	20:2	31, 200
19:1–3	281	20:3	301
19:1–6	281	20:3 5	314
19:1–10	121, 287	20:4	131–32, 213, 307, 308

20:4–6	233	21:19–20	101
20:5	309, 317	21:21	331, 333
20:5–6	41, 309–10	21–22	24
20:6	39, 113, 227, 309, 311	21:22	337
20:7	303	21:23	332
20:7–9	312	21:23–24	338
20:10	293, 315, 321	21:24	342
20:11	316, 317, 325	21:25–27	339
20:11–15	63	21:26	342
20:11–22:21	121	21:27	209, 222, 330
20:12 15	209	22	34, 341
20:12–13	41, 317	22:1	341
20:13	318, 319	22:2	59, 325, 333, 341, 342
20:14	30, 311	22:3	341, 342, 343
20:14–15	320	22:4	341
21	100	22:4–5	343
21 22	86, 327	22:5	307, 341
21:1	317, 325, 326, 331	22:6	37
21:1–2	332	22:6–7	344
21:2	326, 327, 331, 332	22:6–7	12, 20, 38
21:3	226	22:7	38–39, 344
21:3–4	327	22:7 12	347, 349
21:5	286	22:7 14	39, 227
21:5–6	328–29	22:8	14, 37
21:6	88, 329, 347	22:8–9	345
21:7–8	330	22:10–11	345
21:8	321	22:11	346
21:8 27	347	22:12	346
21:9–11	330–31	22:12–13	43
21:10–11	332	22:13	329, 347
21:11	332	22:13–16	347
21:12	333	22:15	222, 330
21:12–14	332–33	22:16	30, 31, 74, 99, 119, 348
21:14	333	22:17	33, 34, 348
21:15–17	178, 334–35	22:18	232
21:16	300, 333	22:18–20	348–49
21:17	333	22:19	209
21:18–21	335–36	22:21	350
21:19	332		

The John Walvoord
Prophecy Commentaries include:

- Daniel
- Matthew
- 1 & 2 Thessalonians
- Revelation

{THE JOHN WALVOORD PROPHECY COMMENTARIES}

1&2 Thessalonians

Walvoord
Hitchcock

John F. Walvoord and Mark H...

Edited by

Philip E. Rawley

{THE JOHN WALVOORD PROPHECY COMMENTARIES}

Revelation

Walvoord

John F. Walvoord

Revised and Edited by

Philip E. Rawley & Mark Hitchcock

MOODY
Publishers™

From the Word to Life